GLOBAL TRANSITION

Other volumes in the Social Dynamics trilogy by Graeme Donald Snooks

ECONOMICS WITHOUT TIME
A Science Blind to the Forces of Historical Change

LONGRUN DYNAMICS
A General Economic and Political Theory

Global Transition

A General Theory of
Economic Development

Graeme Donald Snooks
Coghlan Professor in Economics
Institute of Advanced Studies
Australian National University

Published by
PALGRAVE
Houndmills, Basingstoke, Hampshire RG21 6XS and
175 Fifth Avenue, New York, N.Y. 10010
Companies and representatives throughout the world

PALGRAVE is the new global academic imprint of
St. Martin's Press LLC Scholarly and Reference Division and
Palgrave Publishers Ltd (formerly Macmillan Press Ltd).

Outside North America
ISBN 0–333–77147–8

Inside North America
ISBN 0–312–22370–6

This book is printed on paper suitable for recycling and
made from fully managed and sustained forest sources.

A catalogue record for this book is available
from the British Library.

Library of Congress Cataloging-in-Publication Data
Snooks, G. D. (Graeme Donald)
Global Transition : a general theory of economic development /
Graeme Donald Snooks.
p. cm.
Includes bibliographical references and index.
ISBN 0–312–22370–6
1. Developing countries—Economic policy. 2. Statics and dynamics
(Social sciences) 3. Economic development. I. Title.
HC59.7.S558 1999
338.9'009172'4—dc21

99–13907
CIP

10   9   8   7   6   5   4   3   2
08   07   06   05   04   03   02   01

Printed and bound in Great Britain by
Antony Rowe Ltd, Chippenham, Wiltshire

Contents

Contents

List of Tables

List of Figures

Preface

During the middle decades of the eighteenth century Adam Smith detected a growing unease in Britain about the future. This unease was generated, I argue, by the exhaustion of the commerce strategy that his country had so successfully pursued since the early sixteenth century, together with a growing militarism that suggested a return to an earlier conquest strategy. In response to this concern about the future, Smith developed – in three works (1759 to 1776) on moral sentiments, jurisprudence, and political economy – his famous system of societal change. Through this model he attempted to demonstrate that, if appropriate moral principles were pursued, it would be possible to maintain advances in both prosperity and liberty. His optimism, in the face of much contemporary and subsequent pessimism, was confirmed, perhaps fortuitously, by the subsequent Industrial Revolution.

Today there is a growing unease about the future prospects of global prosperity and liberty. During the last quarter of the twentieth century, long-run growth of the developed world has slowed dramatically; Japan, after three decades of extraordinary growth, is languishing; much of the Third World appears resistant to economic development and democracy; even East Asia, the 'miracle' of the Third World, has stumbled badly; and the former Second World is walking a tightrope between an untenable past and an uncertain future. There are also wars and threats of wars as old empires disintegrate, as the superpowers attempt to maintain control over essential oil supplies in the Middle East, and as African countries assert their political independence. Is the world once more at the crossroads, as it was in Adam Smith's time? Is Western civilization under challenge? What is the future for prosperity and liberity in the Second and Third Worlds? The lesson of this book is that prosperity and liberty can be maintained in the West and advanced throughout the world if, but only if, the appropriate dynamic strategies and strategic policies are pursued.

It is essential to recognize that economic development is a self-sustaining global dynamic process. To ensure that it is not disrupted, even permanently derailed, by inappropriate intervention in the First and Third Worlds alike, we need, as Adam Smith did, to develop a general economic and political model of this dynamic process as a basis for formulating appropriate development policy. In this respect what has orthodox economics, the inheritor of the legacy of Adam Smith, got to offer? Surprisingly little, given the passage of more than two centuries. While orthodox economics has become considerably more professional and technically proficient during that time, it has lost Smith's broad vision. The dominant paradigm of neoclassical economics has become little more than a branch of production engineering. Its central concept, the production function, is merely an engineering relationship between inputs and output. Human society is seen as a giant factory dominated by the machine. By focusing exclusively on the supply side, neoclassical economics fails to recognize dynamic demand (here called **strategic demand**) and, hence, is unable to provide a general model of the dynamic process at the national, let alone, the global level. Not surprisingly, orthodox development policy, which focuses on institutional *outcomes* rather than dynamic *processes*, is misdirected. Accordingly it has little that is useful to say about the future prospects of prosperity and liberty in the Third World.

What is urgently needed is a new approach to economic development that embraces strategic demand, political as well as economic forces, and global as well as national perspectives. An approach that treats human society as a strategic organization rather than a factory and views societal dynamics as a strategic pursuit rather than a production process. It is this broader approach to the subject that has been adopted in the present book, using the dynamic-strategy theory developed in my recent book *Longrun Dynamics. A General Economic and Political Theory* (1998b). It completes the trilogy that began with my manifesto, entitled *Economics without Time. A Science Blind to the Forces of Historical Change* (1993). In the spirit of Adam Smith, it is possible to say that, if we choose the correct dynamic strategies, the global economy can expect to experience steady progress in prosperity and liberty. If not we have cause for considerable unease.

When progress and liberty are challenged at the global and national levels, they also come under attack at the individual institutional level. Many of us have been disturbed by the recent predatory actions of even our own academic instituions. In this difficult new environment the support of close colleagues is essential. It is for this reason that I wish to thank Heinz Arndt, Ross Garnaut, Angus Maddison, and Gary Magee for their intellectual and moral support, Barbara Trewin for her usual expertise with wordprocessing and formatting, and Barry Howarth for his excellent copy-editing and indexing. My wife, Loma Graham, has been a tower of strength throughout these difficult times. I am also grateful for support and assistance on the publication side from Tim Farmiloe, Sunder Katwala, and Keith Povey.

Sevenoaks   GRAEME DONALD SNOOKS
Canberra

List of Abbreviations

ASC   antistrategic country
ESC   emerging strategic country
FASC   former antistrategic country
GCI   gross community income (market plus household income)
GST   global strategic transition
NSC   nonstrategic country
NST   national strategic transition
SC   strategic country

Part I
Introduction

1 Economic Development Redefined

Economic development is one of the most important but least understood issues in the world today. It commands our attention because of the vast chasm in living standards between peoples of the First and Third Worlds. Since the Second World War, considerable effort has been devoted to this issue by intellectuals, public agencies at the national and global levels, and private consultants. While the global development process has expanded steadily, particularly in East Asia, there are still large areas of the world, namely sub-Saharan Africa, that have been bypassed. Many observers, therefore, have become pessimistic about the future of the Third World.

While there is every reason to be pessimistic about the contribution of the 'development industry' to resolving the problems of the Third World, there is no reason at all to doubt that the problem will be resolved. Both issues revolve around the recent discovery of the real nature of the global dynamic process. The reason that traditional development economics is widely regarded as having failed to meet the expectations of its pioneering practitioners (Meier and Seers 1984) is that it has been unable to construct a general model of global economic development. Only when such a model became available – in *The Dynamic Society* (Snooks 1996) and *Longrun Dynamics* (Snooks 1998b) – could it be seen that the economic development of individual countries is part of a global dynamic process that is both systematic and continuing. Development economics may have missed its mark, but economic development is still on course. It is the purpose of this book to demonstrate the truth of these two propositions by constructing and applying a general dynamic model of the development process that I have called the **global strategic transition (GST)**. This chapter will suggest how the GST model requires the redefinition of economic development, and it will outline the book's structure.

1.1   THE TRADITIONAL APPROACH TO ECONOMIC DEVELOPMENT

The existing paradigm of economic development has arisen not from an understanding of the global dynamic process but from a desire to eliminate the observed income gap between the First and Third Worlds. In other

3

words, the problem of economic development is generally viewed as an outcome rather than a process.[1] It will come as no surprise, therefore, that the traditional resolution of this problem is framed in static rather than dynamic terms.

The Traditional Focus

In pursuing its objective the development industry has changed its focus over the past 50 years. The pioneering development economists and development agencies equated economic development with a growth in real GDP per capita, while many today see it in terms of 'poverty reduction', 'equity', 'basic needs', and 'human development'. While this change may appear to be quite subtle, it has important policy implications. As H. W. Singer says: 'we are all agreed – at least theoretically – to attribute more importance to reduction of poverty than to mere growth of GNP' (Singer and Roy 1993: 10). And Paul Streeten (1995: 17–18) asserts that 'the evolution from economic growth, via employment, jobs and justice, redistribution with growth to basic needs and human development, represents a genuine evolution of thinking and is not a comedy of errors, a lurching from one slogan to the next'.

The reasons for this change of focus are that sustained economic growth has been difficult to achieve and, even when it has occurred, poverty reduction through greater equity and human development has not emerged (Dutt 1992: 23–5). But, only those with a naive and shortrun view of the relationship between economic and political change would expect it to. The dynamic-strategy model (Chapters 9, 10 and 16) shows that greater equity emerges only after a country's unfolding dynamic strategy draws a sizeable proportion of the population into its economic and, later, political processes. This requires the passage of some three or four generations. It cannot be achieved overnight.

Whatever the perception of the income gap between the First and Third Worlds, there is little disagreement about the way it can be eliminated. Economic development, it is argued, is the outcome of appropriate international and national development policies – of intervention by intellectuals and bureaucrats. Hans Singer, for example, claims that 'the development process has been shaped by interaction between global and domestic policies, although their relative importance has varied among developing countries' (Singer and Roy 1993: 1). Even neoliberals see an important role for international organizations such as the IMF and the World Bank in shaping national policy in the Third World. The irony of course is that, by forcing non-interventionist policies on national governments, these international organizations have become massively interventionist. I will argue that these policy initiatives are actually employed as substitutes for an appropriate understanding of the global dynamic process.

The failure to develop a model of global dynamics is reflected in the absence of both analytical content in, and consensus about, the basic terminology of economic development. This constantly changing terminology merely distinguishes between those societies that have passed through a process of economic development and those that have not. It does not reflect the changing nature of that dynamic process. A sample of this changing terminology includes: advanced/backward countries; developed/undeveloped countries; developed (DCs)/less-developed countries (LDCs); industrialized (ICs)/newly industrializing (NICs) countries; countries of the centre/periphery; North/South countries; high-/low-income countries; and First-World/Third-World countries. As will be discussed later, the development of a global dynamic model requires the adoption of an entirely new and, for the first time, analytical terminology.

Orthodox and Radical Models

In the absence of a workable model of global change, the development industry has fallen back on one of a number of tangential or partial approaches to the issue of economic development. These approaches, which are discussed in more detail in Chapter 6, include those of the productionists, the poverty-trap theorists, the institutionalists, and the global-polarization theorists.

The only comprehensive body of theory available to development economists is classical and neoclassical growth theory. There are, however, two major problems in employing this theory in development economics. The first is that it was constructed to analyse, in a highly abstract way, the growth of First-World economies. Hence it abstracts from those institutional and political issues that are central to the process of economic development – issues that have been highlighted in the current Indonesian crisis. But as serious as this limitation may be, it is the least of the problems facing orthodox growth theory in a development context. The second, and fundamentally critical, deficiency is its restricted perspective. Growth theory not only lacks global perspective, it also concentrates on the system of production rather than the dynamic core of individual societies. In effect, mainstream economics treats human society as a giant factory dominated by the machine rather than a social organization dedicated to the strategic pursuit as it is in reality. Because economic growth is treated by the 'productionists' as the outcome of a production processes rather than of a strategic pursuit, neoclassical growth models fail to encompass the dynamic core of society. In other words, *'endogenous' growth models endogenize the wrong variables.*

The widespread dissatisfaction generated by orthodox growth models unable to explain the persistence of underdevelopment has stimulated development economists to construct their own theories. The main theoretical explanation for the apparent persistence of underdevelopment concerns the low-level equilibrium, or poverty, trap. Escape from this trap was considered by these theorists to be impossible if left to the self-interest of entrepreneurs working independently. Only through a government-sponsored 'big push' that would generate simultaneous development over a wide front could it be achieved. While these theories address the condition of underdevelopment, they do not model the growth process. They provide no basis for a general theory of global economic development and they focus on the system of production rather than the strategic pursuit. They are merely speculative partial theories and, as such, are of limited use in policy formulation.

A third group of development economists have attempted to explain the persistence of underdevelopment in terms of the failure of institutions in the Third World to evolve efficiently. This is due, the institutionalists claim, to adverse initial conditions inherited from an earlier era of colonization together with path-dependent evolutionary processes. Only a major government initiative to remove, reshape, and replace old and inefficient institutions can eliminate this source of underdevelopment. While this approach takes into account institutional issues neglected by orthodox growth theory, it does so by asserting the dominance of evolutionary rules over more fundamental economic processes. The new institutionalism, however, shares the productionist vision of human society, merely extending the costs-of-production concept to include transaction costs.

The final group of development economists consists of what I have called the global-polarization theorists. They include the 'structuralists' and the 'dependency theorists'. While both are committed to the idea that society is a system of production, they do view economic development as a global process. Underdevelopment is seen as a direct outcome of the expansion and growth of the advanced industrial nations rather than of Third-World problems. The structuralists see the economic problems of the less-industrialized 'periphery' as a direct, if unintentional, outcome of the expansion of the industrialized 'centre', operating through the terms of trade. The solution for the 'periphery' is to minimize contact with the 'centre' through import-substitution industrialization (ISI). Marxist-inspired dependency theorists, on the other hand, view global polarization as the result of a more deliberate exploitative relationship that can be terminated only through a change in global power relationships. Neither explanation of global change is comprehensive or persuasive.

Development policies advocated by intellectuals and imposed by international organizations such as the IMF and the World Bank have reflected these changing fashions in the orthodox consensus. They have also reflected the changing success stories in the development 'game': whatever country is currently successful is the 'model' that all Third-World countries are to follow. From the 1940s to the 1960s, development economists under the influence of Keynesian ideas (Rosenstein-Rodan 1943; Scitovsky 1954) emphasized the roles of investment, government intervention, and planning. This was the era of the 'big push' with its focus on industrialization, particularly in the form of heavy industry and engineering. It was to be achieved by tariff-inspired import replacement and by extracting the necessary surplus from a largely traditional agriculture. The Marxists advocated a similar approach, albeit through different political forms.

While a small group of dissenting neoclassical economists were active at this time (Viner 1953; Schultz 1964; Bauer 1971), it was not until the 1970s that neoliberalism began to emerge as the new orthodox consensus. Owing to the neoclassical resurgence, there was a shift of development policy from government planning and protection to freely operating markets and unrestricted trade, which was adopted from the early 1980s by the Thatcher government in the UK and the Reagan administration in the USA. This, in turn, led to the structural adjustment policies of the IMF and the World Bank during the 1980s aimed at reducing the debt burden accumulated by Third-World countries over the preceding three or four decades. The neoclassical structural adjustment policies have been described as follows:

> It holds that one can temporarily deflate, arrest growth, reduce government expenditures, reduce expenditures on physical and human investments and so on, while at the same time gathering strength for a new and, it is hoped, more sustainable period of growth and development. (Singer and Roy 1993: 44)

It is a faith misplaced. This 'development' policy, which has no underlying dynamic theory, was merely transplanted from the First World where, as I argue in *Longrun Dynamics* (Snooks 1998b: ch. 17), it has been undercutting longrun economic viability. In the Third World the timing, suddenness, and insensitivity of this new policy merely exacerbated the increasing difficulties that most countries, particularly in Africa and Latin America, were experiencing in maintaining the dynamic process throughout the 1980s and early 1990s. Since writing this we have seen further demonstrations of the disruptive nature of neoliberal policies pursued by the IMF in Indonesia in the late 1990s.

As we approach the end of the twentieth century, the bold development experiment begun fifty years ago can hardly be regarded as successful. Despite a massive input of intellectual and financial resources, the global development problem appears to many to be as intractable as ever. Large areas of the Third World, particularly in sub-Saharan Africa and Latin America, have performed poorly in growth terms since the early 1970s. Even the 'miracle' economies of East Asia have stumbled spectacularly. Some of the difficulties experienced must be regarded as an outcome of inappropriate interventions by the development industry, which raised expectations about what could be achieved and led to the waste of scarce resources on a massive scale, and which provided inappropriate neoliberal advice in times of crisis. The argument in this book is that these policy problems could have been avoided if a realist general theory of global economic development had emerged earlier in the century. Such a theory would have provided a realistic understanding of the global dynamic process together with the dangers of large-scale interventions of both the Keynesian and neoliberal kind.

1.2   THE GLOBAL STRATEGIC TRANSITION –
A NEW APPROACH

In *Longrun Dynamics* I argue that real-world dynamic processes can be understood only by abandoning neoclassical growth models, which are based on an inappropriate body of static microeconomic theory, and by employing an inductive approach. This is just as true for the Third World as it is for the First World. By taking an inductive approach in *Longrun Dynamics* it was possible to construct the dynamic-strategy model of economic change that was successfully employed to analyse First World economies and to generate more appropriate policy principles. With further theoretical development, the same model can be employed to analyse the economies of the Third World. The dynamic-strategy theory contains a model of the global mechanism of economic development – a mechanism that I call the global strategic transition (GST).

The dynamic-strategy model characterizes human society as being driven by the biologically determined desires – to survive and prosper – of 'materialist man', who invests in the most efficient dynamic strategy or substrategy. Feedback is provided by the changing material standards of living. Throughout history these dynamic strategies have included four possibilities: family multiplication (procreation and migration), conquest, commerce, and technological change. The last of these, technological change, has included a variety of substrategies such as the pioneering industrial programme of Britain and the recent microelectronic/biotechnological programme. The exploitation of strategic opportunities by materialist man drives the unfolding dynamic strategy, which provides a dynamic form for our model – the strategic sequence of great and long waves – and gives rise to parallel shifts in **strategic demand** and **strategic confidence**. In turn, these two key concepts are responsible for creating **dynamic order** and generating an increase in investment, saving, population, labour skills, ideas of all sorts, and changing institutions and organizations. This strategic demand–response mechanism is orchestrated by rising prices (**strategic inflation**) that provide the necessary motivation for economic change. While it is a self-starting and self-maintaining dynamic process, it will continue only until the dynamic strategy/substrategy has been exhausted – when strategic demand and strategic confidence decline – and will only begin anew when the old strategy/substrategy has been replaced. If this substitution cannot be achieved, the society will stagnate and, eventually, collapse.

The dynamic-strategy model is part of a more general theory of the transformation of human society over vast periods of time. It is a theory based upon systematic empirical study – presented in The *Dynamic Society* (Snooks 1996), *The Ephemeral Civilization* (Snooks 1997a), and *The Laws of History* (Snooks 1998a) – of the emergence of, and change in, human society over the past two million years. It is a general theory that encompasses the dynamics of both the 'developed' and 'developing' worlds. While this theory will be expounded fully in Chapter 2, it should be surveyed briefly here. Over the past two million years, three major technological paradigm shifts (or economic revolutions) have taken place – the palaeolithic, the neolithic, and the industrial. Each economic revolution occurred when the potential inherent in the prevailing technological paradigm had, in terms of the access it provided to natural resources, been exhausted. And each revolution emerged in highly competitive environments where paradigmatic exhaustion first appeared – such as the rift valley in East Africa about 1.6 million years ago (palaeolithic), the Jordan Valley in the Middle East about 10 600 years ago (neolithic), and in Britain just over 200 years ago (industrial) – and were carried to the rest of the known world via the dominant dynamic strategy of the particular historical era. In the palaeolithic era the dominant dynamic strategy was family multiplication, in the neolithic era it was either conquest or commerce, and in the industrial era it is technological change. This is the basis of global strategic transition.

Hence, 'economic development' is merely the process by which additional societies and regions of the world are drawn into the new technological paradigm. In other words, it is an outcome of the global unfolding of the prevailing technological paradigm rather than of policy at the national and international levels aimed at removing the global income gap. Central to this global unfolding process is the adoption by additional societies of the dynamic-strategy approach to pursuing the universal objective of survival and prosperity. The strategic transition of individual societies is the outcome of their transition to the strategic approach.

What we call 'economic development', therefore, is in reality the process of global strategic transition. There is, in other words, nothing unique about the 'problem of economic development'. It has emerged on three earlier occasions in the history of human society and on each occasion it was satisfactorily resolved. What is particularly interesting is that in each earlier case of global strategic transition, it was successfully achieved in the absence of theories and policies about economic development. Indeed, it occurred without anyone being in any way interested in the 'problem' of economic development or making any attempt to resolve it. Earlier GSTs came about automatically (but not inevitably) as the outcome of individuals and the leaders of societies pursuing dynamic strategies that maximized the probability of survival and prosperity.

The implications are breathtaking. If the global strategic transition occurred in the past despite being totally ignored by ruling elites and intellectuals, why does the present GST need to be attended by a large number of functionaries? And why only since the Second World War, when the current GST had been in progress for about 150 years? How do we account for the very recent emergence of the 'development industry'? The answers should not come as a surprise to an industry whose foundation stone is economic rationality. Basically 'economic development' is a game played by four sets of participants: First-World political leaders, bureaucrats, and intellectuals; and Third-World ruling elites. The beneficiaries of this game are the gameplayers and the losers are the taxpayers in both worlds and, of course, the world's poor. No doubt most gameplayers will claim that they are really concerned to improve the condition of the poor in the Third World and are not pursuing their own material advantage. Spectators of the game, however, are entitled to ask why, given the low, indeed largely negative returns on taxpayers money, do the gameplayers persist in this very expensive exercise? If the game were privately funded it would have been wound up decades ago. The game goes on only because political leaders in the First World use it to influence those countries receiving aid in order to facilitate the pursuit of their own dynamic strategies. While this was at its most obvious during the Cold War, it has continued despite the collapse of the former USSR. In the post-Second World War period this form of intervention has been more economical than maintaining colonies for the defence of the technological strategy (Snooks 1997a: 503–6). *It is no coincidence that the interest of the First World in the issue of economic development emerged only as they began dismantling their colonies.* Ruling elites in the Third World (that includes politicians, bureaucrats, and intellectuals) participate in this game because they are able to profit personally from the funds made so lavishly available by the unwitting taxpayers of the First World. And intellectuals and bureaucrats from the First World continue to play the game, despite the failure to achieve their publicly stated objectives, because they receive salaries, research funds, and consulting funds paid by their governments. Of course, as in all other 'industries', there will be altruistic exceptions, but not enough to bring the game to an end.

It is my intention in this book to redefine the objectives and nature of what we have come to know as 'development economics'. The objective should be not to focus on development policy to 'reduce poverty' or to 'close the income gap', but rather to understand the process by which societies are drawn into the prevailing technological paradigm and to formulate policy principles that will remove the barriers threatening to derail this global dynamic process. As the reduction in poverty is an outcome and not an objective of the GST, it cannot be achieved before the transition process has taken place. This new focus on *processes* rather than *outcomes* involves a major reorientation in development economics.

The study of the global strategic transition requires a new vocabulary. In contrast to that of orthodox development economics, the new vocabulary proposed in this book emerges from a model of the global dynamic process. The analytical distinction made here between countries around the world is based on the extent of their participation in the prevailing dynamic strategy. Those societies at the centre of the global strategic transition are called **strategic countries (SCs)**; those at the other extreme who have yet to set out on the path toward strategic participation are called **nonstrategic countries (NSCs)**; those who have begun the journey but have yet to arrive are called **emerging strategic countries (ESCs)**; those who have been hijacked by radical groups interested only in rent-seeking and suppressing the potential strategists are called **antistrategic countries (ASCs)**; and those ASCs that have collapsed and are attempting to transform themselves into SCs are called **former antistrategic societies (FASCs)**. The defining characteristic in each case is their attitude to the prevailing dynamic strategy of technological change.

From this point on, I will avoid using that range of constantly changing development terms that have either no theoretical underpinning or no underlying logic. The exception is when I discuss traditional development theories. For example, no country should be called 'developed' because even the leaders are 'developing' as the industrial technological paradigm unfolds; the North/South terminology encounters difficulties with many poor Asian and European countries in the North as well as rich countries like Australia and New Zealand in the South; and the term LDCs does not make much sense when all countries are 'less developed' than the strategic leader – currently the USA and formerly Britain. Naturally, as the GST approaches its completion at some time in the future, the terminology used here will be temporarily obsolete – but only temporarily as the new technological paradigm shift, which must occur if human society is to avoid collapse, will generate the conditions for a new process of global strategic transition.

There may be some confusion over the use I have made of the word 'strategy'. This is a word much used and abused today, particularly by the development industry. In the existing literature the word 'strategy' is used loosely to mean: approach, plan, perspective, policy, practice, programme, instrument, and even tactic. Very rarely is it used according to its original meaning of: 'generalship, the art of war (literal or figurative)'; which is distinguished from 'tactics' that are devices employed to put any strategy into action. Strategy is used throughout the book in its original meaning. For example, one of the four dynamic strategies, relevant to the ancient world, is conquest, which depended on the art of war. By analogy, 'strategy' has been used to refer to the pursuit of the dominant dynamic activities in other historical eras. Hence, the 'technological strategy' in our own era. The original distinction between 'strategy' and 'tactic' is also followed throughout the book. Words, of course, can be used in whatever way authors and readers wish, provided any eccentric usage is clearly defined. When eccentricity is temporarily the norm, however, it is necessary to redefine any standard usage.

1.3   THE BOOK'S STRUCTURE

The book has been divided into six parts: an overview of the global strategic transition (GST) model; an empirical outline of the progress made during the past two centuries, together with the state of development reached in the Second and Third Worlds; a critical evaluation of the traditional approach to development theory, policy, and prediction; a detailed analysis of the dynamic-strategy model emphasizing both strategic demand and strategic response; and a discussion of the strategic approach to prediction and policy.

Part I consists, in addition to this introduction, of a chapter outlining the GST model. This model shows how, beginning with Britain in the Industrial Revolution (or the industrial technological paradigm shift), an increasing number of countries have been drawn into the vortex of dynamic interaction between the world's most economically advanced nations. This process is part of the global unfolding of the industrial technological paradigm, whereby the economic potential of existing natural resources opened up by the Industrial Revolution is exploited. Eventually the dynamic process will exhaust this potential which, in turn, will create pressures leading to a new technological paradigm shift, probably in the twenty-first century.

This process of global strategic transition is not unique. It has occurred on three earlier occasions in the pre-palaeolithic, the palaeolithic, and the neolithic eras (see Figure 2.1). These earlier GSTs were successfully negotiated despite the absence of 'experts' in the field of economic development, which begs the question of why they are now needed, particularly as they have no knowledge of the global dynamic process. Of course, it also begs the question as to why this book is required. The answer to the latter question is: to show how the development community, owing to its failure to analyse the GST, is endangering the development process. This can be achieved by constructing a realistic general economic and political model of economic development and by establishing appropriate policy principles.

Part II is concerned with the progress made so far by the modern GST. Chapter 3, entitled 'The Unfolding Technological Paradigm', briefly outlines the development achieved by the various regions of the world since the British Industrial Revolution. It provides evidence to show that the GST is a systematic process which is gradually extending throughout the globe. Over the past two centuries the GST has spread throughout Europe and those regions of the world settled by Europeans, and has made considerable inroads into Asia, Latin America, and isolated parts of Africa. Much of sub-Saharan Africa, however, has been passed by. It is argued that the current pessimism about the prospects of Africa, Latin America and, more recently, East Asia and the former Soviet block, owes much to the undue weight given to the dramatic events of the past decade or so.

The claim in this book is that much of this pessimism is unwarranted in the face of our discovery that the GST is a self-generating and self-maintaining process that will ultimately embrace even the poorest regions.

Chapters 4 and 5 consider the current state and future prospects of both the Third and Second Worlds respectively. To provide a framework for this analysis a statistical table has been constructed to rank the main societies throughout the world in terms of their engagement with the GST. On the basis of this GST coefficient, the world's societies have been divided into the analytical categories of NSCs, ESCs, FASCs, and SCs. After discussing the main quantitative characteristics of these strategic categories, Chapter 4 analyses, using the dynamic-strategy model, the current problems and future prospects of NSCs in sub-Saharan Africa and of ESCs in Latin America and Southeast Asia. In Chapter 5 the FASCs – the former Soviet-block countries – are examined by comparing their circumstances with those of ESCs. It is argued that FASCs should be viewed as being in transition from antistrategic to strategic societies rather than from command to market economies. The distinction is fundamentally important as the former focuses on dynamic strategic *processes* and the latter merely on static institutional *outcomes*. It is a distinction essential for policy-making because transition is achieved by targeting not institutions but dynamic strategies. Institutional change is merely a response to changes in strategic demand.

Part III surveys traditional theory, policies, and visions about the future of the Third World. The important conclusion arising from this survey is that because traditional economists, both orthodox and radical, have no general theory of economic development, they have no satisfactory vision of where that process is heading or of how to influence it for the better. Chapter 6 considers the intellectual progress in economic development during the past half-century. After such intensive effort over this long period, it is remarkable that so little progress has been made. The main reason for this disappointing outcome is the limitations of the deductive method employed by both orthodox and radical economists. While the traditional deductive method has considerable strengths in static *production* analysis, it is unable to encompass the broader and more complex study of real-world dynamics. A different approach – the inductive or 'historical method' – is required. Without it we could never understand the dynamic nature of the GST. Traditionally human society is seen not as a strategic organization but as a giant factory. Hence the focus is not on the core dynamic mechanism but on the way its impetus is translated through the production system into a larger GDP per capita. And, as is shown, the system of production is only one of four methods by which this has been achieved in the past. Chapter 7 surveys traditional development policy. It finds that this policy is fragmented into a large number of inconsistent parts, that it is often employed as a substitute for a satisfactory general dynamic theory, and that it is used as an excuse to intervene in the internal affairs of other, less powerful, societies. Chapter 8 examines the traditional visions regarding the future of economic development. As demonstrated, these visions are similar to those held by natural scientists about the future of the universe: some argue that it will continue growing forever, while others believe that it will finally grind to a halt, and even collapse in on itself. Amongst the economists, Ricardo, Malthus, J.S. Mill, Marx, Schumpeter, and Rostow, who see economic growth as a recent and temporary occurrence, argue that the stationary state will eventually prevail, whereas the neoclassical economists imply that it will proceed along an equilibrium growth path – the steady state – forever. These visions are based on either inadequate production models or naive historicism. Further, most traditional economists focus on the national rather than the global level.

Parts IV and V examine in some detail the essential core of the dynamic-strategy model. This is the strategic demand–response mechanism. Chapters 9 to 11 discuss the fundamentally important concept of strategic demand first elaborated in abstract form in *Longrun Dynamics* (Snooks 1998b) and here applied to the global economy, and Chapters 12 to 17 examine, for the first time in detail, the strategic response. Chapter 9 provides a brief outline of the global dynamic-strategy model, which, in a global context, emphasizes the dynamic driving force of materialist man, whose overriding objective is to survive and prosper; the dynamic mechanism which involves a choice of dynamic strategies and substrategies that are alternatively exploited and exhausted by materialist man; the roles of strategic demand and strategic confidence which emerge and change with the unfolding dynamic strategy; and the global strategic demand–response mechanism which is articulated through **strategic inflation** in Third-World countries.

Chapters 10 and 11 focus more closely on the driving force and on the global strategic demand–response mechanism. First, in Chapter 10, a model is developed to explain the mechanism by which Third-World countries participate in the GST. It shows that the unfolding dynamic strategy of the world's leading countries generates a global strategic demand that can, under certain circumstances, be exploited by the Third World. This is the global strategic core–fringe interaction, which operates through strategic inflation in the Third World. To empirically elaborate this model, the growth–inflation curve, first reported in Snooks (1997b; 1998b), has been estimated for Third-World countries.

Part V is concerned with the theory of the strategic response. In Chapter 12 the **strategy function** is presented for the first time. This function, which is a static outcome of the strategic pursuit, defines the relationship between the **strategic outcome** of survival/prosperity and a wide range of **strategic instruments**. These strategic instruments include the familiar factors of production – land, labour, capital, and technology – together with the less-familiar strategic ideas, strategic institutions/organizations, and **strategic leadership**. These instruments respond to changes in strategic demand as the dominant dynamic strategy unfolds, and this response is shaped by **strategic ideas**. It contrasts starkly with the supply-side concept of the production function that, in a factory-like society, is supposed to be shaped by technological change.

Chapters 13 to 17 build on this new concept and show how, in each case, population, capital, technological ideas, strategic ideas, and even strategic leadership respond to strategic demand rather than to forces on the supply side as traditionally argued. The key idea is that the core dynamic in human society is not technological change but rather **strategic change**, which in static terms can be thought of as an inward shift of the strategy function and in dynamic terms as the strategic demand–response mechanism. As suggested earlier, the so-called 'endogenous growth models' endogenize the wrong variable. This has important policy implications.

Part VI concludes the book by discussing, in Chapter 18, the predictions and policies arising from the dynamic-strategy model. It is argued that prediction and policy formation is a critical test for any model of economic development. If a model cannot be employed to make sensible predictions and to propose useful policy, it is unlikely to be able to provide a satisfactory explanation of the present or the past. This inadequacy may not be otherwise discernible, owing to the sophisticated mathematical modelling techniques used by contemporary economists, the difficulties involved in adequately testing this theory, and the widespread refusal to take Popper's refutation principle seriously. The dynamic-strategy theory, which is a general dynamic theory that can explain political as well as economic developments, is able to pass this test. To persuade the reader of this is the objective of the remainder of the book.

2 The Global Strategic-Transition Model

The **global strategic transition (GST)** is the process by which an increasing number of societies are drawn into the vortex of dynamic interaction between the world's most economically advanced nations. It is generated by the global unfolding of the prevailing technological paradigm. This unfolding process is neither inevitable nor smooth, a reality reflected in the fluctuating fortunes of the world economy throughout the history of civilization. The twentieth century, for example, has witnessed the Great Depression of the 1930s, the 'golden age' of the 1950s and 1960s, and slower, more uneven growth during the past twenty-five years punctuated by strategic crises such as those in East Asia at the close of the twentieth century. And as the dynamics of the **global strategic core** has waxed and waned, so has the economic development of the rest of the world. The attempt to model the GST in this chapter is based on my dynamic-strategy theory developed in a recent series of books (Snooks 1996; 1997a; 1998b), and explored further in Parts IV and V of this book. Underlying this process of global development are a set of dynamic laws (Snooks 1998a) that are introduced in later chapters. The existence of laws, however, does not imply historical inevitability because individuals and societies can and do act irrationally.

2.1 THE UNFOLDING TECHNOLOGICAL PARADIGM

There have been four technological paradigms in human history – the pre-palaeolithic (scavenging), palaeolithic (hunting), neolithic (agriculture), and modern (industrial) (Figure 2.1). In each historical era the technological revolution began in a narrowly defined region – a dynamic hot spot – and subsequently spread to the rest of the known world. The Palaeolithic Revolution, which emerged in East Africa about 1.6 million years ago, took about 1.2 million years to spread around the globe; the Neolithic Revolution (Old World), which first appeared in the Jordan Valley about 11 000 years ago, took only 3000 years to extend to the rest of the known world;[1] and the Industrial Revolution, which began in Britain about 200 years ago, is still spreading around the globe but should be completed sometime during the twenty-first century (Snooks 1996: ch. 12). Clearly the GST is accelerating with the emergence of each new technological paradigm.

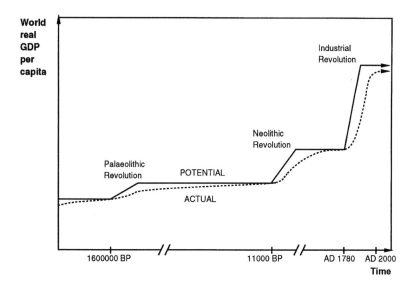

Figure 2.1   Great technological paradigm shifts, last 2 million years
Source: Snooks 1996: 403.

Figure 2.1, which illustrates these technological paradigm shifts, is designed to show two things: the stepped profile of *potential* real GDP per capita at the global level made possible by the three paradigm shifts (heavy line); and the more gradual increase in *actual* real GDP per capita (broken line). As can be seen, potential GDP per capita increases relatively steeply – becoming steeper as we approach the present – but it is then stationary for much longer periods of time that diminish geometrically in length. On the other hand, actual GDP per capita increases only gradually to the potential ceiling tracing out a more wave-like development path. This catching-up process between actual and potential GDP per capita is an outcome of the global strategic transition, involving a highly competitive **strategic core** whose dynamic vortex gradually draws the **strategic fringe** into its orbit. This is an outcome of the voracious appetite of the strategic core for the underutilized natural and human resources of the strategic fringe. These resources are accessed by dynamic strategies specific to each technological paradigm – the family-multiplication strategy in the palaeolithic, conquest or commerce in the neolithic, and technological change in the modern. It is these strategies that have driven each technological paradigm.

This is not a smooth linear process. There are long periods when actual income approaches the potential ceiling, and other periods when it moves away again. Eventually, however, when the current technological paradigm has been fully exploited – when excess capacity has been finally wrung from the globe's natural and human resources, and all its regions have been brought into the strategic process – actual income will press persistently against the potential ceiling. This is when the next technological paradigm shift takes place.

A new paradigm shift occurs because of the continuing drive of economic agents to ensure survival and prosperity – a drive that intensifies owing to constricting geographical conditions. These geographical conditions are what I have elsewhere called the **funnels of transformation** (Snooks 1996: 405). Historically these have been narrow geographical areas through which relatively large numbers of people or commodities have passed, and have included the rift valley of East Africa, the Fertile Crescent of the Middle East, the Meso-American isthmus, and the North Sea. In these dynamic hot spots the changing factor endowments and, hence, relative factor prices act as the catalyst for the introduction of new technologies to further unlock the richness of existing natural resources. There are powerful incentives in these special regions to substitute capital for labour and to invest in new technologies that will save on old natural resources and enable the exploitation of new resources. Once a new technological revolution has been forged, the GST begins anew.

Each technological paradigm with its associated dynamic strategies provides the conditions that determine the characteristic optimum size for the economic systems that flourish within it.[2] This optimum size can be defined in terms of both population and average living standards. In the palaeolithic paradigm the optimum size of economic systems was very small, consisting of forager bands of about twenty-five people operating within tribal structures of about 500 people. While normal nutritional standards were perfectly adequate and leisure standards were relatively high (hunting and gathering took about five hours per day), their consumption of services from durables – such as housing, transport, communications, education, health, and welfare – was very low. This placed a low-level restriction on their total consumption, made them particularly vulnerable to natural disasters, and allowed only a relatively short average life expectancy.

In the neolithic paradigm, owing to an ability to produce sizeable surpluses for the first time in history, the optimum size of economic systems increased dramatically. Urban centres based on agricultural hinterlands supported from 5000 to 30000 people depending upon the region and stage reached in the neolithic unfolding process, which operated within spheres of influence supporting as many people again. But by adopting the dynamic strategies of conquest and commerce, individual societies could, for a number of centuries, transcend those technological limitations. For example, neolithic cities in the Old World increased to 0.4–1.0 million people in empires that could be numbered in tens of millions (Rome had a population of 1 million in an empire of 54 million in AD 14), and in New World cities the population rose to 100 000–200 000 in empires of millions of people. While the normal nutritional standards of the majority of these populations may have been little higher and their leisure standards much lower than those in the palaeolithic era, their consumption of services from durables (including better storage and distribution of food during natural disasters) was much higher and so was their life expectancy. But, of course, the small ruling elites were vastly more prosperous than the earlier tribal leaders. Overall, real GDP per capita rose dramatically but the equity of distribution fell.

In medieval Western Europe, the fine-tuning of the neolithic technological system inherited from classical antiquity appears to have generated a marginal increase in the optimum size of regional capitals from about 30 000 in the early neolithic era to about 50 000 (the size of London) in 1500. This technological optimum was only transcended at this time by leading cities in conquest kingdoms (for example, Paris 230 000) and major commercial states (for example, Milan 100 000). After Western Europe broke out of its traditional confines into the New World and beyond, city size quickly transcended the neolithic optimum through the returns from the expansion of their conquest and commerce strategies. By 1700 the largest cities in Western Europe were London (570 000) and Paris (500 000). Yet cities of this size could not have been maintained in the face of exhausting conquest and commerce strategies had it not been for the Industrial Revolution which transformed the optimum city size. As Britain was the first to adopt the industrial technological paradigm, London increased its population to 2.23 million in 1850, 6.62 million in 1900, and 10.4 million in 1985.

It is not clear that economic systems in the modern technological paradigm have achieved their optimum size. Populations of modern affluent cities can exceed 10 million people (the size of some ancient empires), nation-states can exceed hundreds of millions, and mega-states thousands of millions. In these developed nations real GDP per capita has not only reached very high historical levels but it is far more equitably distributed than before the Industrial Revolution. In the Third World, however, cities have reached similar sizes but both the level and the distribution of income have failed to grow in a corresponding manner.

While this wider historical context is essential for a full understanding of contemporary economic development in this book, our focus here is on the modern global strategic transition, which has been in progress ever since Britain negotiated the Industrial Revolution two centuries ago. In relatively quick succession Britain was followed by the Low Countries, France, Germany, and the USA in the first half of the nineteenth century; by Sweden, Italy, Japan, Austria, and Russia in the second half of that century; by Canada, Australia, Argentina (temporarily), and Spain in the first half of the twentieth century; and a raft of South European, East European, and East Asian countries during the second half of the century. While on the threshold of the twenty-first century no part of the globe remains untouched, many regions have yet to be drawn fully into the dynamic vortex of the global strategic core. These regions include much of Latin America, sub-Saharan Africa, and parts of Southern and Southeast Asia.

Provided we do not derail the global unfolding process, there can be little doubt that the emerging strategic countries (ESCs) and nonstrategic countries (NSCs) will pass through the GST sometime during the course of the twenty-first century. This is not to say that they will do so in their present national form, just that the regions they inhabit will do so. While there is nothing inevitable about this fourth strategic transition, it will only be derailed by the occurrence of a major exogenous shock, such as a physical catastrophe (such as a massive asteroid collision) or a major nuclear war (that could arise from an attempted global takeover bid) or by the persistent attempts of international organizations to undermine the GST in the mistaken belief that sustainable growth can only be achieved in the context of equilibrium and Pareto optimality. A static vision is incompatible with the dynamics of the real world.

2.2 THE DYNAMICS OF GLOBAL STRATEGIC TRANSITION

In order to understand the manner in which a technological paradigm unfolds, is exhausted, and leads on to a new paradigm shift, we need to model this global dynamic process. This can be achieved by adapting my dynamic-strategy theory for individual societies that was first developed and outlined in *The Dynamic Society* (Snooks 1996) and presented as a formal economic model in *Longrun Dynamics* (Snooks 1998b). The global-strategic-transition model is the dynamic-strategy model writ large. It consists of an endogenous driving force; the pursuit of dynamic strategies as part of a strategic struggle between various SCs on the one hand and between ESCs and NSCs on the other; and a transition mechanism involving an interaction between strategic demand and strategic response. This process is explored further in Chapters 9 to 17 below. The outcomes of this dynamic process include a growing number of NSCs drawn into the global paradigm, increasing living standards of both SCs and NSCs, more equal distribution of income throughout the world, and a growing democratization of the world's sociopolitical institutions – outcomes that have been achieved despite, rather than because of, intervention by the development industry.

The Driving Force and the Strategic Struggle

The motive force operating within and between societies is the same. It is the attempt by private individuals and their political representatives to survive and prosper in a world characterized by scarce resources. These circumstances have led to intense competition between individual societies as well as between individuals within societies. A measure of this intensity is the record of regular warfare that has occurred throughout the world even since the Industrial Revolution, which effectively made the conquest strategy obsolete as a means for achieving economic growth (Snooks 1996: 307–14). It is this intense competition that has led to the global **strategic struggle** for the material high ground.

To achieve their objectives, individuals and their strategic leaders adopt and pursue dynamic strategies that comprise families of substrategies. This is discussed in greater detail in Chapters 9 to 11. It is essential to realize that the key to the dynamics of human society is this **strategic pursuit** rather than the way in which the resulting dynamic impulse is transformed into a larger per capita surplus. While the **surplus-generating medium** of our own era is the system of industrial production, in the neolithic era it was either the system of war or the system of commerce, and in the palaeolithic era it was the family system. As we shall see, traditional economics focuses on the system of industrial production rather than the strategic pursuit. Accordingly I call their practitioners the **productionists** and contrast them with the **stratologists**.

Since the Industrial Revolution, the dominant dynamic strategy has been technological change, although some small societies – city-states like Singapore and the former Hong Kong – have been able to grow rich by handling the products of the technological strategy. These small commerce societies depend heavily on the new technologies, and will never develop into nation-states or mega-states as have the technological strategists. Indeed, as we have seen in the case of Hong Kong, they are vulnerable to takeover by the technological mega-states. The strategic struggle for global dominance, therefore, involves competition between rival techno-logical substrategists or between rivals employing the same substrategy.

The industrial technological paradigm has been unfolding now for over two centuries since the beginning of the Industrial Revolution. It is a dynamic process that has been driven by competition between a growing number of new entrants, and which has passed through a number of distinct sub-strategies. The pioneering technological substrategy was pursued by Britain between the 1780s and the 1830s in order to maintain its global surpremacy following the exhaustion by the 1750s of its highly successful commerce strategy that had generated a global empire. It was a response to the general unease of the time that Adam Smith thought was possible. This first-generation substrategy was based on the innovations of practical men and was undertaken through the establishment of small-scale enterprises that focused on a range of basic commodities produced in one or two factories under common ownership. These enterprises began as small partnerships and family firms that gradually gave way to larger public companies. Individual initiatives were transformed into social objectives through the process of **strategic imitation** whereby successful pioneers are imitated by growing numbers of followers (Snooks 1996: 212–13; 1997a: 36–50). This type of development was well suited to the nation-state that had emerged in the pre-modern period in response to the older strategies of conquest and commerce.

The second technological substrategy was initiated by other nation-states in Western Europe between the 1830s and the 1870s. Earlier experi-mentation with industrialization on the Continent had been disrupted by a continued fascination with conquest, particularly by France. But with the failure of conquest, Western Europe as a whole turned its attention to the technological strategy. In order to compete with Britain in the continual struggle to survive and prosper, France and Germany – and later Japan in the East – used tariff protection to imitate the British strategy and to build new capital-intensive industries in engineering and chemicals. These new industries relied to a greater extent than before on scientific ideas and institutional finance. While the enterprises in this second technological phase were more extensive and operated through a wider network of larger factories (except in France), they were able to develop within the existing nation-state, or in the newly emerging nation-states of Italy (1861) and Germany (1871). As competition grew more intense between these nation-states during the second half of the nineteenth century, they embarked on a process of empire-building in order to defend their technological strategies from each other. It was an extension of the balance of power concept from Europe to the rest of the world. The important point is that these nineteenth-century empires were not economically essential to the operation of the technological strategy, in contrast to the empires of the seventeenth and eighteenth centuries that were an integral element of the commerce strategy. It is for this reason that the European empires were dismantled during the mid-twentieth century, a time when the technological strategy could be defended by the mega-states using the threat of nuclear weapons (Snooks 1997a: 503–6).

The third technological substrategy began in North America in the 1870s and flourished during the following century. It had its origins in the determination of American industrialists to drive the Europeans from the large domestic market and, later, to make inroads into the world market. The USA was able to do so by employing existing technological ideas on a scale that no other nation in the late nineteenth century could emulate, rather than by developing a radically different technology. Herein resided the comparative advantage of the world's first mega-state. By large-scale investment in mass-production and mass-distribution techniques, the USA was able to exploit its giant domestic market by supplying goods at prices the Europeans were unable to match. The method was to employ a high degree of specialization through assembly-line techniques in order to produce standardized products that could be distributed in bulk. Once the domestic market had been saturated by the mid-1920s, American entrepreneurs turned their attention – following a hiatus usually called the Great Depression – to world markets. After the Second World War this strategy was highly successful. It was a success based on the earlier development of mega-corporations – which could only emerge within a mega-state – producing an extensive range of commodities and services. When they established branches in overseas markets these mega-corporations became known as multinational or transnational corporations. They are, in effect, agents of the technological strategies of the mega-states, and they play an important role in the GST.

The fourth technological substrategy was developed by innovative nation-states in an attempt to undermine the post-Second World War dominance of the American mega-state. It is particularly interesting that those who were most successful in this new strategic thrust were the nation-states that had failed in the attempt to meet growing American hegemony by developing mega-states of their own through conquest in both Europe and Asia. In the 1960s, the reconstructed Japanese and German nations discovered that they could effectively compete against the USA both in its domestic and overseas markets by fully embracing the new microelectronic technology. If they were unable to transform themselves into mega-states at the expense of their neighbours, perhaps they could economically undermine the foundations of the American mega-state. Through more efficient production and organization, Japan and Germany were able to offer consumers greater variety and choice, even though this meant shorter production runs (only one-quarter of that of the USA in the case of car production). They were able to combine old mass-production methods with the new microelectronic technology to make customized consumer products of a higher quality. These more desirable commodities included cars, households appliances, ceramics, textiles, consumer durables, computer software, as well as food and drink. Consumers, tired of standardized products, responded to this greater choice with considerable enthusiasm. The shift of consumers away from standardized products eventually forced American businessmen in the 1980s to compete with these new dynamic strategists on their own ground.

Finally, we come to the fifth technological substrategy, which is currently driving human society into the twenty-first century. With the conclusion of the Second World War, it became clear to the nation-states of Western Europe, on both the winning and losing sides, that none of them by standing alone could command the economic resources required to successfully compete, either economically or militarily, with America. It also became clear that in the future the USSR would become a mega-state to rival the USA. Mega-status, therefore, would be important for Western Europe not only to defend the technological strategy that they had given to the world but also to engage in economic bargaining on a global scale, to exercise strategic control over a large market, and to effectively control a massive resource base. The future would be determined by economic giants employing a microelectronic/biotechnological programme. Here lies the real driving force behind that remarkable attempt to fashion Europe into a mega-state – remarkable because these societies have been engaged in a ferocious struggle against each other for more than a millennium. And we can expect the USA and the EU to be joined in their mega-club by China, Russia, and possibly others during the twenty-first century (Snooks 1997a: ch. 12).

The Mechanism of Global Strategic Transition

The energy for the strategic transition is generated by this eternal strategic struggle between the peoples of different societies. It powers the unfolding of the industrial technological paradigm that is gradually drawing a growing number of societies into its vortex. This vortex, or global strategic core, consists of a growing number of highly competitive and interacting SCs. The way in which this unfolding process occurs is through the mechanism of global strategic transition.

Central to the transition mechanism is **global strategic demand**. This is the demand generated by the global unfolding of the technological paradigm. While most of this demand is met by SCs in the strategic core, some of it influences NSCs in the strategic fringe. This takes place through international trade. What attracts SCs to NSCs is the latter's stocks of relatively unused natural resources, cheap labour, and their potential supplies of raw materials and foods. The NSCs most able to respond to changes in global strategic demand are those drawn most quickly into the GST. The NSCs respond to strategic demand by providing the labour skills required, making available their natural resources, and exporting primary and, even, manufactured products. And to do this they are required to change the nature of their institutions and organizations. The dynamic-strategy model, therefore, provides a new theory of international trade as well as a new theory of global economic development.

Of course, it is the SCs with their much greater economic and military power that gain most from the GST in the shortrun, but it can be turned to the account of ESCs and NSCs in the longer term. To generate this interaction, the SCs supply capital, technology, and institutions, and Third-World countries use these strategic inputs to construct their new dependent-technological strategy. This is achieved through a process of **global strategic imitation**. As the GST takes place, the living standards of Third-World countries rise, thereby providing markets for capital and intermediate goods from the SCs. In other words, the NSCs, on entering into the GST, pass through their own **national strategic transition (NST)**.

The global strategic demand–response mechanism is orchestrated by rising prices for natural resources, labour, and output in ESCs as it is in SCs. These rising prices provide the incentives for the ESC response. We can expect what I call in *Longrun Dynamics* (Snooks 1998b) **strategic inflation** in ESCs to be considerably higher than in SCs owing to the greater incentives required to induce the strategic response. This is due to the widespread existence of nonstrategic institutions and habits. We can also expect that strategic inflation will be more difficult to recognize in ESCs because the greater political instability in these countries leads to larger errors in policy, particularly concerning the money supply, and generates higher levels of **nonstrategic inflation**. Nevertheless, as shown in Chapter 11, where growth–inflation curves for Third-World countries have been estimated, the initial inflation rate – which is greater than that in SCs by a factor of three or four – is statistically significant. Because NSCs have not entered into the GST, they experience no strategic inflation, only nonstrategic inflation.

Instruments of the Global Strategic Transition

In order to facilitate the interaction between the strategic core and its fringe, characteristic private and public organizations and institutions have emerged. This is part of the response to strategic demand discussed above. Private instruments include a variety of organizations ranging from small companies established to exploit a one-off opportunity in a particular NSC or ESC to 'permanent' giant multinational companies that simultaneously exploit many opportunities in a large number of NSCs and ESCs. Public instruments of strategic transition include national organizations to support local strategists in their international operations; national bodies to negotiate trading arrangements, arrange technological and capital transfer, and secure aid; and world organizations such as the IMF and World Bank (see Chapter 7) to provide assistance to those NSCs that wish, in effect, to participate in the GST. Both SCs and NSCs support these institutions when they believe they stand to gain from doing so.

Outcomes of the Global Strategic Transition

The global strategic transition, as we have seen, has been underway ever since the nation-states of Western Europe began in the early nineteenth century to imitate Britain's Industrial Revolution. It took a century for Western Europe and its former colonies to overtake Britain (see Chapter 3). Southern Europe took even longer – not making significant inroads until after the Second World War. Clearly the GST takes time. Hence, it is not surprising that the income gap between the First and Third Worlds was not eliminated during the second half of the twentieth century. Yet there are positive signs particularly in East Asia, despite the recent crisis, where relatively high rates of economic growth have been achieved since the 1960s. As is well known, the problem areas are sub-Saharan Africa and Latin America, but even here growth rates were improving during the last few years of the twentieth century. And our model of global strategic transition suggests that it is only a matter of time until all these countries are drawn into the vortex of the strategic core. What is required is informed patience because, like it or not, it is not possible for bureaucrats or intellectuals to force the pace of the GST, which is driven by desires rather than ideas.

The main outcomes of the global strategic transition since the Second World War have been higher levels of real GDP per capita and changes in sociopolitical institutions required to adopt and pursue a dependent-technological strategy. These institutions include the rule of law, protection of private property, enforcement of contracts, a range of commercial rules, and a change in political systems and social customs. What it does not include are greater equity in the distribution of income, effective economic and political democracy, or 'human development' in terms of universal education, health, and welfare.

To demand 'human development' is laudable, but merely demonstrates a misunderstanding of the nature of the GST. Just as societies that are inducted into the unfolding technological paradigm gain greater global power, so individuals who are inducted into the ranks of the strategists gain greater political power through the process of national **strategic struggle**. Elsewhere (Snooks 1997a) I have called this the **strategic transfer**. And with this power they are able to influence the distribution of income and the expenditure on education, health, and welfare. The proportion of strategists in NSCs and ESCs will increase steadily – just as it increased in the past in the existing SCs – as the GST progresses. There is for any ESC a causal relationship between the stage reached in the GST, which is driven by the global strategic struggle, and the stage reached in the strategic transfer of political power, which is driven by the national strategic struggle. For intellectuals and bureaucrats to demand 'human development' prior to the strategic transfer will merely endanger the dynamic process through the encouragement of antistrategic revolutions.

2.3   CONCLUSIONS

The global strategic transition is as old as human society. This is the fourth in our history, and it will not be our last. To understand economic development we must understand and model the global unfolding of the industrial technological paradigm. This is absolutely essential for the formulation of development policy. The current fashion – at least in some quarters – of wanting to achieve human development before economic development will, at best, lead to a waste of scarce resources and to delays in the GST. As a systematic study of the past shows quite clearly, human development will occur as, and only as, the GST progresses. The role of policy is to detect the direction of change for individual NSCs, to remove obstacles to that change, and to facilitate its passage. It requires, in other words, perceptive **strategic leadership** that responds to **strategic demand**. This is achieved when political leaders are responsive to the needs of local strategists rather than foreign 'experts', particularly those that come from the IMF and World Bank bearing 'gifts'. It is impossible to achieve the *outcomes* of global strategic transition without passing through the necessary dynamic *process*. Yet it is essential to realize that the requirements of this dynamic process are constantly changing and that there are no static stages through which NSCs must pass.

Part II
Progress of the
Global Strategic Transition

3 The Unfolding Technological Paradigm

The **global strategic transition (GST)** exists in history as well as in theory. It began with the technological paradigm shift, popularly known as the Industrial Revolution, in Britain in the late eighteenth century and subsequently spread throughout much of the world during the following two centuries. As a result, living standards have increased dramatically in a continuously expanding sector of the globe – the global strategic core. True, the distribution of the gains of the GST are unequal, but every region of the world has a higher real GDP per capita now than at the beginning of this process, and there is every opportunity for individual societies to improve their ranking in this respect. The purpose of this chapter is to chart the progress made by the GST since the last technological paradigm shift.

Why, in view of the steady progress of the GST, is there so much frustration about the current state of global economic development? The answer is fourfold. First, most economists, advisers, and policy-makers in the development community take a short-term view. They think about these issues in a timeframe determined not by the reality of the GST but by their period in political office, in the development bureaucracy, or in academia. Secondly, there is little or no appreciation of the dynamic nature of the GST by the development community. Development theorists and policy-makers, as shown in Part III, view underdevelopment as the outcome of a series of supply-side barriers; remove those barriers and rapid and sustained development will be unleashed and the Third World will be transformed. To the contrary, economic development is the outcome of a global unfolding process that cannot be invoked by wishful thinking or by throwing resources at a few perceived barriers to growth. Such action, by wasting scarce resources and inflicting strategic damage, can only delay the GST.

Thirdly, the frustration over the extent and pace of global economic development has much to do with the point of time from which it is viewed. Viewed from the early 1970s, the growth performance of the Third World over the foregoing generation appeared quite impressive. Between 1950 and 1973, Asia (excluding Japan) grew in per capita terms at an annual rate of 2.6 per cent (even higher if we exclude the negative growth of Bangladesh), Latin America at 2.4 per cent, and Africa at 1.8 per cent. The reason for good performance sustained over a generation was the very rapid growth achieved by the principal nations in the global strategic core: Japan grew at 8.0 per cent per annum, Western Europe at 3.8 per cent, and the USA at 2.4 per cent. Only in the subsequent period, 1973 to 1992, when the global strategic core grew more slowly – Japan at 3.0 per cent per annum, Western Europe at 1.8 per cent, and the USA at 1.4 per cent – did the Third World, particularly Latin America (0.4 per cent per annum) and Africa (−0.4 per cent per annum), slump badly. Asia (excluding Japan), growing at 3.6 per cent per annum, was the only exception, and even this region temporarily exhausted itself in the late 1990s. Even the Asian 'tigers' appeared unable to defy strategic gravity for long. The resumption of the GST will require a new effort by the global strategic core. Those viewing global economic development from the vantage point of the late 1990s appear to have short memories. Finally, the development community has an unrealistic view about its ability to resolve the development dilemma. They usually believe that their participation will make a difference. When it does not, as it cannot, these interventionists view the task as hopeless.

3.1   IN THE BEGINNING

While the modern technological paradigm shift took place in Britain, it should be thought of as a Western European phenomenon within a global context. Britain (earlier, England) was one of a large number of small European kingdoms locked in a deadly form of competition for more than a millennium. Throughout much of that time these kingdoms attempted to survive and prosper by pursuing the dynamic strategy of conquest. In turn, Western Europe was subjected to intimidating pressures from without – from Arab societies in the south, Asiatic societies in the east, and the Vikings in the north. Elsewhere I have described this intense situation as a pressure-cooker environment (Snooks 1996: 252–63).

From time to time one of these kingdoms would gain a temporary advantage and extend its territorial influence through conquest. But eventually that kingdom would be blocked and defeated by a new coalition of other kingdoms. In the face of this fluid balance of power, no single kingdom could gain the upper hand for long. While conquest was highly profitable in the shortrun, it could not be relied upon to generate longrun surpluses. This made it necessary for these warring societies to produce the longrun surplus required for heavy investment in the conquest strategy from a continual improvement in agricultural productivity. Hence, the dominant strategy of conquest became the driving force in the longrun improvement in agriculture throughout the Middle Ages as well as providing major shortrun (a generation or so) gains for those who were successful at war. By the mid-fifteenth century, however, the conquest strategy within the old confines had exhausted itself.

In the late fifteenth century, Western Europe, which had been gradually resolving the threats from without, suddenly broke out of its confines and expanded rapidly into the New World and the Orient. The pressure cooker that was Western Europe had finally boiled over. Spain, on the first wave of this boil-over (owing to the military momentum achieved by success-fully pushing back the Arabs), pursued the old conquest strategy in the New World and, with the fabulous wealth it gained, set out to conquer the Mediterranean, where it struggled fruitlessly with the other old conquest societies of France and Austria. Some of the smaller societies, such as Portugal, Holland, and England, however, took advantage of the new com-mercial opportunities that the Western European boil-over had opened up. While the initial returns to the dynamic strategy of conquest were fabu-lously high in terms of gold and silver plunder, their potential was limited. Spain grew rich in the first half of the sixteenth century, but squandered much of its wealth in wars with France over Italian territory. The longrun beneficiaries of the boil-over were the English and the Dutch, who strug-gled desperately with each other throughout the seventeenth century for control over world commerce. This led to three major wars between 1650 and 1674, from which England emerged triumphant. For the next century this left England/Britain free to pursue the dynamic strategy of commerce and to build its first (commerce) empire. By monopolizing world commerce in this way, Britain was able to extract large economic rents and to grow rapidly.

Here we need to focus more closely on Britain, as it was to become the focal point of the modern technological paradigm shift. Figure 3.1 shows England's 'great waves of economic change' over the past millennium. Each of these great waves of up to 300 years (the second was truncated by the Black Death, which was recurrent for more than a century after 1347) is associated with a different dynamic strategy: conquest with the first wave, commerce with the second, and technological change with the third. These waves were generated by England's exploitation and exhaustion of the economic opportunities inherent in each of these three dynamic strate-gies (Snooks 1997a: ch. 10).

How did the technological strategy – the world's first industrial techno-logical paradigm shift – emerge in the aftermath of the exhausted com-merce strategy? By the mid-eighteenth century Britain had completed the construction of a mighty commerce empire, with London, the greatest city in the world since Rome, as its metropolis. But this entire structure was

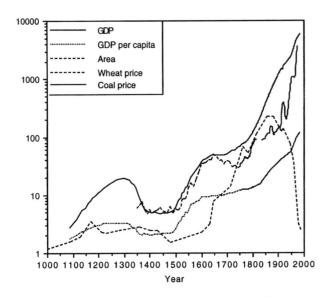

Figure 3.1   The beginning of the global strategic transition (GST): great waves
of economic change in England, 1000–2000
Source: Snooks 1997a: 276.

under challenge as the British dynamic strategy of commerce had been
totally exhausted by this time. In effect, the marginal strategic benefit was
no longer greater than the marginal strategic cost. This is an example of
what I have elsewhere called 'the law of diminishing strategic returns', which
states that investment in a dominant dynamic strategy will ultimately experience diminishing returns that will lead to a deceleration and eventual ces-
sation of societal dynamics (Snooks 1998a: 202–3).[1] Further investment in
the commerce strategy would not pay for itself. For Britain to continue to
survive and prosper it had to develop a new and viable dynamic strategy.
Britain stood at the crossroads – a problem that Adam Smith detected and
attempted to resolve[2] – where great commerce empires of the past like
Greece, Phoenicia, and Venice had once stood. These earlier exhausted
commerce societies did the only thing available to them, they turned once
more to the pursuit of the conquest strategy. And this is what Britain
would have been forced to do had not an entirely new option emerged in
the late eighteenth century.

It is one of those fortunate occurrences of history – rescuing the world
from certain global domination – that just as the commerce strategy
of Britain was being exhausted, so too was the neolithic technological
paradigm that had begun some 10000 years earlier. Britain, the world's

leading power, was able to take full advantage of this fortuitous coincidence. Rather than pursue conquest as its predecessors in Greece, Phoenicia, and Venice had done, Britain found it more profitable to invest in an entirely new technology that enabled it to suddenly gain greater access to existing natural resources both at home and in its colonies. Consequently it was able to sell new manufactured commodities at a price that no country in the world could match. Britain had a new lease on life and was able to resume earlier high rates of economic growth (Figure 3.1) and to become the workshop of the world, without the need, as formerly, to monopolize the world's trading routes.

Britain's second (or technological) empire, built between the 1870s and 1914, was necessary not to generate technological surpluses but to defend the technological strategy. It was an extension of the old balance of power concept from Western Europe to the rest of the world. When a more economical form of strategy defence was developed during the 1940s – the atomic bomb – Britain was able to dismantle its empire and, simultaneously, enjoy historically unprecedented rates of economic growth (Figure 3.1). After the Industrial Revolution, empire was an insurance policy designed to protect the dynamic strategy of technological change (Snooks 1997a: 294–5); after Hiroshima, empire was an encumberance that had to be dismantled in favour of more subtle intervention in the Third World through the 'development community'.

The industrial technological paradigm shift, therefore, took place at the very edge – the leading edge – of Western Europe. Britain, the first to experience the exhaustion of both the commerce strategy and the neolithic technological paradigm, played host to the new paradigm shift between 1780 and 1830, from where it spread to Western Europe and then to the rest of the world through the operation of the GST. This is an example of what I have elsewhere called 'the law of technological revolution', which states that once the potential for an increase in real GDP per capita at the global level is exhausted, a new technological paradigm shift (or revolution) occurs that causes a quantum leap both in *potential* access to natural resources and in *potential* living standards (Snooks 1998a: 217). Indeed, this law underlies the GST model.

3.2   CHARTING THE COURSE OF THE GLOBAL STRATEGIC TRANSITION[3]

Before charting the course of the GST, it needs to be emphasized that countries taking part in this global process will not experience anything like the neoclassical steady state or equilibrium growth path. Countries grow by exploiting substrategies within the prevailing technological strategy. In the early phase of a substrategy, a country will experience rapid rates of economic growth, followed by declining rates, stagnation, and even temporary decline. This describes what I have elsewhere called the **strategic pathway**, which must not be thought of as an equilibrium or optimal concept (Snooks 1997a; 1998b). The period of stagnation will be accompanied by increasing speculation and rent-seeking because, as the substrategy approaches exhaustion, strategic rates of return decline and investors and politicians move into alternative, non-productive activities. Those persisting with investment in the old substrategy can do so only with the assistance of the government and financial institutions, thereby creating unsustainable debts both domestically and internationally. This ensures the occurrence of a financial crisis that distracts attention from the real problem of strategic exhaustion.

While the many follow well-worn paths, the few explore new strategic possibilities. But, prior to the downturn and financial crisis, collectively they have little impact both because of their limited numbers and their limited access to finance, which is being directed into unproductive uses. This situation cannot last. Eventually it becomes widely recognized that the growing debts will never be paid back; credit is withdrawn; attempts may be made by international organizations (IMF) to 'solve' the financial crisis through 'structural reforms' (deflation); and the country goes into decline. Resumption of rapid and sustained economic growth will depend not on 'structural reforms' but on the discovery and adoption of a new dynamic substrategy. In the meantime, the so-called 'experts' who, in the absence of a realistic dynamic model, focus only on the fluctuating pattern of surface events, largely financial, talk unwisely about 'economic meltdown' – an unexplained retreat from equally unwise talk about the 'economic miracle' of a few months earlier. And they suggest policies of 'structural adjustment' (deflation) that only delay the strategic recovery.

The technological paradigm shift that began in Britain at the end of the eighteenth century was quickly transformed into the GST as it spread to the rest of Western Europe. The reason for the rapidity of this transition, which involved a mutually beneficial interaction between Britain and its close neighbours, was the intensity of the relationship between all the nations of Western Europe and between Western Europe and the rest of the world. This highly competitive environment, which had existed for more than a thousand years, ensured that if one country adopted a successful new dynamic strategy it would be quickly followed by the rest. It was a highly contested race in this new **funnel of transformation** in which Britain was the first across the line with the others in close pursuit (Snooks 1994b: 14–15; 1997a: 292–3). In what follows, the entire course of the present GST will be charted by identifying a number of stages: 1820 to 1870; 1870 to late 1929; 1945 to 1973; and 1980 to 2000. These stages are for descriptive purposes and have no analytical implications.

Stage One: 1820–70

Between 1820 and the 1870s, the various nations of Western Europe – particularly France, Germany, and the Low Countries – struggled to overcome Britain's initial technological advantage and to catch and forge ahead of their old rival. Earlier experimentation with industrialization on the Continent had been disrupted by a continued fascination with conquest, particularly by France under the brilliant generalship of Napoleon Bonaparte. But in the longer term the returns to conquest paled in comparison to those of Britain's new technological strategy. Bonaparte was a cul-de-sac for France, and it diverted other Continental countries from the new strategic pathway. In order to make up for this diversion, France and Germany used tariff protection to develop the basic industries of the British Industrial Revolution together with new ideas to introduce a more capital-intensive technology in engineering and chemicals. These new leading-edge industries relied to a greater extent on scientific ideas, institutional finance, and larger-scale operations. As the nations of Western Europe attempted to catch up with Britain they joined the new GST and, as can be seen in Figure 3.2, grew rapidly from the 1820s.

As Britain and, later, Western Europe adopted the technological strategy, they drew both Southern and Eastern Europe, together with the overseas lands that they had settled, into the GST. First, the outward expansion of Western Europe – the world's new strategic leader – had a growing impact on adjacent countries in Southern and Eastern Europe. This can be seen in the growth rates (slopes of curves) of Figure 3.2 for the period before 1870. While they were less impressive in both cases than the growth rates of Western Europe, it was at least a beginning. And after the 1860s, the rates of growth of Eastern Europe (largely Czechoslavakia, Hungary, and Russia) were able to match those of Western Europe. Southern Europe, however, continued to grow at a slower rate during the second half of the nineteenth century.

Secondly, Western Europe was also responsible for drawing the regions of recent European settlement, such as the USA, Canada, Australia, and

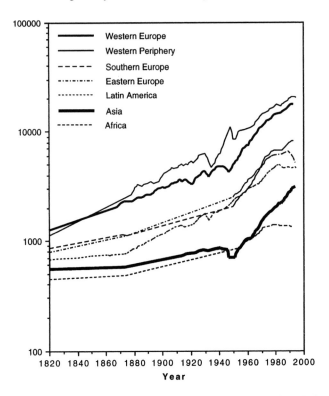

Figure 3.2   Progress of the global strategic transition, 1820–1992
Source: Maddison 1995a: Appendices A, C, and G.

New Zealand, into the GST. This is reflected in the high rates of growth for these regions seen in Figure 3.2. The Western European strategic core had an insatiable demand for raw materials (cotton, wool, and minerals) and food (wheat and, later, meat and dairy products) that were supplied by the land-abundant strategic fringe. In turn the strategic core provided the fringe with capital, labour, technology, and institutions, which were adapted by local entrepreneurs to the local conditions. It is interesting that from as early as the 1840s the European fringe actually performed better than the core. This shows how societies outside the strategic core can be brought into the GST when there is mutual benefit to both sides from strategic interaction. And, as participants in the GST, countries that have all the necessary attributes can, like the USA, go on to pursue an independent technological strategy, surpass the early pioneers, and take over world strategic leadership.

Stage Two: 1870–1929

During this second stage, the GST became more complex and widespread in nature. First, the global strategic core expanded from Western Europe to straddle the Atlantic. This resulted from the USA's successful attempt to develop a technological substrategy to exploit its mega-market. As discussed in Chapter 2, by large-scale investment in mass production and mass distribution techniques, the USA was able to exploit its large domestic market by supplying goods and services to local consumers at prices the Europeans were unable to match. This rapid industrialization in the USA is the main reason for the widening gap in Figure 3.2 between the growth performance of the Western fringe and the Western European core. The subsequent Great Depression was an outcome of the exhaustion of the USA's technological substrategy from the mid-1920s and its reverberation around the world owing to the vulnerable system of international financial and trading arrangements that had emerged from the First World War. And the depression only ended when the USA, as the global strategic leader after the Second World War, was able to redirect attention from its own mega-market to the global market (Snooks 1997a: 387–9).

Secondly, from about the 1860s the GST began to draw in regions from beyond Europe and its dominions. These regions, as shown in Figure 3.2, included Latin America and parts of Asia (mainly Japan) and Africa (mainly South Africa and Rhodesia). These include regions, if not the countries indicated, that are now regarded as part of the Third World, indicating the early if marginal influence of the GST in these areas of relative poverty.

Stage Three: 1945–73

The next stage occurred after the world-wide disruptions of the Great Depression and the Second World War had worked themselves out, and continued down to the early 1970s. During the early part of this period, when Western Europe was devastated by war, the USA became the undisputed strategic leader of the world. The technological substrategy, which the USA had so effectively pursued in its own mega-market until exhausted in the mid-1920s, was pursued after 1945 throughout the world. Only from the 1960s did Europe resume its earlier strategic role after more than a decade reconstructing its war-torn economy. Over the period 1950 to 1973, however, Western Europe (3.8 per cent per annum) grew more rapidly than the USA (2.4 per cent per annum). Figure 3.2 shows that the Western Europeans were able to close the gap with the Western fringe. The key to

Europe's new role was the attempt, particularly by Germany, to employ a new microelectronic technology to undercut the standard mass production approach employed by the USA.

This period also witnessed the catch-up of a number of less advanced regions with the USA and Western Europe. These regions included Southern Europe (mainly Greece, Portugal, and Spain), Eastern Europe (fairly widespread), and Asia (mainly Japan, South Korea, Taiwan, and Thailand). These efforts were so successful that by 1973 Japan's GDP per capita had almost (94.2 per cent) caught up with that of Western Europe, and was as high as two-thirds of that of the USA. Hence, by the mid-1970s, the global strategic core was more diffuse and difficult to define. Indeed, it is more accurate to say that there were two world centres of growth – although one of them was a false strategic (an antistrategic) centre – that of the USA/Western Europe/Japan and that of the USSR. Each core, together with its fringe, had only very limited interaction with the other, but extensive interaction within its own sphere.

While all regions in the world grew quite rapidly throughout the 'golden age' – due to the high growth rates and, hence, high degree of global interaction of the strategic core – the least impressive were Latin America (2.4 per cent per annum) and Africa (1.8 per cent per annum). And, as can be seen from Figure 3.2, African growth rates began to stagnate from the late 1960s.

Stage Four: 1980 to 2000

The current period, following the disruption of the 1970s oil crises, has witnessed a number of dramatic changes in the progress of the GST. First, after 1980 both Latin America and Africa recorded negative rates of growth that continued well into the 1990s. Reversing some 35 years of steady development, it was an outcome that reflected the growing uncertainty in the global strategic core about its own sources of growth and the policies that must be pursued to resume earlier rates of expansion. The major temporary exception to this is the USA which is experiencing a newly won and undoubtedly shortrun combination of good growth and low unemployment and inflation. There are always shortrun exceptions where upswings exceed the trend rate (*The Economist*, 25 April 1998: 31–2). Clearly the longrun technological strategy of the West is decelerating. The typical neoclassical response is to seek security in the state of equilibrium by pursuing 'structural adjustment' policies that, as discussed in Chapter 7, are not only undercutting the longrun viability of the Western World but are being imposed on the Third World through the IMF and the World Bank.

The second dramatic development was the collapse of the USSR, the world's antistrategic core, in the early 1990s. This collapse of the Soviet command system ended the division of the world into two spheres of influence. As shown in *The Ephemeral Civilization* (Snooks 1997a: 440–65), an antistrategic system is unable to generate sustained economic growth within either its core or its fringe and, hence, cannot compete with the strategic countries (SCs). From the early 1990s there has been only one contender for the title of global strategic leader. This collapse has added an entirely new dimension – the former antistrategic countries (FASCs) – to the development dilemma.

The third major development that *appeared* to emerge suddenly in 1997 was the financial crisis in eastern Asia, the only part of the Third World that appeared viable. The 'Asian miracle' has turned into the 'Asian meltdown'. Of course, neither description is appropriate. The so-called succession of 'miracle' and 'meltdown' is merely the process of exploitation and exhaustion of the technological substrategies employed by the ESCs of South Korea, Thailand, Taiwan, Indonesia, and Malaysia. It conforms to the predictions of the dynamic-strategy model outlined earlier in this chapter, particularly when one takes into account the role of ruling elites involved in rent-seeking. Once these societies adopt new and viable technological substrategies they will resume their rapidly growing development paths as part of the GST, which will loosen the grip of the rent-seekers. The main impediment to this is the neoliberal insistence of the IMF and the World Bank that these Asian countries attempt to solve their problems through supply-side 'structural adjustment'. It will merely eliminate strategic leadership and deflate these economies. At best this will lead to unnecessary social unrest and delayed recovery, and at worst it may inflict lasting damage on the dynamic mechanism through **strategic distortion**.

3.3 CONCLUSIONS

This survey shows that the GST has made considerable progress since the technological paradigm shift that occurred in Britain between 1780 and 1830. Over the past two centuries the GST has extended throughout Europe, throughout those overseas regions settled by Europeans, and has made considerable inroads into Asia, Latin America, and isolated parts of Africa. The region on which it has had little impact is sub-Saharan Africa. But, as my realist dynamic model shows, once the global strategic core overcomes its present confusion about the nature and causes of economic dynamics, the industrial technological paradigm will resume its rapid unfolding, and even Africa will be drawn into the GST. It may help to reflect on the pessimism a generation ago about the prospects of East Asia.

The current pessimism about the future of Africa, Latin America and, more recently, East Asia owes much to the undue weight given to the dramatic events of the past decade or so. Ironically, these events owe much in their turn to the poorer performance of the global strategic core – particularly but not exclusively of Japan – brought on by a slowing dynamic strategy and a confusion over the reasons and resolutions of this slowing. Clearly what we need to do in this book is to model the GST and to show how its operation and policy conclusions stand out in contrast to the traditional models and policies. But before turning to this task we need to consider in more detail the current state of both the Third and Second Worlds.

4 The State of the Third World

This chapter considers the progress and prospects of the Third World as part of the **global strategic transition (GST)**. It focuses on those nations that are attempting, with varying degrees of success, to pass through the transition from the status of a **nonstrategic country (NSC)** to that of a **strategic country (SC)**. Those societies that have set out successfully on the transition path – called the **emerging strategic countries (ESCs)** – still have some distance to travel. The remainder – the NSCs – have made little or no progress. Instead they pursue sectional rent-seeking tactics as they wait to gain entry into the global strategic transition. The first part of the chapter considers the state of these Third-World countries by developing a GST index to measure how far they have travelled, and the second part analyses the current problems and future prospects of NSCs in sub-Saharan Africa, and of ESCs in Latin America and Southeast Asia.

A distinction is drawn in this and the following chapter between emerging strategic countries (ESCs) and **former antistrategic countries (FASCs)**, on the ground that they are following different development paths. While sustained economic growth is a new experience for ESCs, it has, until recently, long been part of the experience of FASCs. As we shall see, the development experience of these two 'worlds' is very different. It is misleading, therefore, to lump them together as the World Bank, United Nations Development Programme and, hence, most development scholars do in their publications.

4.1 AN ANALYTICAL FRAMEWORK

To understand the state of the Third World we need to develop an analytical framework. This should involve a set of categories suggested by our underlying dynamic model, rather than the usual static outcomes approach. We shall consider both the conventional-static and the dynamic-strategy approaches to this issue.

The Conventional-Static Approach

Most recent books on economic development follow the World Bank closely by mixing up Second-World and Third-World countries in a simple set of income categories. This reflects their static conception of the development problem. The World Bank development categories in 1995 are shown in Table 4.1. Clearly this classification is based on outcomes rather than processes, and it is factual rather than analytical. Accordingly it cuts across any analytical framework. Further, the results in this table are paradoxical. The best growth performers are the very poorest countries, and the worst performers are the middle-income countries. This paradox unravels when we discover that the middle-income group is dominated by FASCs and the low-income group is dominated by more rapidly growing countries such as China and even India. Only once we apply a suitable dynamic model to this data can we sort out this confusing muddle.

The same can be said for the so-called 'human development index' (HDI) constructed by the United Nations Development Programme. This index, published since 1990, reflects the recent attempt by some to take a wider view of economic development. It is based on four statistical measures: life expectancy at birth, adult literacy, the enrolment ratio in formal education, and real GDP per capita. In theory the index ranges from 0 to 1 and is expressed to the third decimal place. The underlying philosophy of the HDI is that economic development is not just about economic growth but about the wider condition of mankind that the United Nations calls 'human development'. Hence, it incorporates a value judgement about what economic development *should* be rather than what it is, together with a presumption about the nature of its process.

Our objective here is to learn what the HDI has to say about the development process. Like the World Bank's development index, it ranks all countries according to the high, middle, and low categories for human development. This can be seen in Table 4.2. Once again the index tells us

Table 4.1   World Bank development categories, 1995

Category	GNP/capita ($US)	
	Level	*Growth rate*
low-income economies	430	3.8
middle-income economies	2 390	−0.7
• lower middle	1 670	−1.3
• upper middle	4 260	0.2
high-income economies	24 930	1.9
world average	4 880	0.8

Source: World Bank 1997b: 214–15.

Table 4.2   United Nations Development Programme human development
categories, 1993

Category	HDI		GDP/capita ($PPP)
	Average	*Range*	
high human development	0.901	0.804–0.951	14 922
medium human development	0.647	0.504–0.796	3 044
low human development	0.396	0.204–0.481	1 241
world average	0.746	–	5 428

Source: United Nations Development Programme 1996: 135–7.

nothing about processes, only about outcomes. In terms of outcomes it tells us that the HDI gap between the rich and poor countries is significantly less than the GDP per capita gap: the coefficient of multiplication between the low and high categories is 2.28 for HDI but as much as 12.02 for GDP per capita. In other words, the HDI index gives the impression that the hurdles facing the poorest countries are not as high as the income figures suggest. Yet, in reality, the majority of these 'low-income' countries has not even begun the GST process. In this respect, at least, the HDI is highly misleading. What it does show, quite convincingly, is that the scarce resources of poor countries have been directed into the non-growth component of 'human development' without a corresponding increase in economic growth. It is argued below that this only serves to delay the entry of NSCs into the global strategic transition.

The Dynamic-Strategy Approach

This brief survey confirms my earlier suggestion that to understand global economic development we need to develop an appropriate analytical framework. The analytical framework employed in this and the following chapter is based on the dynamic-strategy model outlined briefly in Chapter 2 and developed in detail in Part IV. In my model the GST is a dynamic process involving an interaction between the strategic core consisting of SCs, and the strategic fringe consisting of ESCs and NSCs. The ESCs are societies that have entered into the GST and, barring major accidents, are on the path to economic transition, while NSCs have yet to be drawn into this process on a systematic and sustained basis. Further, and this is the subject of the following chapter, since the collapse of the antistrategic core (USSR) and its satellites (eastern European countries), there has been a group of societies, called FASCs, that have begun the development process all over again, this time on a strategic rather than an antistrategic basis.

In the light of the dynamic-strategy model of global development, four analytical categories can be identified: SCs, ESCs, NSCs, and FASCs. These categories have analytical as well as factual content and, hence, are not empty economic boxes like the categories traditionally employed in development economics. Instead, they inform us about both the relationship between the strategic core and its fringe and the progress made by the GST. It should be noted that FASCs include those countries from Central and Eastern Europe and Central Asia that were part of the Soviet block of countries. These are countries that fully implemented the Stalinist antistrategic system and find themselves in transition from antistrategic to strategic societies. East Asian countries such as China, Vietnam, Cambodia, etc. never completely adopted the Stalinist system and, therefore, find themselves in different circumstances. They are best included in either the NSC or ESC categories depending on their degree of involvement with the GST.[1]

The best statistical measure of the GST and, hence, of the analytical categories into which each country falls is the rate of growth of GDP per capita in both the recent and more distant past. By contrast the HDI is misleading. As NSCs have been encouraged to invest in schooling and literacy ahead of successful economic growth, an index that takes these factors into account will give the false impression that some NSCs have already entered into the GST when this is not the case. As argued later, schooling and literacy are not the forcing ground for economic growth, rather, in the absence of arbitrary government expenditure, they are the response to changes in strategic demand and are required to facilitate the unfolding of the country's dynamic strategy. Hence, the HDI not only misrepresents the reality of economic development, it also provides the wrong signals and leads to further errors in policy.

Table 4.3, which summarizes the position up to 1995, presents the GST coefficient and allocates countries into the fourfold analytical categories of NSCs, ESCs, FASCs, and SCs. It also provides basic factual information on growth rates, GNP per capita ($PPP), population, poverty, HDI, and a comparison between GST and HDI. These countries, located on Figure 4.1, are ranked according to the GST coefficient, which is a simple average of the World Bank PPP estimates of GNP per capita expressed as a ratio of that for the USA, for both 1987 and 1995. The aim of this coefficient is to emphasize the recent past but not to omit the more distant past: this is provided by giving equal weighting both to the eight years before

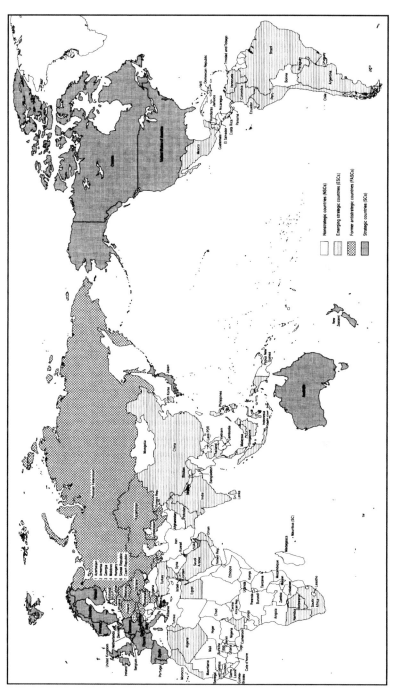

Figure 4.1   Geographical distribution of the global strategic transition (GST) in 1995
Source: Table 4.3.

Table 4.3   Impact of the Global Strategic Transition (GST) to 1995
I   Nonstrategic countries (NSCs)

NSC rank	Country (region)	GST coeff. (USA=100) 1987–95	Growth rate (per capita) 1985–95	GNP/capita ($PPP) 1995	Population (million) 1995	Poverty (% on less than $1/day) 1981–95	GST rank	HDI rank 1993	HDI minus GST rank
		1	2	3	4	5	6	7	8
42*	Ethiopia (Af)	1.85	−0.3	450	56.4	33.8	127	123	−4
41	Mali (Af)	2.15	0.8	550	9.8	n.a.	126	125	−1
40	Tanzania (Af)	2.50	1.0	640	29.6	16.4	125	103	−22
39	Chad (Af)	2.55	0.6	700	6.4	n.a.	124	119	−5
38*	Sierra Leone (Af)	2.70	−3.6	580	4.2	n.a.	123	126	+3
37	Mozambique (Af)	2.75	3.6	810	16.2	n.a.	122	122	0
36*	Burundi (Af)	2.75	−1.3	630	6.3	n.a.	121	121	0
35*	Madagasca (Af)	2.75	−2.2	640	13.7	72.3	120	108	−12
34	Guinea-Bissau (Af)	2.85	2.0	790	1.1	87.0	119	117	−2
33*	Rwanda (Af)	2.90	−5.4	540	6.4	45.7	118	110	−8
32*	Malawi (Af)	2.95	−0.7	750	9.8	n.a.	117	115	−2
31*	Burkina Faso (Af)	3.10	−0.2	780	10.4	n.a.	116	124	+8
30	Niger (Af)	3.20	n.a.	750	9.0	61.5	115	127	+12
29*	Zambia (Af)	3.85	−0.8	930	9.0	84.6	114	97	−17
28	Gambia (Af)	4.00	n.a.	930	1.1	n.a.	113	118	+5
27	Nepal (sA)	4.15	2.4	1170	21.5	53.1	112	109	−3
26	Nigeria (Af)	4.45	1.2	1220	111.3	28.9	111	98	−13
25*	Central African Republic (Af)	4.50	−2.4	1070	3.3	n.a.	110	106	−4

24*	Haiti (LAm)	4.60	−5.2	910	7.2	n.a.	109	104	−5
23*	Togo (Af)	4.85	−2.7	1 130	4.1	n.a.	108	100	−8
22	Bangladesh (sA)	4.95	2.1	1 380	119.8	n.a.	107	102	−5
21	Uganda (Af)	5.10	2.7	1 470	19.2	50.0	106	113	+7
20	Vietnam (SeA)	n.a.	n.a.	n.a.	73.5	n.a.	105	86	−19
19	Yemen Rep. (ME)	n.a.	n.a.	n.a.	15.3	n.a.	104	101	−3
18	Cambodia (SeA)	n.a.	n.a.	n.a.	10.0	n.a.	103	114	+11
17	Laos PDR (SeA)	n.a.	2.7	n.a.	4.9	n.a.	102	99	−3
16	Kenya (Af)	5.40	0.1	1 380	26.7	50.2	101	92	−9
15	Mauritania (Af)	5.85	0.5	1 540	2.3	31.4	100	107	+7
14	Lesotho (Af)	6.35	1.2	1 780	2.0	50.4	99	94	−5
13*	Benin (Af)	6.70	−0.3	1 760	5.5	n.a.	98	112	+14
12*	Angola (Af)	6.90	−6.1	1 310	10.8	n.a.	97	120	+23
11	Senegal (Af)	6.95	n.a.	1 780	8.5	54.0	96	111	+15
10	Côte d'Ivoire (Af)	7.05	n.a.	1 580	14.0	17.7	95	105	+10
9	Ghana (Af)	7.40	1.4	1 990	17.1	n.a.	94	93	−1
8	Honduras (LAm)	7.45	0.1	1 900	5.9	46.5	93	82	−11
7*	Zimbabwe (Af)	8.05	−0.6	2 030	11.0	41.0	92	88	−4
6	Guinea (Af)	n.a.	1.4	n.a.	6.6	26.3	91	116	+25
5	Papua New Guinea (SeA)	8.75	2.3	2 420	4.3	n.a.	90	90	0
4*	Mongolia (eA)	8.90	−3.8	1 950	2.5	n.a.	89	81	−8
3	Bolivia (LAm)	9.25	1.8	2 540	7.4	7.1	88	79	−9
2*	Congo (Af)	9.55	−3.2	2 050	2.6	n.a.	87	89	+2
1*	Nicaragua (LAm)	9.60	−5.4	2 000	4.4	43.8	86	85	−1

Table 4.3 (Continued)

II Emerging strategic countries (ESCs)

ESC rank	Country (region)	GST coeff. (USA=100) 1987–95	Growth rate (per capita) 1985–95	GNP/capita ($PPP) 1995	Population (million) 1995	Poverty (% on less than $1/day) 1981–95	GST rank	HDI rank 1993	HDI minus GST rank
		1	2	3	4	5	6	7	8
39	India (sA)	4.80	3.2	1400	929.4	52.5	85	96	+11
38	Pakistan (sA)	8.35	1.2	2230	129.9	11.6	84	95	+11
37	China (eA)	8.55	8.3	2920	1200.2	29.4	83	78	−5
36	El Salvador (LAm)	8.95	2.8	2610	5.6	n.a.	82	83	+1
35	Philippines (SeA)	0.45	1.5	2850	68.6	27.5	80	69	−11
34	Sri Lanka (sA)	11.35	2.6	3250	18.1	4.0	78	64	−14
33*	Cameroon (Af)	11.45	−6.6	2110	13.3	n.a.	77	91	+14
32	Indonesia (SeA)	11.95	6.0	3800	193.3	14.5	76	75	−1
31	Jamaica (LAm)	12.20	3.6	3540	2.5	4.7	75	63	−12
30	Morocco (Af)	12.80	0.9	3340	26.6	1.1	74	87	+13
29	Guatemala (LAm)	12.80	0.3	3340	10.6	53.3	73	80	+7
28	Paraguay (LAm)	13.40	1.2	3650	4.8	n.a.	72	62	−10
27	Dominican Republic (LAm)	14.00	2.1	3870	7.8	19.9	70	50	−20
26	Egypt (Af)	14.25	1.1	3820	57.8	7.6	68	77	+9
25	Namibia (Af)	15.60	2.9	4150	1.5	n.a.	65	84	+19
24	Ecuador (LAm)	15.70	0.8	4220	11.5	30.4	64	49	−15
23*	Peru (LAm)	15.95	−1.6	3770	23.8	49.4	63	65	+2
22	Botswana (Af)	18.00	6.1	5580	1.5	34.7	58	54	−4

21	Tunisia (Af)	18.40	1.9	5 000	9.0	3.9	57	57	0
20	Syria (ME)	19.10	0.9	5 320	14.1	n.a.	55	66	+11
19*	Jordan (ME)	19.45	−4.5	4 060	4.2	2.5	53	53	0
18*	South Africa (Af)	20.50	−1.1	5 030	41.5	23.7	50	73	+23
17	Turkey (ME)	20.55	2.2	5 580	61.1	n.a.	49	61	+12
16	Costa Rica (LAm)	20.75	2.8	5 850	3.4	18.9	47	24	−23
15	Colombia (LAm)	21.75	2.6	6 130	36.8	7.4	44	37	−7
14	Thailand (SeA)	22.90	8.4	7 540	58.2	0.1	43	39	−4
13*	Brazil (LAm)	22.10	−0.8	5 400	159.2	28.7	42	45	+3
12*	Algeria (Af)	23.05	−2.4	5 300	28.0	1.6	41	52	+11
11	Uruguay (LAm)	24.10	3.1	6 630	3.2	n.a.	39	25	−14
10*	Panama (LAm)	24.15	−0.4	5 980	2.6	25.6	38	33	−5
9	Mexico (LAm)	25.75	0.1	6 400	91.8	14.9	37	36	−1
8	Malaysia (SeA)	28.15	5.7	9 020	20.1	5.6	35	40	+5
7	Chile (LAm)	29.95	6.1	9 520	14.2	15.0	34	26	−8
6	Venezuela (LAm)	31.15	0.5	7 900	21.7	11.8	33	34	+1
5	Argentina (LAm)	31.20	1.8	8 310	34.7	n.a.	32	23	−9
4	Oman (ME)	31.70	0.3	8 140	2.2	n.a.	31	60	+29
3	S. Korea (eA)	34.85	7.7	11 450	44.9	n.a.	30	22	−8
2*	Trinidad & Tobago (LAm)	35.00	−1.7	8 610	1.3	n.a.	29	30	+1
1*	Saudi Arabia (ME)	n.a.	−1.9	n.a.	19.0	n.a.	28	48	+20

Table 4.3 (Continued)

III Former antistrategic countries (FASCs)

FASC rank	Country (region)	GST coeff. (USA=100) 1987–95	Growth rate (per capita) 1985–95	GNP/capita ($PPP) 1995	Population (million) 1995	Poverty (% on less than $1/day) 1981–95	GST rank	HDI rank 1993	HDI minus GST rank
		1	2	3	4	5	6	7	8
20*	Kyrgyz Rep. (cA)	10.15	−6.9	1800	4.5	18.9	81	72	−9
19*	Uzbekistan (cA)	10.70	−3.9	2370	22.8	n.a.	79	68	−11
18*	Azerbaijan (cA)	13.60	−16.3	1460	7.5	n.a.	71	70	−1
17	Albania (eE)	n.a.	n.a.	n.a.	3.3	n.a.	69	76	+7
16*	Ukraine (eE)	14.80	−9.2	2400	51.6	n.a.	67	58	−9
15*	Slovak Rep. (eE)	15.50	−2.8	3610	5.4	12.8	66	31	−35
14*	Georgia (eE)	16.80	−17.0	1470	5.4	n.a.	62	74	+12
13*	Armenia (eE)	16.90	−15.1	2260	3.8	n.a.	61	67	+6
12	Moldova (eE)	n.a.	n.a.	n.a.	4.3	6.8	60	71	+11
11*	Kazakstan (cA)	17.70	−8.6	3010	16.6	n.a.	59	55	−4
10*	Latvia (eE)	18.50	−6.6	3370	2.5	n.a.	56	42	−14
9*	Romania (eE)	19.20	−3.8	4360	22.7	17.7	54	56	+2
8*	Bulgaria (eE)	20.00	−2.6	4480	8.4	2.6	52	47	−5
7*	Lithuania (eE)	20.25	−11.7	4120	3.7	2.1	51	59	+8
6*	Estonia (eE)	20.55	−4.3	4220	1.5	6.0	48	51	+3
5	Poland (cE)	20.75	1.2	5400	38.6	6.8	46	43	−3
4*	Belarus (eE)	20.95	−5.2	4220	10.3	n.a.	45	46	+1
3*	Russian Fed. (eE)	23.75	−5.1	4480	148.2	1.1	40	44	+4
2*	Hungary (cE)	26.35	−1.0	6410	10.2	0.7	36	35	−1
1*	Czech Rep. (cE)	40.55	−1.8	9770	10.3	3.1	27	29	+2

53

IV Strategic countries (SCs)

SC rank	Country (region)	GST coeff. (USA=100) 1987–95	Growth rate (per capita) 1985–95	GNP/capita ($PPP) 1995	Population (million) 1995	Poverty (% on less than $1/day) 1981–95	GST rank	HDI rank 1993	HDI minus GST rank
		1	2	3	4	5	6	7	8
26	Greece (sE)	43.80	1.3	11710	10.5	–	26	20	–6
25	Mauritius (Af)	44.00	5.4	13210	1.1	–	25	41	+16
24	Portugal (sE)	44.30	3.6	12670	9.9	–	24	28	+4
23	Ireland (sE)	51.15	5.2	15680	3.6	–	23	18	–5
22	Spain (sE)	52.15	2.6	14520	39.2	–	22	9	–13
21	Israel (ME)	58.70	2.5	16490	5.5	–	21	21	0
20	New Zealand (AUS)	61.95	0.8	16360	3.6	–	20	13	–7
19*	Finland (wE)	69.35	–0.2	17760	5.1	–	19	6	–13
18	Australia (AUS)	70.15	1.4	18940	18.1	–	18	10	–8
17	Singapore (SeA)	70.25	6.2	22770	3.0	–	17	27	+10
16	United Kingdom (wE)	71.70	1.4	19260	58.5	–	16	15	–1
15	Netherlands (wE)	72.20	1.9	19950	15.5	–	15	4	–11
14*	United Arab Emirates (ME)	72.75	–2.8	16470	2.5	–	14	32	+18
13	Italy (wE)	73.10	1.8	19870	57.2	–	13	19	+6
12*	Sweden (wE)	73.20	–0.1	18540	8.8	–	12	8	–4
11	Germany (wE)	[74.00]	n.a.	20070	81.9	–	11	17	+6
10	Austria (wE)	76.90	1.9	21250	8.1	–	10	12	+2
9	France (wE)	77.80	1.5	21030	58.1	–	9	7	–2

54

Table 4.3 (*Continued*)
IV Strategic countries (SCs)

SC rank	Country (region)	GST coeff. (USA=100) 1987–95	Growth rate (per capita) 1985–95	GNP/capita ($PPP) 1995	Population (million) 1995	Poverty (% on less than $1/day) 1981–95	GST rank	HDI rank 1993	HDI minus GST rank
		1	2	3	4	5	6	7	8
8	Belgium (wE)	78.30	2.2	21 660	10.1	–	8	11	+3
7	Japan (eA)	78.65	2.9	22 110	125.2	–	7	3	–4
6	Denmark (wE)	78.70	1.5	21 230	5.2	–	6	16	+10
5	Norway (wE)	79.95	1.7	21 940	4.4	–	5	5	0
4	Canada (nAm)	81.45	0.4	21 130	29.6	–	4	1	–3
3	Kuwait (ME)	87.25	1.1	23 790	1.7	–	3	38	+35
2	USA (nAm)	100.00	1.3	26 980	263.1	–	2	2	0
1	Switzerland (wE)	100.65	0.2	25 860	7.0	–	1	14	+13

Notes:
1. Region symbols are: Af (Africa); sA (south Asia); LAm (Latin America); SeA (Southeast Asia); ME (Middle East); cA (central Asia); eA (east Asia); eE (eastern Europe); cE (central Europe); sE (southern Europe); wE (western Europe); AUS (Australasia); nAm (North America).
2. GST coefficient/rank has been calculated by averaging the indices of GNP per capita (PPP), with USA = 100, for 1987 and 1995.
3. Countries marked with * experienced negative growth between 1985 and 1995 and are in danger of GST relegation.

Sources: Columns 1 and 6: see note 2.
Columns 2 to 5: World Bank 1997b: 214–15.
Column 7: United Nations Development Programme 1996: 135–7.

1996 and to the longer period prior to 1987, during which the country had some involvement with the global strategic core. The reason for giving greater weighting to the recent past is that we can never take sustained GST progress for granted. Owing to the precariousness of the **strategic pathway**, it is likely that some NSCs and ESCs will slip backwards. These countries, which have experienced a decade of negative growth, have been marked in Table 4.3 with an asterisk. A comparison has also been made between the GST ranking – used to order countries from the least (ranked 127) to the most (ranked 1) successful – and the United Nations' HDI ranking.

Probably the best way to begin an analysis of this detailed database is to summarize the results for each analytical category, as has been done in Table 4.4. This table enables us to draw some interesting conclusions about differential growth rates, the relationship between the GST coefficient and the HDI, the nature of the HDI, the impact of the GST on poverty, regional differences in the GST coefficient, and the performance of the ESC group.

Differential Growth Rates

There are revealing differences in the growth rates presented in Table 4.4 between our analytical categories. The average growth rate over the decade 1985 to 1995 for NSCs (-0.5 per cent per annum) is negative, whereas those for ESCs (1.7 per cent per annum) and for SCs (1.8 per cent per annum) are positive and very similar. And FASCs, which will not be considered closely until Chapter 5, experienced, on average, high rates of negative growth (-6.7 per cent per annum) following the disintegration of the Soviet world. In other words, over the past decade the average NSC experienced a decline in its material living standards, whereas the average ESC and SC improved their living standards at a modest and similar rate. This is a very different picture to that suggested by the World Bank in Table 4.1: the poorest countries are becoming poorer, not wealthier as they suggest.

By reference to Table 4.3 we can explore beneath the surface of average experience. Not surprisingly the proportion of countries experiencing negative growth declines progressively as we move through the rankings from the Third to the First World: it is 48.6 per cent for NSCs, 23.1 per cent for ESCs, and 11.5 per cent for SCs (FASCs are a special case). This suggests that NSCs are twice as likely as ESCs to experience negative growth over a decade interval, and four times as likely as SCs. And for NSCs, negative growth is just as likely as positive growth. In other words, for countries yet to enter into the GST on a systematic basis, positive 'growth' should be interpreted as convergence to the stationary state following an earlier

Table 4.4   Analytical categories in the global strategic transition (GST) to 1995

Category	GST coefficient (USA = 100)	Gowth rate (per capita) 1985–95	GNP per capita ($PPP)	Population (million)	Poverty (% on less than $1/day) 1981–95	GST rank	HDI rank
NSCs	5.12	−0.5	1 266	16.93	45.1	107	106
ESCs	19.08	1.7	5 201	86.62	18.5	56	57
FASCs	19.28	−6.7	3 845	19.08	7.2	57	55
SCs	70.86	1.8	19 279	32.17	–	14	15

Source: calculated from Table 4.3.

exogenous shock. Such exogenous shocks include floods and droughts, epidemics, and external wars. Thus, NSCs, unlike those taking part in the GST, are sensitive to fluctuating fortunes in the natural environment, because they do not possess the surpluses, infrastructure, or technology required to react flexibly and positively to sudden changes.

GST versus HDI Ranking

A convenient overview is provided by Table 4.4. It is important to realize that considerable differences in these two ranking indexes at the individual level are transformed through averaging into quite small differences at the group level. Nevertheless, small differences at the group level are significant.

What Table 4.4 shows is that, while the HDI performance is better (lower score) than the GST performance for the NSC group, the reverse is true for *both* the ESC and SC groups. Table 4.3 provides further detail. For NSCs, the HDI performance of individual countries is better than their GST performance in 61.9 per cent of all cases, whereas for *both* ESCs and SCs this is true in only 46.2 per cent of all cases. The implications are important. Both ESCs and SCs are clearly determined to achieve more in terms of economic growth than of human development. Or, to put it another way, in successful countries economic growth leads human development, rather than the other way around as various international organizations claim. Yet they are the very countries encouraging NSCs to do the reverse. They have persuaded NSCs to devote a relatively greater share of their resources – which are relatively more scarce – to schooling and literacy, particularly of adult females, despite the fact that it is clearly to the detriment of the growth of NSCs. As I will show in Part V, education and literacy should not greatly exceed the strategic demand for these inputs to the development process.

The Ideological Underpinnings of HDI

The HDI is clearly based on Western values that in turn are an outcome of the stage reached by leading SCs in the global strategic transition. By constructing such an index, newly emergent SCs are made to look inferior to mature Western SCs. For example, in the SC group in Table 4.3, Singapore has a GST ranking of 17 compared with Australia's ranking of 18, but its HDI ranking is only 27 compared with Australia's score of 10; and Kuwait has a GST ranking of 3 compared with that for Canada of 4, but its HDI is 38 compared with Canada's 'perfect' score of 1.

There are two important issues here. First, newly emergent SCs owe their success not to human development but to economic growth. To insist on the reverse would provoke failure. Second, why should international organizations make value judgements – implied by the construction of a HDI – about the social performance of countries that have recently achieved considerable economic success? The dynamic-strategy model shows that as a growing proportion of the population in ESCs are transformed into strategists, and as their economic power increases, so will their political and social power. Inappropriate value judgements will just delay the whole process.

The Role of the GST in Reducing Poverty

The role of GST in reducing poverty is reflected in both tables. In Table 4.4, poverty, measured by the proportion of people living on less than $1 (PPP) a day, declines from 45.1 per cent of the population in the NSC group to 18.5 per cent in the ESC group, and to virtually zero in the SC group. Quite clearly the unfolding of the industrial technological paradigm generates not only high rates of economic growth for those involved in it, but also a dramatic reduction in the degree of poverty experienced.

It is essential to understand the causal relationship involved here. The reduction in poverty is the *outcome* of the GST, not of policies to redistribute income in advance of entry into this dynamic process. Indeed, misconceived, if well-meaning, attempts to pursue the reduction of poverty independently of the operation of the GST will not only fail but will delay this essential dynamic mechanism. This is due to a waste of scarce resources and to inappropriate interference with the strategic incentive system. But this is not to argue that ruling elites should be other than sensitive to the needs of their peoples.

Regional Differences in Development

Stark regional contrasts in economic development are reflected by Table 4.3. Of the 42 countries in the NSC category, almost three-quarters are from sub-Saharan Africa. Most of the remainder – such as Vietnam, Cambodia, Laos, and Haiti – are desperately poor because of the devastating effects of civil strife and war. It is, therefore, sub-Saharan Africa (with the exception of the southern tip) that has yet to be inducted into the GST. Africa will be the greatest challenge in the developing world during the twenty-first century.

The ESC category includes much of south, east, and southeast Asia, together with Latin America, and most of the Mediterranean regions of North Africa and the Middle East. India and Pakistan have been included in this category because there are regions within these vast societies that have clearly become part of the GST despite their relatively low national GDP per capita. And, recently, a few former ESCs, such as Singapore, the United Arab Emirates, Kuwait, and the formerly independent territories of Hong Kong (now part of mainland China) have joined the SC club. Needless to say, the technical boundaries between all these categories are fluid and subject to reasonable debate.

Membership of any of these categories is not necessarily permanent. Entry into the GST is certainly no guarantee that rapid economic growth will be sustained. It is highly likely that some countries, particularly those experiencing civil strife, will slip back from the ESC to the NSC category (possibly Cameroon), and even from the SC to the ESC category if they fail, as Argentina did in the mid-twentieth century, to capitalize on their resource bonanzas (possibly Kuwait and the United Arab Emirates) to generate a more permanent basis for sustained economic growth. A place in the GST can never be guaranteed.

The Precariousness of the ESC

The performances of individual ESCs during the decade ending in 1995 are, to say the least, mixed. This category of 39 countries can be divided into four performance groups: negative growth of real GDP per capita; positive growth, but less than the group average (1.7 per cent per annum); moderate growth up to twice the average (1.7–4.0 per cent per annum); and rapid growth (above 4 per cent per annum). Details are provided in Table 4.3.

(1) *Negative growth of real GDP per capita* This group constitutes 23 per cent of all ESCs. While it consists of countries from a range of regions, the largest group (44.4 per cent) comes from Latin America (and the Caribbean), and includes Peru, Brazil, Panama, and Trinidad and Tobago. The worst performers are from Africa (Cameroon, Algeria, and South Africa) and the Middle East (Jordan and Saudi Arabia).

While these countries at one time or another have entered into the GST, their performance over the past decade is such that they could well slip back into the NSC group. There is nothing inevitable or irreversible about individual experience in the global dynamic process.

(2) *Below average growth (0–1.7 per cent per annum)* This group includes 28 per cent of the wider category of ESCs. Once again the largest subgrouping (45.5 per cent) comes from Latin America and includes Guatemala, Paraguay, Ecuador, Mexico, and Venezuela. While these countries appear to have a reasonably secure position in the GST, their future will depend upon improving their rate of economic growth.

(3) *Above average growth (1.7–4 per cent per annum)* Some 30 per cent of the ESCs are in this group, and of these the majority, once again, are from Latin America. They include El Salvador, Jamaica, the Dominican Republic, Costa Rica, Colombia, Uruguay, and Argentina. The remainder are from south Asia (India and Sri Lanka), Africa (Tunisia and Nambia), and the Middle East (Turkey). These countries appear to have a secure place in the GST, but it must be stressed again that there is nothing inevitable about this global process.

(4) *Rapid growth (above 4 per cent per annum)* There are seven ESCs in this group, and they account for 18 per cent of the total. Their growth rates range from 5.7 to 8.4 per cent per annum. The dominant subgroup is east and southeast Asia, consisting of Thailand (8.4 per cent per annum), China (8.3 per cent), South Korea (7.7 per cent), Indonesia (6.0 per cent), and Malaysia (5.7 per cent). The gate-crashers in this east Asian party include Chile (6.1 per cent) and Botswana (6.1 per cent). This is the basis of the much touted 'Asian miracle'. Yet, as we now know, just a year later the same actors were at the centre of the equally inappropriately named 'Asian meltdown'. In the final section of this chapter it will be argued that East Asian ESCs have merely experienced a process of strategic exploitation and exhaustion that should be regarded as normal for this GST category. What should not be regarded as normal is the adoption of deflationary neoliberal policies imposed by the IMF.

4.2 DEVELOPMENT DIFFICULTIES AT THE END OF THE TWENTIETH CENTURY – A NEW INTERPRETATION

In this final section the main problem areas in economic development at the end of the twentieth century, together with their likely resolution in the twenty-first century, will be briefly considered. Detailed case-studies are out of the question in a theoretical treatise. The objective is to show the powerful nature of the dynamic-strategy model in analysis and prediction. More practical advice will be generated for interested parties in future position papers by applying my model and its policy principles to individual countries. Here I review the world's three key development problems: the apparently overwhelming difficulties of sub-Saharan Africa; the retrogressive nature of Latin American development; and the boom and bust of southeast Asia. Each of these problems is due to a different type of crisis: for sub-Saharan Africa it is a **nonstrategic crisis**; for Latin America it is an **antistrategic crisis**; and for Southeast Asia it is a **strategic crisis**.

Sub-Saharan Africa – a Nonstrategic Crisis

In the previous chapter, attention was drawn to the extremely poor growth performance of Africa since independence in the 1960s. This is the case particularly for sub-Saharan countries that dominate the poverty-stricken NSCs in Table 4.3. And this despite the considerable development assistance provided by the IMF, the World Bank, and SCs. These difficulties have attracted considerable comment. We are told, for example, that:

> Three decades of preoccupation with development in Africa have yielded meager returns. African economies have been stagnating or regressing. For most Africans, real incomes are lower than they were two decades ago, health prospects are poorer, malnourishment is widespread, and infrastructure is breaking down, as are some social institutions. (Ake 1996: 1)

And, in more colourful terms it is claimed that:

> From Cape to Cairo, Mozambique to Morocco, Somalia to Senegal, the continent of Africa is beset with life-threatening, large-scale problems. Famine and starvation, civil war and boundary bickering, crippling debt and crumbling infrastructure, plummeting economic performance and soaring population growth, burgeoning human disease and a devastating physical environment are features of everyday life in almost all parts of Africa. (Griffiths 1995: 1)

Africa seems to defy economic development. What is worse, no one seems to know why.

All explanations and proposed remedies from authoritative global organizations and expert individuals lack credibility. The neoliberals in global organizations such as the IMF and the World Bank see Africa's problems in terms of interventionist governments and underdeveloped markets, and they see the resolution of these problems in terms of 'structural adjustment programmes' and 'globalisation'. Other experts see the problem in terms of Africa's colonial inheritance (Griffiths 1995), lack of capital and entrepreneurship (Berman and Leys 1994), unfavourable terms of trade, and of complicated political factors (Ake 1996).

In this respect the first of the writers quoted above claims:

> The problem is not so much that development has failed as that it was never really on the agenda in the first place. By all indications, political conditions in Africa are the greatest impediment to development... African politics has been constituted to prevent the pursuit of development and the emergence of relevant and effective development paradigms and programs. (Ake 1996: 1)

Taking a different tack, our second writer asserts:

> The immediate causes of African misery must be put in the context of basic structural defects, both economic and political, deriving from the comparatively recent and short-lived colonial period when almost the whole of Africa was divided between European powers. The context is by no means the sole cause of Africa's present plight, but the colonial inheritance is crucially important and not easily disowned. (Griffiths 1995: 1–2)

Their views of the African problem and its resolution reflect their training. The political scientist blames the intense struggle between political elites for the marginalization of the development issue and he sees the solution in terms of the creation of democratic political structures. The geographer blames the colonial powers for creating illogical national boundaries that, he claims, have led to civil wars and African imperialism in imitation of earlier European imperialism. These problems can only be resolved, we are told, by changing these artificial boundaries and by creating the transport infrastructure required to overcome the present geographical fragmentation of Africa. And the neoclassical economist blames the perversity of governments for creating an African reality that does not conform to his model. The solution? Change reality to resemble the neoclassical model!

Clearly the problem of sub-Saharan Africa has a political dimension but, as the dynamic-strategy model shows, it is an outcome of the strategic pursuit rather than purely 'political' factors. In order to demonstrate this it is useful to begin with Claude Ake's (1996) coherent but flawed 'political' hypothesis. It is important to detail this argument because the political problem/solution is widely accepted today. Briefly, Ake's argument is that, with the granting of independence, the African struggle against the colonial powers became a struggle between African states and against the African people. During the fight against colonial domination the political elite enlisted the support of the entire population, but on gaining political power they used military force to constrain popular political expression. This led to the increasing power and influence of the military which eventually asserted its own control. The objective of the combatants, we are told, was to capture and maintain political power *as an end in itself.*

To achieve political power, the ruling elite enlisted, in addition to the military, the 'ideology of development', which they exploited as a means for 'reproducing political hegemony' rather than for achieving economic development for their society. Ake (1996: 16) claims that 'political competition tends to assume the character of warfare. So absorbing is the struggle for power that everything else, including the quest for development, is marginalized'. In this development vacuum, responsibility for economic transformation is placed in the hands of international organizations that promote and finance structural adjustment programmes, with a predictable lack of success. In this context Ake sees African development as 'improbable'. The only way to overcome this *political* problem is by providing a *political* solution. This, Ake claims, requires the introduction of democracy – not 'liberal democracy' but 'participative social democracy'.

Ake's argument, which commands wide support (*The Economist*, 3 January 1998: 15) is interesting and coherent, just misplaced. The central objective of human society, as detailed historical study shows (Snooks 1996; 1997a; 1998a), is not the struggle for political power as an end in itself, but a struggle for institutional control over the sources of wealth and income. And Africa's extremely poor development performance is not an outcome of political struggle but rather of insufficient interaction with the global strategic core. As pursuit of the modern technological strategy is not yet possible, ruling elites adopt either the antistrategic objective of rent-seeking or they pursue the traditional pre-modern African strategy of conquest. The essential point to realize is that Africa's problem has fundamental economic origins. While it is true that development has never been on the agenda, the reason is not that it was blocked by purely political forces, but that in the late twentieth century it was not an economic option.

Once again we need to make the key point that political change – in this case the shift towards democracy – is an outcome of the strategic struggle as a society's dynamic strategy of technological change unfolds. This is the only reason democracy emerged in Western Europe after the Industrial Revolution (Snooks 1997a: ch. 10). Hence, political institutions, like all institutions, respond to changes in strategic demand. In those countries that have yet to enter into the GST, there is no unfolding technological strategy, no strategic demand and, hence, no shift of political institutions towards more democratic forms. In these circumstances no amount of Western preaching about the virtues of democracies or of Western investments in democratic organizations in the Third World will hasten entry into the GST. Even the forced introduction of political democracy in a NSC, say by some international organization, would lead neither to greater economic development, nor to greater political freedom, because political freedom is an outcome of a mature technological strategy. Former ruling elites would merely reassert themselves because the people have no economic power. Effective democracy will not occur until the majority of the African people have been absorbed into the company of strategists, and this will only happen long after Africa has joined the GST. At present, modern strategists are few on the ground in Africa and most of these are non-African – Indian, Arab, and European.

How then do we explain the African situation? The central truth of the modern world is that, if an energetic people are unable to enter into the GST, they will seek out and pursue more aggressive ways of achieving their objective of survival and prosperity. These more aggressive ways include rent-seeking at home and conquest abroad.

Conquest was the main dynamic strategy throughout the pre-modern world, including Africa. This traditional African strategy (described in Morris 1994), was outlawed for a hundred years or so from the mid-nineteenth century by European imperialists. During the century of colonialization, Africa was forced to serve the strategic interests of the nations of Western Europe. But with the end of colonialism, the creation of a large number of competing African states unable to enter into the GST established the conditions favourable to the return of the dynamic strategy of conquest.

We have seen in the post-colonial history of Africa the emergence of two versions of the conquest strategy – war between ethnic groups within single countries (such as in Somalia and Rwanda) and war between different countries (such as the recent Nigerian invasions of Liberia, Cameroon, and Sierra Leone). In this way the successful warring groups are able to increase their material living standards, through exploitation of captured resources of oil and timber, without technological change. The outcome for the unsuccessful ethnic groups and nations, however, is disastrous. Sierra Leone, for example, which, according to my GST coefficient, was the fifth poorest country in the world in 1995 (GST = 123), is in dire straits. Owing to the conflict between Nigerian forces supporting the elected but exiled government of President Ahmed Tejan Kabbah and the Armed Forces Ruling Council that overthrew the President in May 1997, the country is in turmoil. Most of its businesses, banks, and schools have closed, hundreds of thousands of people have been forced to leave their homes, essential goods are scarce and prices (nonstrategic inflation) are high, and there is much looting by soldiers and the people alike. Such incursions by more powerful countries like Nigeria (which was ruled by a military class) will continue until they have the opportunity to enter into the GST and partake of more economical ways of pursuing survival and prosperity. Development policy, therefore, should focus on the emergence of a viable dynamic strategy rather than on prematurely imposed political democracy.

Until then sub-Saharan Africa will be at the mercy of exogenous shocks in the form of drought, floods, and disease. Only rapidly growing societies have the resources to respond positively to these external influences. A particular problem for African nations at the moment is the devastating impact of AIDS. This scourge has been particularly severe in the 1990s and particularly in the East African countries of Uganda, Kenya, Zimbabwe, Malawi, Zambia, Swaziland, and Botswana. Life expectancy in this region, which had been rising since the 1950s, stagnated in the 1980s, and plummeted in the 1990s. Botswana provides an instructive case. This country has grown rapidly since 1985 (see Table 4.1), had a GST ranking in 1995 of 58 and, in 1993, a HDI ranking of 54. In the early to mid-1990s, therefore, Botswana was placed in the middle of the ESC category. But, owing to a rapidly declining life expectancy in the 1990s from over 60 years to about 50 years, its HDI ranking in 1997 fell in a single year by 26 places. In terms of life expectancy, Botswana has returned to where it was 30 years ago (*The Economist*, 7 February 1998: 49–50). The impact of such high death rates among young, skilled workers – of all deaths in the 25–35 age group, 80 per cent are HIV-related – is difficult even for a rapidly developing ESC like Botswana (GST = 58) and Namibia (GST = 65) to handle owing to the continual loss of energetic and skilled labour, but for NSCs like Malawi (GST = 117) and Zambia (GST = 114) it is little short of devastating. It is imperative that the poorest countries of Africa join the GST as soon as possible, otherwise their future is bleak as they may well fall prey to African imperialism. But the GST takes its own time.

Latin America – an Antistrategic Crisis

Latin America, as shown in Chapter 3, grew rapidly between 1950 and 1980, but for the following 15 years experienced negative growth and high rates of nonstrategic inflation. Countries such as Argentina, Chile, and Venezuela, which at the beginning of this period gave promise of becoming SCs, slipped back down the greasy development pole. Only since 1995 has the region's growth turned positive and has inflation fallen to strategic levels. In 1997, for example, the growth rate reached 4 per cent and the rate of inflation fell below 10 per cent (*The Economist*, 6 December 1997). Latin America provides a clear illustration of the ever present danger of losing contact with the GST.

How are we to explain Latin America's development performance over the past half-century? It will be argued, in the spirit of my dynamic-strategy model, that Latin America's early attempts to develop through government-assisted import replacement, which were an outcome of the Iberian conquest strategy, led to the emergence of an economic system that made rent-seeking more attractive than profit-seeking. And, because of this, Latin America had only an ambivalent relationship with the GST – like a well-worn engine falling into and out of gear. The skills required in this post-conquest system were those of networking and political lobbying rather than those of innovation and risk-taking. Only once this system ground to a halt and appeared to be on the verge of collapse during the 1980s did business and political interests understand the necessity of dismantling the old rent-seeking system and of engaging fully in the GST. To understand how the Latin American problem emerged, we need to briefly survey its entire history.

Broadly speaking, Latin America has passed through three different phases of economic development that are similar to, but not as successful as, those in other regions of recent European settlement (such as the USA and Australia). They include a land-based export drive between the 1820s and 1920s, a process of import replacement between the 1930s and 1970s, and an urban-based export drive from the 1980s (Alejandro 1970; Bulmer-Thomas 1994).

The first century of independence in Latin America saw its constituent countries responding with varying degrees of success to the dynamic demand for raw materials and foods generated by the world's rapidly growing strategic core. Growth in the New World was imparted through the family-multiplication strategy, which has been pursued by all regions of recent European settlement. This involved procreation/immigration and internal migration to bring the vast land resources of Latin America into the global process of production. In the USA this process, which was known as the westward frontier movement, has been examined in detail elsewhere (Snooks 1997a: ch. 11).

The varying success of different Latin American societies was an outcome of their varying natural resource endowments. Those like Argentina and Chile, possessing a comparative advantage in the supply of wool, beef, and wheat, grew most rapidly. By 1913 Argentina, for example, had achieved a GDP per capita that (in $PPP) was higher than that enjoyed by any country in Western Europe with the exception of the UK and Switzerland, and as much as two-thirds of that in Australia (Maddison 1995b: 23–4). At first sight, therefore, it appears that Argentina had joined the wealthy countries of the world. But on closer examination it is clear that this was an uneven and precarious achievement.

Unlike the USA and Australia, the dynamic strategy of family multiplication pursued by Latin America was unsound and self-limiting. The cause can be found in the way this region was settled by Europeans. While the British settlements in North America and Australasia were commerce colonies, the Iberian settlements in Latin America were conquest colonies. This distinction is essential to an understanding of the very different economic systems developed in these contrasting regions. The Iberian conquest strategy generated a demand for characteristic institutions that favoured rent-seeking rather than profit-seeking, and these institutions were perpetuated even after the initial conquest strategy had been exhausted and colonialism had collapsed. The fundamental reason is that the great bulk of the region's natural and human resources were concentrated in the hands of the small ruling elite. This concentration, together with the military power to maintain it, were inherited by indigenous ruling elites in the postcolonial era.

The former conquest colonies of Latin America were ruled by small economic elites who owned all the natural resources, most of the capital, and who exercised close control over the population. Hence, the rich returns from the land-based export drive accrued largely to the landed elite, with little spill-over (owing to limited strategic demand and linkage effects) to the bulk of the population. This system generated the most inequitable distribution of income in the strategic world. Because the ruling elite was such a small proportion of the total population, maximizing the rate of economic growth was not viewed as a major priority. To substantially increase their surpluses they only had to marginally increase their rate of rent-seeking.

The tension between growth and rent-seeking would only emerge when the rent-seekers became, as they did after the Second World War, a substantial proportion of the total population. By contrast, in the commerce colonies a greater degree of economic and political democracy was generated by the strategic demand of commerce thereby causing greater tension between growth and rent-seeking, and the spill-over effects to the rest of the population were much greater. Latin America's achievement in the century after independence was much more precarious than that by the USA and Australia, because it was based on a system characterized by stronger anti-strategic (rent-seeking) elements. And it was uneven owing to the very different factor endowments. This precariousness was highlighted during the interwar years when the family-multiplication strategy had largely exhausted itself. By the Second World War, therefore, no country in the region had been drawn very deeply or very securely into the GST. Appearances to the contrary were deceptive.

The second phase of economic development, from 1929 to 1980, was a response to the exhaustion of the earlier strategy, which was exacerbated by the deteriorating performance of the global strategic core. The growing reaction to this dilemma, which was reflected in a deteriorating balance of payments, was an attempt to encourage import replacement through tariff protection and state assistance to local manufacturers. This approach was reinforced, as shown in Chapter 6, by the theories of 'structuralists' such as Raúl Prebisch, the foundation director of the UN Economic Commission for Latin America (ECLA).

The import-replacement approach to economic development is misleadingly called 'import substitution industrialization' (ISI) – misleading because it give the impression that this is a dynamic strategy. We must be very clear on this point. *ISI is not a dynamic strategy, only a convenient stepping stone to the real dynamic strategy of technological change.* In fact, if import replacement is pursued on a longrun basis it will actually become an antistrategy, by creating the more or less permanent conditions for rent-seeking rather than those for profit-seeking. The structuralists failed to see this problem because they (like the current crop of neoliberals) did not possess an appropriate dynamic model.

Urban rent-seeking came easily to societies that, owing to their conquest origins, had long practiced the art. In an environment where economic and political competition were severely restricted, rent-seeking was more rewarding than profit-seeking. The ruling elites of Latin American societies continued to monopolize the natural and man-made resources. Where this produced rebellion, as under Peron in Argentina, the new ruling groups merely assumed the mantle of rent-seekers, and redirected existing surpluses to themselves and their supporters rather than creating *greater* surpluses to be shared by *all*. And this preoccupation with redirecting existing surpluses diverted societies like Argentina from the external 'golden age' in world trade in the 1950s and 1960s to the internal struggle between rent-seeking groups. Trade-diverting institutions, which were a response to antistrategic demand, did not cause rent-seeking, they just facilitated it.

The bottom line for an antistrategic society is that it grows less rapidly than a strategic society. Contrast Argentina with Australia. Between 1913 and 1980, Argentina's GDP per capita as a proportion of Australia's (in $PPP) declined from 69 to 59 per cent. Instead of catching up with Australia, as one would have expected, it fell further behind. While slower growth is not a matter of concern for rent-seekers who constitute an insignificant proportion of the total population, it becomes critically important when that proportion increases to significant levels as was the case in Argentina after the rule of Peron. For post-1945 Latin America the tension between rent-seeking and growth became unendurable. Further, an antistrategic society finds it more difficult than a strategic society to replace an exhausted import-replacement programme with a real dynamic strategy.

The exhausting process of import replacement revived interest in export-led growth in some Latin American countries as early as the late 1960s. But the well-developed system of rent-seeking prevented an easy transition. Only when this growing problem was brought home forcibly by the debt crisis of the early 1980s did an increasing number of governments and businessmen realize that major changes had to be made to their economic system. The combined effect of import-replacement exhaustion and debt crisis led to a decade of virtual stagnation. This was an antistrategic crisis of major proportions. Between 1970 and 1980, manufacturing in Latin America (including the Caribbean) grew at 6.2 per cent per annum and real GDP increased by 5.4 per cent per annum; whereas between 1980 and 1993 the respective annual growth rates were 0.8 and 1.9 (World Bank 1993: 240–1; 1995: 164–5). Needless to say, many decision-makers responded to these circumstances by redoubling their networking and lobbying efforts and by a greater involvement in speculative activities. In the process, inflation (of a nonstrategic kind) soared to high levels. Only in the early to mid-1990s were the majority convinced that a new economic way had to be found – that the old antistrategic system, which had given Latin America birth and succour, had to be dismantled.

The standard explanation for Latin America's adoption of and persistence with the import-replacement approach is very different to the dynamic-strategy explanation. It is usually claimed by institutionalists to be the outcome of culture. At the more sophisticated end of the institutionalist spectrum the argument runs along the lines that inefficient institutions and policies become locked into these societies owing to the nature of social evolution rather than to the degree of flexibility in the rent-seeking tactic (determined by the relative size of the rent-seeking group). North (1990), for example, argues that in a world of increasing institutional returns and of deficient informational feedback the conceptual modes of decision-makers do not converge on the 'true' models. In this explanation, increasing returns reinforce the direction of institutional development once a society begins on a particular path, and incomplete markets, which (together with cultural values) reinforce faulty conceptual models, lead to divergence from the most efficient development path. Hence, inefficient institutional systems persist in some societies (but, strangely, not in others) and differential growth rates are experienced.

At the less sophisticated end of the institutionalist spectrum is a recent argument in *The Economist* (6 December 1997, Survey: 7–8) to the effect that Latin American culture together with the weakness of its legal framework favour the development of family-controlled conglomerates that encourage interventionism, rather than market-oriented corporations that promote *laissez-faire*. We are told that 'family businesses in Latin America are strong partly because the extended family itself is strong' and, hence, the clash between profit maximization on the one hand and 'family duty and social status' on the other, will usually be resolved by entrepreneurs in favour of the latter. It is further claimed that:

> Such entrepreneurs were willing collaborators in the development of protectionist and interventionist states in Latin America from the 1930s onwards. Reluctant to stump up large sums of capital themselves, they were happy for the state to invest in capital-intensive industries such as steel, and to become a source of subsidised credit for local private businesses. It was only when debt and inflation became overwhelming and the private sector started being crowded out of the credit market that many Latin American entrepreneurs became grudging converts to economic liberalism.
>
> The logic of the family business and of protectionism combined to discourage growth through specialisation, which might have led such firms to conquer foreign markets and become multinationals in their own right.

What, one wonders, happened in the end to 'the logic of family business' and the 'strength' of the Latin American family. This is institutionalism at its crudest.

One observer of Latin America has claimed:

> No single theory will explain both the intermediate position occupied by
> Latin America on the scale of world income per head and the differ-
> ences that have emerged among Latin American countries over time. Yet
> a theoretical framework is essential if economic history is to be more
> than mere description. (Bulmer-Thomas 1994: 14)

The dynamic-strategy model presented in this book claims to do precisely
this. Certainly it confounds the institutional approach. First, it shows that
institutional evolution as a biological-like process is a myth (Snooks
1997a). In reality, institutional change is a response to changing strategic
demand as the dominant dynamic strategy unfolds. The evolutionary myth
is exploded by the fact that a reversal of the strategic sequence will cause a
reversal of institutional change. In evolutionary biology, which is unidirectional, such reversals cannot occur. Secondly, in the light of this discovery,
the alleged (by *The Economist*) 'weaknesses of the legal framework' and
the existence of 'family-controlled conglomerates' is an outcome of the
antistrategic demand for these institutions generated by Latin America's
import-replacement programme. These institutions were not barriers to
a more outward-looking strategy, they were precisely what was required
to facilitate the path chosen. In these circumstances there is no need for
arguments about 'faulty conceptual models', 'deficient informational feedback', or historical 'lock-in'. Performance depends on the chosen dynamic
strategy.

Since the late 1980s, Latin America has realized the limitations of its
traditional antistrategic (or rent-seeking) approach owing to its increasing
inflexibility (resulting from an increase in the relative size of the rent-
seeking group), and currently it is groping towards a proper strategic
approach. The new export strategy, which promises to integrate it securely
into the GST, has generated a strategic demand for new institutions. And it
is in response to this demand that Latin American countries have recently
dismantled the old antistrategic institutions. This has led to a liberalization
of trade through the removal of tariff barriers, the control of nonstrategic
inflation that masks the essential strategic inflation, the dismantling of the
interventionist state, and the restructuring of the business sector.

The retreat of the state has led to a massive privatization programme,
particularly of public utilities such as telecommunications and electricity.
Over the past decade some 279 companies have been sold by the seven
largest countries in the region for a total of $90 billion (ibid.: 11). This
remarkable sell-off, which echoes that of the FASCs examined in the next

chapter, was initiated by Chile and Mexico in the late 1980s and followed by Argentina and Peru in the early 1990s, and by Brazil in the late 1990s. In addition to restructuring, Latin American firms are, for the first time in more than half a century, aggressively seeking foreign capital to finance their new dynamic strategy.

This is, of course, only the beginning. Latin America needs to pass beyond mere structural adjustment, which is just the first step (as import-replacement should have been from the 1930s) towards a real technological strategy. If this first step is successfully negotiated and the Latin American countries enter fully into the GST, the unfolding dynamic strategy will require additional institutional changes in the economic, political, legal, administrative, and social arenas. The essential point to grasp is that these changes are a response to the demands of the new strategy, not the other way around. Most commentators regard these 'structural adjustments' as the prime mover in economic growth and development. They are not, never have been, and never will be. It is the objective of this book to explain why.

Southeast Asia – a Strategic Crisis

Since the late fifteenth century Southeast Asia has experienced an inter-mittent and partial interaction with the global strategic core. From the early sixteenth to the late eighteenth centuries this interaction was based on the Western European dynamic strategy of commerce, and from the early nineteenth century to the present time it has arisen from the Western European/North American/Northeast Asian dynamic strategy of techno-logical change. The contrast with Latin America, which began its relation-ship with Europe on the wrong end of the conquest strategy, is clear. Although Southeast Asia (with the exception of Siam/Thailand) was sub-jected to Western European and North American colonization, this was the more liberal colonization of commerce and, later, industrial technology, rather than conquest. The implication is important: Southeast Asia did not have forced upon it the infrastructure of conquest which, in Latin America, generated the conditions for antistrategic rent-seeking rather than strategic profit-seeking.

The first of these two phases of strategic interaction has interest here because of the contrast with the current situation. What it shows is that interaction with the global strategic core does not inevitably lead the fringe countries into developing their own dynamic strategies, which are essen-tial if economic development is to be perpetuated. This early strategic core–fringe interaction generated a long phase of economic expansion between 1450 and 1680. A leading expert on this period, Tony Reid (1988; 1993), has called this the Southeast Asian 'age of commerce', based on the export of pepper, spices, resins, tortoiseshell, aromatic woods, and the import of fine cloth, silver, copper, ceramics, and silk from India, the Americas, Japan, and China. This long-distance trade generated considerable wealth in a number of large commercial centres, usually capital cities, and in their hinterlands. While this commerce was controlled by foreigners – including Europeans and Chinese, who provided the entrepreneurship, capital, and commercial networks – it was exploited by rent-seeking local rulers. As the commercial expansion was externally driven, once the global strategic core experienced recession and stagnation from the late seventeenth century, the Southeast Asian age of commerce came to an abrupt end.

Southeast Asian expansion did not revive again until the mid-nineteenth century, this time as a result of a new dynamic strategy pursued by Western Europe – technological change. Once again Western Europe and, later, North America, and Northeast Asia found this region attractive, initially, as a source of raw materials and foods required for industrialization and, subsequently, as an extension of their industrial activities. Once again Southeast Asia was drawn into a GST (the first neolithic, the second industrial) as the world's industrial technological paradigm unfolded. But, for the following century there was little to suggest that this second expansionary phase would be any more permanent than the earlier one. Indeed, whenever the global strategic core faltered owing to exogenous shocks, such as world war (1914–18), or to strategic exhaustion, such as the Great Depression of the 1930s, Southeast Asian prosperity suffered.

Only after the Second World War when old colonial links were severed did a number of these newly independent countries seriously embark on their own industrialization programmes (Booth 1991 and 1998; Warr 1993; Brown 1997). Initially, during the 1950s and 1960s, countries such as the Philippines, Singapore, Thailand, and Malaysia began experimenting with import replacement (or ISI) by employing tariffs, selective foreign exchange allocations, and multiple exchange rates (Brown 1997: 68). This was a first tentative step in developing their own technological substrategy. As we have seen, Latin America got stuck on this step for more than half a century.

While manufacturing in Southeast Asia increased rapidly in the 1950s and 1960s, it soon became obvious to local interests that this type of economic development was severely limited. Owing to the less entrenched rent-seeking interests and the higher proportion of active participants in the economic process (in comparison with Latin America), various countries began pursuing export-oriented manufacturing development using foreign technology. The first to explore export-led growth in the mid-1960s was Singapore because of the limitations for ISI of its small domestic market. In quick succession Singapore was followed by Thailand, Malaysia, and the Philippines in the late 1960s and early 1970s, and by Indonesia in the early 1980s. Accordingly, the contribution of manufacturing to GDP by these five countries increased from between 13 to 28 per cent in 1965 to 30 to 38 per cent in 1986 (ibid.: 67). As this expansion of manufacturing was based on the importation of foreign technology, total factor productivity in the region increased dramatically: between 1960 and 1984 total factor productivity grew at between 0.7 and 1.3 per cent per annum, whereas between 1984 and 1994 it grew more rapidly at between 1.3 and 3.3 per cent per annum (Collins and Bosworth 1996). By the mid-1990s, Southeast Asia had taken the second step towards developing its own technological substrategy. This elevated their GST status to ESCs with considerable future potential – a status that has not been destroyed by the present financial difficulties. Nevertheless, they have yet to take the third and final step on the road to becoming full members of the SC category.

There are a number of aspects of this economic transition that need to be highlighted. First, there was a major change in the nature of Southeast Asia's interaction with the global strategic core in the second half of the twentieth century. During the hundred years from the mid-nineteenth century, Southeast Asia's strategic partners were Western Europe and North America, but increasingly since the 1950s there has been a shift towards Japan and, more recently, South Korea and Taiwan. Secondly, the focus of interest in Southeast Asia by the global strategic core has changed considerably over the past century. Initially the strategic core demanded raw materials and foods but, increasingly from the 1960s, the region's cheap labour made it desirable to relocate some types and stages of industrialization – particularly textiles, clothing, and the assembly of electronic goods – from the core to the fringe. Thirdly, as Southeast Asia's new industrial strategy has unfolded, its ruling elite has shown a considerable degree of flexibility by shifting from exploiting strategists (rent-seeking) to participating directly in the new strategy (profit-seeking). In this they are responding opportunistically to new economic opportunities and to the growing demands, both economic and political, of the new strategists. The ruling elite has discovered that, as they and their fellow travellers have become more significant in the total population, growth rather than stagnation is the best way to increase their wealth. Yet they still attempt to retain direct control over this strategic process and many are closely involved in corruption and cronyism. The interesting issue for the future will be whether they are sufficiently flexible to adjust to changing strategic demand for democratic and strategic leadership or whether they will attempt to hold on to the current sources of their wealth and, in that event, be swept away. The latter is most probable.

What are the implications for Southeast Asia's future economic development arising from the present (March 1998) financial difficulties? Are we witnessing an East Asian 'meltdown' as the doomsters insist or merely a temporary difficulty in the longrun process of transition from NSC to ESC to SC? It is argued here that Southeast Asia's present difficulties are the outcome of the exhaustion of their current technological substrategy. Hence the problem can be regarded as a normal strategic crisis, which will lead quite quickly to a reevaluation of their approach, to a readjustment of sociopolitical institutions to meet newly emergent economic realities, and to the development of a new technological substrategy. This does not mean that there will be no casualties – much will depend on the outcome of the internal strategic struggle between new strategists and old antistrategists. In the process, the strategists are likely to assert themselves more in an effort to gain greater political control over the sources of their new wealth. This contrasts with the antistrategic crisis in Latin America that led to almost two decades of stagnation and regression.

The events, if not the fundamental causes, of the current Asian 'financial' crisis are fresh in our minds. Most observers focus not on the underlying dynamic process, but on the financial outcomes, particularly the currency 'collapse', the escalating foreign debt, and the difficulties experienced by financial institutions. The financial crisis began in Thailand in mid-1997 and spread quickly to Indonesia, Malaysia, and the Philippines during late 1997 and early 1998. A striking manifestation of this crisis has been the 'collapse' of Southeast Asian currencies against the US dollar, which has exacerbated the foreign debt and rendered most businesses technically bankrupt. Between 31 December 1996 and 23 February 1998, the magnitude of the currency devaluation ranged from 35 per cent for Malaysia to about 80 per cent for Indonesia. This rendered impossible any attempt to service the foreign debt, which in June 1997 was, as a proportion of GDP, 45 per cent for Thailand, 35 per cent for Indonesia, and 30 per cent for Malaysia. The problem had been exacerbated by the portfolio and short-term nature of foreign borrowing (*The Economist*, 7 March 1998, Survey: 8). The usual interpretation is that the crisis was caused by financial mismanagement arising from corruption and cronyism and that it was precipitated by the reaction of speculators to the large current-account deficits, ranging in 1996 from 4 to 8 per cent of GDP, and to the growing proportion of short-term debt.

The orthodox explanation of the East Asian crisis is, therefore, a supply-side story about financial mismanagement and corrupt political intervention. The following quotation from the *The Economist* (7 March 1998, Survey: 7) is representative of the neoliberal position:

> Across the region, expectations about future growth became extravagant, and capital became cheap, encouraging overborrowing. Much of the money was squandered on speculative property investment or the overexpansion of industrial capacity. At the same time a fatal combination of pegged exchange rates and an over-hasty opening of economies to short-term foreign capital caused a surge in debt to foreign banks. The resulting financial bubbles were inflated further by inadequate bank regulation and the close, sometimes corrupt, relationship between banks, firms and governments, which encouraged borrowers and lenders to believe that governments would bail them out if need be.

The real economy and the dynamic process receive no treatment at all in this static monetary explanation that is very similar to the neoclassical explanation of the Great Depression of the 1930s (Snooks 1998b: ch. 13). When it comes to analysing the dynamics of human society, neoclassical economists have made little noticeable progress in the past seventy years. They have even managed to forget the lesson taught by Keynes about the role of the demand side. And they still fail to appreciate the dynamic relationship between economic and political variables, which is essential to an understanding of real societies. Everything is judged in terms of static Pareto optimality that I have shown elsewhere (Snooks 1998b: 232–4) is merely a static substitute for dynamic demand (here called **strategic demand**).

The dynamic-strategy approach outlined at the beginning of this chapter involves a demand-side story about the real sector. It is a story that takes into consideration political as well as economic factors. The recent East-Asian pattern of development involving rapid growth followed by stagnation, crisis, and downturn is the typical trajectory of the exploitation and exhaustion of a technological substrategy. This is always difficult for neoclassical economists to accept, because their growth models generate linear equilibrium growth paths. Typically they regard any downturn as a unique crisis emerging from some abnormality (such as inferior moral values on the part of Asian businessmen and politicians or exogenous shocks).

In contrast, my dynamic-strategy model predicts this pattern. The model shows that once a substrategy has been exhausted, business and political interests will attempt to maintain the level of former returns by directing funds to speculative projects. The use of borrowed funds, therefore, is not the outcome of supply-side forces (such as the availability of cheap capital), but of strategic demand. There is nothing unique, or even unusual, about this. It has happened regularly in the West over the past two centuries. The Great Depression, for example, was the outcome of the exhaustion in the mid-1920s of the American technological substrategy of employing mass production and distribution techniques to exploit its own mega-market – an exhaustion that led to growing speculation during the second half of the 1920s and to the collapse of the real economy in the early 1930s (Snooks 1997a: 387–8).

In Southeast Asia, therefore, the speculation process was only exacerbated, not caused, by government encouragement for banks to lend to favoured individuals and projects. My model shows that this 'cronyism' and 'corruption' are not the result of moral failure as many neoliberals imply, but rather the normal outcome of the stage reached in the development process. As involvement in the GST increases and the domestic dynamic strategy unfolds, the growing number of local strategists force the ruling elite to become more responsive to their demands and to abandon their discriminatory policies in favour of genuine **strategic leadership** that treats all strategists equally. In this process of strategic struggle there will be a degree of social unrest as the sociopolitical system is forced to adjust periodically to new economic realities. This adjustment is something that cannot be achieved by 'wise men' from the West (such as leader writers for the *The Economist* or regional directors for the IMF and the World Bank) scolding 'morally deficient' Asian leaders for their foolish behaviour and demanding that they change their ways. And there is no reason for this economic and political behaviour to produce financial crisis: Where were the Western moralists when we were in the midst of the 'Asian miracle'? There is nothing unique about the type of government prevailing in East Asia today. Its like arose in Western Europe whenever the opportunities for rent-seeking emerged (Snooks 1997a: ch. 10). As the Asian crisis is merely part of a dynamic economic/political process, it is pointless for Western observers to pass judgement on political practices that are development-specific and that will only change as strategic demand changes. The desire to do so merely reflects a profound ignorance of the dynamic process.

What is the immediate future for Southeast Asia? The neoliberal position is that the region needs to swallow 'tough medicine' in order to be cured (*The Economist*, 3 January 1998: 13). This medicine – 'structural adjustment' – is of the type advocated by the IMF. Structural adjustment involves balancing budgets and overseas trade accounts, reforming financial institutions, eliminating inflation, deregulating the economy, and reducing government intervention, corruption, and cronyism. This involves 'getting the fundamentals right' in order to grow in the future. Major outcomes of this type of policy are deflation and the abandonment of policies that make rapid economic growth possible. No mention is ever made about 'getting the dynamic strategy right' or of 'providing adequate strategic leadership'. These governments under siege are also told that they must, with some urgency, adopt the democratic institutions of OECD countries. What these wise men from the West fail to realize is that such advice will merely exacerbate the growing political instability because of the strategy-specific nature of institutional development. Democratization, as demonstrated later in this book, is a function of the unfolding dynamic strategy not of an evolutionary political ideology.

The neoliberal argument is that these economic and political reforms must be made quickly and fully. To support their position, reference is usually made to Japan's reluctance to get its fundamentals right, which is supposed to account for its languishing economy. For example, we are told that:

> Economists worry that some tiger countries will follow in Japan's footsteps, refusing to acknowledge the full extent of their banking crises. Japan's sick banking system has still not been cleaned up, eight years after it started ailing, and the economy continues to stagnate in a vicious circle of slow growth, mounting bad loans and shrinking bank lending. (*The Economist*, 7 March 1998, Survey: 10)

They have, once again, failed to correctly diagnose Japan's real problem, which involves a temporary exhaustion of its old technological substrategy, which had been the basis of a remarkable growth record. What is required is strategic revival rather than reformation of the banking system. Once in pursuit of a new technological substrategy the increase in strategic demand for bank finance will lead to an appropriate response from the Japanese banking system. The key is always strategic demand, never independent supply-side reform.

Indeed, the only role that supply-side structural adjustment and premature political 'reform' is likely to play in Southeast Asia's future is one of economic and political disruption. This could arise, in the first place, by provoking short-term social unrest owing to the deflationary nature of neoliberal policy and the destabilizing nature of inappropriate democratization.[2] And, secondly, if these policies are persisted with in the longer term (as a substitute for real dynamic policies), then any attempt by local entrepreneurs to develop new substrategies will be undermined, just as is happening in a growing section of the developed world (Snooks 1998b: ch. 17). What is needed is private investment in strategy exploration together with genuine strategic leadership by governments responding to the new strategists.

4.3   CONCLUSIONS

The Third World embraces a vast range of development experience extending from the poverty-stricken NSCs of sub-Saharan Africa to the vibrant, if currently humbled, ESCs of East Asia. The varied outcomes reflect the very different relationships these countries are experiencing with the steadily expanding GST. An attempt has been made in this chapter to measure these different outcomes by employing a GST coefficient, which, it is claimed, is more suitable for analysis and policy than the UN's HDI. Despite the considerable development differences between Third World countries it is possible to explain their experience by employing a single economic and political theory – the dynamic-strategy theory developed in this book. In particular it has been used to analyse the development problems experienced by sub-Saharan Africa, Latin America, and Southeast Asia and to suggest that new policy principles (to be presented in Chapter 18) are required. In the chapter that follows, this theory is also applied to the FASCs of the Second World.

5 The State of the Second World

Formerly an entity with its own objectives and dynamic, the Second World is currently in complete disarray. While it consists of societies in transition, their paths and destinations are not at all clear at this stage. Some, such as the Czech Republic, Hungary, Poland, the Russian Federation, and Belarus, appear to be in transition from **former antistrategic countries (FASCs)** to **strategic countries (SCs)**. Others, such as the Kyrgyz Republic, Uzbekistan, Azerbaijan, and Albania, could well be in transition from FASCs to **nonstrategic countries (NSCs)**. Those in between may have to be satisfied in the foreseeable future with **emerging strategic country (ESC)** status. It will all depend on their varying abilities to engage with the **global strategic transition (GST)** by developing a viable **dynamic strategy**. This variety of dynamic outcomes is usually overlooked by those who see these societies moving as a group from command to market systems.

In this chapter the state of the former Second World is analysed using dynamic-strategy theory. This involves a discussion of the real nature of FASCs, what the concept of 'transition' actually means, why the Second World rose and fell, and how the performance of FASCs differs from that of other societies attempting to enter into the GST.

5.1   THE REAL NATURE OF ECONOMIES IN TRANSITION

In the broader attempt to provide analytical categories that reflect dynamic reality, a distinction was drawn in Chapter 4 between NSCs, ESCs, FASCs, and SCs according to their relationship with the global strategic transition. The results for FASCs are summarized in Table 4.3 section III, where GST rankings range from the Czech Republic's 27th place to the Kyrgyz Republic's 81st place. These FASC outcomes extend across the entire range of the ESC category from the NSC to the SC thresholds. Yet, while FASCs and ESCs overlap in terms of material outcomes, their relationships with the GST are very different. The ESC is in transition from the NSC to the SC category, whereas the FASC is in transition from the **antistrategic country (ASC)** to the SC, NSC, or ESC categories. In other words, the essence of Second-World transition is from the pursuit of anti-strategic to strategic objectives, rather than from a command to a market economy. The implications of the distinction will become clearer as we proceed.

The FASCs are historically unique. While there have been global strategic transitions before our own – during the pre-palaeolithic, palaeolithic, and neolithic technological eras – there has never been an antistrategic global process. The disastrous Soviet experiment of the twentieth century was an attempt by radical antistrategists to survive and prosper by developing an economic/political/social system that would overwhelm strategists not only in Russia but the entire world. In the attempt, the USSR established itself as an antistrategic force to rival the strategic leadership of the Western World.

The Soviet experiment led to a momentous clash between the great dynamic principle that has generated the progress of human society over the past two million years on the one hand, and the negation of that principle that could have brought civilization to an end on the other. The great dynamic principle is the **strategic pursuit**, and its negation is the anti-strategic containment. More specifically, the antistrategic containment was an attempt to transform individual strategists (profit-seekers) into antistrategists (rent-seekers) who would follow the dictates not of prevailing economic forces but of the ruling antistrategists.

For three generations between the Russian Revolution in 1917 and the collapse of the USSR in 1990, the world consisted of two non-interacting and combative economic systems: the strategic system of the Western World and the nonstrategic system of the Soviet world. These two systems competed with each other for global supremacy, attracting NSCs into their respective orbits. This was less a clash of ideologies than a clash between the forces of dynamics and of stasis because, if the Soviet world had gained global supremacy, there would have been no reason for the ruling anti-strategists to encourage growth. Economic growth was a burdensome necessity if the USSR was to compete effectively with the West. But if they had managed to overwhelm the West, containment of the potential strategists (who are always a threat to the antistrategists) and extraction of rents would have been enough. By the antistrategic negation of the dynamic-strategy principle, flux would yield to stasis. The great intellectual quest for stasis from Plato to Marx would have been realized (Snooks 1998a: ch. 3).

The two opposing principles of flux and stasis cannot coexist over the longer term because the triumph of one requires the elimination of the other. The problem for the antistrategic world is that, although it had developed a system that was unrivalled in suppressing and controlling strategists and extracting rent from them, it was not able to compete with the strategic world at what it does best – the generation of rapid economic growth. Why? Because only strategists operating freely within a competitive environment are able to fully exploit existing strategic opportunities. This is discussed in detail in Part IV. In the end the antistrategic principle failed to negate the strategic principle. In the end the forces of dynamics overwhelmed those of statics. This is the prime modern example of what I have elsewhere called 'the law of antistrategic political collapse', which states that any society in a competitive world that has been hijacked by a party of ruthless antistrategists, who institute a command system to eliminate potential strategists and to economically exploit nonstrategists, will eventually collapse (Snooks 1998a: 238).[1]

Following the collapse of the antistrategic core and its attendent satellites, the West attempted to assist former Soviet countries to make the transition to strategic societies. The interesting question is why did not the West just invade these crippled countries as Germany had attempted to do in the early 1940s? What accounts for this about-face? In *The Ephemeral Civilization* (Snooks 1997a: 504–6), I argue that under the dynamic strategy of technological change, which can be defended with nuclear weapons, it is more cost-effective to trade with than to conquer other countries. Prior to the development of the atomic bomb in the mid-1940s, the technological strategy could only be defended by the leading nations through territorial control. This accounts for the retention of the commerce colonies established by European powers between the sixteenth and eighteenth centuries for trading purposes, and for the extension of these colonial networks in the nineteenth and early twentieth centuries. It was an extension of the balance of power concept in Europe to the rest of the world in order to defend the massive fixed investment in the technological strategy (that is in urban areas). The technological strategy, unlike the other dynamic strategies, generates economic growth from the innovative use of *internal* resources rather than the increasing acquisition of *external* resources. Hence, once the technological strategy could be defended without territorial control, Europe quickly dismantled its former colonies, particularly as the cost of holding them was increasing. It is for this reason that the invasion of the former Soviet world is not economically attractive to the West. What they do find attractive, however, is the market potential of a rejuvenated Central and Eastern Europe.

But what would have eventuated had the antistrategic world triumphed? The Soviets and their allies (possibly China) would have been forced to invade Western Europe and North America, because the antistrategists can only survive by oppressing the strategists and extracting rents. In contrast, the strategic world can only survive through access to markets. There can be no longrun coexistence between those parts of the world that embody the incompatible principles of the strategic pursuit and the antistrategic containment. The West, therefore, was correct in resisting the Soviet world to the end, just as it is now correct in its desire to see those countries become part of the strategic world.

It is important to realize, however, that this conflict has nothing to do with the opposing *ideas* of democracy and communism. This is a false ideological distinction that was employed by the governments of both sides during the Cold War to gain wider support from their peoples for the massive military and foreign-aid expenditures. Essentially the Cold War was a clash between desires that drive the dynamic strategy rather than ideas that merely facilitate it. The Soviet system was an outcome of antistrategic objectives rather than Marxism, and the Western system is an outcome of the mature industrial technology strategy rather than a belief in democracy. This does not mean that the conflict between the strategic and antistrategic cores was any less significant, just that it was a battle between the material interests of profit-seekers and rent-seekers rather than between opposing ideologies.

What this means is that the FASCs were, for the better part of a century, on a false development path – a path that led away from, rather than toward, survival and prosperity. It was a path that led either to collapse or to unendurable stasis. If the Soviets were to win the Cold War, the world would be plunged into chaos arising from enforced stasis and, if they were to lose, their own system would collapse and they would be forced to begin again anew, this time as part of the strategic world.

5.2   THE REAL MEANING OF 'TRANSITION'

It is now possible to evaluate the conventional interpretation of the 'transition' concept and the way in which it is distinguished from the related concept of 'economic development'. The conventional view, I will argue, is flawed. It confuses ends with means, essentially because traditional economists have been unable to construct a workable model of the global dynamic process.

The authors of the European Bank's first *Transition Report* (1994: 3–4) interpret 'transition' as a shift from a command system to a market economy. Essentially it involves a dismantlement of the institutional apparatus of centralized government planning, control, and production in favour of freely operating commodity and factor markets and the primacy of individual enterprise. Essentially, transition is conventionally interpreted as a complete change in a society's economic and political institutions.

While transition is considered to be linked to economic development, the European Bank draws a distinction between the two concepts. We are told (ibid.: my emphasis):

> Development is a summary term which includes as its basic element the advancement, in a number of key dimensions, of the standard of living of individuals. Among these dimensions, education, health and command over resources are central ...
>
> Transition is not only an intermediate goal contributing to economic development. *It may also be regarded as an ultimate objective in itself.* The market economy, in contrast to central planning, gives, in principle, the individual the right to basic choices over aspects of his or her life ... The right to these choices may be seen as a basic liberty and as a fundamental aspect of standard of living ...
>
> The transition from a command to a market economy is *the movement towards a new system for the generation and allocation of resources.* It involves changing and creating institutions, particularly private enterprises. The role of the state in the market economy remains important, although very different from that in a command economy.

Independent scholars take a similar view of these issues (Pomfret 1995: 6–8).

These definitions of 'transition' and 'economic development' emphasize systems of production rather than strategic pursuits, outcomes rather than processes, and institutional change rather than fundamental dynamic mechanisms. As shown in this book, the essence of transition for a FASC is the dynamic process by which it shifts from an antistrategic to a strategic pursuit. Changes in institutional forms of society are merely responses to the emergence of, and changes in, **strategic demand**. To focus on ephemeral institutional forms rather than eternal dynamic processes, and on production systems rather than on strategic pursuits, is to totally misunderstand what is happening in the former Soviet world. And this has very important implications for policy which, for the citizens of FASCs, is a life and death issue.

The conventional policy thrust concerns the dismantlement of the institutions of command together with the creation of the institutions of *laissez-faire*. This is attempted through a programme of privatization, enterprise restructuring, price liberalization, competition, and globalization (European Bank 1994: 10–11). Yet what is the basis for this policy approach? In the absence of a workable dynamic model, the conventional rhetoric focuses on the supposed need to replicate the institutions of the West. There are at least four problems with this approach. First, it is based on the naive assumption that institutions lead rather than follow fundamental dynamic changes. It is implied that if we get the institutions right then everything else will fall into place – Second-World countries will be mysteriously transformed into First-World countries if we can replicate Western institutions there. Secondly, it is assumed, also naively, that current Western institutions are appropriate for the former Soviet world. There are a number of difficulties here: institutions are culture-specific, strategy-specific, and specific to the stage reached in the unfolding dynamic strategy. Economists with any historical understanding will know that current Western institutions would not have been appropriate even in the West a few generations ago. Thirdly, the conventional rhetoric is really a cover. When neoliberal economists say that what is needed is the introduction of Western institutions into the former Soviet world, what they are really proposing (even if they do not recognize the distinction) is the introduction not of real-world institutions but of the institutional assumptions of neoclassical theory. In effect, neoliberal advisers are attempting to make the real world conform to their models.

Finally, and most importantly, the policy focus is completely misdirected. As transition is a strategic rather than an institutional or a production process, the focus of policy must be upon encouraging the emergence of a viable technological substrategy by which FASCs can enter into the global strategic transition. Institutions will only ever be appropriate to individual FASCs, their substrategies, and their stage of development if they emerge in response to changes in endogenous strategic demand. To ignore strategic demand – to place the cart before the horse – will not only cause much unnecessary resource wastage and human suffering but could also result in struggling societies being invaded by their larger neighbours who are also unable to gain early entry into the GST. Unsuccessful strategists regularly succumb to the conquest strategy either as perpetrators or as victims. The evidence of Africa is clear on this.

The conventional confusion over the role of institutional change is highlighted by the claim of the European Bank that transition is 'an ultimate objective in itself', and that this involves 'the movement towards a new system [of production] for the generation and allocation of resources' rather than to a new strategic pursuit. The implication of this claim is that the market economy as a system of production is the end to which history has been inevitably progressing. Ironically this is a metaphysical idea that has much in common with Karl Marx's view that communism as a system of production is the end of history. What both visions overlook is that institutional outcomes are ephemeral and only dynamic processes are eternal (Snooks 1997a); and that dynamic processes are driven by strategic pursuits, not production systems. In reality the market economy did not emerge inevitably, as the European Bank *Report* implies, but merely in response to changing strategic demand as the technological strategy has unfolded in the West over the past two centuries. Rather than being the 'ultimate objective' of human society, it is merely the means, albeit important, for facilitating the modern dynamic strategy. If, for example, the approaching exhaustion of the industrial technological paradigm led to the re-emergence of the conquest strategy, the democratization of societal institutions would be reversed. This is not just a hypothetical possibility, because it has occurred regularly in the past (such as in ancient Greece and medieval Venice – Snooks 1997a: chs 8 and 9). *The bottom line, therefore, is that the transition of FASCs is essentially a strategic transition, not an institutional transition.* To be effective, policy must address this reality.

Finally, we need to comment on the conventional distinction between this new concept of strategic transition and that of economic development. In terms of the theory developed in this book there is no difference. Economic development is the outcome of the strategic transition irrespective of one's starting point – whether as an NSC, ESC, or a FASC. But while the general dynamic process is similar in each case, the specific development path (an outcome rather than a process) will differ according to analytical category and to individual economic circumstances. While there is only one development process, the GST, there are many ways of entering into it.

5.3 THE RISE AND FALL OF THE SOVIET WORLD

In order to understand the present circumstances of FASCs, it is necessary to review briefly the rise and fall of the Soviet world between 1917 and 1990. This is largely an account of the USSR, which became the anti-strategic leader of the world. By the end of the Second World War, the antistrategic core included Central and Eastern Europe as well as the northern half of Eurasia and Central Asia. At the peak of its influence, in the third quarter of the twentieth century, the USSR also provided financial, technical, and institutional assistance to a number of Third-World countries – the antistrategic fringe – including China, Vietnam, and Cuba, and to a number of revolutionary groups in Latin America and Africa. For a brief season many societies seriously looked to the Soviet antistrategic approach as an alternative development model to the Western strategic approach.

The Antistrategic Takeover of Russia

The Russian Revolution of 1917, like all revolutions, was a tragic outcome of the failure to achieve an orderly transfer of political control from the old strategists (aristocratic warriors) to the new strategists (middle classes). But in Russia there was an important difference. In the case of the other revolutions I have studied (Snooks 1997a) – the English Civil War, the Glorious Revolution, and the French Revolution – the new strategists succeeded in gaining and retaining (or at least regaining) control of the revolution against the recalcitrant old strategists. Unfortunately, in the case of Russia in 1917 the new strategists lost control to the antistrategists who successfully hijacked the revolution. This was a disaster for Russia because antistrategists – in this case the Bolsheviks – need to eliminate their opponents in order to establish a political and economic system with which they can exploit society for their own purposes.[2]

Russian society throughout its long history had been under the control of the conquest strategists – the prince or Tsar and his aristocratic support-ers. They attempted to grow rich by acquiring territory and other resources through war. While there was a growing class of merchants from the late sixteenth century who took a leading role in the economic exploitation of Siberia, the Tsar was quick to assert control over this important new source of extraordinary profits. But this bonanza was not to last. When the commerce strategy of Western Europe – which drove the demand for Russian furs – had exhausted itself by the mid-eighteenth century, Russian prosperity also evaporated.

During the century after the 1770s, the Russian ruling class had more success with their conquest strategy, which is reflected in the expansion of the Russian Empire by 46 per cent over this period. The very success of conquest precluded the development of the new technological strategy that swept throughout Western Europe during the nineteenth century. Manufacturing development was restricted by the Tsarist government to those activities that were required for the pursuit of conquest. Only with their defeat in the Crimea by the British and French in 1856 did the Russian ruling elite realize that industrialization and modernization were essential to their longrun survival. But it would be industrialization under their control and subject to their conquest aims rather than at the direction of the new technological strategists. Hence the serfs were set free in 1861, railways were built by government agencies, and manufacturing development was encouraged. Consequently, real industrial output doubled (a factor of 2.03) between 1860 and 1880, and then almost quadrupled (a factor of 3.6) between 1880 and 1900 (Nove 1992: 2). With industrialization came an acceleration in economic growth rather than just economic expansion (see Figure 5.1). While this led to a growing business class in Russia, it was treated largely as an agent of the state.

By the turn of the twentieth century, however, the old conquest strategists had lost their way. The conquest strategy had exhausted itself by the 1880s and, to prove it, Russia was badly defeated both on land and at sea by an upstart Japan in 1905. Without the driving force of conquest, the state-led process of industrialization began to slow down: between 1900 and 1913 industrial output increased by a more modest factor of 1.6. What was needed to redynamize Russian society was a transfer of strategic control from the old warrior class to the newly emerging business class. But the Tsar and his aristocratic supporters refused to sanction this, and the underdeveloped middle classes were not strong enough to force them. It was only the tidal wave of unrest generated by Russia's defeat at the hands of Japan that led to the unexpected establishment of the Russian Duma or parliament in late 1905.

After a few false starts in the experiment with parliamentary democracy, the third Duma of 1907 to 1912 proved remarkably successful. It provided,

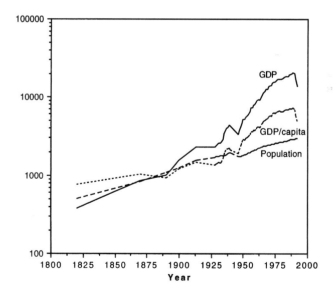

Figure 5.1   The expansion and growth of Russia, 1800–2000
Notes: GDP is in $US 100 m; GDP per capita is in $US; population is in 100,000s.
Source: Snooks 1997a: 449.

for the first time, a public forum for serious discussion of public policy in Russia, and it supported the reforming prime minister Peter Stolypin (Ragsdale 1996). By 1912 not only did this new institution have the support of the Russian people, but it had come to be accepted by the bureaucracy and even the court. As a result the confidence of the country, which had been dashed by the earlier lack of effective strategic leadership, rose substantially during these years, and foreign respect for the Russian government increased. In the absence of the Great War, it is highly likely that Russia would have become a constitutional monarchy with the Duma gaining effective control of the new technological strategy.

But, as we know, war broke out in Europe in 1914. It was a war that devastated Europe and destroyed any hope in Russia of a peaceful transfer of political control to those who were capable of driving the technological strategy. The war placed power back in the hands of the Tsar and the aristocratic warrior class, and their bungling, together with Russia's technological backwardness, led to a disaster of monumental proportions on the battlefield. By taking personal charge of the conduct of the war, Tsar Nicholas ensured that the Russian monarchy would not survive to preside over the transfer of strategic control to a democratically elected Duma.

The disorder created by Russia's military failure led to crowds of people, supported by a disillusioned army, taking over the streets and public buildings of Moscow on 11 March 1917 (new calendar). On 14 March a provisional government was formed to take over the conduct of the war – the middle classes were keen to defend their investment in the technological strategy – and the Tsar abdicated. But, as it was locked in dispute with the Soviet, which represented the proletariat and the radical members of the army, the provisional government did not really rule the country over the following eight months. The middle classes were still not strong enough to assert their authority. Once again the crowds on the street, backed by the army, surged forward to take the initiative (Pares 1966: 467–94). And, as is well known, in November 1917 the Bolsheviks managed to reap the whirlwind of the chaos and to hijack Russia's dynamic strategy.

The Bolsheviks, or antistrategists, gained control of the army and used it to eliminate both the old and new strategists. These victims of Bolshevism were either killed outright or sent to camps in Siberia. This was done initially with the support of the nonstrategists – the peasants – by redistributing to them all the lands of Russia. But when the arch-antistrategist, Joseph Stalin, gained complete control of the institutions of terror, he turned them against the nonstrategists and forced them into collectives. Like Mao Zedong after him, Stalin realized that, given the opportunity, the peasants would transform themselves into small capitalists.

Russia between 1917 and 1990 was ruled by antistrategists – by rent-seeking political opportunists. Their interest was not in pursuing the technological strategy but in using the institutions of command and terror to exploit the entire people of Russia, Central Asia, and Central and Eastern Europe for their own economic advantage. While Stalin physically eliminated the existing strategists, his unacknowledged master stroke was to transform potential strategists – intelligent and energetic risk-takers – into antistrategists by rewarding their talents within the institutions of command. In other words the potential strategists were perverted by the Soviet leadership into supporting the command system from the inside. It is ironic that these people had a vested interest in maintaining the antistrategic system, which in turn prevented them from pursuing the technological strategy in their own right. This is the analytical basis for what has been called the 'paradox of the middle class' (Amalrik 1970). It is recognized that while the middle class had the education and intelligence to understand both the problems plaguing the command system and the remedies required to resolve them, it was also the class that had most to lose from these reforms. Some observers have been puzzled by this paradox, but it can be explained quite satisfactorily by the dynamic-strategy model. Stalin would have enjoyed immensely both the irony and the puzzlement. This was not a dynamic society but rather a parasitic society in which the ruling elite lived on the blood of its own people and of its neighbours. As such it was a society headed for stagnation and collapse (see Figure 5.1).

The Command System of the Antistrategists

The antistrategists of the USSR, like those of the Russian Empire after the exhaustion of the conquest strategy, pursued industrialization not to maximize the material advantage of the Russian people, but to survive and to exploit the great proportion of the population. They took direct control of industrialization in order to prevent the re-emergence of the middle classes that would have posed a threat to their rule of the USSR. To do so, the antistrategists needed to develop an economic system that could promote industrialization but over which they had complete control. Their response was the command system initiated by Lenin but developed by Stalin. Yet, while it was the perfect instrument of exploitation and control, it could not compete in the longrun with the market systems of strategic societies that were developed to maximize economic growth. Only in a world without competition would Stalin's command system have been a total joy to its maker.

The construction of the Soviet command system occurred via a number of distinct steps (Dobb 1960: 97–260; Nove 1992: 39–272). First was the phase of War Communism, from 1918 to 1921, which involved the rapid adoption of central economic control to revitalize the economy to meet the threat of invasion and civil war. But the difficulties experienced during War Communism produced much discontent, leading to disorder and, finally, to rebellion by the Kronstadt sailors in February 1921. In order to survive, the Bolsheviks retreated from their primitive command system during the phase known as the New Economic Policy (NEP), from 1921 to 1928. But by 1926 Lenin had been dead for two years, the economy had been restored largely to the 1913 level, and members of the Party began pressing for a renewed offensive against the remaining capitalist (strategist) elements in society. Also, something had to be done about agriculture to extract a greater surplus. These issues led to the 'great debate', which was really a struggle among the antistrategists for control of their rent-seeking monopoly. This was the last public debate and antistrategic struggle in the USSR until that in the early 1960s, when it became clear that reforms to the Stalin command system were needed. It was a debate skilfully manipulated by Stalin to eliminate at first those on the left, who advocated rapid unbalanced development, and, in the end, those on the right, who wanted gradual balanced development (Nove 1992: 115–32). Having assumed total control over the antistrategists, Stalin announced a renewed drive to 'socialism' through the first five-year plan, 1928 to 1932.

The first five-year plan has been called the 'Soviet great leap forward' (Nove 1992: 137) – rather it was Russia's great leap into purgatory – involving a frontal attack on the 'capitalist' (strategist) elements in society, namely in agriculture, trade, and the consumer-goods industries. It involved the inhuman drive to collectivization of agriculture and to the development of heavy industry. Millions of peasants died from starvation and millions more, often chosen at random from all strata of Soviet society, were murdered or incarcerated in degrading labour camps. Terror was used by Stalin as an instrument to impose his will and to destroy the potential strategists. To engineer the 'great leap', which was to be planned and directed by the Party now controlled by Stalin, *Gosplan* developed its first five-year plan. This was a tremendous task because there was no precedent on this scale that could be imitated by the Soviet – no existing input–output matrices – and very limited information available about the Soviet economy. It was largely a leap of misdirected faith. Needless to say, the plan was over-optimistic and its execution was highly inefficient, but it did generate the first impressive surge in real GDP per capita since the late nineteenth century (see Figure 5.1); and successive five-year plans did enable the USSR to defeat Germany on the eastern front, and to seriously confront the USA in a cold war that lasted four decades. What then was the set of institutions that temporarily rejuvenated a backward and bankrupt empire, how did they work, and why did they ultimately fail?

Our main interest focuses on the policy and planning hierarchy because it is through this set of institutions that the antistrategists attempted to control and exploit the natural and human resources of the USSR, without relying on the technological strategists who alone could challenge their authority. The economic and policy network of the 'classic' Soviet command system in the mid-1960s, prior to the first abortive attempts at reform, was as follows. The legislature consisted of four levels of territorial organization: at the top was the federal government of the USSR; below this were the governments of the national republics; then there were about 50 regional councils; and finally there were the provincial, municipal, and county governments (Snooks 1997a: 454–6). The legislative organs of each of these four territorial levels of government, called Soviets, adopted economic plans and other economic legislation covering their spheres of influence. Enforcement of this economic legislation was the responsibility of the Council of Ministers at every level. Each of the ministries, which were concerned with various sectors of the economy (such as railways, agriculture, finance, and so on), worked through a number of 'economic councils' or *sovnarkhozy* under the control of VSNKн, and 'planning committees' or *Gosplan*. The economic councils prepared the annual plans for their designated sector, and the planning committees prepared the five-year plans (and the longer plans) and coordinated the individual annual plans.

How did the antistrategists attempt to make this complex system work? The essential underpinning of the command economy was the terror Stalin maintained throughout his brutal rule, which was directed against anyone who was even suspected of questioning his commands. Against this background of fear the main, although not exclusive, positive incentives in the classic command system were of a material nature, involving bonuses for fulfilment and overfulfilment of output targets. While this incentive system enabled the Soviet leaders to achieve their broad objectives, it led to excessive wastage of resources and to unacceptable levels of inefficiency. In effect it was just a massive system of production with no dynamic (or strategic) motivation – a caricature of a real strategic system. But, until this inefficiency posed a threat to the survival of the antistrategists, from internal and external sources, it was not a matter of serious concern. Their objective was to maximize not the material advantage of the nation but the economic rent they could extract through this command system. Nonetheless, a minority of conscientious planners and economists, who did believe that the Soviet system should serve more than just the Party functionaries, were concerned about wastage arising from: the deliberate understatement of enterprise capacity in order to meet targets and obtain bonuses with a minimum of effort; the falsification of reported production; the dilution of product quality; and the fulfilment of output targets specified in weight units by making fewer but heavier items of production. But these concerns only surfaced when the leadership became anxious about their longer-term survival.

During the first three decades of its operation, the Stalin command system served the Soviet leadership well. It suppressed the new strategists, redistributed income from the people to Party functionaries, enabled Russia to collectivize and industrialize, defeated Hitler, launched the world's first artificial satellite into space in 1957, established the world's second most powerful mega-state, and created a global antistrategic core that seriously challenged the existing global strategic core of the West. Yet why was the USSR able to crush Germany but was unsuccessful in its struggle against the West? The dynamic-strategy model suggests that the command economy is ideal for feeding the war machine but not for generating longrun economic growth. Basically the problem for a wartime economy is how to develop a system of production (rather than a strategic pursuit) to maximize the amount of output from a given supply of inputs. The Soviet command system was better designed to achieve this objective than the unplanned Nazi economy, at least until Albert Speer took control in 1942. Even the democracies temporarily assumed some of the core characteristics of the command economy during the Second World War, because during this short-term crisis maximization of output (which depended on engineering efficiency) rather than maximization of extraordinary profits (which depended on innovation) was a more effective method of survival. As the reverse was true during the Cold War, the USSR was unable to compete with the USA and Western Europe after the mid-1940s.

The Reform That Could Never Be

The Stalin command system was ideal for imitating the production (but not the strategic) system of the technologically advanced nations because it was run by engineers and accountants who were skilled in implementing technical and economic plans. They just followed the blue-prints handed to them, and practised a little embezzlement on the side. The initial results in terms of growth rates were impressive (just like those of China at the end of the twentieth century), because they had a great deal of catching up to do. But this was achieved at great cost in terms of human lives, human oppression, and gross inefficiency in the use of resources.

On bridging much of the technological gap between itself and the USA, the USSR faced even greater difficulties. How were they to proceed in the future? This is a major problem for a system that has effectively eliminated the potential strategists who would normally explore and invest in new technologies in order to achieve extraordinary profits. By the 1960s, imitation of the West was no longer enough. To forge ahead in the Cold War the USSR needed to become an innovator rather than a follower. But the command system mitigated against this: the incentives were perverse; the enterprise directors were engineers not entrepreneurs; the most intelligent and energetic section of the population was materially committed to supporting a vast system of rent-seeking; and, as factor and commodity markets had been abolished, there was, as foreseen by Friedrich Hayek (1935), no reliable information on which to base innovative decision-making. Stalin had developed a system of control and production that had no dynamic core.

Only when Soviet growth rates began to decline after the late 1950s and to stagnate in the early 1960s (see Figure 5.1), in the midst of a cold war with the West, did the Soviet leadership begin to openly express concern about the nature of Stalin's command system. Khrushchev, on gaining power in 1953, attempted to make the command system more responsive to his perception of the needs of the Russian people, and in the early 1960s he began to consider reforming the command system itself to make it more efficient. This led in 1962 to the publication in *Pravda* of an article, originally written in 1956, by the Russian economist E. Liberman on the planning process. Liberman's concern was to improve the enterprise incentive system, to encourage the introduction of new technology, and to improve the quality of output: 'in a word, in achieving the greatest production efficiency'. To achieve these objectives, he advocated greater decentralization of decision-making power by linking enterprise bonuses to profitability once the output target had been achieved. This *Pravda* publication began the second great debate in Soviet history, during which a large number of issues were enthusiastically discussed, including the need for a rate of interest to enable the more rational allocation of capital, for greater innovation, and for a formal recognition of consumer demand. This debate was concerned with how to modify the *system of production* rather than how to build into it the *strategic pursuit*.

In 1965, the year after Khrushchev had been removed because of the adverse impact of his impetuous and ill-informed initiatives on the economy and foreign affairs (Ragsdale 1996: 240–8), the first major reforms of the command system were announced by Aleksei Kosygin, co-premier with Leonid Brezhnev. The fact that the military–industrial complex had reasserted its control after the dismissal of Khrushchev in October 1964 was not a good omen for the fate of these reforms. In general the reforms followed the Liberman proposals and were framed to provide enterprises with greater independence and motivation. To do this they 'reformed' the pricing system, introduced profit-related bonuses, and recognized a rate of interest in financial dealings. Yet despite these 'reforms', the enterprises did not act more entrepreneurially because the ministries refused to give up their powers, and enterprise directors did not wish to be released from them as it would either undermine their existing privileges or would expose them to risks that, as engineers, they were not trained to handle. As Alec Nove (1972: 357, 354) has said: 'The system has an inner logic which defies gradual change'; and these changes were 'the reform that never was'. While growth rates (Figure 5.1) did pick up in the second half of the 1960s, they stagnated again in the 1970s, and all further 'reform' attempts proved to be futile.

None of this is surprising. It is just not possible to fine-tune the institutions of an antistrategic command system of production to enable it to compete in the longrun with market systems run by dynamic strategists. The fundamental reason is that command systems and market systems are not alternative institutions for achieving the same objective as is generally assumed. They have entirely different objectives. The command system is an excellent antistrategic instrument for repressing and perverting potential strategists and for extracting economic rent from the people; and the market system is the best available vehicle for dynamic strategists wishing to maximize their material advantage through economic growth. But the market system is a total failure as an instrument of mass repression and exploitation; and the command system is hopeless when it comes to longrun innovation and growth. Both are a response to the requirements of the dominant economic decision-makers – one strategic the other antistrategic.

If a society wishes to achieve rapid and sustained economic growth there is no point in trying to reform the command system of production, not only because the oppressive mechanisms will merely reassert themselves owing to vested rent-seeking interests at all levels but also because there is no way of building into it the essential strategic pursuit. Innovation and sustained growth can only be achieved by destroying the entire antistrategic structure in order to allow the reemergence of the dynamic strategists who will generate strategic demand for the most appropriate institutions for their culture and degree of engagement with the GST. Until the command structure is destroyed, the potential strategists will not be released. They will continue to hold onto their privileges based on rent-seeking. Rather than 'the reform that never was' the longrunning attempt to modify the Stalin command system was 'the reform that could never be'.

Destruction of the Antistrategic Command System

For 25 years after the Kosygin initiative, the antistrategists attempted to 'reform' the command system without really changing it. During this time they were involved in a struggle for survival on two fronts – the international front and the home front. Internationally the Soviet leadership was involved in an escalating confrontation with the West in military and space-exploration terms, and at home they were faced with the growing dissatisfaction of the populace over the general standard of living. But because the economy had been performing so badly for a generation there was little the Soviet leadership could do about either problem. If they continued to compete with the USA, as Brezhnev had attempted to do, they would need to squeeze the living standards of the Russian people and could be faced with rebellion, even revolution; and if they attempted to increase the consumption levels of the people, they could be faced with international humiliation, military revolt, and even invasion. It was against this background that Mikhail Gorbachev was elected general secretary.

While Gorbachev was recognized as a 'liberal', and only narrowly came to power in 1985 with a mandate to revitalize the old system, none realized how radical he was to become. He began predictably enough, attempting to reform the system from within. His initial anti-alcoholism programme, aimed at increasing labour productivity, was an expensive failure. Undaunted he followed up with his programme of *glasnost*, or 'openness', aimed at exposing corruption in government, encouraging good civic behaviour, and enhancing confidence in public bodies. He also encouraged open criticism of the existing system, which led to calls from economists and an increasingly free media for radical reform.

Gorbachev was determined to use markets to make state enterprises more responsive to consumer requirements, and more innovative. In this programme of *perestroika*, or 'restructuring', enterprises were to be given greater independence, the bureaucracy was to be pruned, research was to be geared more closely to production, and price reforms and self-financing were to be introduced. Privatization, however, was not part of the restructuring programme. As always the command system reasserted itself. By mid-1990 the reforms had ground to a halt.

This failure stimulated an even more radical demand for reforms including privatization. In response, Gorbachev publicly advocated greater enterprise freedom, radical price reform, and even the creation of stock and commodity exchanges (Nove 1992: 408). Naturally this was strongly resisted by those who had most to lose, including the military–industrial establishment. In the face of this determined opposition Gorbachev hesitated and seemed to lose his nerve. This led to his famous 'shift to the right' between October 1990 and April 1991, during which he lost the support of the intellectuals to Boris Yeltsin who already enjoyed the confidence of the working classes (Dunlop 1993: 52–4). While moving back to the left again after April 1991 to compete with Yeltsin's growing power, Gorbachev failed to regain control of the revolution he had started.

The USSR in 1991 was rushing headlong into chaos and collapse (see Figure 5.1). The various captive nations together with the USSR republics were demanding independence, central authority was collapsing, new strategists were demanding their independence, and trade between enterprises, individuals, and regions was breaking down. In January 1991 radical price reforms were finally introduced; in April a law was adopted to allow individuals to trade and employ others; and commercial banks and stock exchanges were emerging. Owing to the impossibility of reforming the command system, Gorbachev, through his *demokratizatsiya* programme, had finally unleashed the forces of chaos that had been contained by Stalin in 1928. He attempted to use the people to force through the reforms that were being resisted by the antistrategists in the command structure, but was surprised by their general apathy and ill will. What he did not realize was that the potential strategists who could revitalize the economy would be released from Stalin's bonds only once the antistrategic command system had been completely destroyed. Reform was not enough. In the end he inadvertently destroyed what he had hoped to save – the system of 'Leninist socialism' (as opposed to Stalinist coercion). By mid-1991 the antistrategic system was no longer effective, and in August the military–industrial complex staged an unsuccessful coup, after which the Communist Party was dissolved, all the republics and captive nations declared their independence, the USSR ceased to have any meaningful existence nor Gorbachev any effective role. Boris Yeltsin, who had been President of Russia since June 1991 and had the confidence of the majority of the people, emerged as the decisive leader of the day.

Gorbachev was not alone in failing to understand that the command system was incapable of reform. Even detached and seasoned observers like Alec Nove have, after the event, made a similar judgement. Nove (1992: 418–19) writes:

> Looking back, one is struck by a paradox, or dilemma. To carry through the fundamental *perestroika* of the economy required strong government. In the first three years of Gorbachev's rule the mechanism for imposing a policy did exist, but the apparatus ... was not inclined to do the job, since marketization threatened its powers and privileges. So Gorbachev set about dismantling the apparatus, changing its personnel, allowing criticism of its privileges ... *Glasnost* and *demokratizatsiya* doubtless weakened the powers of resistance and obstruction of the *apparatchiki*. However, the effect was also to undermine the power to implement policy. So by the time the reform programme was radicalized, the means to enforce it no longer existed.

The point is not that the command system could have been reformed had Gorbachev retained the power to implement policy, but rather that the system was incapable of reform. Only an entirely new economic system and a new society dominated and led by the dynamic strategists could achieve the rapid and sustained growth that was necessary to compete with the other mega-states.

This is an interesting illustration of the central thesis in my book, that institutional change responds to strategic demand and not the other way around. It was not possible to establish a set of institutions to arrange the transition from antistrategic to strategic control of Russia. The old system had to be destroyed and the new strategists had to take over from the anti-strategists – a change from rent-seeking to profit-seeking – before the appropriate institutions could be rebuilt in response to strategic demand. This is also the experience of some of the more perceptive Western advisers who helped to reconstruct Russia's economy from 1991 to 1994. Anders Åslund (1995: 10–11), for example, tells us that new laws, institutions, and property rights 'are undertaken more easily and appropriately after liberalization [i.e. dismantlement of the old system]; it is extremely difficult to carry them out in advance'.

For similar reasons many Western experts failed to predict the collapse of the Soviet system. Those at the grandly named Centre for Strategic and International Studies at Georgetown University wrote boldly in the early 1980s:

> All of us agree that there is no likelihood whatsoever that the Soviet Union will become a political democracy or that it will collapse in the

foreseeable future, and very little likelihood that it will become a conge-
nial, peaceful member of the international community for as far ahead
as one can see. (Byrnes 1983: xvii)

Clearly they could not see very far. And Paul Kennedy, the historian who
wrote *The Rise and Fall of the Great Powers* (1989: 663–4), said in the
late 1980s just a few years before the complete collapse of the USSR:

> However one assesses the military strength of the USSR at the moment,
> therefore, the prospect of its being only the fourth or fifth among the
> great productive centres of the world by the early twenty-first century
> cannot but worry the Soviet leadership, simply because of the implica-
> tions for long-term Russian power.
>   This does *not* mean that the USSR is close to collapse, any more than
> it should be viewed as a country of almost supernatural strength. It *does*
> mean that it is facing awkward choices.

They and most other observers missed predicting the greatest societal collapse of modern times because they did not recognize what might be
called the 'antistrategic paradox': the use of the antistrategic command
system in an attempt to achieve the outcomes – innovation and economic
growth – of strategic societies. While my dynamic-strategy model can
only explain what has happened in the USSR (although it would have predicted it), it can be used in a predictive sense for China and other ESCs.

Russia's Future

To see what Russia might become we should focus briefly on the dynamics of transition from a collapsing antistrategic system to an emerging
strategic system. The driving force in this transition is strategic demand –
the demand of the new strategists for control over the economic resources
and income of Russia. The dynamic process of transition involves a struggle for economic and political control between the new strategists and the
remaining elements of antistrategists (the *nomenklatura*). It was a struggle
between the profit-seekers and the rent-seekers – between those with a
vision of a new Russia and those who yearned for the privileges of the old
USSR. The new strategists demanded privatization so that they could control Russia's resources, marketization so that they could pursue their economic objectives as efficiently as possible, democratization so that they could
gain control of the dynamic strategy, and legalization so that they could be
protected from intimidation by bureaucrats and the Russian Mafia.

By the mid-1990s the strategists had achieved many of these objectives: the rate of inflation was reduced from 2,510.4 to only 48.3 per cent per annum between 1992 and 1994; unemployment was reduced to 2.4 per cent by 1994; the transition-induced recession reached its nadir in 1995; and government revenue as a proportion of GDP was reduced from 41 to 28 per cent between 1989 and 1994 (Fischer *et al.* 1996; Murrell 1996). A major reason for this achievement is that a number of Russian politicians closely identified with the interests of the new strategists. These politicians included Boris Yeltsin, the Russian president, who came to power on the reform platform and who chose the team and the plan for transformation; Yegor Gaidar, who developed and implemented the transformation programme; Boris Fedorov who, as minister for finance, helped to stabilize the new market economy; and Anatoly Chubais, whose privatization programme was highly successful (Dunlop 1993: 38–66; Åslund 1995: 314–16). While the usual response is that these changes were the outcome of a period of high ideals on the part of a few extraordinary men, the truth is that it was a response by these few extraordinary men to a growing strategic demand. Their remarkable skill was to successfully ride the surging strategic wave. But there are some worrying signs. In particular, between 1995 and 1998 the powers of the Russian president have been growing relative to those of the Duma, the courts, and the prime minister. Most recently (March 1998) Yeltsin, without any warning, sacked the entire Russian government. Such arbitrary action, despite being constitutional, could destabilize the entire transition process.

The main opponents of the new strategists were the old bureaucrats and enterprise directors rather than the military–industrial complex (VPK) as many expected. This was because the massive structural change after 1991 slashed the size and status of the VPK and elevated that of agriculture and energy which were responsive to consumer demand. The antistrategists were able to retain vestiges of their old economic power because of the time it took to totally deregulate the Russian economy and to introduce a democratic form of parliamentary government. In the interim they gained considerable concessions from Yeltsin at a time (1992) when the populace was disoriented and unusually passive (Dunlop 1993: 296). It was the struggle for survival between these two groups that slowed down the transition process.

With the reduction in the influence of the state and of workers' organizations, enterprise directors assumed control of their economic units and through their well-organized associations – such as the Russian Union of Industrialists and Entrepreneurs – they became a powerful government lobby before democratic reforms, including a new constitution, were introduced in December 1993. While these reforms finally gave political control to the new strategists, some of the old antistrategists had become well entrenched. During the two years from late 1991 to late 1993, many enterprise directors became very wealthy by exploiting the system of price control, trade barriers, multiple exchange rates, and subsidized financial support (ibid.: 303–6). But, once the new strategists had achieved their goal of destroying the old command apparatus, the opportunities for this type of rent-seeking were reduced to something approximating normal levels and profit-seeking began to assume the role it plays in other market economies. Accordingly, in the democratic election of December 1993, the first in almost four generations, the electoral representatives of the industrial enterprise directors – Arkady Volsky's Civic Union Party – captured only 2 per cent of the vote. No doubt many of the old antistrategists have switched their talents from rent-seeking to profit-seeking. They have finally been released from the ensnarement Stalin so cleverly planned for them.

The important conclusion to come from this examination is that, without the demands generated by the new strategists, none of these reforms would have succeeded even to the limited extent that they have and the antistrategists would have continued their rent-seeking activities until the entire system collapsed. As it is, Russia has been converted into something approximating a strategic society. There will be further attacks from the remaining antistrategists who will attempt to exploit the mistakes and difficulties of the present regime, and there will be temptations for ambitious politicians to advance their personal power. But now that Russia is largely under the control of the new strategists and is in receipt of financial and technological assistance from the West, there is every reason to be optimistic about its ability, over the next generation or so, to enter fully into the GST.

5.4   THE BEGINNING OF STRATEGIC TRANSITION

With the collapse of the USSR, the world's antistrategic core, the former countries of the Soviet world were finally free to begin the perilous strategic transition. It is far too early to say how successful they will be, but at least they have been released from antistrategic control that could only have one outcome – exploitation and eventual collapse. The conventional economists' inability to understand this is the outcome of their failure to develop a general dynamic model. The most recent data available when this chapter was written (presented in section III of Table 4.3) only measures the extent of the economic decline of FASCs following the collapse of the Soviet world. Only the next decade will demonstrate which of these countries are able to develop dynamic strategies and enter into the GST. Nevertheless, there are some indicators of possible future success.

Table 4.4, which summarizes the latest published data for all analytical categories, shows that the GST coefficient for both ESCs and FASCs is, on average, almost identical at just over 19 compared with that of 100 for the USA. But it is a coincidence brought about by a modest *positive* growth rate over the past decade of 1.7 per cent per annum for ESCs and rapid *negative* growth of −6.7 per cent per annum for FASCs. This convergence has left ESCs with a GNP per capita about one-third higher than that for FASCs. It is hard to say if or when this convergence will be reversed; or how difficult it will be for former antistrategic societies to transform themselves into strategic societies.

A further interesting difference between these two transition categories is that the relationship between the GST and HDI rankings is reversed: for ESCs the GST ranking is better (smaller) than the HDI ranking, but for FASCs it is reversed and the difference is greater. In other words, prior government investment in education in FASCs does not help them find an appropriate dynamic strategy. Rather, in growing societies (ESCs), HDI lags behind GST, which indicates that education is a supply response to changes in strategic demand.

Greater detail on these issues is provided in section III of Table 4.3. As suggested earlier, the FASCs' range coincides with that of the ESCs. But in contrast to individual country experience in the ESC category, all FASCs, with the sole exception of Poland, experienced negative growth, which for Azerbaijan, Georgia, Armenia, and Lithuania ran into double-digit figures. The top five FASCs in GST ranking, which are the Czech Republic, Hungary, Russia, Belarus, and Poland, probably have the best prospects of entering into the GST in the near future. Something similar could be said also about the next five countries that include the Baltic states of Estonia, Lithuania, and Latvia, together with the Black Sea states of Bulgaria and Romania. One may wish also to include Kazakhstan, the one Central Asian state with considerable development potential based on oil and minerals, in this group (Pomfret 1995: 73–97). In contrast, the bottom five countries, consisting of the Central Asian states of the Kyrgyz Republic, Uzbekistan, and Azerbaijan, together with Albania and the Ukraine, could well end up as NSCs. Similarly, the fate of some Eastern European states, such as the Slovak Republic, Georgia, and Armenia, also hangs in the balance. These countries at the bottom of the GST ranking, which were heavily subsidized by the more advanced Soviet states, will find it difficult to enter into the

GST at an early date, particularly due to their high degree of specialization (for example, cotton-growing in Uzbekistan), the unsustainable nature of their past development (salinated and poisoned soils and depletion of water sources), and the possibility of ethnic civil war (Pomfret 1995: 63–74). Russia and the advanced Eastern European states, on the other hand, should respond positively to the falling away of the dependent territories of the Soviet world.

An evaluation of progress in transition is conventionally measured in terms of the relative size of the private sector, together with the degree to which privatization, enterprise restructuring, price liberalization, banking reform, and trade deregulation have been undertaken (European Bank 1994: 10–11). In view of the argument in this chapter, such measures can only be regarded, at best, as an indirect indication of the strategic transition. At worst they can be completely misleading, because it is possible to forcefully push through these institutional forms without even kindling the beginnings of a viable dynamic strategy. The continuing economic and political problems of FASCs is evidence enough of this. Only the emergence of dynamic strategies in FASCs can be regarded as evidence of transition. This is best reflected in the growth rates of productivity and real GDP per capita.

5.5   CONCLUSIONS

The transition of the old Soviet block countries should be seen not as a shift from a command to a market system but a shift from an antistrategic to a strategic society. It is a vitally important distinction owing to the very different policy and, hence, welfare implications. In reality, successful institutional change is a response to changing strategic demand that is generated as a FASC enters into the GST and its dynamic strategy unfolds. It is impossible, therefore, to determine in advance what type of institutional structure is appropriate for any FASC without knowing what the requirements of its strategic demand will be. Considerable material damage and human suffering will be created by placing the institutional cart before the strategic horse. Ironically, this dilemma is very similar in kind to that facing central planners in a command system attempting to frame economic plans without any strategic information.

Transition policy advisers wrongly impose modern Western institutions on FASCs – wrongly because they are not appropriate to the country's type or stage of dynamic strategy, nor to its historical background. To make matters worse, this institutional 'reform' is based not on reality but on the assumptions of neoclassical theory. In essence it is an attempt to make a complex dynamic world resemble the world of simple, static neoclassical models. The reason for this inappropriate policy is the failure of orthodox economics to develop a dynamic model that encompasses both economic and political change.

What is urgently required is a policy emphasis on strategic transition rather than institutional transition. As we have seen, the Soviet world collapsed because it adopted an antistrategic approach to economic and political organization. Accordingly, the key requirement for the transition of these countries is the rapid adoption of the dynamic strategy of technological change. This objective is shared with the NSCs; only their respective starting points are different. To do this they need to select and pursue an appropriate technological substrategy that will depend upon factor endowments, competitive environment, and historical background. This substrategy, which will differ between FASCs, will determine the nature of the institutional response through a changing strategic demand. Relevant policy principles are discussed in Chapter 18.

Part III
Traditional Theory, Policy, and Visions

6 Traditional Development Theory

Despite massive scholarly attention devoted to the issue of underdevelopment over the past fifty years, it remains a daunting problem. This dilemma raises questions about the intellectual and practical significance of traditional development theory. In particular we wish to know whether this body of ideas constitutes a general theory of economic development and whether it can resolve the problems of Third-World poverty. These issues are explored in this chapter by considering the nature and scope of existing development theory under four main headings: the productionists; the poverty-trap theorists; the global-polarization theorists; and the institutionalists.[1]

6.1 THE PRODUCTIONISTS

The only comprehensive body of theory available to development economists is classical and neoclassical growth theory. There are, however, two problems with this body of ideas. First, growth theory has been developed by scholars interested in the growth process of 'developed' rather than 'underdeveloped' societies. It would be surprising if this theory had much relevance to the Third World. In fact, despite the ritualistic survey of growth theory undertaken in every textbook on economic development, the usual admission is that it has little relevance. We hardly need a body of technical growth theory to tell us that capital (Solow–Swan model), technological change, and human capital (endogenous-growth model) are relevant to the growth process. These facts have been known by economic historians since Arnold Toynbee Sr (1884–1969) began lecturing on the Industrial Revolution at Oxford in the early 1880s. Possibly the main role of growth theory has been to perversely encourage development economists to ignore key components of the dynamic process: such as human capital and technological change before the late 1980s; and dynamic demand before *Longrun Dynamics* (Snooks 1998b).

The second, and as yet unrealized, problem with orthodox growth theory is its highly restricted outlook. Not only does growth theory lack a global focus, but it concentrates solely on the *system of production* in human society. Mainstream economics, in effect, treats human society as a giant factory dominated by the machine. While many will concede the failure of growth theory to throw light on the wider development process, even they do not realize the limitations of building growth models from static production theory. These limitations translated into reality are seen in Chapter 5 where we examine how the USSR failed in its attempt to use a command system of *production* to generate social dynamics. In both cases the core dynamic process has been overlooked.

The central assumption underlying all growth theory is that the dynamics of human society is the outcome of changes that occur within the system of production. This is a widely held, fundamental misconception of the nature of the dynamic process. As explained in detail in Parts IV and V, the core of the real-world dynamic process is the **strategic pursuit**, whereas the productive system is *a* medium by which the objectives of this pursuit can be achieved. In the modern world the productive system is the main, but not exclusive, medium for the technological strategic pursuit. We need only think of the dynamic success of innovative commerce city-states such as Hong Kong and Singapore to realize this. And, as I show elsewhere (Snooks 1996; 1997a), prior to the Industrial Revolution, the commerce or conquest systems, and not the production system, were the **surplus-generating mediums** of these societies. In other words, if we are to understand the dynamics of human society we must be able to model the core process that all societies, both past and present, have in common. And that common core process is the strategic pursuit, not the production system.

It is helpful, of course, to know how the strategic pursuit is translated into larger per capita surpluses. But a knowledge of the productive systems of the present is no more helpful than a knowledge of how military imperial systems operated in the Assyrian or Roman empires, or how commerce/imperial systems operated in the Greek, Phoenician, Venetian, or early British empires. Models of these surplus-generating systems are little more than technical 'how-to-do-it' manuals for astute managers rather than pioneering strategists in the past and present. What they leave out is far more important than what they include. What they leave out is the universal core of the dynamic process.

Exactly what do the classical and neoclassical growth models tell us? Surprisingly little. The classical model, for example, includes a production function together with functions for technology, investment, profits, labour, and wages. As such it is, rather interestingly, more comprehensive than the more recent neoclassical models. Here I focus on the Ricardian–Malthusian variant. Adam Smith's broader dynamic model is reviewed in

Chapter 8. The classical model can be presented in a series of eight simple equations:

$$Y = f(L, K, N, T) \tag{6.1}$$

$$T = T(I) \tag{6.2}$$

$$I = dK = I(R) \tag{6.3}$$

$$R = R(T, L) \tag{6.4}$$

$$L = L(W) \tag{6.5}$$

$$W = W(I) \tag{6.6}$$

$$Y = R + W \tag{6.7}$$

And for longrun equilibrium:

$$W = wL \tag{6.8}$$

In these equations Y is total output, L is the labour force, K is the capital stock, N is the amount of land, T is the level of technique, I is investment, W is the wages bill, and R is the profit level.[2]

But what does this circular system really tell us? Merely what we assumed it would; that, if for some unspecified reason profits (R) were to increase, the following sequence would occur: an increase in investment (I) → increases in technology (T) and the wages fund (W) → increase in the rate of population growth → decline in wages and profits, and so on until the stationary state is reachieved. Even Marx's growth model is merely a variation on this classical theme. He accepted the central importance of both the production system and the role of capital in this system, but gave greater emphasis to technological change ('progress of the machine'). Even the outcome of Marx's model was much the same as the classical model (Snooks 1998b: ch. 3).

The only reason that 'growth' (or, more accurately, convergence to equilibrium) occurs in this interactive system of production is because of exogenous shocks. The productive system is merely the medium by which the dynamic impulse is translated into increased per capita surpluses in modern economies. If Roman society had had a school of classical economics, no doubt it would have emphasized a 'fighting function' rather than a production function, while Venetian society would have focused on a 'conjuring function' (Snooks 1996: ch. 11). What all these classical models would have overlooked is the core dynamic process – the strategic pursuit. As suggested in Chapter 12, this can be thought of in comparable static terms as a 'strategy function'.

Much the same is true of the neoclassical growth model in both its Solow–Swan and 'endogenous' versions. The Solow–Swan model emerged in the mid-1950s as a response to Harrod's famous 'knife-edge' problem which, as it turned out, depended on his assumption of fixed ratios between *production* inputs. The Solow–Swan model solved this by introducing substitution between *production* inputs. Clearly the growth outcomes of all these simple models are highly sensitive to the underlying production theory rather than to the core dynamic process which is inadequately represented by random exogenous shocks.

The simple Solow–Swan model, as discussed more fully elsewhere (Snooks 1998b: ch. 3), is based on a closed economy with a Robinson-Crusoe-type producer/consumer who owns all the resources, who controls the production process, and who consumes part of the output and saves the rest. There are just three fundamental equations in the model: the production function, with two inputs of capital and labour; the investment function; and the labour function. As usual with orthodox growth models, the most important of these is the production function. In fact, in the case of the Solow–Swan model the production function is even more crucial, because minor differences in its underlying assumptions produce entirely different models of economic growth. 'Growth' outcomes depend, therefore, on assumptions about the nature of production.

The main defining characteristics of the Solow–Swan production function are: each input exhibits positive and diminishing marginal products; the production function generates constant returns to scale; and as each factor approaches zero its marginal product approaches infinity and vice versa. A popular production function of this type is the Cobb–Douglas production function that can be expressed as:

$$Y = AK^{\alpha}L^{1-\alpha}$$

where Y is output, A is technological change, K and L are capital and labour respectively, and α and $1-\alpha$ are returns to the factors of production. It can be expressed in intensified form as:

$$Y = Ak^{\alpha}$$

The contribution made independently by Trevor Swan (1956) and Robert Solow (1956) was to employ a limited form of this type of production function, which allows factor substitution. They assumed that as technological change is exogenous to the model, the production function can be written:[3]

$$Y = F(K, L) \tag{6.9}$$

or in intensive form:

$$y = f(k)$$

The fundamental 'dynamic' equation for the Solow–Swan model is derived from the change in the capital stock over time. This depends heavily on the assumption that the saving rate is exogenous and constant. Change in capital stock is given by:

$$\dot{K} = I - \delta K = s \cdot F(K, L, t) - \delta K \tag{6.10}$$

where $\dot{K}$ is the increase in capital over time. This can be expressed in per capita terms by dividing equation (6.10) through by L (labour):

$$\dot{k} = s \cdot f(k) - (n + \delta) \cdot k \tag{6.11}$$

In equation (6.11), $s \cdot f(k)$ is the saving rate and $n + \delta$ is the effective depreciation rate for the capital/labour ratio. Basically the Solow–Swan model suggests that the steady-state capital/labour ratio (k^*) is determined by the intersection of the investment and depreciation functions. The steady state occurs when the variables K, Y, C, and L grow at constant rates and, hence, *per capita quantities do not grow at all!* This is why the Solow–Swan model cannot explain longrun economic growth.

The Solow–Swan model, by excluding technological change, is even more unrealistic than the much earlier classical model. But it shares with that model an exclusive focus on the surplus-generating medium of production rather than the driving dynamic impulse. The approach is similar to undertaking a formal examination of the mechanics of an electric motor without understanding the nature and role of electric power; or failing to realize that in other times and places motive power has been generated by different types of engines, such as mechanical, steam, water, and nuclear. What is true of the electric motor is not true of the others. *In other words, even the translating mechanism is not universal.* But is this the case with the 'new' or 'endogenous' neoclassical growth model?

The endogenous growth model has passed through two main development stages. The first stage involved an attempt by Romer (1986), Lucas (1988), and Rebelo (1991) to introduce technological change in the form of learning-by-doing as an unintended consequence of investment. Yet this was not really a theory of technological change. In the learning-by-doing models, which were inspired by Arrow (1962) and Sheshinski (1967), pioneering discoveries immediately 'spill over' to the entire economy through an entirely unrealistic instantaneous diffusion process. The advantage of this assumption is that monopoly profits do not arise and, hence, the earlier competitive framework required to determine the equilibrium rate of technological change can be retained. But the outcomes are not Pareto optimal because they can be improved through appropriate policy. Nevertheless, the 'knowledge spill-over' assumption leads to increasing returns that overcome the tendency for diminishing returns to capital accumulation in the Solow–Swan model, generating longrun growth at a growing rate. Of course, this assumption is highly unrealistic for at least two reasons: technological diffusion takes place gradually in reality not instantaneously; and innovation requires intentional action by economic agents investing in research and development (R&D) in search of monopoly profits. Nor is it empirically correct (Snooks 1993: 84–7). And, of course, by avoiding monopoly profits it neglects the motivation for growth decision-making.

The second stage in the development of endogenous growth models began in the late 1980s and early 1990s with the introduction of theories of R&D and of imperfect competition by Romer (1987; 1990), Aghion and Howitt (1992), and Grossman and Helpman (1991). In these models, technological change is the outcome of deliberate investment in R&D to achieve monopoly profits. The outcome of R&D investment is positive longrun growth, but only for as long as this investment continues. Owing to the generation of monopoly profits, the outcomes are not Pareto optimal and these models are usually accompanied by policy prescriptions for 'improving outcomes' through taxes and subsidies. These 'improved outcomes', however, undermine the dynamic process, replacing societal flux with stasis.

One way of endogenizing technological change is, as Romer (1990) has done, by analysing its operation through an expansion in the variety of producer or intermediate goods. An increase in product variety is used as a proxy for innovation. Firms are motivated by anticipated monopoly profits to invest in R&D with the objective of discovering new intermediate products. The production function – the central feature of these models – adopted as a basis for the R&D model specifies diminishing marginal productivity for each input and constant (rather than increasing) returns to scale for all inputs together. The form of the production function for firm i employed by Romer (1987 and 1990) and others is:

$$Y_i = A \cdot L_i^{1-\alpha} \cdot \sum_{j=1}^{N} (X_{ij})^\alpha \tag{6.12}$$

where $0 < \alpha < 1$, Y_i is output, L_i is labour input, and X_{ij} is the employment of the jth type of specialized intermediate good. Technological change is introduced in the form of 'expansions' in the intermediate good N, and can be expressed, in terms of equation (6.12), as:

$$Y_i = A \cdot L_i^{1-\alpha} \cdot N \cdot X_i^\alpha = A \cdot L_i^{1-\alpha} \cdot (NX_i)^\alpha \cdot N^{1-\alpha} \tag{6.13}$$

Now, if the increase in NX_i takes the form of a rise in N for given X_i, diminishing returns do not arise and endogenous longrun growth occurs. Hence, endogenous longrun growth arises from this particular property or *assumption* of the production function.

The huge number of contributions to the neoclassical growth model during the second half of the twentieth century has taken us little further than the classical model developed by a handful of economists some two centuries ago. The major differences between these two orthodox models are merely the outcomes of assumptions made about the production function. *As the 'endogenous' growth model, like its classical predecessor, omits the strategic pursuit, it cannot be regarded as endogenous at all.* All this misdirected effort is evidence that the deductive method cannot cope with real-world dynamic processes. There has to be a better way.

Because of this limited focus, the traditional growth model has limited real-world applicability. Certainly no claim for generality can be made, because it has no relevance to any society not employing the industrial technological strategy. This includes modern commerce societies such as Hong Kong and Singapore, all pre-modern dynamic societies and, most relevantly, all nonstrategic countries (NSCs) because they are pursuing non-dynamic rent-seeking objectives. And even for those societies pursuing an industrial technological strategy, the limited focus of this model means that, while it can tell us something about the surplus-generating medium, it cannot inform us about the core dynamic process.

Orthodox growth models ignore not only the core dynamic process in individual societies, they also fail to consider the global development process. In the main they fail to place the growth of individual countries within a wider process of global economic change. A recent attempt to employ the neoclassical model to explain global patterns of growth rates has failed. How could it possibly have succeeded when these models view economic growth as convergence to equilibrium arising from the structural conditions of production in a single economy?

A model analysing convergence to the steady state is not really a dynamic model. The convergence concept is concerned not with the longrun improvement in material living standards, but merely with recovery from some sort of crisis such as war, depression, or drought. Accordingly it is not valid to employ the Solow–Swan model to explain or predict the nature of convergence of longrun growth rates between nations, as many applied economists have attempted to do. To reiterate something that appears to have been forgotten by some applied economists, Solow–Swan convergence is concerned with recovery from crisis, while global longrun growth rates reflect more fundamental dynamic forces usually associated with not only technological change but also the strategic pursuit.

The applied convergence literature shows that evidence (see Snooks 1998b: 40) on global growth rates does not confirm the hypothesis that poor nations, which are further from some sort of notional steady state, will grow more rapidly than richer countries. Only when similar countries, such as those in Western Europe or regions within the same nation, are examined does a strong inverse relationship between 'initial' income level and annual growth rate of real GDP per capita emerge.[4] These contrasting results are explained by growth theorists in terms of similar production functions, saving rates and, hence, steady-state conditions in closely related countries and regions of the same country. Only through allegedly holding constant the different steady-state conditions throughout the world by including the proxies of human capital in their regression equations, are growth theorists able to conclude that 'the cross-country data support the hypothesis of conditional convergence' if not absolute convergence (Barro and Sala-i-Martin 1995: 30). In effect this is an admission that they cannot explain the pattern of growth outcomes at the global level using the Solow–Swan model – the model does not predict different steady states. Hence, the Solow–Swan model is unable to explain either real-world dynamic *processes* or even real-world dynamic *outcomes*.

What appears to concern some growth theorists (Barro and Sala-i-Martin 1995: 237) is that while the endogenous model can 'explain' longrun growth in individual countries, it cannot explain conditional convergence. Owing to the scale effects – larger nations can better afford the fixed costs of innovations – larger nations should grow faster than smaller nations. As this prediction is not borne out by evidence of global growth rates, the new growth theorist is tempted to borrow ideas about national leadership and catch-up through imitation from economic historians, rarely acknowledged, like Alexander Gerschenkron (1962). This is a departure from the method, normally followed quite rigorously, of deriving results deductively from the existing body of neoclassical theory. The greater pragmatism of some new growth theorists, while it may be applauded by some empiricists, is unlikely to receive the approval of core neoclassicists. Theoretical models begin to lose their coherence when they can be applied to reality only with the support of *ad hoc* ideas borrowed from elsewhere. It is like a Gothic cathedral that only holds together because it is supported by a series of flying buttresses. But, more importantly, these theorists attempt to explain the global pattern of growth outcomes in terms of different production relationships rather than different dynamic strategies. As always they adopt a supply-side rather than a demand-side approach.

6.2 THE POVERTY-TRAP THEORISTS

The widespread dissatisfaction generated by orthodox growth models unable to explain the persistence of underdevelopment stimulated some development economists interested in remedial policy to develop their own theories. Yet, while these theories address the condition of underdevelopment, they neither model the growth process nor provide any basis for a general theory of global economic development. They are merely speculative partial theories and, as such, are of limited use in policy formulation.

The main theoretical explanation for the persistence of underdevelopment is the low-level equilibrium, or poverty, trap hypothesis. No attempt will be made here to examine the various versions of this hypothesis in detail as they are dealt with fully in the chapters on population (Chapter 13) and capital accumulation (Chapter 14). These theories have a long history that can be traced back to the population model of Thomas Robert Malthus (1986; 1st publ. 1798), but which probably owe most to John Maynard Keynes (1936). As is well known, Keynes' theory of effective demand was developed to explain the persistence of high levels of unemployment during the Great Depression of the 1930s. It is a model to explain how equilibrium can be achieved at less than the full-employment level of GDP. It is, in effect, a low-level employment trap hypothesis.

Keynes' theory was on everyone's mind during the 1940s and 1950s when the low-level development trap was expounded by writers such as Paul Rosenstein-Rodan (1943), Ragnar Nurkse (1953), Richard Nelson (1956), Hans Singer (1958), and Albert Hirschman (1958). Like Keynes they argued that a Third-World country could only break free from the poverty trap if its government sponsored a 'big push' to achieve simultaneous development over a wide front. In this way they could effectively exploit the hidden development potential arising from surplus labour in the economy's traditional sector (Lewis 1954; Fei and Ranis 1961).

While these poverty-trap theories are more realistic than orthodox growth theories – because their authors were committed to resolving important real-world problems – they are still framed by the aggregate production function. They are caught in a trap of their own making. The poverty-trap theorists have no doubt that economic growth is generated by the production process rather than the strategic pursuit. Rosenstein-Rodan's (1943) theory of underdevelopment, for example, includes a discussion of 'indivisibilities in the production function', and Nelson's (1956) theory includes an 'income determination equation' that is really a production function. Also their common emphasis on the central role of capital in the 'big push' is a reflection of the way in which this production variable was treated in the prevailing Keynesian and neoclassical growth models. They also saw society as a system of production – a factory – and failed to develop a general theory of global economic development.

6.3   THE GLOBAL-POLARIZATION THEORISTS

There are a number of distinct 'schools' of development economics less wedded to traditional ideas. These include the 'structuralists' and the 'dependency theorists'. While they are still committed to the idea that society is a system of production, they draw attention to the important fact that economic development is a global process. They view underdevelopment as a direct outcome of the productive expansion and growth of the advanced industrialized nations rather than the internal problems of Third-World nations.

The Structuralists

Less committed to neoclassical ideas, the structuralists argue that, while orthodox economics might be relevant to the advanced nations of the 'centre' they are less relevant to the underdeveloped nations of the 'periphery'. The reason is that nations in the 'centre' are structurally and institutionally different to those in the 'periphery'. Accordingly, notions of international comparative advantage and free trade are detrimental rather than advantageous to the nations of the 'periphery'.

The grounds for this opposition to neoclassical theory are not hard to find. Structuralism was initiated by a group of Latin American economists associated with Raúl Prebisch (1901–86), the foundation director of the UN Economic Commission for Latin America (ECLA). Like all concerned thinkers in primary-producing countries, they were sensitive to the problem of global competition from advanced industrial nations. There is nothing novel in this opposition to orthodox economics from policy-makers in less-developed nations. It is part of a tradition that can be traced back to the work of Friedrich List (1789–1846) in the 1830s and 1840s. List realized that Germany could only compete with Britain, the first industrial nation, if it rejected free trade and adopted a protectionist policy. Such policies have exercised the minds of economists and political leaders in all nations attempting to industrialize. In Australia import substitution was advocated during the 1850s and 1860s by David Syme (1871; 1876), a newspaper proprietor and historical economist, and was officially introduced in the colony of Victoria as early as 1871; and in Latin America tariff protection was introduced in the 1890s.

Our interest in the structuralist hypothesis – often called the Prebisch–Singer hypothesis – arises from its claim to provide a global view of the development process.[5] Essentially this hypothesis draws a distinction between the economic structure and institutions in the developed 'centre' and those in the underdeveloped 'periphery'. Owing to these alleged differences, technological change and free trade between these two regions may lead to the stagnation and regression of the less-developed nations. The structuralist claim, therefore, is that economic growth of the 'centre' is responsible for the perpetuation, rather than the elimination, of global underdevelopment.

Yet, why is technological change beneficial for the 'centre' but disadvantageous for the 'periphery'? The Prebisch–Singer argument is that it leads to the progressive movement of the terms of trade against either primary products or, as stressed in more recent work (Singer and Sharma 1989), the exports of less-developed countries. This is because technological change has quite different consequences for the production of secondary and primary products. The developed 'centre', we are told, is dominated by oligopolistic corporations that are able to set prices, and by powerful unions that are able to push up real wages; whereas primary producers and workers in the underdeveloped 'periphery' have little control over prices or wages. Hence, while technological change leads to higher prices and wages in the 'centre', it produces the reverse in the more competitive 'periphery'. Also technological change saves on material inputs and leads to the replacement of organic materials with synthetics. In this way the 'centre' gains at the expense of the 'periphery' and, as the gap between them increases, the problem of underdevelopment becomes more firmly entrenched. This international polarization is reinforced, it is argued, by Engel's Law – as income rises the proportion spent on food falls or, in other words, the income elasticity of demand for food is less than unity.

The Prebisch–Singer hypothesis has been highly controversial and has generated considerable empirical work on historical changes in the terms of trade (Higgins 1968: 282–4). This evidence, which indicates wide variation in the terms of trade on commodity (manufacturing as well as primary), regional, and secular bases, provides greater support for my dynamic-strategy hypothesis than for the Prebisch–Singer hypothesis. What can be concluded is that strategic opportunities change with time and place, and those nations that are sufficiently perceptive or lucky to make the correct choices are able to profit and develop. Those who make and maintain the wrong strategic decisions must endure the consequences of the terms of trade moving against them.

The policy implication of the Prebisch–Singer hypothesis is that 'periphery' countries should respond to declining terms of trade by pursuing the 'development from within' approach. This has become more generally known as the policy of import-substitution industrialization (ISI). In other words, nations of the 'periphery' must transform their structure and institutions to more closely resemble those of the nations of the 'centre'. Like the big-push theorists, they advocated large-scale intervention by 'periphery' governments; but unlike them, Prebisch (1950) and Singer (1950) advocated artificially changing the incentive structure. Hence, the structuralists, in advocating protection and trade diversion, departed from the neoclassical approach, which rejected such policies on the grounds that they were not Pareto optimal and advocated free trade, now referred to as 'globalization' (Arndt 1992). This represents a clash between advocates of the concepts of static and dynamic comparative advantage.

The main achievement of the structuralists was their vision of economic development as a global process. Unfortunately they were not able to build a general theory of economic development, largely because of their conviction that the economic struggle between the 'centre' and the 'periphery' is a zero-sum game. They merely identified a problem – global polarization – that they were convinced was responsible for underdevelopment and suggested policy to alleviate it. When we strip away the 'centre'– 'periphery' terminology – which is not really a model – we can see that the structuralists are in fact part of the historicist tradition that stretches back for almost two centuries. As argued and demonstrated in Chapters 2 and 3, they are incorrect in claiming that global development is a zero-sum game between the 'centre' and the 'periphery'. Also, their focus on differences between manufacturing and primary products or even the structure of developed and less-developed societies is too broad. In the end the structuralists miss the point that the difference between rich and poor countries is an outcome of the dynamic strategies chosen and the success with which they are pursued.

The Dependency Theorists

Another group of scholars, who became prominent in the 1960s and 1970s, also theorized about the zero-sum nature of the interaction between developed and underdeveloped regions and nations. What distinguishes them from the structuralists is their total rejection of neoclassical theory, together with the inspiration, in varying degree, that they derive from Karl Marx. Some of the prominent individuals in this category include Paul Baran (1957), Gunder Frank (1967), and Fernando Cardoso and Enzo Faletto (1979). Their views will be briefly surveyed.

What these writers have in common is the belief that underdevelopment is not only persistent but that it is an outcome of capitalist growth, which necessarily involves the permanent exploitation of the Third World. It is claimed by Frank (1967: vii–xv), in the tradition of Baran, that capitalism with its monopolistic structure possesses persistent 'underdevelopment-generating contradictions'. By expropriating the 'surplus' of the Third World, capitalist development leads to local, national, and international 'polarization'. This polarization is reflected, in particular, in the 'metropolis–satellite' structure of the world. Underdevelopment, in other words, is a persistent outcome of the global process of capitalist development.

The only way underdeveloped nations can escape this world structure, Frank (ibid.: xii) tells us, is through socialist revolution. He asserts that this can be achieved only by 'the masses of the people', because 'the historical mission and role of the bourgeoisie ... is finished'. Others have suggested that such action in individual nations can be coordinated through a New International Economic Order (NIEO) that would restructure the world economy in favour of the Third World (Hadjor 1993: 225–7). Only through direct action is it possible, they claim, to disrupt the global process of capitalism that is the cause of underdevelopment.

What the dependency theorists have in common with all other traditional schools of thought is the idea of society as a system of production – a factory. This permeates the radical as well as the orthodox tradition because of the influence of Karl Marx's *Capital*. As is discussed in detail in Chapter 15, Marx treated capitalist society as a giant factory dominated by the machine. Machine production, which is the driving force in his growth model, not only determined capitalist 'value' but also the production relationships between the two classes of capitalists and workers. Economic change is the outcome of 'the progress of machinery'. The destiny of capitalist society, therefore, is determined by the machine and the factory. Hence, the radical tradition, like the orthodox tradition, suffers from the fundamental misapprehension that economic growth is driven by, and only by, the capitalist process of production.

6.4 THE INSTITUTIONALISTS

The final traditional explanation of underdevelopment focuses on the failure of institutions in Third-World nations to evolve efficiently. This is due, it is claimed, to adverse initial conditions resulting from an earlier era of colonialism, and to a path-dependent evolutionary process. This cause of underdevelopment can be eliminated only by a major government initiative to remove, reshape, and replace old and inefficient institutions. This institutionalist approach encompasses the 'cumulative causation' hypothesis of Gunnar Myrdal and the 'path-dependent' hypothesis of the new institutional economics of Douglass North.

Myrdal and 'Cumulative Causation'

Gunnar Myrdal (1957; 1968) explains persistent underdevelopment in terms of the difficulties involved in transmitting the trade-induced growth impulse from the small prosperous export sector to the large poor traditional sector of a less-developed society. By taking up where Hla Myint (1954) left off, Myrdal elaborates the concept of the dual economy that emerges due to the influence of international trade. In doing so he, like the structuralists, departs from the orthodox theory of international trade based on Ricardian comparative advantage.

Myrdal argues that while international trade stimulates the growth and prosperity of the modern sector of a less-developed country, this will not cause the traditional sector to follow suit. Over time, therefore, the gap between rich and poor regions within such an economy will grow increasingly large. The reason for this 'vicious spiral' is that the 'backwash' effects (or negative externalities) will overwhelm the 'spread' effects (or positive externalities). The backwash effects include the undercutting of traditional handicraft industries, the transfer of the society's best and most able workers from the traditional to the modern sector, and higher rates of fertility prevalent in the traditional sector. The spread effects – or backward and forward linkages in the terminology of Albert Hirschman (1958) – are limited by the institutional structure of most underdeveloped countries owing to their colonial legacy. Under the colonial rule of Europe, Myrdal argues, the traditional society was structured so that the colonial power could maximize the exploitation of its resources. The opportunities created by European investment in a colony – in the form of processing, manufacturing, shipping, finance, and insurance of its natural resources – accrued to imperial rather than colonial interests.

But why did this pattern, as Myrdal claims, persist after decolonization? Myrdal's (1957: 13) answer is that in the former colony:

> The system is by itself not moving towards any sort of balance between forces, but is constantly on the move away from such a situation. In the

normal case a change does not call forth countervailing changes but, instead, supporting changes, which move the system in the same direction as the first change but much further. Because of such circular causation a social process tends to become cumulative and often to gather speed at an accelerating rate.

This 'cumulative circular causation' hypothesis is very similar to the currently popular path-dependence hypothesis. In Myrdal's terms, an ex-colonial nation will find it difficult to escape its colonial past. The metropolis and the small colonial sector will continue to develop, in response to international trade, at the expense of the large traditional sector, because of the 'attitudes and institutions' firmly established in the colonial period. It is interesting that Myrdal developed this concept a generation or more before it was reinvented as the path-dependence hypothesis (Arthur 1988) and, subsequently, adopted by Douglass North (1990). Whatever the formulation, the concept is not a persuasive explanation of underdevelopment.

According to Myrdal, the only way to break this vicious cumulative circle is by decisive government intervention. In reflecting upon his career in a World Bank lecture, Myrdal (1984: 153) said:

> The institutional approach meant enlarging the study to include what in a summary way I referred to as 'attitudes and institutions.' They were found to be largely responsible for those countries' underdevelopment and would have to be changed in order to speed up development.

But he acknowledges that this is difficult to do, because the governments in less-developed countries are either ineffective or they serve only a small ruling elite.

What Myrdal does not acknowledge is that the real reason for the lack of development in Third-World countries is that they have yet to enter into the global strategic transition, with the result that they are ruled by rent-seeking antistrategists rather than profit-seeking strategists. The only reason that colonial institutions appear to be barriers to development is that they are just what is required to facilitate the ruling elite's rent-seeking activities. As the society enters into the global strategic transition, local strategists gradually gain the upper hand and discard restrictive colonial institutions, replacing them with new institutions that facilitate their strategic pursuit. Difficulties do emerge, however, in former *conquest* colonies (in contrast to former *commerce* colonies – see Chapter 4) where rent-seeking groups, owing to their inherited control over natural and human resources, retain political control and generate a demand for antistrategic institutions; at least until they become a substantial proportion of the total population, at which time their materialist objectives can only be maximized by replacing rent-seeking with profit-seeking, antistrategic objectives with strategic objectives, stasis with growth (see Chapter 4). Therefore both 'cumulative circular causation' and 'path-dependence' are unhelpful supply-side concepts. Institutions do not operate as barriers to development when strategic opportunities are being exploited – they are just invoked by scholars who have no sense of dynamic demand. It is, as we shall see in Parts IV and V, strategic demand rather than supply-side strategic instruments that drives the development process.

Douglass North and Path-dependence

As the new institutional economics is discussed in detail in Chapter 16, where the institutional response to strategic demand is examined, it will be reviewed briefly here. Douglass North, in contrast to Gunnar Myrdal, does not wish to reject neoclassical theory. Indeed, his new institutional economics is based on the Walrasian general equilibrium model. And he accepts the neoclassical model of production. In order to introduce institutions into the neoclassical model (the reason he received the Nobel Prize), North releases a number of restrictive assumptions concerning the availability and processing of information by economic agents: namely that decision-makers have perfect information, correct conceptual models of reality, and are able to process all relevant information accurately.

North (1990) argues that because information about reality is fragmentary, individual decision-making involves significant costs. These are transaction costs which include costs both of obtaining information and of enforcing agreements. Only if information is perfect will transaction costs be zero. North argues that the neoclassical concept of production costs, which he embraces, should be widened to include these costs of transactions together with the more familiar costs of what he calls 'transformation'. North (ibid.: 34) explains:

> Institutions provide the structure for exchange that (together with the technology employed) determines the costs of transacting and the cost of transformation. How well institutions solve the problems of coordination and production is determined by the motivation of the players (their utility function), the complexity of the environment, and the ability of players to decipher and order the environment (measurement and enforcement).

North identifies a number of 'general types' of exchange. The first, which encompasses most of human history, is what he calls 'personalized exchange', and is characterized by small-scale production and local trade. It involves a common set of cultural values, repeated exchange dealings, and no third-party (state) enforcement. In this system, transaction costs are low (abundant information and trust), but transformation costs (limited specialization owing to small scale) are high. The second general type, which North identifies as 'impersonal exchange without third-party enforcement', is based on either kinship ties, hostage exchange, or merchant conduct codes. This type is associated with larger markets, more complex production and exchange, and long-distance trade. The third general type, 'impersonal exchange with third-party enforcement', involves a complex system of contracting which makes the role of a coercive third party essential. This large-scale complex system generates high transaction costs but low transformation costs.

To reduce transaction costs, societies, according to North, adopt informal (customs) and formal (laws) constraints. Formal constraints emerge as societies become more complex and transaction costs rise. In other words, he adopts a supply-side hypothesis to explain the emergence of institutions, which contrasts with the strategic-demand hypothesis in this book. Formal constraints, North tells us, include political and judicial rules, economic rules, and specific contracts. These formal rules, which 'descend from polities to property rights to individual contracts' (ibid.: 52), provide the wealth-maximizing opportunities for human actors, which can be realized through economic or political exchanges (or bargains). In other words, human organizations are developed to exploit the profitable opportunities contained within institutions. North emphasizes that inefficient systems of property rights may persist owing to high political transaction costs and to inaccurate conceptual models of decision-makers. This, he claims, accounts for the absence of economic growth in much of the Third World.

The role of enforcement costs receives special consideration because North believes that 'the inability of societies to develop effective, low-cost enforcement of contracts is the most important source of both historical stagnation and contemporary underdevelopment in the Third World' (ibid.: 54). This is because some societies appear unable to make a successful transition from the self-enforcing contracts of 'personalized exchange' to the more complex world of 'impersonal exchange' – a world that requires effective state intervention to monitor property rights and to enforce contracts. Often the problem, according to North, is an inability to resolve the conflict of interests faced by those running the state.

North's system is disconcertingly circular and devoid of any driving force. The sequence of events is as follows: unexplained economic progress → greater societal complexity → increased transaction costs → institutional change → new wealth-maximizing opportunities → organizational change → increased production → economic progress → and so on. When this system breaks down, owing to unexplained costs of developing effective political systems and to muddle-headedness (wrong conceptual models), economic development grinds to a halt. How, one might ask, is it possible to derive a set of dynamic economic laws from this type of explanation? In the absence of dynamic laws there can be no scientific explanation of the dynamics of human society.

It is on this institutional foundation that North attempts to explain the *persistence* of underdevelopment. Third-World societies, he claims, get locked into their institutional structures owing to the nature of their evolutionary processes. This, he tells us, is a path-dependent process. In a world of increasing institutional returns and deficient informational feedback, the conceptual models possessed by decision-makers do not converge on the 'true' models. Increasing returns reinforce the direction of institutional development once a society begins on a particular path (the result of historical accident), and incomplete markets, which reinforce faulty conceptual models, produce a growing divergence of the actual from the most efficient development path. This sequence leads to the persistence of inefficient institutional systems in Third-World nations and, hence, to relatively poor economic performance.

According to North, therefore, the persistence of underdevelopment is a product of its institutional past (initial conditions) together with the existence of deficient conceptual models and imperfect information. There are a number of problems with this hypothesis. First, why have so many countries been able to break out of this vicious circle? They have been doing this for the past two hundred years. And continue to do so (see Chapter 3). His hypothesis, like the rest in this chapter, attempts to explain only the barriers to development, making no attempt to show how Third-World countries enter into the global development process. Secondly, he appears to be suggesting that some societies are able to understand reality – that is they possess 'true' conceptual models – and others are not. This amounts to saying that the ultimate answer is cultural and that some cultures are superior in this respect to others. I reject this view on historical grounds. Thirdly, like Myrdal, he falls back on the supply-side argument that Third-World societies are prisoners of their past; that they get locked into processes that are not in their best interest. Not only does this suggest that Third-World societies are irrational over the longer term, but it is clearly ahistorical. As I have demonstrated elsewhere (Snooks 1997a), human societies throughout history have shown a remarkable ability not only to change their institutional development relatively rapidly, but to even completely reverse it in a non-evolutionary manner, whenever strategic opportunities exist. In all cases this has been a response to changes in strategic demand and not to supposed supply-side developments.

Finally we need to ask ourselves how the new institutionalists view human society. How does their vision relate to that of the production theorists? The short answer is: quite closely. Both schools of thought see human society as a system of production – a factory dominated by the machine and its input requirements. The major difference is that the new institutionalists have a wider conception of the costs of production because they do not assume that transactions between buyers and sellers are costless. They view the dynamics of human society as an outcome of interaction within the overall framework of total production costs between arrangements required to reduce both the costs of transaction and the costs of transformation. There is no hint here of a strategic pursuit. North's decision-makers exploit institutional opportunities rather than strategic opportunities.

6.5 CONCLUSIONS

Owing to the vast amount of intellectual effort that has been devoted to the problems of economic development, it is remarkable that greater progress has not been made. It is hardly controversial to conclude that traditional development theory, both orthodox and radical, has failed to provide a general theory to explain the global development process. And without such a theory it is impossible to analyse the development process, predict future outcomes, or to formulate relevant remedial policy.

The major reason for this disappointing outcome is the method employed by both orthodox and radical economists. While the prevailing deductive method has considerable strengths in static production analysis, it is unable to handle real-world dynamics. That requires an entirely different approach – the inductive or historical method. Without it we will never understand the nature of the global strategic transition. As we have seen, the traditional theorists focus not on the real-world strategic pursuit but on the mechanical system of production. They see society not as a strategic organization but as a giant factory. What is required is a new method and a new vision.

7 Traditional Development Policy

The objective of development economics is to explore the reasons for persistent underdevelopment and poverty, and to frame policies that can be employed by Third-World governments and international organizations to resolve these problems. Typically the role of development policy is viewed as removing those obstinate economic, political, and social barriers to transformational change in the developed world (World Bank 1993: 116). In this chapter the nature and scope of development policies are reviewed, and their theoretical and empirical foundations are discussed. It is argued that the extensive disagreement between experts on most policy issues, together with its fragmented nature, has risen because of the failure to construct a satisfactory general economic and political theory of the global development process. Policies are based on severely constrained partial theories, a good deal of casual empiricism, and unrestrained economic ideology. And much of the resulting policy lacks integration into a consistent whole. In order to resolve these problems it is essential to construct a general theory of economic development.

This chapter focuses on three broad policy formulation issues. The first involves the fundamental issue of whether practical development policy should be pursued at all. This concerns the seemingly endless debate over the role of the state versus the role of the market in economic affairs. The second issue concerns the broader dynamic problem of how it might be possible for Third-World countries to break free from the poverty trap. And the final issue concerns the efficacy of policies relating to population, human capital, technological change, domestic and foreign resources, equity versus growth, and environmental degradation.

7.1 THE STATE OR THE MARKET?

This fundamental policy issue has been of central concern to the economics profession since the time of Adam Smith (1723–90). It arises from the apparent paradox that individuals pursuing their own self-interest unintentionally create orderly institutional structures that, in many instances, not only operate surprisingly efficiently but also facilitate the generation of relatively high rates of economic growth. But inevitably the question arises: Why is it not possible to achieve even greater efficiency and higher rates of economic growth by devising more effective dynamic institutions? This question appears most pertinent to the Third World where growth and efficiency are particularly disappointing. A brief survey of ideas on this issue from Adam Smith to now will demonstrate this concern.[1]

Smith was the first political economist to treat spontaneous order as central to his grand societal system. He did so by introducing the famous concept of the 'invisible hand', by which individuals pursuing 'self-love' were guided to create institutions that restrained their selfish desires in order to enable the emergence of liberty and economic growth. Smith constructed a theoretical system in which the driving force of self-love – the 'principle of motion' – was constrained by the Stoic virtues embodied in the 'impartial spectator', an instrument of divine forces (Smith 1976; orig. publ. 1759). Hence, the Stoic virtues – self-command, prudence, justice, and beneficence – planted in the breast of every 'reasonable' man, operated as a constraint on desires and enabled the construction of just laws, which are the 'main pillar that upholds the entire edifice' (Smith 1776/ 1961, II. ii: 3–4). Only if the impartial spectator were denied by the leading individuals of a particular society would the laws of the jungle, rather than justice, prevail.[2] While other classical economists, such as David Hume (1711–76), David Ricardo (1772–1823) and John Stuart Mill (1806–73), rejected Smith's mystical argument about the impartial spectator as unscientific, they agreed with his views about the pursuit of self-interest being in the best interest of society. In effect they secularized the concept of the invisible hand by equating it with the hidden directives of the market.

The first systematic attack on the classical view of the role of markets came from Friedrich List (1789–1846), who was a citizen of the then underdeveloped 'country' of Germany in the early nineteenth century. He rejected the Ricardian concept of comparative advantage and free trade, claiming that countries such as Germany, Russia, and the USA could only industrialize and compete with Britain if they adopted protectionist policies. List also claimed that if a country wanted to be prosperous it required a powerful government prepared to intervene in the market economy to promote economic projects (Blaug 1986: 129–31). This marked the beginning of the great debate about economic development between liberals and interventionists.

The balance of opinion between these two competing ideas has fluctuated widely over the past 150 years. Until the 1930s the liberal view prevailed in the economics profession despite the fact that policies of protection were adopted by various European nations, the USA, and other regions of recent settlement for prolonged periods. At the same time the historical school of economics, which rejected the deductive approach of mainstream economics together with its *laissez-faire* policies, fought a rearguard action in the Anglo-Saxon world, gaining most ground in the USA (Snooks 1993: 26–9). Only with the Great Depression of the 1930s and the Keynesian Revolution did mainstream economics change its policy emphasis from the liberal to the interventionist position. Keynesians argued that full employment and stable growth could only be achieved through extensive government involvement. During the 1950s and 1960s the concept of the mixed economy became fashionable. It was at this time that economists also became increasingly interested in the problem of underdevelopment and, in the tradition of Friedrich List, they argued that escape from the poverty trap could only be engineered through large-scale government intervention. As discussed earlier, only when the end of colonialism was in sight did the great powers begin to think about the poverty of the Third World.

But not all economists accepted the interventionist view. Neo-Austrians such as Friedrich Hayek (1899–1922), and monetarists such as Milton Friedman (1912–), held to their libertarian beliefs and waited in the wings for their opportunity on centre stage. Like Adam Smith, Hayek treated the coordination problem as central to his conception of economics. He called the complex order of human society, which he believed was more sophisticated than could be consciously planned by individual decision-makers, 'spontaneous order'. Not surprisingly, Hayek rejected Smith's belief that human institutions were the result of divine intervention, but maintained they were the outcome of myopic human action in the pursuit of self-interest. Yet how is this outcome possible? Hayek (1988) argues that human institutions or rules, which constrain the demands generated by animal instincts, are not foreseen or planned by the human intellect but evolve in a Darwinian manner. He adopts a simple neo-Darwinian explanation involving the adaption of institutional variation through a process of group selection under competition which, if successful, becomes dominant in the 'rule pool' by an increase in the population and power of the innovative society. The more populous society absorbs the least successful societies.

With the emergence of major and unfamiliar economic problems – slower, even negative, rates of growth and high rates of both unemployment and inflation – following the 'golden age' (1950 to 1973), the status and influence of interventionist orthodox economics declined. This made it possible for dissenting members of the profession to finally move onto centre stage. Some, like Milton Friedman, revived interest in the quantity theory of money and reshaped it (by turning it into a theory of the demand for money) to fit the new circumstances of the 1970s and 1980s. They also reaffirmed the old liberal belief in the primacy of markets (Friedman and Schwartz 1982). Others, like the 'new classical macroeconomists', attempted to resolve problems in the prevailing neoclassical synthesis by unrealistically assuming that markets are highly competitive and that they clear instantly. By doing so they thought they had eliminated the need for government intervention. While this was true in the case of their models, they needed to do more to eliminate this need in reality. Could this be why they have, through neoliberal policy, unsuccessfully attempted to make reality conform to their simple market models?

The decade from the early 1980s represents the high-water mark for neoliberalism. Libertarian ideas were employed by Britain's Prime Minister Thatcher (1979–90) and the USA's President Reagan (1981–9), who were desperately seeking solutions to the economic and political turmoil of the second half of the 1970s. As these policies spread around the world, the neoliberals flourished, making inroads into the disciplines of political economy and economic development. 'New' political economists like James Buchannan (1987: 586) adopted the libertarian ideas of Hayek, such as methodological individualism, which treats individual choice as the basic unit of analysis and 'collectivities', or social groups, as the outcome merely of individual choices and actions. Hence, he and other public choice/constitutional economists reject any proactive role for government in the pursuit of national objectives. Governments, we are told, should exist only to facilitate private enterprise by protecting individuals and property rights, and by enforcing privately negotiated contracts. But, in contrast to Hayek, Buchannan claims that it is possible for mankind to frame better political rules than those that might evolve spontaneously.

Neoliberalism also emerged during the 1980s and early 1990s in the ranks of development economists and the staff of international development organizations such as the IMF and the World Bank. The most prominent neoliberal development economists are Peter Bauer and Deepak Lal. Bauer's (1984) neoliberal outlook is based upon his detailed fieldwork on the rubber industry in Malaysia (Bauer 1948) and on trade in West Africa (Bauer 1954). He claims that the development of these regions in the 1940s and 1950s was due not to the forced mobilization of resources, nor to forced changes in attitudes and institutions, nor to large-scale, state-sponsored industrialization or any other form of big push, nor to national consciousness. Rather, he claims:

> What happened was in very large measure the result of the individual voluntary responses of millions of people to emerging or expanding

opportunities created largely by external contacts and brought to their notice in a variety of ways, primarily through the operation of the market. These developments were made possible by firm but limited government, without large expenditures of public funds and without the receipt of large external subventions. (Bauer 1984: 30–1)

Deepak Lal's attack on interventionist development economics is of a more polemical nature (Lal 1983). He argues that development economics had committed the grave mistake of supporting state-led development at the expense of market considerations and that it had focused on macroeconomic issues rather than microeconomic efficiency. The latter – getting the fundamentals right – is a typical neoliberal attitude based on a blinkered analysis of the modern system of production in human society. Nevertheless, in Lal's words:

Most of the serious distortions in the current workings of the price mechanism in Third World countries are due not to the inherent imperfections of the market mechanism but to irrational government interventions, of which foreign trade controls, industrial licensing and various forms of price control are the most important. (Ibid.: 77)

Even international development organizations, such as the World Bank and the IMF that are dominated by the superpowers, were influenced by neoliberalism in the 1980s. The World Bank (or more correctly the International Bank for Reconstruction and Development) underwent a major transformation in its vision and role during this decade. In the 1970s, under the direction of Robert McNamara (1968–81) the World Bank became a major player in global economic development. Initially McNamara, influenced by calls from a number of internationally significant organizations (the Dag Hammarskjöld Foundation in 1975 and the ILO in 1976), adopted a 'basic human needs' approach to development – an approach that aimed to eliminate poverty, hunger, and misery throughout the world. Owing to the vigour with which this policy was pursued, annual World Bank loans increased fivefold over the period 1970 to 1979 from $US8.9 billion to $US44.8 billion (World Bank, *Annual Reports*). In real terms this amounted to a 2.7-fold increase in Third-World debt.

As the World Bank increased in size and influence, so it attempted to gain more direct control over the development programmes of Third-World countries. This was effectively achieved from the late 1970s, through so-called 'structural adjustment loans' (SALs), which were designed not for development projects but to reshape the economic policies of participating

Third-World countries. These loans, which amounted to about one-third of the total, were conditional on the developing countries achieving pre-specified policy changes. Between 1980 and 1986 the most important conditions, in terms of frequency of stipulation, were:

- to strengthen public investment programmes (specified in 86 per cent of all loans);
- to improve export incentives (76 per cent);
- to revise agricultural prices (73 per cent);
- to improve financial performance of public enterprises (73 per cent);
- to reform the government budget or taxes (70 per cent). (Mosley *et al.* 1991, vol. I: 44)

In 1987 the Bank strengthened this programme through an 'integration policy', which effectively subordinated all loans to its structural adjustment programme.

The main objectives of this structural adjustment programme are to substantially reduce the role of state intervention through a process of privatization and to promote globalization. In effect this policy was designed to transfer strategic leadership from national governments in the Third World and to invest it in global markets dominated by the superpowers. Those governments stubbornly refusing to relinquish their leadership received little Bank support. Hence, in the name of minimal government intervention, the World Bank sought maximal intervention for itself in the affairs of the NSCs and, more recently, ESCs experiencing financial difficulties. And to what effect? While this policy appears to have led to an improvement in export and balance of payments performance, growth rates have not improved and living standards have declined in the countries involved in this programme (Mosley *et al.* 1991).

Since the early 1990s this global leviathan has begun to curtail its activities owing to the growing criticism both of its ironically interventionist policies and of its neoliberal philosophy. Between 1990 and 1996, Bank lending increased in nominal terms by only 19.2 per cent, while in real terms it actually declined by 0.7 per cent (World Bank, *Annual Reports*). This process of contraction began under the direction of Lewis Preston and, since 1995, has continued under James Wolfensohn. Currently the Bank preaches sustainability – defined in terms of relieving poverty, controlling population, and saving the environment – and, if the 1997 Bank report on the role of the state is any guide, it is rethinking its stance on government intervention. Policy, therefore, swings in time to the pendulum of fashion in the debate over the state versus the market.

The International Monetary Fund (IMF), which was established in 1945 to provide technical assistance and short-term funds to resolve the balance of payments and currency problems of the advanced nations, turned increasingly to the problems of the Third World from the 1960s. Initially the IMF provided only 'stand-by' arrangements by which member nations could draw from its quota over a period of 12 to 18 months according to certain agreed conditions concerning budgetary and monetary performance monitored at regular intervals. But from 1963 the IMF initiated a programme by which additional loan 'facilities' were provided to poorer nations for coping with: exogenous shocks to export earnings and food exports (1963); stabilization of raw material prices (1969); oil price shocks (1974–75); and structural adjustment (1980s and 1990s). Also, in the mid-1990s, the IMF extended its stand-by facilities to handle massive financial crises by Third-World countries, such as Mexico in 1995 ($US17.8 billion), South Korea in 1997/98 ($US57 billion), and Indonesia in 1997/98 ($US43 billion). But the price of this 'helping hand' for East Asian nations is the surrender of their dynamic strategies to the neoliberals. Financial stability has been purchased at the cost of involuntary structural-adjustment policies that will undermine their longrun growth prospects.

This vast expansion of lending facilities during the last quarter of the twentieth century has enabled the IMF to extend its power and influence over the most successful Third-World countries as well as the least successful. And it took place just at a time when there were signs that the interventionist power of the World Bank was being contained. The irony is that this expansion of interventionist power has been conducted in the name of neoliberalism. It would seem that intervention is only wrong when it is undertaken by national governments rather than international organizations dominated by the superpowers or when it is employed for economic development rather than structural adjustment. Presumably international organizations in contrast to Third-World governments, and neoliberals in contrast to interventionists, are regarded as possessing a monopoly on the truth. This is an interesting presumption in view of the pendulum swings that have taken place in the policy stance of these international organizations over the past half-century.

What has been the policy thrust of the IMF since the early 1980s? The objective of their stabilization programmes is 'compression' of the economy, to be achieved by removing 'excess demand' generated by the public and private sectors. This is, in other words, just good old-fashioned deflation. The neoliberal philosophy appears to be that, unless these remedies hurt in the shortrun, there can be no longrun return to economic health. It is a philosophy regularly expressed in influential journals such as

The Economist (29 November 1997: 13) – on this occasion in relation to the Asian financial 'crisis': 'pain is necessary, and pain must be meted out'. This pain involves a reduction of government expenditure to reduce inflation and to reverse alleged crowding-out of the private sector; a reduction in real wages to improve their international competitiveness; devaluation of the currency to eliminate the deficit on current account; and tighter control of the money supply to further reduce inflationary pressures. Even as recently as February 1998 the financial ministers of the Group of Seven welcomed the IMF's 'emphasis on structural reforms to reduce inappropriate government interference in the market economy', called for 'continued action to strengthen the financial system and regulatory reforms of the financial and other sectors so as to increase openness', and suggested that the IMF develop a new global code of conduct to 'forestall any future economic collapse' (AFP 23 February 1998).

But what are the practical outcomes of neoliberal policy and the pain it has caused? The short answer is that the outcomes are extremely disappointing and hardly justify the misery that has been inflicted on underdeveloped societies. Studies undertaken by the IMF (Morrison 1995) and independent observers (Pastor 1987; Killick *et al.* 1992; Killick 1995) suggest the following:

- There was a high rate of (about half) abandonment of these programmes in the 1980s, confirming their unsuitability.
- Those groups enduring the most pain in the longrun as well as the shortrun are the wage earners and the poorest classes in Third-World societies.
- While there is generally some improvement in the balance of payments and exports in the shortrun, performance declines in the longer run. Growth rates and living standards also decline, particularly in the longer term.
- While some countries possessing 'very high rates' of inflation achieved substantial reductions following these programmes, most continued to experience 'moderately high' inflation.
- Although there has been a substitution of private for public investment, few countries have also experienced an increase in total investment/ GDP ratios.

At best, structural adjustment programmes should be regarded only as very shortrun emergency measures aimed at resolving *some* crises of mismanagement. They must never be regarded as universally applicable or be maintained in the longer term in the pretense that they constitute viable development policies. They do not.

The fundamentally important issue that must be addressed is: Why have neoliberal policies at the IMF failed to promote economic development? It is possible to answer this question with the dynamic-strategy model presented in this book. What follows is a summary of the more detailed argument developed in subsequent chapters.

- The neoclassical vision on which this policy is based is at variance with reality. It is a vision of a perfectly competitive society which achieves optimal efficiency, measured in Paretian terms, when it is in equilibrium. The problem is that economic development is a disequilibrium process – an opportunistic strategic pursuit rather than an efficient production process. This would not matter – the human race has generated many unrealistic ideas – if neoclassical economists were not in a position to impose their vision on reality, as they have done through the IMF and the World Bank.
- More specifically, IMF/World Bank stabilization policies, where they are effective, are responsible for disrupting the strategic demand–response mechanism that generates strategic inflation. They do this by failing to discriminate between strategic and nonstrategic inflation when they insist on reducing nominal inflation to zero.
- By exerting power over economic policy in Third-World countries, the IMF/World Bank have destroyed any semblance of strategic leadership, which is essential to achieve economic development.
- By enforcing the zero budget deficit rule, the IMF has made it difficult or impossible to import capital and technology, thereby disrupting the unfolding of the dynamic strategy in the ESC concerned.

7.2   GENERAL POLICY ISSUES

The policy issue for neoliberals is seductively simple: there should be *no* government interventionist policy. The greatest good for the greatest number will be achieved by individuals pursuing their own self-interest in domestic and international markets. Governments should not become involved in development issues because they will merely distort markets and extract rent. That is in theory. In reality, as we have seen, the only way to eliminate interventionist policy at the national level is to impose it at the global level where the scope for error is monumental. This is the great paradox of neoliberalism. The world is not as simple or as paradoxical as this for the interventionist who believes that governments can assist in the development process. The complexity arises from framing policies that might just be able to do this. For this purpose development economists have turned to the general growth and development models discussed in Chapter 6. We review their policy implications here.

The Policy Implications of Growth Models

This is not a large section precisely because neoclassical growth models have not been particularly useful for policy purposes. How could they be when they are constructed from static production theory? There are only two theory–policy connections: the tenuous claim that these growth models have been responsible for the policy approach to economic development since the 1940s; and the fact that some of these growth models have found limited use in development planning.

The first of these connections need not detain us long. Since the 1940s, development policy has focused on the role of investment and, more recently, on technological change. It hardly requires a mathematically specified growth model to demonstrate the importance of capital, both physical and human, or of technological change to the process of economic development. These relationships have long been understood by those interested in historical economics, such as the German historicists from the early nineteenth century, Karl Marx in the mid-nineteenth century, and Arnold Toynbee (snr) in the 1870s. After all, the study of the Industrial Revolution has traditionally focused on investment, inventions, and new factory skills. The strange fact that most economists only see reality in terms of simple (and seriously flawed) mathematical models is a major weakness of mainstream deductive economics. The point requiring emphasis is that growth theory has less to tell us about the nature of real-world dynamics than a careful reading of economic history.

It is sometimes claimed that growth models have been useful in economic planning. A number of points can be made in this respect in addition to the comment that most neoliberals would be horrified by the claim. First, these 'production' models have nothing to say about the global development process or about the strategic pursuit that is central to that process. Accordingly they cannot offer any advice to planners or other development groups about the wider objectives or dynamic strategies that a society should be pursuing. As a result, strategic leadership, which is essential to economic development, degenerates into establishing a set of directives for expanding the *production process* rather than in facilitating the dynamic *strategic pursuit*. The ultimate expression of the poverty of this production approach can be seen in the former Soviet planning system (Chapter 5), which failed because it excluded the strategists, and substituted engineered production for the strategic pursuit (Snooks 1997a: 451–65).

Secondly, even the use of neoclassical growth models in *production* planning is severely limited owing to their highly aggregated nature and, more importantly, lack of reality. We are told that the Harrod–Domar model was employed by Indian planners to help formulate their Five-Year Plan of 1950/51 to 1955/56 (Ghatak 1995: 367). It was used to provide rough estimates of the investment/saving required to achieve predetermined growth rates of output and vice versa, presumably on the grounds that they expected no technological change, which the model omits entirely. But its high degree of aggregation meant that it could not be employed for more detailed calculations of inputs and outputs over a range of sectors.

The limitation of theoretical growth models led to their abandonment by development planners in favour of empirical models of an engineering nature. Initially planners turned to the input–output analysis invented by Wassily Leontief (1951); then, owing to the limitations of this static analysis, to linear programming that solved the problem of 'choice' of the optimal technique of production; to cost – benefit analysis that takes externalities into account; to social accounting that includes income and expenditure flows as well as production quantities; and to computable general equilibrium (CGE) models that capture substitution possibilities in supply and demand as well as price adjustments. Planning economic development, therefore, degenerated into an engineering exercise involving the manipulation of the inputs and outputs of the production process. What was required to carry out this exercise was the engineering ability to manage production flows rather than the strategic ability to creatively exploit dynamic opportunities. The machinery of production was substituted for the dynamic strategic pursuit. And in the process economics became the study of production engineering.

Underdevelopment Policy

The models of underdevelopment, as shown in Chapters 13 and 14, are concerned with how to break free from the poverty trap. As such they have clear policy implications. If these models have any claim on reality, then their policy implications, unlike those of neoclassical growth models, should be important. To evaluate their policy implications I will review the big-push, structuralist, dependency, institutionalist, and 'imitation' models. As we shall see, these policy proposals seek to provide a blueprint – a step-by-step plan – for the development process. They are, in effect, employed as substitutes for a general theory of economic development.

The Big-Push Models

The poverty-trap theorists argued that a special effort was required by the government of an underdeveloped economy if it were to break free from the low-level equilibrium trap that, to their mind, caused persistent underdevelopment. As they accepted the Keynesian/neoclassical focus on the role of capital as the central component in the growth process, poverty-trap theorists argued that escape required a big investment push that could exploit the society's 'hidden' resources.

Rosenstein-Rodan (1943) argued that the big push should be planned by the state to coordinate large-scale and simultaneous investment in a broad range of industries as well as in social infrastructure. This big push would exploit underemployed labour and would generate the technological external economies necessary for rapid and sustained economic growth. Arthur Lewis (1954) developed this argument further in his famous work on the dual economy. Similarly Ragnar Nurkse (1953), who believed that trade would lead to conspicuous consumption rather than economic growth, advocated that a process of balanced industrialization through import replacement be pursued and coordinated by governments. Albert Hirschman (1958) also accepted the big-push idea but, owing to scarce resources in underdeveloped countries, he was sceptical about their ability to proceed in a balanced way. Accordingly he advocated a policy of unbalanced growth that would also provide the incentives necessary to call forth hidden resources to achieve rapid and sustained growth.

Big-push policy is particularly interesting because it is a substitute for knowledge about the wider dynamic process. Instead of modelling the process of economic development, either in a national or global context, and basing policy on that firm foundation, these theorists have hypothesized why growth has not occurred in the Third World. Essentially they were saying that whatever the nature of the development process, Third-World nations might be able to join it through the big push. They were attempting to provide a kick-start to the *production* process in underdeveloped countries without understanding the connection between that process and the forces driving it. Central to their mystification about the dynamic process is their failure to see that at its core is a strategic pursuit rather than a production process. It is the strategic pursuit that generates and sustains economic growth, which is something that the production system can never do. They were trying to kick-start the wrong thing. As I argue in Part V, it is not possible for a production system to generate a self-maintaining growth process, just as it is not possible for an electric engine to produce motion without an exogenous power source. The electric engine and the production system are merely means by which a dynamic source is translated into a more desirable output. In the pre-modern era, that surplus-generating role was provided by either a military–imperial system, a commerce–imperial system, or the family system.

A major problem with the big-push approach is that it is not part of a realistic model of longrun economic development. The only attempt to provide a broader framework, by W. W. Rostow (1990; orig. publ. 1960), was not successful because, like the big-push theorists, he viewed societal dynamics as a process of *production*. Rostow's stages of economic growth are a descriptive account of how the big push might be achieved over the longer term by proceeding via a number of manageable steps: pre-take-off in which the investment/GDP ratio rises to 5 per cent; the take-off in which it rises to 10 per cent or more; and the drive to maturity in which it rises to 20 per cent or more. Unfortunately, Rostow fails to provide a persuasive dynamic model to explain how or why this would occur. It is merely a long-run policy blueprint to show how a big investment push might be implemented over time. It is also the classic example for my argument that policy is employed as a substitute for analysis of the dynamic process. The problem is that Rostow wanted to believe that his step-by-step policy was actually a dynamic model, and when pressed on this issue referred to his very brief treatment of what he called 'a dynamic theory of production' involving a discussion of leading manufacturing sectors that trace out rise-and-fall trajectories or 'optimal sectoral paths'. His so-called dynamic model, however, has no driving force or dynamic *process* (as contrasted with *outcomes*), and it is fixated with the dynamics of human society as a production process rather than a strategic pursuit (Snooks 1998a: ch. 4).

Structuralist and Dependency Policy

The structuralists and dependency theorists viewed underdevelopment as an outcome of the global process of capitalist growth. Structuralists such as Raúl Prebisch and Hans Singer regarded the expansion of the developed 'centre' as responsible for the adverse movement of the terms of trade against commodities produced by the less-developed 'periphery'. They argued that this cause of underdevelopment could only be overcome by a policy of import substitution industrialization (ISI). Third-World governments, therefore, should engineer development through the use of tariff barriers, investment in infrastructure, and the use of planning techniques compatible with the market. Clearly there are similarities here with the big-push policies, although the structuralists emphasize government protection and coordination rather than direct investment and foreign as well as domestic resources. These differences arise from different global perspectives.

Dependency theorists on the other hand tend to see underdevelopment as a conspiracy between the capitalist nations and between these and the capitalist classes in the Third World. This is not a particularly helpful model of global economic development because it focuses on institutions and organizations rather than dynamic processes. Accordingly its policies tend to be equally unrealistic involving advocacy of socialist revolution and the development of a New International Economic Order (NIEO). The NIEO idea arose in the 1960s and 1970s from the demand of numerous Third-World countries for a major restructuring of the world economy in their favour to overcome the perceived First-World conspiracy (Hadjor 1993: 225–7). This demand included proposals for greater aid, redeployment of certain industries from the 'centre' to the 'periphery', lower tariffs on manufactured exports to the First World, cheaper technology transfer, price stabilization schemes for primary products, compensation for natural resource damage during colonialization, and so on. But owing to the unrealistic nature of this idea – asking the First World to return a substantial proportion of the surplus that they had allegedly extracted from the Third World in the past – it has remained just an idea.

Institutionalist Policy

Underdevelopment to the institutionalist is the outcome of inefficient and ineffective institutions and attitudes in the Third World. This inefficiency is generated by unfavourable initial conditions created by the colonial age and by an adverse evolutionary process that makes it difficult for individuals to change these institutions and attitudes. To overcome this problem institutionalists advocate positive government intervention to reshape these defective institutions – in effect to redirect the evolutionary process to resemble that in the developed world. But, how can this be managed when national governments are part of this path-dependent process? Clearly it is necessary to apply outside pressure to recalcitrant Third-World nations. Recently institutionalists appear to have persuaded the World Bank that ineffective institutions and attitudes should also be part of their responsibility (World Bank 1997b). As yet the World Bank is merely encouraging governments to make appropriate institutional changes, but eventually this may become part of their structural adjustment programme.

It is clear that institutionalists have also adopted the familiar supply-side approach of identifying and advocating the removal of barriers to economic development. In this case the supply-side focus is on ineffective institutions. Once these institutions have been reshaped, reformed, and redirected the development process, we are told, will begin. Once again there is no sense of a global process of economic development or of the strategic pursuit.

The Policy of Imitation

There is a large group – larger than usually realized – of pragmatic development economists who are moved more by events than ideas. They are influenced not by which models, but by which countries, are successful. Basically they ask themselves: What developing countries are growing rapidly, and what are the characteristics that have led to this success? Having answered these two simple questions, they advocate that the less successful Third-World nations follow the most successful. Underdevelopment to these economists can be explained as an outcome of failing to imitate the most successful developing nations (Amsden 1994).

I propose to call this approach the policy of development imitation. It is an example of my concept of **strategic imitation** used in this series of books on the dynamics of human society to explain the way in which a successful dynamic strategy spreads throughout society (Snooks 1996: 212–13), and to develop a new theory of decision-making (Snooks 1997a: ch. 2). It is a process that enables one to economize on the scarcest resource in both nature and human society – the intellect. Clearly it is easier to identify successful developing countries than successful dynamic models of the global process of economic development. The problem in the policy context, however, is that it lacks context owing to its shortrun focus on what is a longrun issue.

These pragmatic economists were quick to latch onto the 'East Asian miracle' and to advocate that less successful nations should follow either (or both) their policies or culture (Amsden 1994). We are told that the success of the Asian tigers in the 1990s has been due to their industrialization policies (import replacement rapidly followed by export promotion); to their particular mix of state and market; to the nature of their financial, labour, corporate, bureaucratic, educational and professional organizations and institutions; or to their standards of honesty in the public and private sectors. Some have even attempted to generalize from East Asian experience to map out a set of policy stages through which a developing nation might do well to pass (World Bank 1993).

There are a number of critical problems with this approach that will be more obvious today (May 1998) than they were a year ago. First, this approach is guilty of the old historicist fallacy of extrapolating past patterns of events into the future. No doubt some advocates of the 'East Asian miracle' are a little more sensitive to (perhaps even a little embarrassed by) this problem since the mis-called 'East Asian meltdown', but others are now telling us why these same countries should *not* be followed. Either way, the reversal of fortunes will not faze these enthusiastic advocates of success. Success is eternal even if its identity is ephemeral. The only way to make sensible predictions and to formulate useful policy is by constructing inductive models that underlie the ephemeral nature of events. We must focus on the eternal *processes* rather than the ephemeral *outcomes*. This is the only way to understand the dynamics of human society. Secondly, this attempt to establish a set of policy stages that an underdeveloped country should pass through is a substitute for understanding the real nature of the development process. It focuses on the changing structure of production achieved by a few successful nations rather than upon the universal qualities of the strategic pursuit.

7.3 SPECIFIC POLICY ISSUES

The major part of development policy is concerned with specific issues such as population, human capital, technological change, savings, taxation, inflation, foreign resources, welfare, and environmental degradation. Usually these specific issues are dealt with in isolation from each other. Once again the problem is the failure to develop an overall theory of economic development that could integrate these apparently diverse and, often, conflicting issues. Both a dynamic and a static framework is provided in this book. The dynamic framework is the strategic demand–response mechanism discussed in Chapter 11, and the static framework is the strategy function discussed in Chapter 12. These have been used to integrate policy in these diverse areas and to sort out the present inconsistencies. An integrated set of strategic policy principles is presented in Chapter 18. What will be attempted here is a brief outline of the way these policy issues have been traditionally handled.

Population

Population is an issue of major concern to all those interested in the development of the Third World. Generally those developing countries with the lowest rates of economic growth have the highest rates of population expansion. Population, therefore, is seen as a major barrier to economic development. This is reflected in the population-trap model developed by

Richard Nelson (1956), which is discussed in detail in Chapter 13. Nelson treats population as a major obstacle to economic growth and a major reason for persistent underemployment. The model suggests that, while-ever GDP per capita remains below a notional threshold level, the rate of population expansion will exceed the rate of economic growth and any less-developed economy will gravitate back to a low-level equilibrium trap. Only through a determined effort by the state to reduce fertility levels and to promote economic growth can this obstacle to development be removed.

The traditional economic analysis of changing fertility and mortality draws heavily on the work of demographers. Central to this work is the 'demographic transition' concept, which is a generalized description of historical changes in fertility and mortality rates in the Western world over the past two centuries. It is often wrongly regarded as a model rather than a generalized description and it is used to predict population change in the Third World. As explained in Chapter 13 the 'demographic transition' is not a model and certainly should not be used for prediction. This is the old historicist fallacy once again. Population change in reality is a response to strategic demand and can be predicted only by using the dynamic-strategy model.

Within this descriptive framework, demographers have observed a cor-relation in the Third World between an increase in the education of adult females and a decline in fertility. This simple quantitative observation has led to the widely held policy view that a government-sponsored increase in adult female education will lead to a reduction in fertility at a greater rate than the fall in mortality thereby leading to a slow-down in the growth of population. This policy recommendation is repeated in every development text book despite the fact that there is no underlying economic–theoretic model, and it has become universally accepted by policy-making bodies. *The only problem is that there is no causal relation-ship between female education and fertility.* As shown in Chapter 13, theo-retically and econometrically, both the reduction in fertility and the increase in adult female education are responses to changes in strategic demand. But this should not be regarded as also challenging the suggested causal relationship between adult female education and declining infant mortality rates which is responsible for population pressures.

Family planning is also advocated as a means of reducing fertility and, thereby, of controlling population expansion. This can take the form of advice about contraception together with the provision of family-planning support as in India, or the form of oppressive government directives as in China's one-child family programme. The important point is that neither approach will work in the longer term, and scarce resources will be wasted, *unless there is a reduction in strategic demand for children*. In the absence of such a strategic change these policies will either be ignored or evaded where possible because the strategy of family multiplication is the only way that ordinary individuals in NSCs can attempt to maximize the probability of survival and prosperity. Forced programmes will, in the longer term, only generate much misery, bitterness, and perverse and undesirable outcomes (such as female infanticide). Hence, relative reductions in birth rates over the longer term cannot be used to evaluate these different policies.

Human Capital

The treatment of human skills and education in the development literature is curious. Despite the fact that education and training have long been regarded by both economists (Petty 1691; Adam Smith 1961, orig. publ. 1776; Marshall 1920, orig. publ. 1890) and economic historians (Toynbee 1969, orig. publ. 1884; Coghlan 1918; Clapham 1926) as important to economic growth, this key issue, like technological change, was largely ignored by development economists until the 1970s. This can be illustrated by the treatment this subject receives in good development textbooks such as those by Benjamin Higgins.

In the first edition (1959) of Higgins' *Economic Development*, education was completely ignored, whereas in the second edition (1968) it was considered sufficiently important to have a long chapter (40 pages) of its own. Yet even in the late 1960s, education, along with public health, was regarded by Higgins as part of 'social development' rather than 'economic development' (although he was clearly uncomfortable with this distinction) and he did not refer to it as human capital. What is the reason for this change in approach to education? The answer is to be found in the growing attention that was given to the empirical sources of growth – particularly the 'residual' – by mainstream economists such as Robert Solow (1957), Massel (1960), Kendrick (1964), and Denison (1962); and the increasing focus on that part of the residual that could be accounted for through schooling by Mincer (1958) and Schultz (1960; 1961). The conceptual framework for these studies was provided later by Gary Becker (1964). Yet it is interesting that only since the 'endogenous' growth models from the late 1980s has the role of human capital in growth been taken for granted in development texts. This is a case of professional amnesia, which is a recurring problem for a discipline that refuses to take history – even its own history – seriously.

But when the pendulum of fashion swings it swings hard. Today, in the late 1990s, human capital is expected to perform development miracles, just as physical capital was expected to do in the 1940s and 1950s. It is now widely expected that any increase in schooling investment will generate economic growth. Of course this is no more true than the earlier claim about investment in physical assets made by the big-push theorists. In both cases policy is a substitute for knowledge about the global process of economic development. It is the familiar attempt to kick-start the system of production. The focus on human capital has even led to the inclusion of schooling variables in the HDI, widely employed as a measure of economic development in the 1990s. As shown in Chapter 4, the HDI is an inappropriate and misleading index that can divert policy attention from the real development issues.

The usual argument about human capital is that education should be pursued by governments owing to market failure. If left to the market, less than the socially optimum level of education will be provided because, owing to externalities, the private benefits accruing to investment in education will be significantly less than the social benefits. Accordingly Third-World governments are expected to provide universal education at the primary and, later when resources allow, secondary levels, with greater selectivity at the tertiary level where the focus should be on education of an elite in science and technology.

As argued in Chapter 13, there are no miracles associated with the big schooling push any more than with the big investment push. When these countries enter into the GST, strategic demand will be generated for growing levels and sophistication of education and training. In these circumstances governments can provide **strategic leadership** by providing the amount of public education that will maximize the unfolding of the dominant dynamic strategy. To pursue a big schooling push ahead of strategic demand will merely waste scarce resources and generate unfulfilled ambitions and, hence, a sense of failure and bitterness amongst the people. This will lead to social unrest and to a deceleration of the development process. The big schooling push is just a wasteful way of filling the gap in traditional knowledge about the real development process.

Technological Change

Development textbooks have been even slower to recognize the role of technological change than that of education. While the second edition (1968) of Benjamin Higgins' text included a chapter on education, technological change continued to be largely ignored: it was discussed in only a few scattered pages on sections dealing with the classical growth model and techniques of planning. Today the pendulum of fashion has swung to the other extreme, with technological change now regarded as the very core of the development process and given due treatment in most modern texts.

How do we account for this pendulum shift in the popularity of technological change? Essentially, as mainstream economics employs a deductive methodology, it has an unfortunate tendency to ignore even the most important variables in the dynamic process if these variables have not been integrated into the discipline's theoretical models. While this is always a danger in any discipline more interested in virtual rather than actual reality, it is difficult to understand in the case of development economics as its practitioners are more likely to encounter real-world problems. Why has development economics failed to construct its own models of technological change and economic growth? It seems that ultimately they too treat their research as an intellectual game. If technological change is not part of the rules of this game then it can be validly ignored.

This begs the question as to why mainstream economics, which has had a dominating influence over development economics, did not include technological change in its models until the late 1980s and early 1990s. Clearly the importance of technological change has long been recognized by economists in the classical tradition such as Adam Smith, Karl Marx, and Joseph Schumpeter. The problem appears to be that, just as the profession was becoming interested in the issue of development economics, it was diverted by the Keynesian revolution which focused attention on the shortrun rather than the longrun. Even once the neoclassical mainstream had come to grips with the implications of *The General Theory*, growth theorists were constrained by the limitations of the building blocks of their theoretical models – static production theory based largely on the idea of perfect competition. The introduction of technological change required the abandonment of perfect competition. The difficulties that this introduced helped delay the development of endogenous growth models until the late 1980s when some mainstream theorists thought that the vast evidence regarding the importance of technological change accumulated by growth accountants and historical economists could no longer be ignored.

Only since the emergence of endogenous growth models have the majority of development economists felt comfortable discussing the role of technology. Yet, even as late as the mid-1990s, some of the more advanced and mathematical textbooks in development economics (Ghatak 1995) felt justified in continuing to ignore this central issue. Neoclassical theorists appear happiest when using simple models that exclude real-world complexities.

Mainstream economists, therefore, have now provided theoretical justification for focusing on technological change, but they have not constructed useful models for dealing with it in a development context. Accordingly, development economists treat the subject in a pragmatic manner, by drawing heavily on the work of applied economists and economic historians. Development economists examine pragmatic issues such as technological transfer (including the role of transnational corporations); the development of a domestic capability to absorb external technical ideas (through technical education); the further development of a domestic capability to create new and innovative technologies (through the training of scientists and engineers); and the creation of a social environment conducive to innovation through microeconomic reform. And growth theorists, in the wake of Kenneth Arrow (1962), focus on 'learning by doing' as a source of increasing returns. This is a supply-side approach which treats these issues as prerequisites for economic development. The underlying belief is that supply creates its own demand. Say's Law is alive and well in modern development economics, as it is in neoclassical economics.

In order to support this supply-side view, which is the basis of technology policy, development economists usually provide data that demonstrate a statistical correlation between education and growth, and between the proportion of scientists/technical researchers and economic development (United Nations Development Programme 1994: 138–9). But this does not prove their supply-side argument that government investment in R&D generates economic development, particularly as they cannot provide a dynamic model that theoretically demonstrates this relationship. It is merely a matter of casual conjecture.

Indeed, the real relationship between these supply-side variables and economic growth is far more complex than this – it also involves strategic demand. The dynamic-strategy model presented in this book suggests that the proportion of scientists, engineers, and technicians in a population ideally should be a response to strategic demand that is generated as the pioneering strategists explore the available strategic opportunities that open up when their country participates in the global strategic transition. It is this strategic demand–response mechanism that generates economic growth. Accordingly, government policies directed at providing these skills before entry into the GST will inevitably fail and will probably delay the development process. Supply cannot create strategic demand.

Once again, what is lacking in the traditional approach to technological change is a dynamic model showing how strategic demand for new technological ideas and skills is generated, and how growth and development actually occur. This dynamic model is provided in Chapter 15, *which also challenges the recently accepted idea that technological change is the central feature of societal dynamics.*

Domestic and Foreign Development Resources

A major concern in development economics is where the resources needed for financing economic growth are to be found. We have seen that the big-push theorists were convinced that sufficient resources could be transferred from the traditional sector – where they were thought to be underemployed – to the modern industrial sector, without any reduction in the former's productivity. The only question was how these 'hidden' resources might be redirected through voluntary savings, taxation, or inflation. Others, such as the structuralists, were less convinced that a large-scale effort could be financed from domestic sources and advocated that use be made of foreign investment, foreign aid, and assistance through the World Bank and IMF. I will briefly review some of the policies in these fields.

Voluntary Savings

Economists seem perpetually concerned about the rate of saving, not just in the Third World but also in the First World. It is usually lamented that in underdeveloped countries the lower socioeconomic 'classes' are unable to save much from their low incomes, while the upper 'classes', who have the capacity to save, use their surpluses for conspicuous consumption. Even when some groups save, this surplus is used to finance the consumption of other groups. Higgins (1968: 505) tells us that the 'pawnshops, the landlord who lends to tenants during the growing season on a sharecropping basis, the village moneylender, divert the savings of one group to financing consumer expenditures of others'. The explanation, he tells us, is that the return to money lent for consumption is greater than that for longer-term investments.

What Higgins does not tell us is that the reason for this, apparently perverse, situation is the absence of strategic demand for investment because of the country's failure to enter into the GST. Saving for the purpose of productive investment will not occur unless, and until, this strategic demand emerges. The answer is not, as most development economists argue, to artificially increase savings to generate productive investment and economic growth. Higgins (ibid.: 506), for example, argues that: 'Voluntary savings amounting to only 2 to 3 per cent of national income might well prove to be the critical margin in permitting a take-off'. This is the usual supply-side response. Rather, the answer is to encourage our Third-World nation to enter into the global strategic transition. A systematic study of history (Snooks 1996; 1997a) shows that, whenever there is strategic demand for savings, those savings are forthcoming. The deficiency is always in strategic demand, not in the multi-faceted supply-side response.

Taxation

If voluntary savings are inadequate, but underemployed resources are known to exist, it is usually argued that forced savings can be mobilized for development purposes through taxation. This presupposes that there is wide acceptance of the government's role in the development process, otherwise there will be persistent attempts to avoid paying taxes. Also, if the government perception of the availability of underemployed resources is wrong, the taxation they propose might reduce the existing incentives for economic growth. An extreme example of this disincentive effect was Stalin's drive to collectivization in the USSR in 1930, which led the wealthier peasants, or *kulaks*, to hide their food surpluses and to destroy and, where possible, consume their livestock.

Of course, taxes used intelligently can provide positive incentives for investment in avenues considered important for economic development. But there will be tensions between the incentive and the revenue objectives of a taxation system. Tensions also exist between revenue and equity issues. Development economists interested in this area draw upon the traditional body of taxation theory (Ghatak 1995: 134–44), but their policy prescriptions are flawed because they do not consider the issue within the context of a general theory of the development process.

The main problem for underdeveloped countries in raising forced savings is the narrowness of the tax base. Direct taxes usually fall heavily on salary earners, particularly civil servants, who are unable to disguise their main sources of income. Owing to this narrow base, marginal tax rates are high and the disincentives for greater work effort are correspondingly low. Some, like Nicholas Kaldor (1956) and Benjamin Higgins (1968), have suggested widening the direct tax base to include 'expenditures' (income minus saving), wealth, land, and gifts. While an expenditure tax has, we are told, some advantages – it encourages saving – it is difficult and costly to raise, as experience in India and Sri Lanka has demonstrated (Ghatak 1995: 135–6). Similarly, indirect taxes fall narrowly on imports (customs duties) and consumers (sales and excise taxes) and they can be highly regressive. There is considerable discussion in the literature about moving to a value-added tax (VAT), which is broader in scope and has a neutral effect upon production and distribution, but it suffers from administrative difficulties (Ibid.: 140–1). Once again this traditional discussion focuses on supply-side considerations – optimality, equity, neutrality of impact – rather than on the strategic demand for development funds, which is the core of the dynamic process.

Inflation

The so-called 'inflation tax' is a revenue-raising instrument advocated by the structuralists, but vehemently opposed by the monetarists, to enable governments to finance their development programmes. Under certain conditions it amounts to a transfer of resources from fixed income earners to a government prepared to print money or, the same thing, to sell government debt to the central bank. The main assumption underlying this argument is that inflation is moderate so that the public remains willing to hold non-interest-bearing money balances rather than buying assets or spending their cash balances. In these circumstances the government gains in real terms what the public loses. This transferred surplus can then be used to finance public development projects.

Needless to say, the monetarists oppose the whole concept on the grounds that it will be ineffective and dangerous. They argue that, owing to the vertical aggregate supply curve, any increase in the money supply will impact only on prices and not on output. Their advice to governments of Third-World countries is to budget for a zero deficit each year and, thereby, avoid any temptation to resort to money creation with all its inflationary consequences. They also argue that the target inflation rate should be zero because positive inflation generates costs but no benefits.

In *Longrun Dynamics* (Snooks 1998b: ch. 11) I presented a new model of inflation which shows that **strategic inflation** is a natural outcome of the dynamic process. It is generated by the strategic demand–response mechanism that is central to the dynamic process in both developed and underdeveloped countries. Only **nonstrategic inflation** is the outcome of supply-side exogenous shocks and monetary mismanagement. This theoretical conclusion (Chapter 9) is supported by the discovery of the **growth–inflation curve** (Snooks 1998b; and Chapter 11 below) which is valid for the past (going back 700 years) and the present, as well as for developed and underdeveloped countries. Hence, I reject the monetarist notion that the target inflation rate should be zero. If such a target were achieved and maintained, then longrun growth would also approach zero.

Yet I also oppose the concept of the 'inflation tax' because it distorts the pattern of price changes that are central to the supply response to strategic demand. Every attempt should be made to reduce **nominal inflation** to the level of strategic inflation by squeezing out the nonstrategic component. This can be achieved through a monetary policy in tune with the requirements of the global strategic transition. As demonstrated in Chapter 11, a viable dynamic strategy will not lead to hyper inflation, just a prosperity-generating strategic inflation.

Foreign Resources

The enormity of the development task for Third-World countries that have yet to embark on economic development, but who have been persuaded that it will follow automatically from a big 'push', has led them to rely heavily on foreign resources including private foreign savings and foreign aid. The traditional argument is that foreign resources should only be used if they generate sufficient export income to at least meet the required repayment of principle and interest over the life of the loan. This income flow might arise from investment in the export sector that increases the supply of foreign currency or from the import replacement sector that reduces the demand for foreign currency. In this way the debt burden (as a percentage of GDP) will not get out of control.

Owing to the optimism about immediate development possibilities, however, this sound criterion is usually overlooked. Typically it is assumed that, if enough funds are invested in an underdeveloped country, eventually it will be possible to kick-start its economy. The available evidence, however, confounds this simplistic idea. As Table 7.1 shows, the long-term debt burden of the Third World rocketed out of control during the

Table 7.1   Long-term debt of the Third World, 1970–96
(\$US billions)

Year	Debt
1970	59.2
1975	161.9
1980	452.3
1985	809.3
1990	1 184.5
1995	1 626.4
1996	1 708.4

Sources: World Bank 1997a and World Bank (various years), *World Debt Tables, vol. I.*

1970s and 1980s, increasing twentyfold in nominal terms and sixfold in real terms, and yet, apart from a select group of developing nations in East Asia, the problem of underdevelopment remains. Interestingly, until the Asian financial crisis of 1997/98, those countries that were able to achieve high rates of economic growth experienced declining debt burdens.

What accounts for the unproductive expansion of the debt burden of the Third World? It is usually explained as the outcome of supply-side issues, such as the glut of petro-dollars following the OPEC price increases in 1973 and 1979. The story goes that these OPEC oil price increases led to a sudden glut in export earnings for oil-exporting countries as reflected in the amazing increase in their combined current account surpluses by a multiple of 15.3 between 1973 and 1980 (World Bank 1985, *Annual Report*). Unable to digest these funds, somewhere between half to two-thirds were deposited with private international banks, primarily in European financial centres. Keen to find an outlet for this new liquidity, the private banks discovered willing borrowers in the Third World who were experiencing difficulties in maintaining the real value of imports required to feed their development and/or consumption programmes, owing to the massive shift of terms of trade against them. This process has been referred to as petro-dollar recycling.

As the old saying goes: you can lead a horse to water but you cannot make it drink. Yet the Third World drank deeply at the well of these petro-dollars because it was imbued with the idea from the 'development community' – academics, advisers, bureaucrats, the IMF and the World Bank – that economic development was just a matter of following the text book prescriptions and investing heavily in a big push that would ensure their rapid escape from the low-level income trap. (More cynically, the rent-seekers knew that a proportion of these funds would end up in their hands.) The private banks involved in recycling believed the same rhetoric. They had to if they hoped to remain solvent. What no one appeared to understand was that economic development cannot be turned on and off like a tap, because it is a gradually occurring global process. The Third-World debt crisis is a monument to the myopia of the development community and the greed of the private banks.

The crisis came in mid-1982 when Mexico, struggling with a growing debt burden, made public its decision to suspend payment on its external obligations in August that year. By this time the velocity of private-bank petro-dollar recycling was declining, owing to the impact of the international recession induced by the restrictive monetarist policies of the UK, USA, and elsewhere in the Western world. The resulting reduction in demand for Third-World exports made it difficult if not impossible for underdeveloped countries to meet their obligations to the private banks. Widespread collapse was only averted through pressure applied by the IMF and the USA to the large banks to continue supporting their Third-World clients. This was the beginning of the 'involuntary lending' scheme, which prevented wholesale financial crisis and bankruptcy.

The proper criteria for incurring foreign debt is that it be employed only to pursue a viable dynamic strategy once the GST is underway. In other words, foreign borrowing should be a response to strategic demand. It should not be assumed, as has been done in the absence of a general theory of global economic development, that all Third-World countries are in a position to use these funds to achieve rapid and sustained economic growth. If this criterion is not employed, borrowed funds will be largely, if not completely, wasted, and will only add to the debt burdens of Third-World countries and delay their strategic transition. What public and private institutions need to do is to discriminate between those nations (ESCs) who have entered into the global strategic transition and those nations (NSCs) who have not. An attempt is made in Table 4.3 to draw a distinction between NSCs and ESCs by constructing a GST index. Failure to make such a distinction will disrupt the GST.

Foreign aid, like national welfare payments, is provided for a variety of reasons that vary with the donor nation and with time. While the official rhetoric is that aid is granted for altruistic reasons, closer inspection suggests that, in reality, strategic reasons – involving the survival and prosperity of the donor nation – dominate. In any case the level of foreign aid is insignificant and it is directed at middle-income nations rather than the poorest nations. The United Nations Development Programme (1993) reports that the leading developed nations, on average, direct only 0.33 per cent of their GNP into foreign aid, compared to the UN target of 0.7 per cent, and that the largest recipients (both absolutely and relative to their GNP) tend to be countries like Egypt, China, and India (ESCs) rather than the poorest African countries (NSCs). This meagre outcome for the least developed nations is usually explained as an outcome of their low 'absorptive capacity' created by their inappropriate skills and institutions.

There is an important truth here, but it is rather heavily disguised. While it is correct that the poorest nations have a low absorptive capacity for aid (or any other injection of foreign resources), it is due not to an institutional/resource mismatch but to a lack of strategic demand in these countries. It also reflects the strategic interests, both political and commercial, of the wealthy donor nations. Until NSCs enter into the global strategic transition, no amount of institutional reshaping will change this situation. Only those nations actually participating in the global dynamic process have any productive use for development funds. In the poorest nations, aid serves as an instrument not of economic development but of political, military, and, sometimes, humanitarian ends.

Growth versus Equity

The issue of growth versus equity is highly controversial, and attitudes to it have fluctuated widely over the past 50 years. Initially, in the period from the 1940s to the 1960s, it was assumed that economic growth in the Third World would lead automatically to an improvement in equity. Despite the large injection of private and public capital in development programmes, little growth and even less equity has been achieved in the underdeveloped world.

It was probably the natural frustration of the development community arising from the failure of these early development programmes that led in the 1970s to a shift in emphasis from growth to equity. If growth could not be generated, at least basic needs, such as clean water, health, education, and housing, could be provided for the poor in undeveloped nations. This led to the 'basic needs' approach, initially supported by the Dag Hammarskjöld Foundation in 1975, taken up by the International Labour Organisation in 1976, and thereafter adopted by the World Bank. Academic development economists, such as Paul Streeten (1980; 1995; Streeten *et al.* 1981), also took up the call. This new policy stance was responsible for recycled petro-dollars being employed on welfare rather than growth-inducing programmes. Basically it was an implicit admission by the development community that it had no understanding of, or control over, the global dynamic process. Instead of seeking solutions to the causes of persistent underdevelopment, they turned in frustration to the alleviation of its worst symptoms.

Only in the 1980s, when it became clear after the OPEC crisis that alleviation of symptoms would not solve the escalating crisis of the Third World, did the development community turn in desperation to the new liberal prophets. If they could force Third-World societies to get their 'economic fundamentals' right, then surely economic growth or at least equity would emerge, even if they still did not understand the global process of economic development. All but the fanatical few in the late 1990s really believed this to be true. Today there is a new uncertainty that is expressing itself in a more cautious approach to the continued commitment of funds to issues of both growth and equity. It is imperative, therefore, that a new way be found.

The shifting debate between the supporters of growth and of equity also arises from the lack of a general economic and political model of development. By contrast, the model developed in this book shows that the unfolding dynamic strategy in an ESC leads to a growing proportion of strategists in the total population. These strategists invest in and benefit from the prevailing dynamic strategy and, through the **strategic struggle**, gain political influence. This is the way that economic growth leads inevitably to greater equity: no growth, no equity. If the development focus shifts from growth to equity, the strategic process will be disrupted. It is essential that the strategic response does not anticipate strategic demand in this artificial manner. The only way to accelerate the process of faster growth and greater equity is to remove obstacles to the unfolding of the dominant dynamic strategy and to the progress of the strategic struggle. In the end, equity must be 'taken' through the strategic struggle, not 'given' by, even well-meaning, interventionists. The entire history of economic development is one of wasted resources and disruption of the GST on a massive scale. For the sake of the poor nations of the world this must stop.

Environmental Degradation

Recently economists have addressed two major environmental issues: the benefits and costs of maintaining or restoring natural resources; and the benefits and costs of resolving the so-called 'greenhouse effect'. Since the early 1960s, the major issues of concern among environmentalists have been the need to preserve wilderness areas, to reverse the degradation of natural resources, to preserve 'biodiversity', and to achieve 'sustainable development'. Orthodox economists tackling these issues have been concerned largely with exposing and removing the inefficiencies in markets for environmental services that have been responsible for the overexploitation of natural resources. It is argued that the reason natural resources are overexploited is that environmental values – the regard people have for nature – are not taken into account when economic decisions are made to use natural resources (Kelman 1981). Some environmental economists go further than this. They argue that sustainable development cannot be achieved unless decision-makers take into account not only the environmental preferences of the exiting generation but also of future generations (Howarth and Norgaard 1992: 473). This requires the recognition of inter-generational equity – each generation making a commitment to transfer to the next sufficient natural resources and capital to make economic development sustainable.

Since the late 1980s a new major environmental issue has emerged. It is the so-called greenhouse effect. The pioneering neoclassical economic research on this issue was undertaken by William Nordhaus (1991a, b, c) and it has since attracted growing interest from other economists (Dornbusch and Poterba 1991; Cline 1992; Manne and Richels 1992; Schelling 1992; Bagnoli *et al.* 1996). The problem is well known, involving the production of greenhouse gases – including carbon dioxide, methane, nitrous oxide, chlorofluorocarbons (CFCs) – through the burning of organic and fossil fuels. These gases build up in the atmosphere, absorb sunlight radiation in the red spectrum, and increasingly warm the atmosphere. It has been estimated scientifically that a doubling of carbon dioxide in the atmosphere will probably lead to an increase in temperature by approximately 3 degrees Celsius. At present the amount of carbon (which is 26.9 per cent as large as the amount of carbon dioxide) in the atmosphere is increasing at the rate of 0.5 per cent per annum, and it is thought that there is enough carbon fuel in the world to generate three doublings. This is relatively straightforward. The difficulties arise when it is asked what this implies for world climates and the global economy. All that can be said with certainty is that some regions will become warmer, others cooler (if warm currents are deflected), some wetter, and some drier. And it is not clear that the net effect of these complex regional changes would be unfavourable for world agriculture, particularly as an increase in carbon dioxide would enhance photosynthesis (Schelling 1992: 1–4). Recently it has been suggested (World Health Organisation 1996) that changing weather patterns, particularly in tropical areas, may increase the geographical spread of certain diseases such as malaria. But nothing is known about future disease patterns with any certainty, and the gradual nature of change provides ample opportunity to establish remedial measures. The alarmists generally assume that human society is unable to adjust to climate change – that it is essentially static rather than dynamic. This flies in the face of our entire history.

The change in global climate will have differential effects in the First and Third Worlds. Its influence on SCs will hardly be significant. As is well known, the proportion of GDP generated by agriculture in SCs is generally less than 5 per cent, and in some nations less than 3 per cent, and greenhouse climate change would have little effect on the other 95 to 97 per cent of the economy. Hence, in the First World the greenhouse effect would probably not even be noticed (ibid.: 5–6). But in the Third World, where the contribution of agriculture to GDP is as high as 30 per cent and where disease control is less effective, the economic impact of climate change would be greater, but still not overwhelming. Yet clearly this is the part of the world that could afford it least. Nordhaus (1991a: 931) has estimated that by 2050 the impact of greenhouse climate change on GDP would be as low as 0.25 per cent per annum for the USA and no more than 2.0 per cent per annum for the entire world. This is a worst-case scenario because the net effect of greenhouse warming actually could be economically advantageous (Nordhaus 1991c).

While the orthodox comparative–static approach is helpful in sorting out the main issues and providing rough orders of magnitude, it does not take into account the longrun dynamic dimension. If it takes 50 to 100 years for temperatures to increase by 3 degrees Celsius, there will be two offsetting dynamic issues to consider. First, by the second half of the twenty-first century, today's Third-World countries will be far more developed and the relative importance of their agricultural sectors will be much smaller. In addition, these countries will be wealthier and, hence, in a better position to fight off any increase in the incidence of disease. This will limit the adverse economic and health effects of climatic change. Second, as factor endowments change, so do relative factor prices which provide incentives for technological change. Human society is never static, it is always changing and responding in a positive way to its changing physical and economic environment. In this way the structure of human society will change even faster than global warming, thereby minimizing the impact of climatic change.

The only persuasive argument in support of expensive attempts to stabilize the build-up of greenhouse gases is that we may be prepared to pay heavily to slow the change in our physical environment – although it must be realized that the history of the Earth is a story of continuously changing ecosystems – and that, for some totally unforseen reason, the greenhouse effect may lead to a sudden catastrophe. We might wish to respond to the unlikely possibility of a natural catastrophe in this respect by investing in measures designed to stabilize or even to reduce the stock of greenhouse gases in the atmosphere. This would amount to 'buying greenhouse insurance' (Manne and Richels 1992).

Nordhaus (1991a: 923), in analysing how to 'efficiently' slow the greenhouse effect, develops a comparative–static model involving a 'greenhouse damage' function (which takes account of changes in crop yields, land and capital losses to rising seas, and damage to ecosystems) and an 'abatement cost' function (including the cost of phasing out fossil fuels and CFCs, raising coastal structures, building dykes, planting trees). He then uses this model to calculate the size of greenhouse taxes that would need to be imposed on US citizens to achieve varying reductions in the stock of greenhouse gases. Nordhaus suggests a modest tax of $US 7.3 per ton of carbon, which would reduce greenhouse gases by 11 per cent, including a substantial reduction of CFCs, and a cut in carbon dioxide by about 2 per cent. A more radical approach aimed at substantially removing the problem involving trillions of dollars per annum would be totally unacceptable to taxpayers and their governments because, on present information, the likelihood of a sudden natural catastrophe is very low. To take the radical option would, even if it could be sold politically, be economically irrational, because at best it would amount to a massive waste of GDP that could be used for other, more immediate purposes, and at worst it could derail the GST. It is essential, therefore, to view this important issue in a dynamic as well as a comparative–static perspective.

7.4 CONCLUSIONS

From this brief survey of traditional development policy we can draw a number of conclusions that will be addressed later in the book. First, it is clear that there exists no integrated approach to development policy. It has fragmented into a large number of conflicting parts. The underlying cause of this unsatisfactory situation is the failure of economists to develop a general economic and political model of the development process. The objective of this book is to provide such a model (Chapters 9 to 17), and to suggest (Chapter 18) an integrated approach to development policy. Secondly, traditional policy is employed as a substitute for any analysis of the dynamic core of the development process. Policy is employed, in other words, to short-circuit the necessary dynamic process by kick-starting the stationary 'engine' of production. Thirdly, policy is an excuse to intervene for materialist ends in the affairs of others even when it is, in a development sense, totally unnecessary. This is just as true of the superpowers that dominate international development organizations as it is of rent-seeking governments in Third-World countries. The central point – totally ignored by neoliberals – is that minimal intervention can only be achieved if we understand the global dynamic process rather than the conditions of static efficiency. Finally, the concept of minimal intervention includes strategic leadership (in response to strategic demand) as well as the need to remove the obstacles to the global strategic transition.

8 Traditional Visions of the Future

A powerful dynamic theory should provide a clear and realistic vision of the future. Any model with pretensions to explain the past and the present must be able to offer profound insights about the path ahead for human society. This will be important as a basis for framing wider policies concerning infrastructure and environment. If, however, a model has nothing worth while to say about the future, then it will be equally impotent in relation to the present and the past. In this chapter we need to ask: What can the traditional theory of growth and development tell us about the future? To answer this question I will briefly review traditional visions of the future from the classical economists of the late eighteenth century to the neoclassical economists of the late twentieth century.

What we find is that traditional economic thinkers have little useful to say about the future prospects of human society. And what they do have to say often arises not from their dynamic models but from unconvincing exercises in casual historicism – of attempting to read the direction of movement in human society in the past and extrapolating that into the future. This is the case particularly with Marx, Schumpeter, and Rostow. Not only have these visions been proved wrong by the passing of time but, owing to the nature of their 'models', there was no reason from the very beginning for expecting them to be right. The essential problem is that they did not construct realistic dynamic models of the global process of economic development. In Chapter 18 an attempt will be made to show what can be said about the future using a general economic and political model of the global strategic transition.

This chapter is organized around two main groups of authors: those who see the future in terms of the outcomes of their production models, and those who provide historicist visions. While the first group, which includes the classical and neoclassical approaches, has little to say about the future that is either interesting or convincing; the second group, which includes Adam Smith, Karl Marx, Joseph Schumpeter, and W. W. Rostow, has much to say that is interesting but none of it is convincing.

8.1 THE PRODUCTIONIST VISION

The growth models of both the classical and neoclassical schools are constructed, as discussed in Chapter 6, from the building blocks of production theory. They see economic growth as a production process rather than a strategic pursuit, and they view human society essentially as a factory (or farm) rather than a strategic organization. It will come as no surprise therefore that any vision the productionists might have of the future will be limited to what can be seen from the factory floor.

The Classical View

The standard classical 'growth' theory of Ricardo and Malthus has a number of severe limitations: it is a model not of growth but of convergence to the stationary state; it is a model not of the dynamics of human society but of a simple system of production; and if you attempt to kick-start this system of production it runs down and stagnates. The model merely analyses how an exogenous growth impetus is translated temporarily into increased GDP per capita and how this surplus is distributed between the owners of the factors of *production*. In other words, Ricardo and Malthus were concerned to model only the surplus-generating mechanism in a 'modern' society.

To generate a continual improvement in real GDP per capita with the classical productionist model it is necessary to continually kick-start it – to apply a continuous series of exogenous shocks to this lifeless mechanism. Clearly such a model has nothing to tell us about the nature of dynamics of human society either future or past. The most important dynamic issue is the one that the classical productionists ignore completely – how the continuous dynamic impulse is generated. Adam Smith, who will be discussed along with the historicists, is the only early economist who attempted to address this central issue.

What does the classical model imply about the future? Essentially it is pessimistic about the future growth of 'developed' economies. Economic growth is a temporary phenomenon that occurs after a random external shock displaces an economy from its stationary longrun equilibrium position. Once an economy has converged on this equilibrium position it will remain in the stationary state until it is disturbed by a further random exogenous shock. The stationary state, therefore, is the norm in classical thinking.

It is curious how many intellectuals are prepared to enthusiastically embrace the idea of stasis. Yet they are only able to do so because they fail to realize that stasis is impossible and that no society in history has been able to achieve it in a normal competitive environment without being reduced to poverty or to destruction (Snooks 1996). In a competitive world it is just not possible to stand still.

One of those who embraced the stationary state was J. S. Mill. In his *Principles of Political Economy* (1909, orig. publ. 1848), Mill used the Ricardian model to explain growth generated by the Industrial Revolution as merely convergence to the stationary state. He even came to believe that the stationary state would be a kind of Mecca in which mankind would pursue moral improvement rather than material prosperity. It did not seem to occur to him, as it did to Adam Smith, that those societies unable to grow through industrialization would turn from peaceful pursuits to military activities. An important question for Mill (1909/1848: 746) was: 'Towards what ultimate point is society tending by its industrial progress?' For this he had the ready answer: 'It must always have been seen, more or less distinctly by political economists, that the increase in wealth is not boundless: that at the end of what they term the progressive state lies the stationary state, and that each step in advance is an approach to it.' For Mill this outcome was not to be feared but to be welcomed:

> It is scarcely necessary to remark that a stationary condition of capital and population implies no stationary state of human improvement. There would be as much scope as ever for all kinds of mental culture, and moral and social progress; as much room for improving the Art of Living, and much more likelihood of its being improved, when minds ceased to be engrossed by the art of getting on. (ibid.: 751)

While Mill takes the idea of the stationary state from the classical growth model, his vision of self-restraining individuals pursuing moral rather than material ends is an outcome of his own wishful thinking about the nature of man.

This acceptance of the Ricardian model was a major retreat by Mill from the stance he had made in *Logic* (1843), only six years earlier. There he had proposed the use of induction (the 'historical method') to develop the new discipline of 'social dynamics' as distinct from the existing deductive discipline of 'social statics', of which Ricardian convergence was an integral part. Unfortunately, Mill's 'social dynamics' project failed because he had no comparative advantage in the historical method. Owing to the absence of a realistic dynamic vision of the future, Mill had to convince himself that he was satisfied with the static classical conception of the stationary state. Had he been able to see the real future of the following 150 years he would have been surprised at the high rates of growth achieved and dismayed at the recalcitrance of human nature.

The Neoclassical View

As this approach to dynamics has been considered in detail in Chapter 6, it can be dealt with briefly here. This group of growth models includes the basic Solow–Swan and the 'endogenous' growth models. The Solow–Swan version is a simple production model concerned with convergence to the longrun equilibrium growth path known as the steady state. It emerged to solve the problem of instability in the Harrod–Domar model. Technological change is treated as an exogenous and unanalysed force. The more recent 'new' growth theory, which attempts to endogenize technological change, also focuses on the equilibrium growth path. In both versions of the neoclassical model the concept of the equilibrium growth path is employed to provide the model with dynamic structure in the absence of a real-world dynamic form (Snooks 1998b: ch. 3). It also provides the basis for a 'vision' of the future.

It is something of an overstatement to talk about a neoclassical *vision* of the future. Like their classical counterparts, the neoclassical productionists treat societal dynamics as the outcome of society's production system. Their views about the future are based on the assumption that economic growth in the longrun will occur at the equilibrium or steady-state rate. This, of course, contrasts with the Harrod–Domar conclusion that economic growth is likely to be unstable in either an upward or downward direction. The only prediction concerning Third-World countries is that in the shortrun they will converge to the steady state at a rate determined by their initial conditions and the nature of their production functions.

Clearly such predictions are completely unrealistic. It is no secret that the growth path of developed and developing nations fluctuates over time, a fact which the neoclassical model totally ignores. This model is unable to predict the *conditions* under which the longrun (steady state) and shortrun (convergence) rates of growth are likely to break down in either First-World or Third-World countries. Hence, the neoclassical model is unable to explain either the problem of deflation that is beginning to emerge in developed countries or the economic crisis overtaking East Asian nations. A model with no vision of the future has no relevance to the present or the past.

8.2 HISTORICIST VISIONS

Have the historicists succeeded where the productionists have failed? To answer this question we need to review the visions of the future by influential writers such as Adam Smith, Karl Marx, Joseph Schumpeter, and W. W. Rostow. We shall find that their visions, based on the old historicist fallacy rather than the 'historical method' advocated (but not followed) by J. S. Mill, are interesting but badly flawed.

Adam Smith: the Rise of Prosperity and Liberty

When we think about the classical growth model we usually focus on the Ricardian–Malthusian version. But there is another, infinitely more complex dynamic model – that developed by Adam Smith in a series of works that include *The Theory of Moral Sentiments* (1976, orig. publ. 1759), *Lectures on Jurisprudence* (1978, orig. written. 1760s), as well as the widely known *The Wealth of Nations* (1961, orig. publ. 1776). Smith's dynamic model has dimensions that are moral and political as well as economic. This model has been convincingly reconstructed by Athol Fitzgibbons (1995).

The foundations of Smith's model were moral. Different moral principles, such as utility, virtue, and authority, would, Smith argued, lead to different political systems, such as (respectively) democracy, aristocracy, and monarchy. In turn these political systems would lead to different social and economic outcomes, such as (respectively) liberty and economic stagnation, social cohesion and economic stagnation, and nihilism and economic growth (ibid.: 120). There is a strong likeness here to the dynamic system in Plato's *Republic* (Snooks 1998a: 42–5).

In applying this model to the past, Smith divided history into four stages – prehistory, Greek civilization, Roman civilization, and medieval Europe – and argued that each stage passed through a political sequence from democracy to monarchy to aristocracy, each with its own underlying moral principle. This sequence was driven not by the material class conflict of Plato's model, which influenced Smith's approach, but by the moral shortcomings of each political stage. It is because the characteristic moral principle of each political system was insufficient to achieve both liberty *and* economic growth, that their host society declined culturally and, ultimately, collapsed, to be replaced by a more opportunistic political system. Smith believed, therefore, that both the rise and fall of human civilization was due to the inherent potential together with the fatal flaw in the underlying moral principle. Only in a society able to effectively combine all three moral principles could both liberty and economic growth be effectively achieved. Britain, Smith claimed, was such a society, owing to its integrated political institutions of monarchy, aristocracy, and democracy. While this continued to be so, Britain, he believed, would continue to be both prosperous and free.

Owing to his historicist approach, Smith did not suffer from the same intellectual myopia as the productionists of the classical and neoclassical schools. Realizing that societal dynamics transcended what happened in the system of production, Smith was able to place his well-known discussion of industrial specialization and division of labour in a wider political and moral framework. The only problem is that Smith, due to a metaphysical rather than a realist historicist approach, reversed the real-world sequence of causation. He saw causation flowing from a society's moral outlook to its political institutions to economic and social outcomes. In reality, as shown elsewhere in a series of historical studies (Snooks 1996; 1997a; 1998a), causation flows from strategic outlook to societal institutions to economic and moral outcomes. Smith's deductive dynamic model is driven by a moral sequence, whereas my inductive dynamic model is driven by a strategic sequence. The possibility of reversing the real-world sequence is an ever-present danger of the deductive method.

Marx: the Rise of Communism and the End of History

Unlike the classical economists with whom he is often associated, Karl Marx had a clearly articulated vision of the future. It is a vision about the end of history and the process by which he believed it would be achieved. Marx, as is well known, claimed that human society must necessarily pass through a number of historical stages – tribal society, feudalism, and capitalism – that would ultimately and inevitably lead to the final stage he called communism, which would generate prosperity and freedom. This bears a strong resemblance to the historicist vision of Adam Smith, except that the latter saw his own society as the beneficiary of this dynamic sequence. For Marx, 'capitalism' was just one of the stages in a process of social evolution driven by dialectical materialism. Each stage had its own defining technology, economic base, sociopolitical superstructure, unique set of economic laws, and its own characteristic struggle between economic classes that leads to its breakdown and to the emergence of the next stage on the high road to communism. Marx borrowed the idea of material class struggle from Plato's *Republic*, and the dialectical concept from Hegel's *Philosophy of History*.

Marx's dynamic model, which has been analysed in greater depth elsewhere (Snooks 1998a: 49–55), will be briefly surveyed here. Although Marx claimed that his system was grounded in the material conditions of society, his dynamic principle is metaphysical rather than scientific. The driving force in his model is the dialectical process of class struggle, which takes place not in the economic conditions of society but in the sociopolitical superstructure that emerges from these conditions. Economic foundations are important in Marx's system, but only because they carry higher things. Contrary to popular opinion, the real source of the dynamic in Marx's vision of inevitable historical change is sociopolitical rather than economic. The capitalist in Marx's penultimate stage, for example, is driven by his destiny rather than by his desire to maximize material advantage. Marx's 'general law of capitalist accumulation' is revealingly reflected in the well-known statement: 'Accumulation for accumulation's sake, production for production's sake: by this formula classical economy expressed the historical mission of the bourgeoisie' (Marx 1961, orig. publ. 1867: 558).

There is a fatal circularity in Marx's model. While the sociopolitical superstructure is determined by capitalism's economic conditions that are in turn driven by technological change, a society's changing techniques of production are a function of the profit rate that in turn depends upon competition both within and between the social classes of capitalists and workers which takes place in the sociopolitical superstructure. The circle is complete. History is driven not by an economic or technological dynamic but by the forces of destiny that Marx *believed* were carrying human society toward an ideal state of being in which prosperity and freedom for all would be achieved. These are the metaphysical forces that determine the declining longrun profit rate, the introduction of labour-displacing machinery, the growing reserve army of unemployed workers, the growing concentration of industrial wealth, the increasing severity of economic fluctuations, the growing poverty of the majority of the population and, finally, the breakdown of capitalism through revolution. All countries, including the less-developed, are destined to pass through this stages' process.

Marx wanted to explain the process by which the ideal state of communism would inevitably emerge, but he was not interested in the details of that system. This he regarded, somewhat ironically, as the province of utopian socialism. Yet he did suggest, largely in his *Critique of the Gotha Programme* (1947, orig. publ. 1891), that the rebelling workers will seize power and replace capitalism with a socialist state under the 'dictatorship of the proletariat' in which each citizen will be rewarded according to ability rather than birth. In this classless society the inner contradictions will finally and mysteriously disappear, bringing the dialectical process to an end. The socialist state will take charge of the means of production and, with the elimination of class conflict, the economy will grow without crisis until scarcity has been eliminated, human nature transformed, the state dissolved, and the distribution of outputs altered from 'to each according to his labour' to 'to each according to his needs'. And with the end of both scarcity and the inner contradictions of human society will come the end of societal dynamics. Finally, at the end of history, the stationary state beloved of all classical economists will establish itself.

Schumpeter: the Emergence of Socialism

Joseph Schumpeter began with the classical growth model and extended it by including the *process* of technological change. But essentially, like the orthodox economists, he treated technological change as an exogenous shock and economic growth as an interlude between normal periods of stasis. Later Schumpeter generalized his model by providing it with a superficial historicist form. In the end his vision of the future of capitalism was very similar to that of Marx.

In *The Theory of Economic Development* (1934, orig. publ. 1912), Schumpeter's analysis begins with a discussion of economic activity in the classical state of longrun equilibrium. Economic growth occurs only when this equilibrium is disturbed by an exogenous shock, namely by an innovation embodied in new plant and equipment introduced by the 'New Men'. The resulting supernormal profits induce a 'cluster' of complementary innovations financed by credit expansion that causes price increases, structural change (from consumer to capital goods) and, after a lag, increases in employment and output. Once innovation ceases, the continued expansion of investment (the 'over-investment' assumption) reduces profits to normal levels. Eventually new investment ceases, credit contracts, the price level falls, recession emerges and, finally, the economy settles back into the stationary state. Further growth requires additional exogenous shocks. Economic development, therefore, proceeds via a series of long booms and recessions. In *Business Cycles* (1939), Schumpeter replaces the term 'economic development' with 'economic evolution', tightens up his discussion of the nature and sequence of cycles, and introduces the concept of the production function. Hence, like the authors of neoclassical growth models that were to follow, Schumpeter interpreted economic growth as the outcome of a technological shock to the system of production.

Schumpeter provides a broader historical framework for his entrepreneurial growth model in his later book *Capitalism, Socialism, and Democracy* (1943). His objective in this book was to discover the future of capitalism. While he regarded this framework as 'evolutionary' – and it has been interpreted as such by some latter-day evolutionists (Witt 1993) – it is really an old-fashioned historicist exercise. While possessing many features in common with Marx's model, it belongs to what I have elsewhere (Snooks 1998a) called positive historicism in contrast to metaphysical historicism. Marx's model is 'metaphysical' because it is driven by the forces of destiny, whereas Schumpeter's is 'positive' because it merely describes his perception of the 'tendency' in history and extrapolates it into the future. This is the old historicist fallacy.

Schumpeter begins with his entrepreneurial model of 'economic progress' which he views as the 'prime mover' of the sociopolitical transformation of capitalism. But he has no model of the interactive mechanism between economic and institutional change. Instead he merely claims, like the positive historicists of old, to see a 'tendency' in the pattern of sociopolitical change as capitalism evolves. It is only this that distinguishes his model from that of Marx – that prevents it from being metaphysical. But it comes at the cost of having no driving force in his model. According to Schumpeter the historicist, the 'progress' of capitalism not only earlier helped to break down the institutions of feudalism and to form a protective sociopolitical framework of its own but, in the interwar period, had already begun to undercut its own institutions and to create those favourable to socialism. In Schumpeter's (1943: 135, 162) words: 'Capitalist evolution first of all destroyed, or went far toward destroying, the institutional arrangements of the feudal world – the manor, the village, the craft guild' and later 'the capitalist process not only destroys its own institutional framework but it also creates the conditions for another [that is, socialism]'. This is Schumpeter's famous 'creative destruction' process.

The main elements in Schumpeter's self-destructive capitalist process include: the 'obsolescence of the entrepreneurial function' as salaried managers take over from owner-managers, and as the mechanical routines undertaken by teams of researchers employed by mega-corporations replace the heroic activities of risk-taking individuals; the destruction of capitalism's 'protective' sociopolitical framework as the bourgeoisie is displaced by the masses; and the growing hostility of the educated and intellectual classes to the base materialism of capitalism. While he regretted the fact, Schumpeter was convinced that the next stage (or 'civilization') in the progress of human society will 'inevitably' be socialism. And under socialism, once scarcity is eliminated, the stationary state, which in the late 1930s he thought was far in the future, will emerge. Though this has a Marxian ring to it, Schumpeter was adamant that socialism would arise not from the failure but from the success of capitalism.

The important point to emphasize is that Schumpeter's vision emerged not from his formal growth model but from his historicist attempt to identify the 'tendency' in human affairs and to extrapolate that into the future. In his own words:

the various components of the tendency we have been trying to describe, while everywhere discernible, have as yet nowhere fully revealed themselves. Things have gone to different lengths in different countries but in no country far enough to allow us to say with any confidence precisely how far they will go, or to assert that their 'underlying trend' has grown too strong to be subject to anything more serious than temporary reverses. (Ibid.: 163)

In other words, Schumpeter was unable to employ his formal economic models to frame such a vision of the future. His vision was more comprehensive than his model but, as is always the case with naive historicists, his vision was wrong.

Rostow: Beyond Consumption

The last of the stages theorists is W. W. Rostow who, in view of the self-conscious comparisons he makes between his *The Stages of Economic Growth* (1990, orig. publ. 1960) and Marx's model, clearly saw himself as the orthodox successor to the great radical economist. Yet, as we shall discover, while Marx's model involves a complex mechanism and driving force, albeit metaphysical, Rostow's stages are devoid of analytical content. His stages of economic growth are, at best, merely descriptive categories through which societies are supposed to pass, mysteriously propelled by some unknown dynamic force. Rostow provides no dynamic model – no driving force and no mechanism of change. There is absolutely no logical reason why one stage should succeed the one preceding it in Rostow's hierarchy; we merely have his insistence that this is what has happened in the past. Hence, his future stage – beyond the age of high mass consumption – is pure guesswork. Rostow's vision of the future has neither a logical connection with the penultimate stage nor the imprimatur of history.

Despite these critical problems, Rostow has high ambitions for his stages hypothesis and the vision he claims for it. In *Stages* (1990: 1) he tells us:

This book presents an economic historian's way of generalizing the sweep of modern history. The form of this generalization is a set of stages-of-growth ...
They constitute, in the end, both a theory about economic growth and a more general, if still highly partial, theory about modern history as a whole.

While focusing on the nature of the growth process, Rostow is also concerned with its direction and, ultimately, its destination. One of the questions that *Stages* was designed to answer is: 'Where is compound interest taking us? Is it taking us to Communism; or to the affluent suburbs, nicely rounded out with social overhead capital; to destruction; to the moon; or where?' In attempting to answer this question, Rostow admits to regarding *Stages* as 'an alternative to Karl Marx's theory of modern history' (ibid.: 2).

The central feature of Rostow's schema is a set of five generalized historical stages through which all societies making the transition from the 'traditional' to the 'modern' must pass. These stages include:

- 'the traditional society' which is characterized by longrun stagnation and low rates of investment;
- 'the preconditions for take-off' that exhibit rising rates of investment (to 5 per cent of GDP), 'new production functions' based on the 'insights of modern science', 'new types of enterprising men', and more 'flexible' institutions;
- 'the take-off', taking about a decade or so, that occurs when investment rises to 10 per cent or more of GDP, new techniques are employed by an expanding entrepreneurial class, leading sectors emerge, the institutional framework is transformed, and 'compound interest' becomes built into society;
- 'the drive to maturity', taking about 40 years, that involves an increase in the rate of investment to 20 per cent of GDP and the extension of new technology and institutions to the rest of the economy;
- 'the age of high mass consumption' that is based on the redirection of surpluses from capital accumulation to mass consumption and welfare.

To meet the charge that these stages are merely descriptive (and there are many who contest his claim that they are accurately so), Rostow asserts that they are driven by a 'dynamic theory of production' (ibid.: 12–16). But this discussion, which covers no more than four pages of *Stages*, does not constitute a dynamic model, merely a few suggestions about what such a model might involve: such as a framework of demand and supply forces that might determine 'a set of sectoral paths, from which flows, as first derivatives, a sequence of optimum patterns of investment' that might trace out a rise and fall trajectory. The only thing we learn from this sketch is that Rostow, like all our traditional economists, regards societal dynamics as being generated by the capitalist system of production. This model has no driving force whatsoever – it is supposed to kick-start itself – as Rostow rejects the concept of economic rationality. We are told that 'net human behaviour is seen not as an act of maximization, but as an act of balancing alternative and often conflicting human objectives' (ibid.: 149): which merely begs the question of how his society might achieve *'optimum* patterns of investment' and *'optimum* sectoral growth paths' (my emphasis). Also he neglects to tell us how his stages and the 'dynamic theory of production' are related.

A critical test for any dynamic model is what it can tell us about the future as well as the past. Certainly his optimism about the development of the Third World has not been vindicated. In this respect Rostow shares the failure of the big investment push advocates, of which he was one. But he had a vision of the future that reached beyond the fate of the Third World. In *Stages* (ibid.: 11–12) Rostow speculates about what might be beyond the age of high mass consumption:

> Beyond, it is impossible to predict, except perhaps to observe that Americans, at least, have behaved in the past decade as if diminishing relative marginal utility sets in, after a point, for durable consumers' goods; and they have chosen, at the margin, larger families... But even in this adventure in generalization it is a shade too soon to create – on the basis of one case – a new stage-of-growth, based on babies, in succession to the age of consumers' durables... But it is true that the implications of the baby boom along with the not wholly-unrelated deficit in social overhead capital are likely to dominate the American economy over the next decade rather than the further diffusion of consumers' durables.

There are two striking features in this statement. First, had Rostow developed a dynamic stages model with an inner logic as a viable alternative to that of Marx as he claimed, he would have found it possible to formulate a clearly articulated final stage rather than this very vague scenario. Marx had a model, albeit driven by metaphysical forces, that could logically formulate a future stage to follow capitalism. If, as he claimed, Rostow had a dynamic model based upon real historical forces, then he could have done no less. After all, as we have seen, that was the objective of the book. Rostow's uncertainty about the next stage reflected his inadequate model.

Secondly, the suggestion made in 1959 that the stage beyond high mass consumption would involve households in a shift from the consumption of durables to the creation of larger families severely undermines the credibility of his 'model'. The very reverse of his prediction took place, indeed was already well under way when he wrote those words. From the 1950s to the mid-1970s the entire Western world saw the first permanent reduction in the average size of households – from about five to three people – in the entire history of human society (Snooks 1996: 230–1). This was a response to the shift in the gender demand for labour in favour of married women, as an outcome of technological change (the automation and, later, computerization of market activity), by households wanting to increase their consumption of durables and market services (Snooks 1994a: 81–90). Rostow's dilemma is similar to that of Ricardo in the middle of the Industrial Revolution – the modern technological paradigm shift – when he excluded technological change from his dynamic model. When Rostow wrote *Stages* he was in the middle of the greatest structural change in developed countries since the time of Ricardo.

Thirdly, the implication of Rostow's (incorrect) view that households will shift their expenditures from durable goods to more children is that the next (final?) stage will see the achievement of the stationary state. It is hardly surprising, therefore, to discover that Rostow concludes *Stages* (1990: 166) by claiming that 'on one point Marx was right – and we share his view: the end of all this is not compound interest for ever; it is the adventure of seeing what man can and will do when the pressure of scarcity is substantially lifted from him.' This conclusion arises from an assumption rather than the logical operation of his model. The idea that scarcity is supply-determined rather than demand-determined is an outcome of Rostow's view of man as a non-maximizer – as essentially economically irrational.

8.3   CONCLUSIONS

The traditional vision of the future of human society is a little like the scientific vision of the future of the universe: some argue that it will continue growing forever, whereas others believe that it will finally cease, possibly even collapse in on itself. Historicists, such as Malthus, J. S. Mill, Marx, Schumpeter, and Rostow see growth as a recent and temporary occurrence that will lead in the not-too-distant future to the stationary state. Some of these even believe that this will usher in an ideal state of being for human society, whereas recent neoclassical economists appear to believe that the future is the steady state rather than the stationary state. Yet some of these, if pushed, may see an end to the equilibrium growth path, as they regard economic growth as a modern invention rather than as an inherent characteristic of human society. But even these visions apply only to individual *developed* nations and do not encompass the global process of economic development. This is hardly surprising as they are based on either inadequate production models or naive historicism. In either case they provide unpersuasive and flawed views of the future of human society.

A very different vision of the future, which will be discussed in Chapter 18, is provided by my dynamic-strategy model. It is a model that focuses on the strategic pursuit rather than the process of production, and is derived from the underlying dynamic process in human society rather than the superficial pattern of events or deductive guesswork. As this model encompasses the dynamic process at the global as well as the national level, it embraces the Third World as well as the First World. It is a vision that arises logically from a realistic dynamic model.

Part IV
Strategic Demand

9 The Global Dynamic-Strategy Model

Strategic demand is the central feature of both the dynamic-strategy model first presented in *Longrun Dynamics* (Snooks 1998b) and the theory of the **global strategic transition** (**GST**) developed in this book. To understand this concept, which is explored throughout Parts IV and V, it is necessary to review the complete model. As the dynamic-strategy model has been developed in detail in the earlier companion volume, no more than an outline is provided here. The main focus of this chapter is to place the model in a global context in order to explain the fundamental mechanism underlying the GST.

9.1 THE GLOBAL CONTEXT

The broad contours of the GST – a process by which an increasing number of societies over time are drawn into the vortex of dynamic interaction between the world's most economically advanced nations – are discussed above in Chapter 2. To show how the GST works we need to explore the strategic demand–response mechanism in a global setting. This is the objective of Chapters 9 to 17. Our review here of the operation of the global dynamic-strategy model focuses on the way it works in the different analytical categories developed in Table 4.3 (p. 48). The central conclusion is that only strategic societies – both SCs and ESCs (Type I) (explained below) – generate their own endogenous dynamic mechanism, as well as responding to global strategic demand through international trade. The rest – both NSCs and ESCs (Type II) – grow only in response to the strategic demand generated by the **global strategic core**.

The SCs are involved in an intensely competitive struggle with each other for survival and prosperity. To achieve their objectives they need to gain an advantage over their competitors by effectively exploiting their existing strategic opportunities and by pioneering new technological substrategies. In this way they generate their own endogenous dynamic mechanisms of which the centrepiece is strategic demand. Individual SCs also benefit from the expansion of global strategic demand via its impact on trade between First-World countries. In other words, strategic demand operates both endogenously and exogenously, and the balance between them varies with our analytical categories.

175

The ESCs – societies that recently have entered into the GST – are of two kinds. ESCs (Type I) pursue a relatively independent, if not pioneering, technological substrategy. Accordingly they generate their own strategic demand. In the main they are caught up in the process of **global strategic imitation** and, as demonstrated in Chapter 4, are experiencing rates of economic growth higher than those in SCs. Together with SCs they constitute the global strategic core, and like them they benefit from the expansion of global strategic demand operating through international trade. But there are also ESCs (Type II), which respond through international trade to external strategic demand – demand generated by the global strategic core. Endogenous sources of strategic demand are limited. ESCs (Type II), therefore, pursue a dependent **dynamic strategy**, generally through satisfying the demand of the strategic core for raw materials, foods, and cheap labour. The implication is that when this external demand evaporates so does the ESC (Type II) dynamic process, which results in regression to NSC status.

The NSCs are not involved systematically in the GST and, hence, they fail to grow over the longrun. From time to time NSCs will interact with the global strategic core and they will experience temporary bursts of growth. But just as often the GST will pass them by. It all depends on the changing requirements of the strategic core and the relative ability of NSCs to meet these requirements. When caught up temporarily in the GST they respond to an external strategic demand. They generate none of their own.

The strategic demand–response mechanism, discussed below, is orchestrated by strategic inflation. This process differs between our various analytical categories. In the case of SCs and ESCs (Type I), strategic inflation is generated by an endogenous dynamic process, whereas in ESCs (Type II) it is the outcome of global strategic demand. And, of course, NSCs do not experience any systematic strategic inflation because they have not entered into the GST. Conversely, nonstrategic inflation is rampant in NSCs and ESCs (Type II) owing to the rent-seeking activities of their ruling elites, whereas it is considerably less important in SCs and ESCs (Type I) owing to their pursuit of profit-seeking strategies. Nonstrategic inflation in the latter is a product of policy mistakes and exogenous supply-side events such as the OPEC oil crisis of the 1970s.

This model has important implications for the dynamic theory of international trade. The orthodox static theory is based on the principle of comparative advantage or comparative production costs. Although the analysis is usually dressed up with a discussion of indifference curves (preferences) as well as production–possibility curves (supply), this is essentially a supply-side analysis. Preferences operating through indifference-curve analysis is a passive concept that fails to qualify as a candidate for real-world demand. It is merely a device, employed more generally in neoclassical economics, to enable the solution of utility maximization. Pareto optimality is an artificial concept required by a discipline with no sense of real-world demand (Snooks 1998b: 232–3). Orthodox trade theory totally overlooks the driving role of dynamic demand. In fact, orthodox 'dynamic' trade theory focuses merely on the logical impact of given changes in the factors of *production* – technology and factor endowments – in their static model. They fail to see that international trade is part of the strategic *pursuit*. In the dynamic-strategy model, by contrast, global strategic demand is the driving force behind international trade. This constitutes a new dynamic theory of international trade.

9.2   THE DRIVING FORCE

The endogenous driving force in strategic societies, both SCs and ESCs (Type I), is the competitive struggle by **materialist man** to survive and prosper. This is the major outcome of our biologically determined desires that have been shaped by genetic change over almost four billion years. In the dynamic-strategy model, as in life, ideas are an effective way of achieving the object of our desires, but they do so in a passive way. Two major implications emerge from this reality: that altruism is not a prime determinant of human behaviour; and that the decision-making process is not dominated by the neoclassical rationality model. Because these implications are borne out by history, it is necessary to develop realist models of both human behaviour and decision-making.

The **concentric spheres model of human behaviour**, outlined in Chapter 10, is based on the notion of genetically determined desires, but it allows for the exercise of human freedom of action (unlike the sociobiological model). In this model, the way an individual relates to other individuals and groups depends on their potential contribution to maximizing his or her material advantage. This potential contribution is measured in the concentric spheres model by the **economic distance** between the self and other individuals and groups who occupy positions on a set of concentric spheres that radiate outwards (see Figure 10.1 below). Underlying this model are two balancing sets of forces, one centrifugal and the other centripetal. The centrifugal force is the incessant desire of the self to survive and prosper, which leads the typical individual to consistently pursue his or her own self-interest. This is the energizing force. The centripetal force, which can be thought of as the economic gravity holding society together, is generated by the self's need to cooperate with other individuals and groups in order to achieve its own objectives through the pursuit of a dominant dynamic strategy. It is through this interaction of competition and cooperation that the individual maximizes the probability of his or her survival and prosperity and that the society prospers. But the underlying condition for the trust required for cooperative activity, which should not be confused with altruism, is the generation of **strategic confidence**.

If ideas do not drive society, but merely facilitate the desires of its members, we need to replace the neoclassical rationality model with a realist model. Through the inductive method it is possible to derive such a model, which I have called the strategic-imitation model. In reality decision-making is based on the need to economize on nature's scarcest resource – intelligence. Rather than collect vast quantities of information on a large range of alternatives for processing through a mental model of the way the world works, the great majority of decision-makers – whom I have called **strategic followers** – merely imitate those people and those projects that are conspicuously successful. The only information they require is that necessary to answer the questions: Who and what are materially successful and why? Hence the important information required by decision-makers is **imitative information**, not cost–benefit information. Even the **strategic pioneers** do not employ rationalist techniques when seeking new ways of exploiting strategic opportunities. Rather than exhaustively seeking out the 'best' investment projects, they believe that their investment projects are the best. It is the market that adjudicates.

The strategic-imitation model has global implications. In a global context, societal strategic pioneers are to be found in the global strategic core, and the followers amongst the ranks of the remaining SCs, ESCs, and FASCs. The societal followers, who are caught up in the process of strategic imitation, merely need to know which are the most successful countries and what paths they are treading. In contrast to the neoclassical growth model, dynamic-strategy theory relevant to individual societies can be applied to global change. While some economists have observed the existence of imitation at the global level, none has developed a general model to explain it. Simple imitation mechanisms, usually picked up from unacknowledged economic historians, are just grafted onto orthodox growth models (Snooks 1998b: 45).

9.3   THE DYNAMIC MECHANISM

The endogenous driving force, therefore, is provided by the dynamic concept of materialist man. It is a self-starting and self-sustaining force that drives a dynamic mechanism that has at its centre the pursuit of a dominant dynamic strategy and its component substrategies. This begins as an individual or family activity but, if successful, it is adopted by wider social groupings, at first local, then regional and, finally, national. And it is through the strategic-imitation mechanism, by which successful pioneering initiatives are imitated by a growing number of individuals and groups, that this aggregation process takes place. In this way a successful dynamic strategy becomes the object of political policies controlled by the ruling strategists both in individual countries and progressively throughout the world. This involvement of human society in a **strategic pursuit** marks my theory off from orthodox models that emphasize the productive activities of mankind. Human society is a strategic organization, not a factory.

The choice of **dynamic strategy** – from four possibilities including family-multiplication, conquest, commerce, and technological change – depends on the underlying economic conditions, such as factor endowments and the nature of external competition. This arises from 'the law of strategic optimization', which states that a competitive society will adopt the dynamic strategy that achieves its materialist objectives more efficiently (Snooks 1998a: 201).[1] The important point to realize is that investment in these various dynamic strategies is undertaken for the same objective and involves a broadly similar process. The main difference is that investment in family-multiplication, conquest, and commerce is undertaken to achieve economic growth through gaining control of new *external* resources, while technological change is used to achieve growth through greater efficiency in the use of existing *internal* resources. As far as the strategist is concerned there is nothing special about technological change. Similarly, within the context of a particular dynamic strategy, entrepreneurs attempt to gain a competitive advantage through the adoption of new substrategies which, where successful, generate new technological styles.

As individuals and governments seek to exploit their physical and social environment, setting in train a mass movement orchestrated through strategic imitation, the dominant dynamic strategy unfolds in the sense that its opportunities are progressively exploited and, finally, exhausted. And it is this unfolding dynamic strategy that shapes the expectations of decision-makers. The eventual exhaustion of a dynamic strategy, as argued in Chapter 3, is the outcome of 'the law of diminishing *strategic* returns' (ibid.: ch. 8). The rise and fall of dynamic strategies and their substrategies traces out a distinctive **strategic pathway**, which provides the dynamic form for my model. This supersedes the arbitrary dynamic forms – the equilibrium growth path and path-dependence – adopted by supply-side neoclassical and evolutionary growth theorists. A dynamic form cannot be deduced logically from a set of assumptions about the production function, particularly when production is only indirectly relevant to one type of dynamic strategy. As already mentioned, human society is a strategic organization, not a factory. A general dynamic form can only be arrived at empirically.

From historical observation we can derive a general dynamic form for individual societies that encompasses a series of wave-like surges in economic growth that are separated by intervals of stability or retreat. This sequence consists of 'great waves' of about 300 years and, within each of these, 'long waves' of about 40 years. The great waves are generated by dynamic strategies and the long waves by a series of substrategies. Our great waves sequence reflects the sequence of dynamic strategies, each of which passes through a wave-like surge of exploitation and exhaustion. The phase of strategic exploitation is characterized by high rates of participation in profit-seeking, while the phase of strategic exhaustion is characterized by increasing rates of participation in rent-seeking and speculation. It should be realized that these wave-like surges are *not* part of a dynamic 'cycle', because the intervals between them are *not* systematically related to the surges before and after. Each of these intervals is a hiatus following the exhaustion of a dynamic strategy during which the strategic pioneers search desperately for a replacement strategy. If they are successful the sequence will continue (often by reverting to an earlier strategy) but, if they are not, the sequence comes to an end and the society collapses. The latter happened in the case of all ancient societies. Unlike the neoclassical equilibrium growth path, the strategic pathway is not an optimizing concept. It can be identified only retrospectively.

At the global level the dynamic strategies and substrategies pioneered by leading SCs and imitated by the rest are responsible for driving the unfolding industrial technological paradigm. As discussed in Chapter 2, this constitutes the GST by which individual countries will eventually exploit to the full the technological potential of the existing paradigm. Over the entire history of human society, this has generated a series of technological paradigm shifts (Figure 2.1) that will extend indefinitely into the future. This is where the current GST is leading.

9.4   STRATEGIC DEMAND AND STRATEGIC CONFIDENCE

The unfolding dynamic strategy, driven by the competitive energy of materialist man, plays a central role in the dynamic-strategy model. Not only does it provide the model with a realist dynamic form, but it gives rise to two important new concepts in economics that I have called **strategic confidence** and **strategic demand** (Snooks 1998b: ch. 11). These concepts explain not only the dynamics of longrun investment and saving that are left hanging in orthodox, comparative–static macroeconomics, but also how dynamic order is generated.

Strategic confidence, which rises and falls with the dominant dynamic strategy and its various substrategies, explains the changing investment climate in any strategic society. It even provides a dynamic explanation for Keynes' 'state of long-term expectation'. Accordingly, it plays a central role in determining the willingness of strategic pioneers and their followers to invest, because of its influence on the longrun expected rate of return and in the creation of dynamic order (through encouraging cooperation and an orderly institutional structure). Confidence and expectations rise as the dynamic strategy unfolds, and they decline, stagnate, and possibly collapse as it is progressively exhausted. Strategic confidence also binds society together. This concept is discussed more fully in Chapter 10.

Strategic demand also rises and falls with the dynamic strategy. It is the effective demand exercised by decision-makers for a wide range of physical, intellectual, and institutional inputs required in the strategic pursuit. In exploiting the strategic opportunities, entrepreneurs need to invest in new infrastructure; to purchase intermediate goods; to employ labour skills; to acquire or construct the necessary buildings, machinery, and equipment; and to develop new facilitating social rules and organizations. Also governments need to provide strategic leadership to facilitate the exploitation of strategic opportunities. Strategic demand, therefore, is the central active principle in society. Naturally the supply response of population, capital formation, and technological change, which depends on relative prices, will contribute to the way in which the strategic opportunities are exploited, but they do so passively. Thus we must turn Say's Law – which was accepted explicitly by classical economists and implicitly by neoclassical economists – on its head: in SCs and ESCs, strategic demand creates its own supply.

Strategic demand and strategic confidence together explain the variables that Keynesian macroeconomics either assumes to be given or leaves in the swamplands of 'psychological propensities' and institutional arrangements. The 'state of long-term expectation', the propensity to consume, and the liquidity-preference schedule are all left unexplained in Keynes' comparative–static model of employment. By contrast, in the dynamic-strategy model they are treated as economic rather than psychological or institutional issues, and can be readily explained in terms of strategic demand and strategic confidence. The dynamic-strategy model treats investment, saving/consumption, the rate of interest, employment, and real GDP as joint outcomes of these two concepts. Hence, the saving required to finance investment – one of the great problems for neoclassical economics – is generated by the growth process rather than being its precondition.

The dynamic-strategy model, therefore, is able to encompass *The General Theory* as a special case. This possibility, I like to think, would not have surprised Keynes, who was acutely aware that he was painting a static picture at a point in time rather than exploring a moving picture over time. To do so he was forced to invent psychological laws which filled the gap left by a lack of historical observation. Laws, however, should explain what we know, rather than obscure what we do not know.

The claim made in *Longrun Dynamics* is that the dynamic-strategy model resolves the difficulties experienced in employing Keynesian economics during the volatile conditions of the 1970s. These difficulties drove most orthodox economists back into the neoclassical, supply-side camp. And because of this, macroeconomic policy is currently based on the misplaced microeconomic notions about the desirability of balance – of equilibrium – in internal budgets, external trade accounts, and prices. In order to place Keynesian macroeconomics in a wider framework and to sensibly address issues of macroeconomic policy we need to develop a persuasive dynamic model. The dynamic-strategy model also plays a central role in global development. As we have seen, the strategic demand generated by the world's leading SCs plays a central role in driving international trade and in drawing NSCs into the global transition. Hence, it is essential to develop a general model of global economic development.

9.5   STRATEGIC DEMAND AND STRATEGIC RESPONSE

With the dynamic-strategy model, we can shift focus from comparative–static macroeconomics to longrun dynamics by considering the interaction between strategic demand and the **strategic response** of supply-side variables. It is this interaction that gives rise to the strategic pathway – the dynamic form of our model – and to the dynamic role played by inflation in facilitating the strategic response. These are the major differences between strategic theory and orthodox theory. In neoclassical economics the supply-side is, by default, treated as the active force in society (supply creates its own demand), which has no place for inflation, while in Keynesian economics the supply-side variables are merely assumed to be given. By contrast, in the dynamic-strategy model, strategic demand provides the active force to which the supply-side variables respond. Strategic inflation, which provides the incentive system in this strategic-response mechanism, is a stable, nonaccelerating function of economic growth. This is the basis for the **growth–inflation curve** introduced in *Longrun Dynamics* (ibid.: 151–9).

Population, labour supply, capital formation, and technological, institutional, and strategic ideas all respond to the unfolding dynamic strategy. Changes in these supply-side variables, both in terms of composition and growth rates, are a function of changing strategic opportunities. These variables expand and become more complex as the dominant dynamic strategy is exploited, and they stagnate, decline, and sometimes collapse, as the dynamic strategy is progressively exhausted. Naturally, supply-side costs play a role in shaping the strategic response, but this is a passive rather than an active role. In this way the supply-side variables are treated endogenously in the dynamic-strategy model. Strategic demand creates its own supply.

This strategic demand–response mechanism also has global implications. Strategic demand generated by the world's strategic core elicits a response from the owners of natural and human resources in the Third World. Not only is it the driving force behind international trade and the GST, but it also plays a central role in the generation of strategic inflation in ESCs and FASCs. This theoretical relationship between strategic demand and strategic inflation can be empirically estimated, as in Chapter 11, in the form of the growth–inflation curve for the Third World as well as the First World. It has radical implications for policy as shown in Chapter 18.

9.6 CONCLUSIONS

In summary, the Dynamic Society is characterized as being driven by the biologically determined desires – to survive and prosper – of materialist man, who invests in the most efficient dynamic strategy or substrategy. Feedback is provided by the changing material standards of living. This exploration of strategic opportunities drives the unfolding dynamic strategy that provides a dynamic form for our model – the strategic sequence of great and long waves – and gives rise to parallel shifts in strategic demand and strategic confidence. In turn, these two key concepts are responsible for creating dynamic order and generating an increase in investment, saving, population, labour skills, ideas of all sorts, and institutions and organizations. This self-starting and self-maintaining dynamic process continues only until a dynamic strategy/substrategy has been exhausted – when strategic confidence and strategic demand decline – and will only begin again anew when the old strategy/substrategy has been replaced. If this substitution cannot be achieved, the society will stagnate and, eventually, collapse – it will have failed in its strategic pursuit.

At the global level this model can account for the progress of the GST. The world's SCs are involved in a competitive struggle to survive and prosper. To do so they adopt new technological substrategies, thereby gaining an advantage over their competitors. Strategic demand generated by the leading SCs plays a central role in driving international trade, the levels of strategic inflation in the Third World, and the unfolding of the industrial technological paradigm. In the following chapters we turn to these issues in greater detail.

10 The Driving Force

To understand **strategic demand**, which is the central concept in my theory of the global strategic transition (GST), we need to explore the forces driving it. This requires the development of a realistic theory of human behaviour that can explain the exploitation of strategic opportunities and, hence, the **unfolding technological paradigm**. The failure to analyse the driving force in society is a major weakness of orthodox economics. Neoclassical growth models are neither self-starting nor self-maintaining (Snooks 1998b: ch. 3). In these production models 'dynamics' can only be generated from unsystematic exogenous shocks, whereas in the dynamic-strategy model the driving force – the **strategic pursuit** – is endogenous.

The objective of this chapter is to report a more realistic model of human behaviour developed elsewhere (Snooks 1997a: 25–50; 1998b: 109–25). This model, which is based inductively on historical investigation rather than on guesswork or laboratory experiment, provides an endogenous driving force for my strategic model of longrun dynamics. Owing to its general nature it is relevant to both the First and Third Worlds. And, in the course of this chapter, it is demonstrated that social dynamics is an outcome of the strategic pursuit.

This new model has three main characteristics. The first is concerned with motivation, the second with the decision-making process, and the third with the role of rules in decision-making. Briefly, the driving force in this model is the biologically determined desires (but not behaviour) of mankind; its objectives are to satisfy these desires by maximizing the probability of survival and prosperity; its process involves an interaction between the unfolding dynamic strategy and the investment decisions of strategic pioneers and their followers; and societal rules are an outcome, not of the cost of information but of strategic demand and the costs of analytical thinking for a species which, despite its intellectual achievements, is essentially intuitive rather than cerebral in nature. Institutions, therefore, are employed to facilitate the dominant dynamic strategy and to do so in a way that economizes on the scarcest of all resources in nature – intelligence.

10.1   THE DRIVING FORCE

The Nature of Materialist Man

An extensive study of the dynamics of human society, the results of which are presented in *The Dynamic Society* (Snooks 1996) and *The Ephemeral Civilization* (Snooks 1997a), make it clear that human decision-makers are not the passive sort embodied in the orthodox concept of *homo economicus*. In reality, decision-makers are driven by an intense desire to survive and prosper. This can be seen operating throughout the history of human civilization and, indeed, throughout the past two million years since the emergence of mankind. Elsewhere I have called this 'the law of human motivation' (Snooks 1998a: ch. 8).[1]

Historical analysis suggests that biologically determined desires – the result of genetic change over almost four billion years – are far more important than intellectual ideas in human motivation and, hence, in human behaviour. Indeed, human decision-making is driven not by intellectual objectives but by animal desires. John Maynard Keynes' intuition about the importance of 'animal spirits' is borne out by historical research. The desire to survive and, having survived, to satisfy our biological appetites is the driving force in society. In recognition of the difference between the passive decision-maker in orthodox economics and the dynamic decision-maker in reality, I draw a distinction between *homo economicus* and **materialist man**.

Of course, the human intellect does play an important role in the operation and progress of human society, but that role is limited to facilitating the satisfaction of our basic desires. In fact, as demonstrated elsewhere (Snooks 1997a: 121–7), the difference in the pursuit of this objective between human and non-human species is not a matter of kind but a matter of degree. Human beings merely rely to a greater degree on the intellect to satisfy their genetically determined desires than other species do, because of their larger and more complex brains.

Intellectuals are loath to accept the primacy of desires as a driving force and the relegation of ideas to a facilitating device. Economists are no different. When discussing the relative importance of ideas and desires in determining the progress of civilization, economists, even of the calibre of J. S. Mill (1875 orig. publ. 1843, vol. I: 257) and F. A. Hayek (1988: 12–18), always choose ideas. Why? A major reason, as suggested elsewhere (Snooks 1996: ch. 6), is that the status and wealth of intellectuals depends on their success in persuading the rest of society, or at least the ruling elite, that ideas are primarily responsible for the achievements of human civilization.

Intellectuals also find it difficult to accept the self-centred nature of human beings. They have a faith in the fundamental altruism of mankind, despite all the evidence to the contrary. It is a faith that rises above the ever-present exploitation, physical and psychological abuse, betrayal, abandonment, dishonesty, corruption, and theft not just in society in general but in the family in particular; and that rises above the exploitation and war between nations and even between regions or ethnic/political groups within nations.

The issue of altruism needs to be re-evaluated. According to general usage, 'altruism' is a principle for action by which an individual will deliberately attempt to improve the welfare of others even if it reduces his or her own welfare. Altruism, therefore, is an end in itself rather than a means to a different end. Hence, any act aimed at maximizing the welfare of self, but which in the process improves the welfare of others, cannot be regarded as altruism. To do so would be to confuse ends and means. If the end is the maximization of individual material advantage, and the means is cooperation with other individuals who also gain, then self-interest rather than altruism is the driving force. Much of the recent writing in economics has confused ends with means. Cooperation is not the same as altruism. This does not deny that some individuals are altruistic in the proper sense of the word, just that they are in a small minority.

Economists have long debated the altruism–selfishness issue. A relatively new element in this debate (Becker 1976; Frech 1978; Samuelson 1983; Bergstrom 1995) is the concept of 'kin selection' borrowed from sociobiology where it emerged about thirty years ago (Hamilton 1964). It is rather curious that some economists should take this idea from sociobiology rather than directly investigate the issue historically, because sociobiology is a science in which individual *behaviour* (rather than desires) is genetically determined owing to the mechanical selection process of differential reproduction (Snooks 1997a: ch. 5). When applied to the social sciences, sociobiological theories generate models that provide no freedom of choice (for example, Bergstrom 1995).

A Realist Model of Human Behaviour

By using the historical method, I have been able to develop a more realistic model of human behaviour – the concentric spheres model – that is based on the notion of genetically determined desires and is consistent with individual freedom in both human and non-human species (Snooks 1994a: 50–1; 1997a: ch. 2). It can be used to sort out the altruism–selfishness

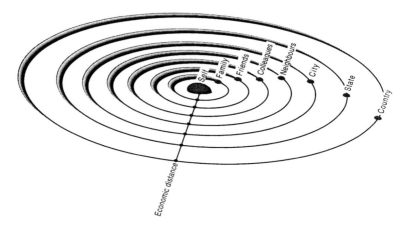

Figure 10.1   The concentric spheres model of human behaviour
Source: Snooks 1997a: 30.

issue. In this model, the way in which an individual behaves in relation to
other individuals depends not on the 'genetic distance' between them as in
the kin selection model, but on the **economic distance** or importance of
other individuals or groups in maximizing the material interests of the
self.[2] In this model, represented in Figure 10.1, the individual is at the centre of a set of concentric spheres that define the varying strength of cooperative relationships between the self and all other individuals and
groups in society. The strength of the economic relationship between the
self and any other individual or group – which is measured by the economic distance between them – will depend on how essential they are to
the maximization of the self's utility. Those aspects of the self's objective
function that require the greatest cooperation – such as the generation of
love, companionship, and children – will be located on spheres with the
shortest economic distance from the centre. For the typical individual,
spouse and children will occupy the sphere closest to the centre, with other
relatives, friends, workmates, neighbours, members of various religious
and social clubs, other members of his or her socioeconomic group, city,
state, nation, and group of nations, occupying those concentric spheres
that progressively radiate out from the centre. As the economic distance
between the centre and each sphere increases, the degree of cooperation
between them diminishes.[3]

Underlying the concentric spheres model are two balancing sets of forces,
one centrifugal and the other centripetal. The centrifugal force is the incessant desire of the self to survive and prosper – a desire that leads the

typical individual to place himself before all others. This force provides individuals with ambition and competitive energy. The centripetal force – the economic gravity holding society together – is the need of self to cooperate with other individuals and groups in order to more effectively achieve its objectives, through the pursuit of the dominant dynamic strategy. It is through this interaction between competition and cooperation that the individual maximizes the probability of his or her survival and prosperity, and that social order is created from the primordial chaos. These forces find expression in the 'primary laws of history' (Snooks 1998a: ch. 8).

But exactly what is it that enables self-seeking individuals to cooperate with each other? The usual answer is that it is something called 'trust'. This response, however, merely begs a further question: What generates trust? Institutionalists argue that trust is an outcome of the evolution of formal and informal rules that determine predictable and cooperative conduct. Yet no one has proposed an evolutionary model that can convincingly explain the changing nature of societal rules, particularly when sharp institutional reversals occur, as they do quite regularly in history.

The dynamic-strategy model presented in this book tackles the problem from a different and more realistic direction. It suggests that the reason chaos, which results from the breakdown of the centripetal force, does not occur in any given society is that it is successfully pursuing a viable dynamic strategy. This successful dynamic strategy leads to a workable network of competitive/cooperative relationships, together with all the necessary supporting rules and organizations. Individuals in this society, therefore, relate directly to the successful dynamic strategy and only indirectly to each other. It is not a matter of mutual trust as such – of having confidence in the nature of other individuals – but rather having confidence in the wider dynamic strategy in which they are all vitally involved.

Hence, it is not individual trust, but **strategic confidence** that keeps society from flying apart. What we know as 'trust' is merely derived from strategic confidence. And as the dynamic strategy unfolds, the nature of strategic confidence and, hence, trust changes in subtle ways. The dynamic-strategy model, therefore, can explain the nature of investor confidence that was left hanging in Keynes's *The General Theory* (1936).

Strategic confidence – the economic gravity of the concentric spheres model of behaviour – lasts only as long as the success of a society's dynamic strategy. Once the dynamic strategy has been exhausted and cannot be replaced, strategic confidence declines and, in extreme cases, vanishes entirely. And as strategic confidence falls, so too does social trust and cooperation, leading to the fragmentation of society as families turn in on themselves and, in extreme cases, as individuals begin to abandon even their families. This implies, in terms of Figure 10.1, the stripping away of the concentric spheres one by one until the self is left isolated, attempting to live by his/her wits alone. This announces the victory of centrifugal over centripetal forces and the destruction of the society.

Strategic confidence, which is the outcome of a successful dynamic strategy, is communicated to the citizens of that society in two main ways. The first and most important mechanism involves a continuous increase in material standards of living. While this flow of material returns is maintained, so is strategic confidence. But once this stream is interrupted, confidence begins to decline. This is why Western governments that are inspired by neoliberal policies are playing a very dangerous game by deliberately disrupting growth through their deflationary policies in the hunt for a fictional enemy called inflation. The second, and less important, mechanism is the use of ideology to draw society's citizens into acceleration of the dominant dynamic strategy.[4] It is less important than the income mechanism because it is only effective, and then only in a reinforcing manner, when living standards are rising or, at least, not falling. Nonetheless, it is a mechanism that is employed more extensively, yet less effectively, when the dominant dynamic strategy begins to fail.

10.2 THE STRATEGIC-IMITATION MODEL OF DECISION-MAKING

In reality there is little fundamental difference between the basic neoclassical model of decision-making and the bounded-rationality or institutional extensions of it (Snooks 1998b: ch. 8). Both sets of revisionists accept the view that each decision-maker makes each and every decision in isolation by collecting as much information as is economically possible about the subject under consideration, by applying an appropriate conceptual model to that data, and by computing a rational outcome. The major difference between the parent neoclassical model and the various revisionist versions is reflected in the degree of perfection they are willing to assume about the responses of economic agents to the present and their foresight about the future. While the neoclassicists assume a perfect world, the revisionists assume a world that is less than perfect. Their response is merely to release some of the assumptions of the basic neoclassical model. But this is not the way to develop a better theory of human behaviour.

To develop a better theory we need to abandon the present view of human decision-making – developed by atypical individuals with a comparative advantage in abstract thinking – as a problem-solving process of information processing. Despite the inevitable protestations of scholars, human beings are not intellectual game-players of the digital computer variety. Also, the average person makes no attempt to model the world in his or her head. The only 'models' they possess are non-functional, such as conspiracy models (which ascribe their difficulties to various minority groups), religious models (which provide divine justification and support), or models of self-justification (which convert selfish motives into altruistic ones). And these survive largely because they are *not* confronted by information about reality. A comprehensive, rather than a selective, study of history demonstrates quite clearly that human decisions are just not made in that way. Ironically, even neoclassical economists abandon their models and rely on intuition when involved in national policy-making (Snooks 1997a: ch. 13). A better theory must be based not on psychology or institutionalism, but on historical experience.

Historical experience suggests that the decision-making process is imitative rather than isolationist, and is dualistic rather than holistic. While this cannot be established in the psychology laboratory, it can be observed in historical reality. Unlike the established models, it can explain the remarkable cycles of fashion – the bandwagon effect – in decision-making in all aspects of human life. Many have commented upon curious fashions in dress, diet, popular and classical culture, art, architecture, customs, rituals and ceremonies, technologies, religions, and lifestyles (Plato, *Republic*: paras 395–7; Schumpeter 1934; Mises 1958; Dawkins 1989). To this we can add the current fashion in OECD countries and international organizations (the IMF and the World Bank) of economic policies that focus on price stability at the expense of unemployment and growth (Snooks 1997a).

None of these fashions has been adequately explained in terms of the established models of decision-making. But they can be explained by the strategic-imitation model. In this model, the decision-making process can be divided into the pioneering and routine phases, with each part of the process being dominated by a different type of decision-maker – the strategic pioneer and the strategic follower. Each phase will be dealt with separately. As shown in Chapter 9, this model can also explain the strategic imitation of 'pioneering' societies by 'following' societies at the global level.

The Pioneering Phase

Investment in new ideas and projects is an extremely uncertain activity because little information of any kind about likely outcomes is available to the **strategic pioneers**, and it is a risky activity because of the high probability of failure for new ventures. As innovative ideas are without precedent, and as these ideas can change society in unpredictable ways, pioneers can only make informed guesses about likely outcomes. While they may use the limited information available to gauge the benefits and costs of what they are proposing, the pioneers operate more on intuition

about outcomes and on faith in their own abilities. They have no foresight as assumed by the supporters of rational expectations. Individuals,
mainly family and friends, supplying support in the form of financial
and human capital do so because they share this belief in the pioneer's
abilities. This is not an area of economic activity in which conservative
financial institutions will want to be involved. They only finance routine
decision-making.

The essential point to realize is that the strategic pioneers do not make
their decisions in a vacuum. They work within the boundaries of an
unfolding dynamic strategy, and respond to the changing incentives that it
generates. In other words, the pioneers operate at the leading edge of the
unfolding strategy, actively exploring its economic potential and generating strategic demand. This involves the development of new substrategies
which, within the technological strategy of the modern era, can be thought
of as new **technological styles**. Hence, there is an interaction between the
strategic pioneers and the unfolding dynamic strategy, which gives direction and meaning to their activities. While these activities are not random,
many pioneers misread the signs and fail. Only a few succeed, but these
provide the example for the many to follow. And it is this mass following
that provides the driving energy for the strategic unfolding. The core of the
dynamic-strategy model, therefore, is the interaction between the unfolding dynamic strategy and the strategic pioneers, which provides a dynamic
structure that marks it off from other theories of economic growth (Snooks
1998b: ch. 10).

The pioneers are few in number and even less significant in proportion
to the total population of decision-makers. They are more ambitious, possess greater imaginative and intellectual skills, are prepared to take greater
risks, have greater faith in themselves and, most importantly, have a
greater perception of how the dynamic strategy is unfolding than the vast
majority of routine decision-makers. They are driven by a greater abun-
dance of biological desires that drive all life. When conspicuously successful, the pioneers are followed by large numbers of imitators. Needless
to say, they are not always successful. Indeed, owing to the risks that
attend untried ways, only a very small proportion of the pioneers are able
to achieve their objectives. But, as the material rewards that fall into the
hands of those who do succeed are very great, there is always a steady
stream of those willing to test their ambitions, skills, and faith.

We are now in a position to discuss the mechanism by which successful
pioneering decisions are made. There are two parts to this mechanism – the
drive and ambition of imaginative risk-takers, and the competitive process
of alternative investment projects. The pioneers invest most of their time

not in the collection of information about alternative projects, nor in the development of conceptual models of reality, nor in the computation of optimal solutions, but rather in developing imaginative ideas that they believe will bring windfall gains and in demonstrating the successful outcomes of their ideas. These ideas may be arrived at from an awareness of the unfolding dynamic strategy achieved either through contemplation or, more likely, through a practical involvement in, or association with, a particular industry or activity. In essence, the pioneers provide the driving force required to propel their ideas and projects into the market place. And it is the market place of competing ideas and projects, shaped by the dominant dynamic strategy, that determines the outcome. Only a very small proportion of pioneers will successfully realize their material ambitions.

Success breeds success. The pioneers who get it right are provided with the rationale for what they have done. Successful feedback leads to further developments along the same lines. There is no need to examine alternatives while-ever individual pioneers are achieving the outcomes they desire. Only when the feedback is less favourable will they even consider alternative investment projects, and these will only be pursued if the benefits of the alternative exceed not only the costs of the new project but also the costs of scrapping the initial one. And this will probably only occur in the generation following the successful pioneering phase. By then the, initially pioneering, organization will have entered the routine phase of imitating the success of its forefathers or of others – unless a second generation pioneer comes to the fore.

It is this pioneering mechanism – involving an intense competition between individuals pursuing competing ideas and projects – rather than the attempts by individuals to calculate the benefits and costs of alternative strategies that produces what might be regarded as optimal outcomes. In an important sense, the individual pioneers embody the alternative projects that the existing model either assumes to be given (neoclassical) or assumes that each individual attempts to determine and evaluate (revisionist). The effort of each pioneer is directed to the 'discovery' of a single project. Of course many of these projects will be duplicated or will involve some overlapping with other projects. What the pioneers require to become involved in this competitive process is not vast amounts of information and superhuman computing abilities, but rather great energy and imagination. They do not shop around for the best idea, they believe their idea is best. The market of competing pioneers, which is shaped by the unfolding dynamic strategy, will do the rest. It is from this competitive process that the most appropriate ideas will emerge.

The Routine Phase

Investment in routine ideas and projects by the **strategic followers** is characterized by far less uncertainty and by greater predictability than investment in entirely new ideas and strategies by the pioneers. After the pioneering phase, it is clear which projects are the most profitable. The successful pioneers, and their supporters, earn supernormal profits on their strategic investments. This provides, for the first time, positive information about the rates of return on investments in various alternative projects. The central question is how this information is used. In the routine phase, decision-makers do seek information but not of the kind envisaged by the traditional behavioural model. They do not seek detailed information on the costs and benefits of all possible alternatives. Rather they seek information on who and what is successful and why they are successful. Who is earning supernormal profits on what investments, and how can I get in on the act? Their aim is to imitate not the mechanism of digital computers, but the projects of the successful pioneers. This process, which I call **strategic imitation**, is based on the systematic observation of both human society and animal life in *The Dynamic Society* (Snooks 1996) and *The Ephemeral Civilization* (Snooks 1997a). The 'law of strategic imitation' is one of the 'primary laws of history' (Snooks 1998a: ch. 8).

Strategic imitation, of course, is more complex and interactive than this suggests, because once the followers apply imitated ideas to a commercial area, they will make further modifications of their own in the light of their own circumstances and experience. There are still many smaller battles to be fought, lost, and won in the attempt to work out the ideas of the pioneers for new environments. This will involve small changes and (lower order) innovations in response to slightly different economic and competitive environments in order to successfully (and sometimes unsuccessfully) apply these new ideas. The microeconomic process of strategic imitation, therefore, does involve scope for degrees of imagination and independence. It is an important characteristic of human nature that it is able to find scope for imaginative responses on even the smallest scale. This process of adaption has received considerable attention from others (Tunzelmann 1994; Magee 1997). But the important point to be made here is that the wider decision-making process has at its core an imitative mechanism.

This is not to say that some information on benefits and costs is not collected, just that it is collected to justify rather than to determine routine investment decisions. Such a procedure has three major advantages: it reduces the time taken to collect and process cost–benefit information; it provides the investor with additional confidence; and it is used to persuade conservative financial interests to make funds available for the enterprise.

As the decision on what investment strategy to employ is made before any serious attempt to collect and process information, the difficulties involved in the formal cost–benefit calculation are reduced to manageable levels. The collection of data is highly selective, and the desired outcome is known in advance. The object of the exercise is to confirm decisions made on the basis of entirely different information – information about successful strategists and strategies. This confirmation provides additional confidence in the task ahead.

A major reason for at least attempting benefit–cost calculations is to obtain funding for investment proposals. This occurs in both the public and private sectors. More recently the public sector has, under pressure from taxpayers, adopted the procedure of commissioning feasibility studies on large public projects. These studies, however, are generally undertaken after, rather than before, major projects have been chosen. Their purpose is to justify rather than to determine public decision-making. And those undertaking the feasibility studies are chosen accordingly.

In the private sector, individuals and firms must convince financial organizations that the investment proposal is sound. These organizations have standard forms for roughly estimating likely income flows that are based upon the past financial performance of the individual or organization and on the value of any realizable assets. Even banks do not attempt to gather vast amounts of information nor do they employ complex computer models to calculate likely future returns on proposed investment projects. They merely look at whether or not this individual or firm has previously succeeded or failed, usually by consulting computerized data banks on credit rating, and how successful others have been in the past when pursuing similar projects. In effect, this exercise is merely a formalization of the imitative procedure undertaken by all routine decision-makers. It does not attempt to calculate the benefits and costs of all alternative projects as required by the neoclassical and revisionist models.

The information required for strategic imitation is, in contrast to that required in the neoclassical model, readily available and is easily evaluated. We gain it from direct observation of those around us, from professional advice, from the media, and from books, magazines, and electronic sources. In the past the main form of imitation was through direct observation of local celebrities. While this was probably more important then than it is today in sophisticated societies, we are still only too aware of the *nouveaux riches* in our midst. Mankind possesses a primitive and unquenchable need to display the objects of material success. The intense desire to imitate the successful is matched only by an intense desire to display the fruits of success. It is true that imitation is the sincerest form of flattery. The only difference between sophisticated and primitive societies, apart from the scale of material success, is the way in which this interactive mechanism of display and imitation is effected. While in the past the main mechanism was word-of-mouth, today the media play a major role. Most of us gather a large proportion of our **imitative information** from the media which specialize in watching the rich and successful and in sharing this information, often in the most crudely voyeuristic form, to its readers and viewers. We are treated to a continuous parade of the successes to be imitated – and the failures to be avoided. This information is not the stuff of cost–benefit calculations, but of who we should imitate if we are to be successful in life.

Popular books and magazines are also important sources of information for routine decision-making. Once again these sources supply not the type of information required to undertake cost–benefit calculations, but information about who or what should be emulated and how we should do so. This type of imitative information covers all aspects of our lives, not just investment decision-making. Hence it is a fertile source of data for the fashions that continually sweep through human society. By browsing the shelves of popular bookshops and newsagencies, we discover an almost endless range of specialized magazines and books on every facet of our lives at work, at home, and at leisure. We are shown who are the most successful in material terms, what their opulent lifestyles are like, and how we can imitate them in even the most modest ways. We are told about their businesses and investments; about their houses, gardens, swimming pools, and tennis courts; about their motor vehicles, yachts, holidays, clothes, hairstyles, lovers, children, and their various leisure interests. And we are told how to obtain some of these things for ourselves. These magazines and books are not just for entertainment. They are also for instruction – to enable us to imitate the successful. It is this information that feeds our desires and thereby fuels the driving force in human society.

Increasingly the imitative information obtained through popular books and magazines is being provided through computer software and international computer network systems. This has been called, somewhat extravagantly, the 'information superhighway'. I say 'extravagantly', because it is a function already provided through the media and popular books and magazines, and because its promoters like to give the impression that this information will be the basis for some sort of intellectual revolution. In fact, what the 'information superhighway' will provide in the main is popular entertainment and imitative information, not the type of intellectual information originally carried on the Internet. There is no mass market for hard ideas and facts, and there never will be. What will not receive pride of place on the 'information superhighway' is information that will enable subscribers to undertake detailed benefit–cost calculations of the type envisaged by the neoclassical model. Why? The answer is that there is little demand for this type of information, either in electronic or book/magazine form, precisely because materialist decision-making is not made in this way. But what the Internet has achieved is a revival of the role of word-of-mouth as a means of distributing imitative information; this time globally rather than locally.[5]

What is it that drives the followers to imitate the pioneers? There appears to be a genetically determined desire to do as well if not better than our neighbours, and the fear that if we do not run with the herd something nasty will happen (possibly perpetrated by the herd itself which mistrusts dissidents). This is something we share with all other species in nature. It is a central part of the desire to survive and prosper, which always emerges in competitive environments. In the case of our own species it amounts to good old-fashioned envy regarding the prosperity of others. Imitation comes easily and pleasurably to us. It is a natural outcome of one of our most conspicuous characteristics – mimicry. And, as discussed elsewhere (Snooks 1997a: 122–6), it is a characteristic we share with other animal species. In childhood we learn through mimicry, in youth we amuse ourselves and our peers by mimicking others, and in our later years we laugh along with professional comedians whose stock-in-trade is mimicry. It has a more serious purpose, too, as the basis for human decision-making.

There is a darker side to the process of imitation that reinforces the natural desire to be part of the crowd. In every society there are some who react against the crowd. These are the dissenters, the original thinkers, those who dare to be different. They would appear to be less well adapted genetically to survive and prosper. And as such they will either be forced to conform or will be rooted out of society. Although the dissenters are always in a small minority, they are seen by the crowd as a threat to the survival and prosperity of the majority. This can be seen throughout history in the way society has turned against highly original thinkers like Socrates, Galileo, and Darwin; it can be seen in the widespread persecution of religious and political minorities; it can be seen in the vilification of individuals who speak out against prevailing attitudes on issues like race, sex, gender, and immigration; and it can be seen in the attempted repression by academic societies and organizations of original thinkers who challenge the conventional wisdom. This predictable intolerance works to strengthen the mechanism of strategic imitation.

In sum, what is the imitative process of decision-making? It comprises two elements. The first of these involves the immediate strategic followers who, in the pursuit of survival and prosperity, attempt to imitate the actions of successful pioneers. The second of these is the market of innumerable

opportunists, all jostling for a share of the supernormal profits first generated by the pioneers. Only the most skilful or the most fortunate of the followers will reap more than normal profits – and even then only for a
limited period – while some will fail completely. The eventual outcome
for any society operating in a competitive international framework will
approach the optimal, not because individuals were able to estimate that
outcome, but because they followed the successful pioneers and were
tested in the market place. There is, therefore, no place in this realist
model for rational expectations.

The strategic-imitation model has more in common with the theory of
J. A. Schumpeter (1934, 1939) than any other. The reason is, no doubt,
that Schumpeter's theory of innovation and economic development also
incorporates historical observation. Schumpeter argues that innovations
emerge from an economy in equilibrium when the 'social climate' favours
the emergence of 'New Firms' led by enterprising 'New Men'. Owing to
the creation of monopoly profits, opportunistic imitators enter these new
fields in 'clusters'. This leads to an upswing in economic activity that continues until the monopoly profits are driven down to normal levels and the
supply of innovations dries up. These innovations include new goods, new
processes, new markets, new resources, and new industrial organizations.
   This was not the source of my strategic-imitation model. Indeed, there are
important differences between us. First, the dynamic-strategy model incorporates a theory of decision-making (the strategic-imitation model) that is
relevant to the entire society, whereas Schumpeter's model only attempts to
explain why the class of 'New Men', who have a propensity to innovate,
emerge, and why they are imitated by others. Secondly, the dynamic-
strategy model attempts to explain the emergence and development of broad
strategies and substrategies, while Schumpeter's model is really only an
explanation of the upswing of the business cycle; it does not really explain
the longrun growth rate (Higgins 1959: 137). Third, in my model the strategic pioneers respond to the incentives generated by an unfolding dynamic
strategy, whereas Schumpeter's innovators emerge in response to a vaguely
defined 'social climate'; my model has a dynamic structure that is lacking in
Schumpeter's model. Finally, the dynamic-strategy model incorporates a
theory about the fundamental reason for imitation in decision-making –
which I have called **intellectual economizing** – and Schumpeter's does not.

10.3 THE ROLE OF RULES

What is the role of rules in human decision-making? The existence of
rules is widely assumed to be evidence for the institutionalist argument

about the costs of information. To the contrary, the theory of human behaviour developed here suggests that rules are evidence not of the costs of obtaining information, but of the costs of thinking. Decision-making rules, in other words, emerge from an attempt to economize on nature's most scarce resource – the intellect. The human race is the only species in the last four billion years that has had the capacity to think creatively but, I claim, even we are basically intuitive rather than intellectual in nature. We respond to desires rather than ideas. Ideas are only used by society, and then sparingly, to facilitate the achievement of our desires.

Despite the fact that modern man emerged at least 100 000 years ago, thinking is not an activity that comes easily to us. Systematic thinking can only be achieved after many years of training. While originality in highly formalized thinking – using symbols and a set of simple rules as in mathematics – can be achieved after 15 to 20 years of training, originality in less formalized thinking – the detection of complex relationships between variables in real-world processes – can only be achieved after about 40 years of intensive training. As abstract thinking is a very scarce resource, most people develop routines and rules in order to conduct their daily lives. Even academics, who deal with ideas on a professional basis, go through much of their professional work and their daily lives using formal and informal rules. While intensive thinking may be undertaken when designing research programmes and in drawing conclusions from research results, the major part of scholarly activity involves routine data collection and highly repetitive experiments. And even much of the interpretation of evidence relies on mechanical rules of statistical inference, such as the diagnostic tests in econometrics. The old saying that research is 99 per cent perspiration and 1 per cent inspiration is not far from the mark. Even pure research relies heavily on the existing body of knowledge. Intellectuals, like everyone else, are forced to economize on this extremely scarce resource. We reserve thinking for any unfamiliar or critical problems that arise – yet even here we prefer to follow others who have successfully negotiated these problems rather than think about them ourselves – and we employ rules and customs, which are flexible rather than rigid, for the rest. There are parallels here with the way scarce brain cells are employed in nature. Animals at the top of the food chain (lions and tigers) are able to devote a higher proportion of their brains to the problem of survival than to the production of fatty acids by consuming animals (cattle and sheep) that specialize in this type of production.

Could artificial intelligence (AI) be the answer? Although progress since the mid-1950s (the international conference on AI at Dartmouth College in 1956) has been much slower than expected, critical observers suggest that recent developments have been encouraging and that the 'goal of a general artificial intelligence is in sight, and the 21st-century world will be radically changed as a result' (Lenat 1996: 18). While this will certainly help us to economize on that scarce resource, 'natural intelligence', it will not radically change the way we make decisions. We shall continue to imitate the successful and will employ AI to gather imitative information rather than cost–benefit information, not only because there are no data about the future but also because we just do not make decisions as neoclassical economists believe. AI will merely become an important instrument in the timeless process of strategic imitation.

Yet, despite the fact that intelligence is a very scarce resource, those who specialize in its development – scholars, academics, and intellectuals – receive no more than a modest return for their services. These specialists do not possess a relatively high marginal product because their services are not in great demand. Why? The answer is obvious. Despite the size of our brains, humans are not intellectual beings. We do not use complex systems of thought to make day-to-day decisions, and we do not pursue intellectual leisure activities. The size of the market for intellectual ideas and hard facts about reality, even in the most highly educated societies, is pathetically small. On the one hand, the best decision-makers are decisive 'men (or women) of action' who operate more on intuition than intellect, and on the other we prefer uncomplicated entertainment to intellectual pursuits. Certainly both our leaders (political and business) and our entertainers (popular culture and sport) receive much higher material returns than our intellectuals.[6]

What we need to consider here is exactly who needs rules? There are three main groups who find rules, or institutions, attractive – the **strategists** in pursuit of profits, the strategic imitators, and the **antistrategists** in pursuit of rents. The strategic pioneers have only a limited need for rules, because they do not need to economize so heavily on things intellectual and because they have great confidence in their own ideas and abilities. They are convinced they can take on all comers, and win. They are the rule-breakers of society, who find the conventional way of doing things impossibly restrictive. Those who seek rules are the strategic followers. They need rules to facilitate the dynamic strategy because they are forced to economize heavily on thinking and because they have little confidence in their own ideas. They are the rule-makers in society. When something goes wrong with their plans they believe someone else is to blame and that they should be compensated for their loss. Those who follow others are rarely able to accept responsibility for their actions. They even devise rules to be exercised through the courts of law to ensure this. They are able to do so because they – the strategic followers – are in the majority. A species that must economize so heavily on intelligence is not the type of decision-maker envisaged by supporters of rational expectations.

Secondly, the political representatives of the dynamic strategists use rules to encourage and direct the population to support their initiatives. This is the reason for the strategic struggle in society – so that the strategists can gain control of the instruments of policy to secure the sources of their wealth and income. Finally, rules are demanded by the antistrategists who pursue rent-seeking through the establishment of exploitative systems. The representatives of order, who are the rule-makers in society, wish to direct other individuals to support or comply with their objectives. This is achieved through formal rules, informal conventions, and centralized religion and propaganda. On the other hand, the representatives of chaos, who constitute the creative forces in society, attempt to break down these rules. There is, therefore, a strategic and tactical element in the rules of society.

10.4 CONCLUSIONS

Materialist man, who, in a typically competitive environment, struggles to survive and prosper, provides the endogenous driving force required for a realistic theory of longrun dynamics, which is the centrepiece of the global process of economic development. It is a dynamic principle motivated by biologically determined desires that can only be satisfied through the pursuit of an appropriate dynamic strategy. The resulting dynamic process involves an interaction between the unfolding dynamic strategy and the investment decisions of the strategic pioneers and their more numerous followers. At its core is a decision-making mechanism, called strategic imitation, whereby what is economized is the scarcest resource in nature – intelligence – rather than cost–benefit information. This concept explains the imitation of the few by the many at both the societal and global levels.

At the same time the unfolding dynamic strategy generates the confidence – strategic confidence – required to form the necessary cooperative relationships in order to channel the energy of materialist man into an effective societal strategy. Institutions, therefore, are required to facilitate the dynamic strategy in a way that economizes on intelligence. And the unfolding dynamic strategy gives rise to changing strategic demand – examined in detail in the chapters that follow – which is the key concept in my general theory of the GST.

11 The Global Strategic Demand–Response Mechanism

It is now time to explore the empirical dimensions of the dynamic-strategy model by focusing on the process by which the industrial technological paradigm unfolds. The unfolding paradigm generates a changing **global strategic demand**, which is exploited in varying degree by both First-World and Third-World countries through international trade. While **strategic countries (SCs)** are in the best position to respond to this demand, considerable economic opportunities also exist for **emerging strategic countries (ESCs)** and **nonstrategic countries (NSCs)** with appropriate resources. Opportunities to participate in the **global strategic transition (GST)** vary as global strategic demand waxes and wanes and as its structure changes. This, together with the strategic demand–response mechanism by which it is effected, are the subjects of this chapter.

11.1 FLUCTUATIONS IN GLOBAL STRATEGIC DEMAND

A quantitative impression of the fluctuating fortunes of global strategic demand can be gained by measuring the unfolding technological paradigm. As shown elsewhere (Snooks 1997a), this can be achieved by employing real GDP and real GDP per capita – in this case for the world's most advanced economies, the global strategic core. Figure 11.1 provides a picture of the paradigmatic pathway during the twentieth century. As this is a semi-logarithmic graph, the slopes of the real GDP curves indicate the rates of economic change. The first point to note is that the per capita curve grew more rapidly than the absolute curve, which suggests that, as the twentieth century progressed, technological change played an increasingly important part in the growth process. Secondly, Figure 11.1 suggests that there have been three watershed periods in the unfolding process: the 1940s, the 1970s, and the 1990s. The modest growth of global strategic demand achieved during the first half of the twentieth century more than doubled in the 1950s and 1960s, but fell back to the earlier rate of progress during the 1970s and 1980s, and then, in the 1990s, began to stagnate.

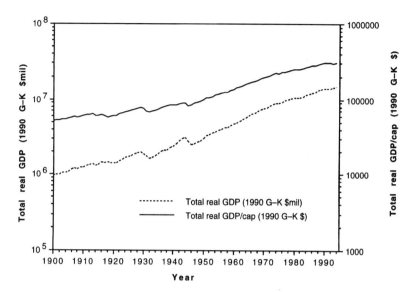

Figure 11.1   Development of the global strategic core: real GDP and real GDP per capita, 1900–94 (Geary Khamis $)
Source: Maddison 1995a: Appendix.

Of course, in the shortrun, strategic demand fluctuated within this longrun framework. Most notably it declined sharply during the 1930s, the mid-1940s, the mid-1970s, and the early 1990s.

These longrun and shortrun changes in global strategic demand had implications for NSCs as well as SCs. As can be seen in Table 11.1, the rate of the strategic transition in Asia (excluding Japan), Latin America, and Africa almost tripled in the 1950s and 1960s, but halved again after 1973. Quite clearly the overall pace of economic development in the Third World depends on the dynamism of the global strategic core. The GST in other words is driven by the world's most advanced economies. This is why the Third World has much to lose from the current neoliberal anti-growth policies of the First World, which have acted as a brake on the expansion of global strategic demand.

11.2   THE CHANGING STRUCTURE OF GLOBAL STRATEGIC DEMAND

Global strategic demand is subject to change not only in its levels but also its structure. Structural change is an outcome of the changing nature of the

Table 11.1 Global growth rates, 1820–1992 (% p.a.)

	The strategic core	Western Europe	European settlements	Southern Europe	Eastern Europe	Asia (excluding Japan)	Latin America	Africa
1820–70	n.a.	0.9	1.4	n.a.	n.a.	0.1	n.a.	n.a.
1870–1913	n.a.	1.3	1.5	0.9	1.2	0.6	1.5	n.a.
1913–50	1.2	1.2	1.3	0.7	1.0	−0.4	1.9	1.0
1950–73	3.3	3.8	2.4	4.8	4.0	2.8	2.4	1.8
1973–92	1.5	1.8	1.2	2.2	−0.8	3.6	0.4	−0.4

Note: The strategic core includes: Australia, Austria, Belgium, Canada, Denmark, Finland, France, Germany, Italy, Japan, the Netherlands, New Zealand, Norway, Sweden, Switzerland, UK, USA.
Sources: Regions from Maddison 1995a: 62–3; strategic core calculated from individual country data in ibid.: Appendix.

technological substrategies pursued by the world's strategic core, which are reviewed in Chapter 2. As the structure of strategic demand changes, so too do the opportunities facing the nations of the world within a given level of strategic demand. Individual nations will respond differently to this changing structure of strategic demand because they possess different factor endowments.

Structural changes that are of interest here are those that have occurred since the Second World War. The golden era of the 1950s and 1960s was dominated by the technological substrategy pursued so successfully by the USA. This involved the redirection of large-scale production and distribution techniques that were developed to exploit the domestic market during the 1910s and 1920s, to supplying the global market after the Second World War. The success of this technological substrategy, which was imitated by other advanced nations, was responsible for the golden era in which many NSCs also participated.

The world economic hegemony exercised by the USA in the 1950s and 1960s came under attack towards the end of the golden age. It was an attack mounted by those societies, Japan and Germany, that had failed in the early 1940s to compete with the USA by developing their own mega-states through conquest. Through the application of a new microelectronic technology, Japan and Germany were able to offer consumers greater variety and choice even though this meant shorter production runs. They were able, as discussed above, to combine the older American mass-production methods with the new microelectronic technology to produce customized consumer products in the form of cars, household appliances, ceramics, textiles, consumer durables, computer software, and food and drink. The resulting shift during the late 1960s and the 1970s away from standardized American products, opened the door for other enterprising societies that had the resource endowments to pursue this new dynamic substrategy. Extraordinary profits were to be made from the value added to inputs rather than the mass use of inputs. Hence the prizes went to those Third-World countries that could supply the new *outputs* rather than those supplying the old *inputs*. Those countries were to be found not in Latin America, South Asia, or Africa, but in East Asia which had the resource endowments to follow in the footsteps of Japan.

The impact of the changing structure of global strategic demand can be seen reflected in Table 11.1 While the growth rate of the global strategic core halved between the golden age and the last quarter of the twentieth century, the rate of growth of Asia (excluding Japan) increased by more than a quarter. The remarkable growth of Asia in these difficult times was centred in East Asia, particularly Singapore, South Korea, Taiwan, Hong Kong, and China. Also, as shown in Table 11.2, growth in East Asia was

Table 11.2 Growth rates in Asia, 1913–92 (% p.a.)

(a) Regions

	East Asia	South Asia	Southeast Asia	Japan
1913–50	0.0	−0.3	−0.4	0.9
1950–73	4.8	0.9	2.3	8.0
1973–92	6.1	2.4	2.6	3.0

(b) Countries

	South Korea	Taiwan	China	Pakistan	India	Bangladesh	Thailand	Indonesia	Burma	Philippines
1913–50	−0.2	0.4	−0.3	−0.3	−0.3	−0.3	0.0	−0.1	−1.3	−0.2
1950–73	5.2	6.2	2.9	1.8	1.6	−0.6	3.2	2.5	1.8	1.8
1973–92	6.9	6.2	5.2	2.7	2.4	2.2	5.3	3.1	1.3	0.7

Source: Based on Maddison 1995a: 63.

about 2.5-fold greater than that in either South Asia or Southeast Asia, despite the impressive performance of Thailand. By contrast, growth in Latin America fell to very low levels, while that in Africa, despite the modest performances of Egypt and Morocco, was negative. Hence, while a number of Asian countries were able to exploit the slow-down in global strategic demand, it was at the expense of the old primary producing countries in Latin America and in Africa that either employed import-replacement policies or had yet to enter into the GST.

While there is some evidence in the late 1990s that the growth rates for societies in Latin America and sub-Saharan Africa may be picking up again, this is unlikely to be sustained if policy-makers in the global strategic core continue to pursue neoliberal antigrowth policies. As we have seen, growth in these countries relies on a strong expansion of global strategic demand. Only those ESCs possessing both the resources to exploit the present difficult global circumstances and the sense to reject the structural adjustment and stability policies of the First World have any chance of participating in the GST.

11.3 THE STRATEGIC DEMAND–RESPONSE MECHANISM

The interaction between strategic demand and strategic response is, as demonstrated in *Longrun Dynamics* (Snooks 1998b), central to the dynamic process in human society. Clearly, the response to strategic demand depends on those conditions concerning the supply of factors of production and of technological and institutional ideas. These conditions are discussed in detail in Chapters 12 to 17. This is necessary because in neoclassical economics the supply side is treated as the active force in society – supply creates its own demand – and in Keynesian economics the supply-side variables are treated as given. Herein lies the fatal flaw of orthodox economics.

Central to the strategic demand–response mechanism is the role of prices. Systematic inflation in the dynamic-strategy model is an outcome of the pressure of strategic demand on existing resources, ideas, and institutions. Generally, the more rapid the strategic unfolding – and, hence, the more rapid the growth of strategic demand – the higher the rate of inflation. The rising levels and relativities of prices (including wages), which create opportunities for extraordinary profits, provide the incentive for the resulting strategic response. It should be noted that the artificial complications introduced by rational expectations theory, a theory introduced to support the flawed Phillips curve, have been swept away by the strategic-imitation model of individual decision-making discussed above. In any case rational expectations would not significantly modify changes in strategic demand, which are driven by biologically determined desires.

It is essential to draw a distinction between different types of inflation. As shown in *Longrun Dynamics*, **nominal inflation** is merely the aggregation of **strategic inflation** and **nonstrategic inflation**. This distinction is particularly important in the case of NSCs and, to a lesser extent, ESCs. Strategic inflation is, as discussed in Chapter 7, the inflation required to generate the strategic response. It is both an essential component and a natural outcome of the dynamic process. In other words, strategic inflation is a stable, non-accelerating function of economic growth. Nonstrategic inflation, on the other hand, is the outcome of exogenous shocks (such as wars, epidemics, and resource bonanzas/ crises) and institutional problems (such as inappropriate action by unstable governments, central banks, and pressure groups). The greater the impact of exogenous shocks, the more difficult it is to see the role played by strategic inflation (ibid.: ch. 11). While this proved to be a minor difficulty when examining SCs, it can be expected to become more significant in the case of NSCs. This lack of clarity in the available data, however, does not invalidate our model.

11.4   THE GROWTH–INFLATION CURVE

The dynamic-strategy model predicts that strategic inflation will be a stable, non-accelerating function of economic growth. This was borne out in the data on SCs for the very longrun (1370–1995), the longrun (1870–1995), and the shortrun (1961–95) (ibid.: ch. 11). It was the attempt to verify the strategic demand–response mechanism that led to the discovery of the growth–inflation curve in the companion volume. The question here is: Does the growth–inflation curve exist for NSCs and ESCs? The dynamic-strategy model predicts that in NSCs nonstrategic inflation will overwhelm strategic inflation owing to their failure to achieve sustained economic growth, and in ESCs strategic inflation will dominate owing to sustained growth generated by successful strategic pursuits. As I am merely seeking some empirical confirmation for these theoretical conclusions rather than building an econometric model, no attempt will be made to maximize the goodness-of-fit coefficient. It is essential to realize that the growth– inflation curve is an empirical reflection of my dynamic model, not the model itself.

Reasonably reliable data on the rates of economic growth and inflation for NSCs and ESCs are restricted to the last few decades. Nevertheless, it has been possible to marshal data for 28 countries for the period 1961 to 1992, and 54 countries for 1983 to 1993. I will deal separately with these two data sets. Figure 11.2 contains scatter diagrams showing the different growth–inflation experience of a large number of Third-World countries, both NSCs and ESCs. Owing to the different roles predicted for strategic inflation in NSCs and ESCs by the dynamic-strategy model, we cannot regard this figure as representing a growth–inflation curve for the Third World. Rather it shows the changing growth–inflation experience as NSCs are transformed into ESCs – as Third-World countries begin to experience rapid and sustained economic growth. As NSCs begin to participate in the GST the nominal rate of inflation falls to less than 10 per cent per annum because nonstrategic inflation, which is the outcome of political and institutional instability, is reduced to the levels experienced by SCs. Nominal inflation will not be reduced to zero because, as nonstrategic inflation falls, strategic inflation, which is required to orchestrate the strategic demand–response mechanism, rises.

A major problem with existing empirical work on inflation and growth in the Third World is that no allowance is made for the transition from

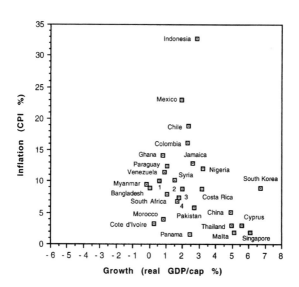

Figure 11.2   Global transition from NSC to ESC: growth and inflation
(a)   1961–93
Notes: 1. Philippines, 2. India, 3. Egypt, 4. Kenya.

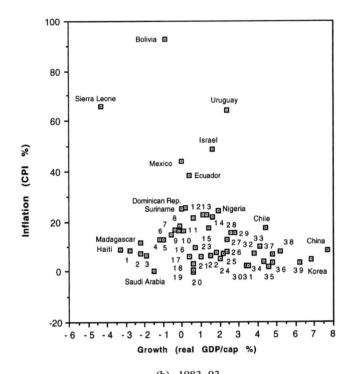

Figure 11.2   Global transition from NSC to ESC: growth and inflation
Source: Calculated from data in IMF, *International Financial Statistics Yearbook*
(various years); and Maddison 1995a.

Notes:							
1	Trinidad & Tobago	11	Paraguay	21	Morocco	31	Malaysia
2	Ethiopia	12	Ghana	22	Tunisia	32	Indonesia
3	Jordan	13	Jamaica	23	Bangladesh	33	Botswana
4	Philippines	14	Colombia	24	Papua New Guinea	34	Cyprus
5	South Africa	15	El Salvador	25	Pakistan	35	Singapore
6	Kenya	16	Honduras	26	India	36	Dominica
7	Myanmar	17	Vanuatu	27	Lesotho	37	Mauritius
8	Syria	18	Venezuela	28	Costa Rica	38	Tonga
9	Guatemala	19	Panama	29	Egypt	39	Thailand
10	Malawi	20	Bahrain	30	Belize		

NSC to ESC, or for the difference between strategic and nonstrategic inflation. The critical problem is that this orthodox empirical work is not informed by any dynamic modelling. Accordingly the growth–inflation experience of Third-World countries is invariably misinterpreted. The usual argument is that growth rates increase because inflation is reduced to lower levels (De Gregorio 1993). By drawing a distinction between

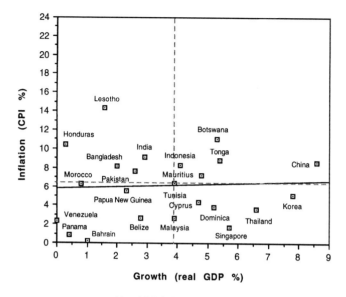

(a)   15% inflation ceiling

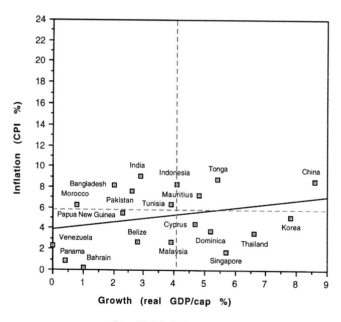

(b)   10% inflation ceiling

Figure 11.3   The growth–inflation curve for ESCs, 1983–93

strategic and nonstrategic inflation and between NSCs and ESCs we can show the fallacy in this work.

An approximate way in which this distinction can be made without involving any value judgements is by imposing an inflationary ceiling on our sample of 54 Third-World nations. This can be expected to eliminate those NSCs experiencing high levels of nonstrategic inflation (if not those experiencing low levels of both inflation and growth). This rough procedure cannot be expected to generate clear-cut growth–inflation curves of the type detected for OECD countries, but they should exhibit a family resemblance. Figure 11.3, which provides the results of imposing an inflation ceiling of 10 per cent per annum, bears out this conclusion.

The growth–inflation curve in Figure 11.3 is both stable and positive, and it exhibits striking similarities with the growth–inflation curves for OECD countries presented in Figure 11.4. But, because of the greater political instability of the Third World, the curve in Figure 11.3 has a low goodness-of-fit coefficient (0.1), and only the constant is significant at the one per cent level.[1] The problem for Third-World countries is that we are unable to successfully filter nonstrategic inflation out of the data in this manner. By introducing regression variables such as the money supply and the wage rate, to allow for nonstrategic inflation, the goodness-of-fit (R^2) increases to 0.45 and the t values improve.[2] This suggests that there is a meaningful strategic growth–inflation curve for Third-World countries, but we cannot see it clearly because it is not possible to isolate strategic inflation. Nevertheless, in the case of both the SCs and the ESCs, the initial inflation requirement for the period 1983 to 1993 is very similar (and significant), at between 4 and 6 per cent per annum. This suggests that, as far as the strategic demand–response mechanism is concerned, SCs and ESCs have a great deal in common. It is the NSCs that are very different.

Closer inspection, however, reveals some interesting differences between SCs and ESCs. First, the SCs appear to require a lower price incentive than ESCs to crank up their growth rates. This is the result of greater resource and institutional difficulties in ESCs in responding to changes in strategic demand. Secondly, owing to a greater clustering of SCs at the lower end of the growth-rate scale, the *typical* rather than the *initial* rate of inflation is somewhat different from that of the ESCs. For the SCs, typical rates of growth and inflation are 1.7 and 4.6 per cent per annum, while for ESCs they are 3.8 and 6.0 per cent per annum respectively. Hence, the typical ESC experiences both higher growth and higher inflation than the typical SC. Yet, while the typical ESC experiences

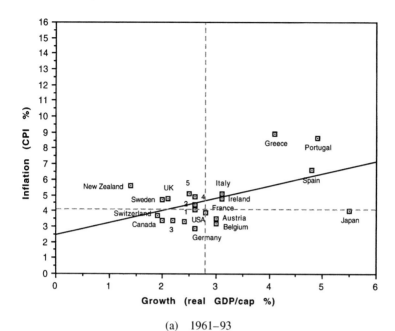

(a)   1961–93

Notes: 1. Australia, 2. Denmark, 3. Netherlands, 4. Norway, 5. Finland

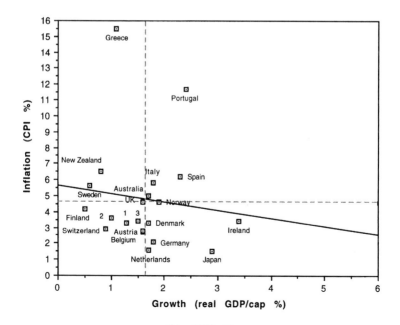

(b)   1983–93

Notes: 1. France, 2. Canada, 3. USA

Figure 11.4   The growth–inflation curve for SCs

a growth rate double that of the typical SC, its inflation rate is only one-third higher. Clearly there is a message here for SC policy-makers: it is possible that the typical growth rate in the First World could be doubled with only a marginal increase in inflation.

This message is underlined by comparing the OECD growth–inflation curves for 1961 to 1993 and 1983 to 1993 in Figure 11.4. While the growth rate for the typical SC in the period 1961 to 1993 was double that for 1983 to 1993, the typical rate of inflation was about the same – just over 4 per cent per annum. In other words, while rapid and sustained growth may generate marginally higher strategic inflation, it also leads to markedly lower nonstrategic inflation owing to the reduced need for government intervention. While we are examining Figure 11.4, it should be noted that the majority (62 per cent) of OECD countries in the period 1983 to 1993 occupied the growth–inflation space in the south-west quadrant formerly (1961 to 1993) occupied by a minority (33 per cent) of these countries. Hence, economic policy in the SCs since the early 1980s, which has been directed at containing inflation, has merely managed to reduce economic growth to very low levels without significantly reducing nominal inflation. Strategic inflation has certainly been reduced but, to compensate for this, nonstrategic inflation has risen. These new results reinforce the conclusions and policy implications drawn in *Longrun Dynamics* (Snooks 1998b).

The important conclusion to arise from this empirical analysis is that the dynamic process of the ESCs is, in terms of the strategic demand–response mechanism, very similar to that of the SCs. Clearly this is not true of the NSCs, which experience low growth, low strategic inflation, and high to very high nonstrategic inflation. Clearly the time has not yet come for the NSCs – they have yet to successfully embark on the GST. Therefore they remain dominated by rent-seekers who find their rewards in nonstrategic inflation, rather than by profit-seekers who respond to strategic inflation.

11.5 CONCLUSIONS

A model has been developed in this chapter to explain the mechanism by which Third-World countries participate in the strategic transition. It shows that the unfolding dynamic strategy of the world's most advanced countries – its strategic core – generates strategic demand that can be exploited by the Third World. Those societies that react to global strategic demand and, thereby, become part of the GST, do so by responding to changes in strategic inflation and relative factor prices. The predictions of the model have been tested against the real world. From the empirical analysis emerges the critically important growth–inflation curve. The major conclusions are that the dynamic process of ESCs is very similar to that of SCs, and that SCs have something to learn from the growth–inflation experience of ESCs. Both findings have important implications for policy.

Part V
Strategic Response

.

12 The Strategy Function

In order to understand the **strategic response** we need a new vision concerning the objectives of human society and its macroeconomic relationships. New visions are reflected in new metaphors. The neoclassical metaphor for modern society is the factory dominated by the machine. Orthodox economists see society as an organization that maximizes its economic output from a given set of inputs and state of technology. They see society working out its objectives within the context of the aggregate production function. This, I argue, constitutes a distorted vision of reality. Human society is not a factory but a strategic organization, and social dynamics is not a production process but a **strategic pursuit**. Accordingly we need to replace the neoclassical production function in our dynamic models with what I propose to call the **strategy function**.

12.1 WHAT IS THE STRATEGY FUNCTION?

The strategy function describes the relationship between the **strategic outcome** of survival and prosperity and the **strategic instruments** by which it is achieved. While this is a static concept, it is determined by the unfolding dynamic strategy. Clearly it involves a more complex macroeconomic relationship than envisaged by orthodox economists. On the one hand, the strategic outcome, which is measured by real GDP per capita (or, better, real Gross Community Income – market plus household income – per household), is considered as an indicator not of 'wellbeing' but of **economic resilience** – the ability to survive and prosper. The strategic instruments, on the other hand, include both the familiar natural resources of capital stock (both physical and human), population, and technological ideas; and the unfamiliar **strategic institutions and organizations**, **strategic leadership**, and **strategic ideas**. The strategy function can be expressed formally as:

$$O = f(N, K, R, A, E, So, Sl, Si)$$

where O is strategic outcome proxied by GDP (or GCI), N is population, K is capital stock, R is natural resources, A is technology, E is economies of scale, So is strategic institutions and organizations, Sl is strategic leadership, and Si is strategic ideas.

219

A New Purpose and a New Way

The strategy function is based on a new vision of mankind's social objective. As suggested above, neoclassical thinking is restricted by the need to see everything in terms of physical production. According to this outlook, the social objective is associated with the technological relationship between aggregate output and the aggregated factors of production including land, labour, and capital. Orthodox economists see human society essentially as a unit of production. It is a vision with a long history in the discipline of economics (see Chapter 15) and it is a vision rejected in this book. Human society, I argue, is an organization dedicated to the creative pursuit of strategic objectives. As such it embraces a set of novel strategic factors that require further consideration here and in subsequent studies.

Strategic Ideas

The concept of strategic ideas is presented for the first time in this book. Essentially this concept concerns the ways in which the strategic instruments can be integrated in order to pursue the strategic objective of survival and prosperity. The accumulated flow of strategic ideas can be regarded as the state of **strategic knowledge**, which defines the strategy function. Strategic ideas are not planned in advance, they arise in a pragmatic manner as individual strategists and their leaders attempt to exploit strategic opportunities in the face of competition and scarce physical and human resource endowments. They are, in other words, a response to changes in strategic demand. These strategic ideas operate at a number of levels, including that of the dynamic strategy and its various substrategies.

At the highest level, strategic ideas are responsible for defining and facilitating the major dynamic strategies of family multiplication, conquest, commerce, and technological change. They include ideas by individuals and their political leaders about how to exploit the prevailing physical and competitive environments by establishing and pursuing viable dynamic strategies. These are the ideas that facilitated Rome's pursuit from the sixth century BC of the conquest strategy in a highly competitive Mediterranean world; that facilitated the Venetian pursuit from the eleventh century of a commerce strategy; and that facilitated Britain's pursuit of the technological strategy from the late eighteenth century. These strategic ideas changed with the demands of an unfolding dynamic strategy.

Each dynamic strategy, which is played out over three or more centuries, consists of a number of substrategies of shorter duration. The technological dynamic strategy, for example, has passed through five substrategies, each of which has involved different combinations of strategic instruments. As these technological substrategies have been outlined in Chapter 2, I will draw attention only to the different characteristics of each here. The pioneering technological substrategy pursued by Britain between the 1780s and 1830s was, as we have seen, based on the strategic ideas and innovations of practical men rather than systematic investment in research and development by large organizations and was undertaken through small-scale enterprises that focused on a limited range of basic commodities in one or two factories, which minimized the degree of capital investment. And these enterprises were based on small partnerships and family firms rather than large public companies. These developments did not just evolve, they were the outcome of the emergence of strategic ideas in response to strategic demand. This was part of the pioneering industrial strategy function. The state in its turn showed strategic leadership by dismantling restrictive mercantilist institutions, providing industrial strategists with new supporting institutions in the form of patent and company law, and by establishing military support and colonial administration for British interests overseas.

The second-generation substrategy was developed by other European countries between the 1830s and 1870s in order to compete with Britain. They, in effect, developed an alternative strategy function that reflected their different physical and competitive environment. Strategists in these countries employed the latest capital-intensive technology in heavy industry, engineering, and chemicals; they invested more heavily in science and research and development; they sought greater assistance from large financial organizations; and they operated through larger corporations that controlled wider networks of larger factories, thereby reaping economies of scale. All this was the outcome of new strategic ideas. Strategic state leadership was provided not only by establishing protective tariffs and infrastructure for the provision of human capital and scientific research, but also by extending the network of their overseas empires, particularly in Africa.

The third-generation substrategy was based on the scale of industrial activity, thereby producing an entirely different strategy function. It was the outcome of determined American industrialists in the late nineteenth century to drive out the Europeans from the world's first mega-market and, later, to make inroads into the global market. The USA was able to achieve this objective by employing existing technological ideas on a scale that no other nation in the late nineteenth century could emulate. This was a triumph for American strategic ideas. By large-scale investment in mass-production techniques, US strategists were able to exploit their large domestic market through the provision of goods and services at prices that Europe was unable to match. The key was the high degree of specialization and division of labour that could be achieved using assembly-line production techniques pioneered by Henry Ford to produce standardized products that were delivered to customers through mass distribution methods. Once the domestic market had been saturated in the 1920s, new strategic ideas were required as the US economy stagnated and descended into depression. Consequently America turned its attention to the global market, particularly during the 1950s and 1960s. This effective new substrategy employed systematic investment in R&D, mega-corporations with high degrees of vertical, horizontal, and geographical (including multinational) integration, together with institutionalized finance. Strategic state leadership was provided in the form of tariffs and subsidies, particularly in the earlier decades, public infrastructure for education and science, as well as military support for strategic interests overseas. America's success was the outcome of effective public and private strategic ideas rather than of technological ideas. It was an outcome of **strategic change** rather than technological change.

The fourth-generation substrategy was pursued by innovative societies to effectively undercut the seemingly impregnable global position of the USA after the Second World War. In the 1960s both Germany and Japan, who had failed in their earlier attempt to meet the American challenge through conquest, adopted the new microelectronic technology. This was a triumph for strategic ideas over sheer size. They were able to seduce consumers away from standardized products by efficiently offering consumers greater variety and choice, even though this meant shorter production runs.

Yet while smaller societies with innovative strategic ideas will always be able to find a temporary niche in the global economy, the future lies with the mega-states (Snooks 1997a: ch. 12). Hence, the fifth substrategy involves emulating the US mega-state status. This is the real force driving the remarkable pace of the European Union over the past generation – remarkable because of the former 1500 years of intense competition between its member nations. And it is the force that will catapult China and a reconstructed Russia into that company during the twenty-first century. The mega-state will replace the nation-state. Yet even these mega strategy functions will reflect the different combinations of strategic instruments that are the outcome of strategic demand operating on different physical and sociopolitical environments.

Strategic Substitution

The central point, therefore, is that societal objectives can be achieved using many different combinations of a wide selection of strategic instruments.

As the above account suggests, the key instrument in this dynamic process is strategic ideas, which are responsible for coordinating the supply response to changes in strategic demand. The implication is that we need to reassess the emphasis currently placed on the dynamic role of technological change. The dynamic-strategy model clearly demonstrates that technological change is merely one way of facilitating the strategic pursuit. We have seen how strategists in the USA were able to achieve world economic hegemony not through the development of a superior technology but, through the use of strategic ideas, to exploit the unprecedented size of their domestic market. And, of course, in the pre-modern era, technological ideas played virtually no driving role in the dynamics of human society.

Strategic substitution – or more correctly the substitution of strategic instruments – can be presented graphically in the limited case of two strategic instruments, A and B, in the two-dimensional Figure 12.1. Strategic instrument B can be substituted for strategic instrument A by moving along any given strategy function while maintaining the level of the strategic outcome. An increase in the level of strategic outcome is achieved by an inward shift of the strategy function from Sf_0 to Sf_1. This strategy function is driven towards the point of origin as the dynamic strategy unfolds and new strategic ideas are forthcoming in response to the resulting changes in strategic demand. An inward shift of the strategy function is an outcome of what I have called strategic change.

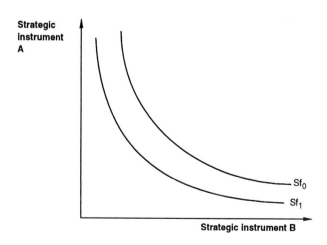

Figure 12.1   The strategy function
Source: Based on discussion in the text.

While this is a limited and static graphical representation, it does illustrate the essential substitutability of strategic instruments. This concept is important when we come to discuss, in the following chapters of Part V, the response of various strategic instruments to changes in strategic demand. In discussing the role of capital formation, for example, a frequent theoretical explanation provided for the persistence of underdevelopment is the low-level equilibrium trap, which is based on the idea that a barrier to economic development is provided by a 'capital requirement' that persistently exceeds the quantity of aggregate saving. What our concept of strategic substitution – which could be examined in the usual marginal terms – suggests is that in an ESC with a low level of aggregate saving, it will be possible to substitute either other sources of funds, namely foreign, or, more interestingly, other strategic instruments for physical capital stock. A familiar form of technical substitution is of labour for capital, but it is also possible to employ strategic ideas to change the design of the existing strategy so that the 'capital requirement' is reduced to equality with aggregate saving. An obvious way of doing this is through the process of borrowing ideas, technological and otherwise, rather than investing in R&D infrastructure.[1] Hence, the low-level equilibrium trap model is an entirely artificial construct that is required in a discipline that has no sense of the strategic transition.

12.2   DOES THE AGGREGATE PRODUCTION FUNCTION EXIST?

The aggregate production function exists only in the minds of neoclassical economists – economists who see human society as one big 'factory' producing goods with varying combinations of 'factors of production', including land, labour, capital, and technological change. Needless to say, the production function is not something that has been observed in society, rather it is a concept that has been extrapolated from the factory (or farm) to the economy. Rather than ask: How does society work and how can we model it?, the neoclassical economist asks: How can we employ our existing body of microeconomic production theory to model the entire society? These are very different questions and they lead to very different interpretations of human society and its macroeconomy.

The aggregate production function approach has led to the idea that any change in real GDP that cannot be accounted for by changes in the main factors of production – capital stock, labour, and land – is the outcome of 'technological progress'. This is a measure not of the dynamic objectives of society but of total factor productivity (TFP). As can be seen from

Table 12.1, estimates of the contribution of technological progress to the growth of real per capita GDP in the 1950s and 1960s range from a remarkably high 73 per cent in the case of Japan to 95 per cent in the case of Germany. Owing to the vagueness of the concept of 'technological progress', the 'sources of growth' school have heroically attempted to allocate this total between improvement in the quality of factors of production (particularly in human skills), economies of scale, and the 'residual' usually regarded as 'advances in technical knowledge'. It is this residual that orthodox economists regard as the key to economic growth. Table 12.1 suggests that the contribution of the technological residual to growth ranged from 23 per cent in Germany to as much as 49 per cent in the USA.

Considerable scholarly effort has been lavished on the estimation of TFP since the pioneering work of Edward Denison (1962) in the early 1960s. One of Denison's books is even tantalizingly entitled *Why Growth Rates Differ* (1967). But instead of modelling the dynamics of human society arising from the pursuit of different dynamic strategies and substrategies, Denison presents a detailed breakdown of the 'supply-side determinants' of economic growth as suggested by the production function analogy. This is an accountant's version of the sources of growth. While it is widely conceded that much of this work is based on arbitrary assumptions (Hayami 1997: 146), it is not recognized that *the whole approach is misconceived*.

The growth accounting results presented in Table 12.1 are the arbitrary outcome of imposing a static production function, derived from the individual firm, on society as a whole. It is an approach that fails to recognize not only that growth takes place in a dynamic rather than a static context, but also that the changing production of goods and services is the least important part of this dynamic process. The strategy function, as we have seen, suggests that we need also to take into consideration changes in strategic institutions/organizations, strategic leadership, and strategic ideas. All these strategic instruments are included in the 'residual'. In other words, the most important components of the strategic response are left unexplained. Even if we accept the static framework implied by the aggregate production function, it will be clear that the role of technological knowledge in the dynamic process is both quantitatively and qualitatively much smaller than is generally assumed.

Strategic ideas, as suggested above, are more central to the modern dynamic process than are technological ideas. While technological ideas are an important dynamic facilitator, they are shaped by strategic ideas. In the pre-modern era, strategic ideas held the same central dynamic role, whereas technological ideas were of minor importance and were subject to the requirements of either conquest or commerce. Hence, we need to

Table 12.1 'Sources of growth' in NNP per employee, selected developed nations, 1950s and 1960s (percentages are in parentheses)

| | 1950–62 | | | | 1948–69 | 1953–71 |
	UK	France	Germany (FR)	USA	USA	Japan
Growth rate per year (%)						
(1) National income	2.38	4.70	6.27	3.36	4.00	8.81
(2) Employment	0.65	0.11	2.43	1.17	1.55	1.46
(3) Income per employee	1.73(100)	4.59(100)	3.84(100)	2.19(100)	2.45(100)	7.35(100)
Contribution to the income growth rate per employee[b]						
(4) Total conventional input	0.21(12)	0.74(16)	0.20(5)	0.40(18)	0.20(8)	1.99(27)
(5) Work hours	0.15(−9)	−0.02(0)	−0.27(−7)	−0.17(−8)	−0.21(−9)	0.21(3)
(6) Capital[c]	0.36(21)	0.76(16)	0.47(12)	0.57(26)	0.41(17)	1.78(24)
(7) Output per unit of conventional input	1.52(88)	3.85(84)	3.64(95)	1.79(82)	2.25(92)	5.36(73)

(8) Age-sex composition	0.04(−2)	0.10(2)	0.04(1)	−0.10(−4)	−0.10(−4)	0.14(2)
(9) Education	0.29(17)	0.29(6)	0.11(3)	0.49(22)	0.44[d](18)	0.36[d](5)
(10) Improved allocation of resources	0.12(7)	0.95(21)	1.01(26)	0.29(13)	0.30(12)	0.95(13)
(11) Economies of scale	0.36(21)	1.00(22)	1.61(42)	0.36(17)	0.42(17)	1.94(26)
(12) Residual (advances of knowledge)	0.79(45)	1.51(33)	0.87(23)	0.75(34)	1.19(49)	1.97(27)
(13) Education (9) + Residual (12)	1.08(62)	1.80(39)	0.98(26)	1.24(66)	1.63(67)	2.33(32)

Notes: [a] Net national product at the factor cost adjusted for irregularities in weather and resource utilization rates.
[b] Relative contributions in percentages with the growth rate of income per employee set as 100 are shown in parentheses.
[c] Total national assests including inventroy, land, and external assets.
[d] Includes 'unallocated'.

Source: Hayami 1997, based on estimates in Denison and Chung 1976 and Denison 1967.

reevaluate the role and importance of technological change. To do so we must abandon the production function in favour of the strategy function.

The temptation to adopt and employ the static aggregate production function to examine the growth of modern nations is difficult to resist in a deductive discipline that has ignored real dynamic processes. It is important to realize that it is impossible to build an insightful body of macroeconomic theory from microeconomic production theory. The reason is that the macroeconomy is not the simple aggregation of firms and farms, rather it is the outcome of the strategic pursuit. Macroeconomics is not microeconomics writ large. It is, however, possible to work back down from the dynamic macro level to the micro level and to relate all the parts through the strategy function. This will lead to a detailed focus on aspects of microeconomics that have been ignored by neoclassical economists.

12.3   CONCLUSIONS

The strategy function – a relationship of strategic pursuits rather than production outcomes – is employed in the remainder of this section both to evaluate the production-function approach normally employed in development economics and to explain the response of strategic instruments to changes in strategic demand. In doing so we provide new explanations for the familiar 'factors of production' of capital, labour, and natural resources and, for the first time, examine the unfamiliar instruments of strategic ideas, strategic leadership, and strategic institutions/organizations. This involves replacing the traditional societal metaphors of the giant factory with that of a strategic organization, and of the production process with the strategic pursuit.

13 Population

The mechanism by which a Third-World nation responds to changes in **global strategic demand** is discussed in Chapter 11, and the role of **strategic ideas** in coordinating the supply response is examined in Chapter 12. We turn now to an analysis of that response. How does a nation's resource endowment change as the global technological paradigm unfolds? To answer this key question we need to examine the **strategic response** of population and labour supply, capital stock (both physical and human), the state of technology, strategic institutions and organizations, strategic ideas, and strategic leadership. Orthodox economists typically treat the major production variables – namely population and technological change – as exogenously determined. They are regarded, therefore, as the sources of societal change. From this springs the idea that supply creates its own demand. By contrast, in this and the following chapters it will be argued that the supply-side variables respond to changes in **strategic demand** and that they possess no driving force of their own.

What determines population increase, and what is its relationship to economic growth? Is population expansion an incentive or a brake upon economic growth? Or neither? Scholars from different disciplines in the social sciences have very different views. In economics the classical (or Ricardian/Malthusian) model assumes that population is a function of real-wage levels and that its expansion brings economic growth to an end through diminishing returns; the Keynesian and neoclassical models deal with it as an exogenous shock that, together with technological change, drives capital formation; and the endogenous growth model treats it as an outcome of family income and education. In each case these arbitrary assumptions are, as argued in *Longrun Dynamics* (Snooks 1998b), the supply-side alternative to modelling dynamic demand. Only in development economics has an attempt been made to examine the relationship between economic growth and population increase. But even here attention is focused on simple supply-side conceptions, such as the low-level equilibrium trap model (Nelson 1956). Even demographers see population growth as exogenously determined by forces that impact on fertility and mortality in a process known as the 'demographic transition'.

None of these approaches to the causes and consequences of population expansion is particularly persuasive. It will be argued that a new explanation is required. In the dynamic-strategy model, population expansion is largely a response to changes in strategic opportunities. Effective decisions about fertility and participation in the market sector are made by families in response to incentives generated by a changing strategic demand. The requirement for additional workers depends on the nature of the dominant **dynamic strategy** and the stage reached in its exploitation. These issues form the focus of the remainder of the chapter.

13.1 DEMOGRAPHIC OR STRATEGIC TRANSITION?

The concept known as the 'demographic transition' has taken on the status of a dynamic model. In demography it is widely regarded as having both explanatory and predictive power. The 'demographic transition' concept owes its origins to the observation of changes in mortality and fertility rates that have taken place in the Western world over the past two centuries, and it has been used to predict changes in these variables for the Third World. Despite its popularity there is a problem. In reality the 'demographic transition' is merely a generalized pattern of historical events and can make no valid claim to being a dynamic model. Those who make this claim are blind to the old historicist fallacy (Snooks 1998a: ch. 5). I will outline the demographic and neoclassical approaches to this important but confused issue, and then outline and econometrically test the strategic approach which employs a realist dynamic model.

The Demographic Approach

Not surprisingly, the most detailed research on the causes and consequences of population change has been undertaken by demographers rather than economists. The latter wrongly regard this as being outside their field of expertise. A characteristic of the demographic approach to societal change is the failure to employ a dynamic model to sort out the causal links between population expansion, economic growth, and sociopolitical change. Variations in mortality and fertility are generally seen as the outcome of exogenous shocks and are not modelled endogenously. They are treated as the outcome of biological and environmental forces. Massimo Livi-Bacci (1992: 2), for example, tells us:

> To begin with, we can categorize these [demographic] forces and obstacles as biological and environmental. The former are linked to the laws of mortality and reproduction which determine the rate of demographic growth; the latter determine the resistance which these laws encounter and further regulate the rate of growth. Moreover, biological factors

affect one another reciprocally and so are not independent of one another.

This is, in other words, a supply-side approach which suggests that population will approach as closely to its biological maximum as various environmental barriers including nutrition, heating – which in turn depends on the available biomass – and disease will allow. These constraints, we are told, can be modified in the longrun by human adaptation, including body size and immunity to disease, and in the shorter term by controlling access in society to sexual partners, by sexual taboos, the duration of breastfeeding, and the frequency of abortion and infanticide (ibid.: 36–7).

This type of supply-side analysis is not well suited to explaining the relatively sudden change in Europe's historical relationship between mortality and fertility, which resulted in a rapid increase in population from 111 million in 1750 to 395 million in 1950. Clearly this dramatic change, which has become known as the 'demographic transition', cannot be explained in terms of changing biological or environmental forces. Instead it is explained in terms of non-demographic forces, which are exogenous to the demographic-transition 'model'. Once again Livi-Bacci (ibid.: 104–5) tells us:

> The mortality decline which began in the second half of the eighteenth century is generally ascribed partly to exogenous factors, including the reduced frequency of epidemic cycles and the disappearance of the plague; partly to the reduction of famine due to better organization; and to sociocultural practices which helped to reduce the spread of infectious diseases and improve survival, especially of infants. Mortality decline spurred demographic growth and so increased pressure on available resources, which in turn led to lower fertility by means of both reduced nuptiality and the spread of deliberate attempts to limit births.

Hence, the exogenous impact on mortality leads to Malthusian pressures that are resolved through individual fertility control measures that are an outcome of urbanization generated by the Industrial Revolution (namely the growing costs of child bearing in an urban industrial society – an argument that appears to have been taken from neoclassical economists such as Gary Becker, whose model is discussed in the next section).

Rather than develop a dynamic model to explain the 'demographic transition', demographers treat the superficial pattern of demographic events as if it were a dynamic model. Figure 13.1, adapted from Livi-Bacci (ibid.: 103), is regarded as 'an abstract model of transition', when in reality it is

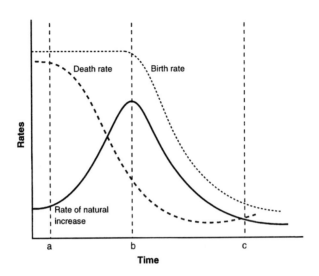

Figure 13.1   Demographic-transition 'model'
Source: Based on Livi-Bacci 1992: 103.

merely a generalized description of changing rates of mortality, fertility, and population. Economists would regard this figure as a diagrammatic representation of 'stylized facts'. It shows merely that in Europe during the past 200 years the rate of natural population increase rose rapidly owing to a decline of death rates at a time when the birth rate retained its earlier levels, and then declined rapidly as the birth rate fell to join the new low death rates. Some (Birdsall 1988) have attempted to embellish this descriptive framework with a theoretical gloss by dividing the demographic transition into three phases: in the first phase the death rate begins to fall from a traditional situation where both birth and death rates are high; in the second phase the death rate stabilizes; and in the third phase the birth rate begins to fall more rapidly than the death rate. The only problem with this more prescriptive form of the demographic transition concept is that very few societies actually passed through these phases (Hayami 1997: 56–7). By using this 'model' to predict demographic change in the Third World, demographers are guilty of the old historicist fallacy of expecting superficial patterns of historical events to hold in the future.

An obvious limitation of the 'model', which is recognized by demographers, is its inability to explain the considerable variation at the national level of the 'demographic transition'. Some nations experienced long transitions that involved relatively small population increases, whereas others passed through shorter transitions involving larger expansions of population. It is claimed, for example, that France took 185 years (1785–1970) to complete its 'transition', during which time its population increased by a factor of 1.62, whereas the German 'transition' took only half that time – 90 years (1876–1965) – and population increased by the larger factor of 2.11 (Chesnais 1986: 294, 301; Hayami 1997: 58). Variations of this nature pose difficulties for demographers wishing to examine the causal relationship between population expansion and economic growth.

And it is a problem that assumes greater proportions when the demographic-transition 'model' is applied to the Third World. As Table 13.1 shows, there are vast demographic differences between the various regions of the Third World, and even more between its individual societies. These differences encompass crude birth and death rates, total fertility rates, mortality rates, and rates of population increase. Take the total fertility rates for example: in the early 1950s, most Third-World countries experienced a rate of about six children per average female, whereas in the early 1990s this ranged from 1.9 in East Asia to 5.7 in Africa, with compound rates of population growth ranging widely from 1.0 to 2.7 per cent per annum. Clearly the demographic-transition 'model' cannot explain these differences. It can only suggest that *if* the Third World responds in a broadly similar way to the First World, then fertility rates will *eventually* fall to match the decline in mortality rates that began in the mid-twentieth century.

Even so, the 'model' cannot predict when or explain why. Nor should it be expected to. Demographers really see the 'demographic transition' as a self-contained biological process. We are told that it is 'a complex process of passage from disorder to order and from waste to economy' (Livi-Bacci 1992: 101). The move from biological 'waste' to 'economy' involves a reduction in birth and death rates of between 30 and 40 per thousand to about 10, together with a consequent decline in the average number of children per woman from five to less than two. And the shift from biological 'disorder' to 'order' is seen in terms of children routinely surviving their parents rather than the reverse. These may be states of existence recognized by demographers but they have no objective standing in the real and dynamic world.

It is hardly surprising, therefore, that demographers experience difficulties in establishing a quantitative relationship between population expansion and economic growth. After examining the statistical relationship between population change and economic growth for 16 industrialized countries between 1870 and 1987, Livi-Bacci (ibid.: 138) was forced to acknowledge that 'the long-term experience of wealthy nations, whose

Table 13.1 Demographic indicators of world population, 1950–96

Region	Population (millions)		Annual rate of growth (%)		Birth rate (per 1000)		Death rate (per 1000)		Fertility (per woman)		Life expectancy at birth	
	1950	1996	1950–90	1990–5	1950–5	1990–5	1950–5	1990–5	1950–5	1990–5	1950–5	1990–5
Global	2515	5768	1.86	1.5	37.4	24	19.7	9	5.00	3.0	45.9	64
First/Second World[a]	832	1175	0.93	0.4	22.6	12	10.1	10	2.84	1.7	65.7	74
Third World	1683	4593	2.22	1.8	44.6	27	24.3	9	6.18	3.3	41.0	62
Africa	224	739	2.63	2.7	48.9	41	27.0	14	6.61	5.7	38.0	52
North America	166	299	1.27	1.0	24.6	15	9.4	9	3.47	2.0	69.0	76
Latin America	165	484	2.50	1.7	42.5	25	15.3	7	5.86	2.9	51.2	68
East Asia	671	1434	1.72	1.0	40.8	18	23.3	7	5.72	1.9	42.7	70
Southeast Asia	182	490	2.24	1.7	44.1	26	24.4	8	5.99	3.2	41.2	64
Southern Asia[b]	479	1392	2.30	1.9	44.9	29	25.1	10	6.11	3.7	38.8	60
Western Asia[c]	42	171	2.86	2.2	47.5	30	23.4	7	6.78	4.1	43.5	66
Europe	393	729	0.59	0.2	19.8	11	11.0	11	2.59	1.6	65.3	73
USSR	180	—	1.18	—	26.3	—	9.2	—	2.82	—	64.1	—
Russian Federation	—	148	—	0.0	—	11	—	13	—	1.5	—	66
Oceania	13	29	1.73	1.4	27.6	19	12.4	8	3.83	2.5	60.8	73
China	555	1232	1.80	1.1	43.6	18	25.0	7	6.24	1.9	40.8	68
India	358	945	2.17	1.8	44.1	27	25.0	10	5.97	3.4	38.7	60

Notes:
[a] Europe, USSR/Russian Federation, North America, Australia, New Zealand, Japan.
[b] India, Pakistan, Bangladesh, Afghanistan, Iran.
[c] Middle-eastern countries.
Sources: United Nations 1989; United Nations 1996.

populations grew at different rates, does not allow us to attribute a particular economic role to demographic growth'. For the demographer, the problem is that, although these wealthy countries have experienced similar rates of economic growth, their demographic changes are very different. *In other words, each of these industrialized countries was able to achieve its growth objective by employing different demographic programmes.* Although the demographic-transition 'model' cannot explain these different demographic outcomes, the dynamic-strategy model, which embodies the concept of **strategic substitution**, can do so.

Demographers are convinced, however, that the general, if not specific, role played by population in economic development has changed over time. For Europe during the eighteenth century, population is seen in Malthusian terms with population pressing on natural resources and leading to a decline in living standards. But after the Industrial Revolution, they claim, population became, in some sort of vague and non-quantifiable way, a positive force for economic growth. Livi-Bacci (ibid.: 132), for example, asserts that the earlier

> difficult balance between population and land was broken as economic and demographic growth became not competing but complementary forces. This, however, is only a general picture; clearly the attempt to describe more specifically the nature of the relationship between population and the economy is a difficult undertaking.

It is particularly difficult without the assistance of a realist dynamic model. By developing such a model – the dynamic-strategy model – it is possible to consistently account for periods of *both* declining and increasing living standards. They are the outcome of exhausting (or non-existing) and expanding dynamic strategies respectively. Hence, the so-called Malthusian crisis is, in reality, a **strategic crisis**.[1]

Some scholars of agricultural development, however, have challenged the strict Malthusian view. Both Clark and Haswell (1964) and Boserup (1965) have suggested that under certain conditions population expansion in a non-industrial society can lead to positive economic development. Basically the model suggests that the slow increase in population generates a growing demand for food and raw materials that encourages the development of a more intensive agricultural technology that leads to increased production and, hence, to further population expansion. In the process the agricultural society is transformed. This is something like the Ricardian convergence model with technological change added, leading to slow and continuous economic development. The only problem is that the model has no driving force. What is it that generates population increase in the first place? We are not told. Population has not been modelled endogenously.

This is a typical problem with the demographic approach. While it is not difficult to account for changing mortality, at least in an informal way, fluctuations in fertility are a different matter. In the European 'demographic transition' the decline in mortality is seen as the outcome of the reduced frequency of epidemics (plague and influenza), together with a growing control over infectious diseases (measles, scarlet fever, diphtheria), respiratory diseases (bronchitis, pneumonia, influenza), and intestinal diseases (diarrhoea, enteritis) as living standards rose. Higher living standards gave rise to better personal and social hygiene, better medical knowledge, better waste disposal and water supply and, ultimately, the introduction of vaccination and immunization. The resulting reduction in mortality rates arose in particular from the impact of these changes upon the health of infants. In the Third World the fall in mortality, which occurred after the Second World War (see Table 13.1), has been attributed to the improvement in medical knowledge and basic services transferred to poorer countries from the global strategic core.

What is more problematical for the demographer is the explanation of declining fertility in Europe in the past and in the Third World in the future. The basic reason is that declining fertility is an outcome not of obvious changes in human activities but of more obscure changes in human preferences and attitudes. General observations are usually made to the effect that the average number of children per woman ('total fertility') falls as real GDP per capita rises or as the degree of adult, particularly female, education or literacy rises (Livi-Bacci 1992: 121–3, 165–6). But these relationships, shown in Figure 13.2, are not very precise, and, in the absence of a dynamic model, they lead scholars into the mire of spurious correlation. It is a problem with serious implications, because these spurious correlations are used as a basis for population policy in poor countries that cannot afford to waste scarce resources. As it is absurd to suggest that governments attempt to reduce fertility by increasing real GDP per capita (when the reason they want to reduce fertility is to increase living standards), policy-makers insist that fertility can be reduced by a programme of adult female education. While such a programme may be regarded as important for a number of other reasons, *it will have no significant impact on fertility.* The problem is an outcome of confusion regarding causation.

The Productionist Approach

The neoclassical approach to fertility decline in the modern world was pioneered by Gary Becker. His most well-known work on this subject is

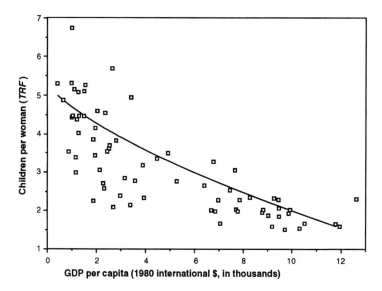

(a) Relation between real GDP per capita and children per woman (*TRF*) in 16
industrialized countries (1870, 1913, 1950, 1973, 1987).

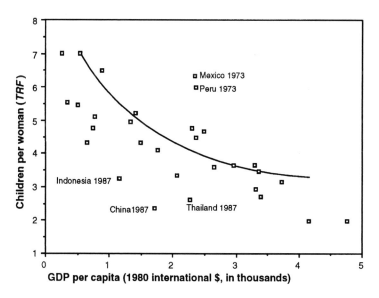

(b) Per capita GDP and average number of children per woman (*TRF*) in
15 less-developed countries of Asia and Latin America (1973 and 1987)
Figure 13.2   The conventional explanation of fertility change
Source: Based on Livi-Bacci 1992: 123, 165.

A Treatise on the Family (Becker 1981). As we have come to expect of this approach, it is static in nature and employs the supply-side focus of the ubiquitous production function. Hence, when Becker talks about the demand for children, he really means how changing net costs of 'producing' children affect the decision to have them. There is no attempt to construct a dynamic model in which dynamic demand is the centrepiece.

Becker, like most supply-side analysts, treats the demand for children as an ever-present force. As such it can be passed over for the supply side. He does not recognize that the demand for children is determined by strategic demand, which changes as the dynamic strategy unfolds. Becker begins by asserting that 'men and women strongly prefer their own children to children produced by others' (Becker 1987, II: 281). It is this unexplored 'preference' that enables economists to adopt a supply-side and, in particular, a production-function approach. Here Becker is firmly in the productionist tradition. He further asserts that 'the desire for own children means that the number of children in a family is affected by supply conditions' (ibid.). The so-called demand side encompasses only family 'preferences' for children and other commodities, and it is made operational through the static utility maximization concept.

Family utility is maximized subject to the household production functions for children and other commodities, and to the constraints on family resources. These resource constraints include money income (a product of the wage rate and time spent in market work) and the time available for household production. In explaining the decline in fertility, Becker focuses exclusively on the production costs for children. This is rationalized in the following way (ibid.):

> The basic theorem of demand states that an increase in the relative price of a good reduces the demand for that good when real income is held constant. If the qualification about income is ignored, then, in particular, an increase in the relative price of children would reduce the children desired by a family.

Becker further tells us that the net cost of children is increased and, hence, the demand for them is decreased, when opportunities for child labour 'as in traditional agriculture' decline or when the value of a mother's time rises. He then concludes that:

> During the past one hundred years, fertility declined by a remarkable amount in all Western countries ... Economic development raised the relative cost of children because the value of parents' time increased,

agriculture declined, and child labour became less useful in modern farming. (Ibid.: 282)

This is Becker's explanation of the demographic transition. It is, to his mind, the outcome of any set of forces that causes the net production costs of children to rise and, hence, of fertility to fall. The limitations of this approach are obvious. He does not try to model these forces, because that would require a dynamic theory that is lacking in neoclassical economics. It is enough for Becker that a few random outcomes of this dynamic process – the decline in traditional agriculture and the rising value of women's work – are consistent with his static production model. Nor does he try to systematically examine all the important outcomes of this dynamic process. He appears unaware of the increased employment opportunities for children in urban sweatshops and mines in ESCs. More fundamentally, he does not realize that family demand for children is not an ever-present force but that it fluctuates in response to changes in strategic demand as the dominant dynamic strategy unfolds.

My initial dissatisfaction with this supply-side approach to changing fertility led to an attempt in *Portrait of the Family* (Snooks 1994a) to develop a dynamic model.[2] This was attempted by constructing and testing data on household size and the value of household work for Australia over the period 1788 to 1990. By developing a model to analyse household change as a function of the unfolding technological strategy or of strategic demand (although these terms were not precisely defined at that time), proxied by the capital/labour ratio, and of the supply response of households, proxied by the female/male wage ratio, it was possible to explain 99 per cent of the decline in the size of families between 1946 and 1990. The detailed results, given in the notes, show that all variables are significant and have the correct sign and that the diagnostic tests are satisfactory.[3] This model, and others like it in *Portrait*, was the direct ancestor of the dynamic-strategy theory centred on strategic demand that was first developed in *The Dynamic Society* (Snooks 1996). It was the first step in a move away from the simplistic, supply-side, neoclassical production models employed by orthodox economists – by the productionists.

The Strategic Approach

In contrast to the 'demographic transition' concept, the dynamic-strategy model embodies a demand-side approach. Population change is interpreted as a response by families in any society to changes in its strategic demand. It will be argued that this dynamic model can explain not only the growth of population but the relationship between demographic and economic variables that cannot be adequately explained by demographers or orthodox economists. Accordingly the dynamic-strategy model provides a better basis for population policy in the Third World than the demographic-transition 'model' and the neoclassical human-capital model.

The demographic-transition 'model', as we have seen, is unable to explain either the fluctuating fortunes of fertility or the different demographic experience of nations within either the First or Third Worlds. In contrast, the dynamic-strategy model is able to explain both. It interprets the different fertility and population experience of different nations experiencing similar growth rates in terms of the different strategies and substrategies they employ in their efforts to survive and prosper. In the Western World since the seventeenth century a number of different dynamic strategies have been pursued by different nations, including the commerce strategy by England and the Dutch Republic in the seventeenth and eighteenth centuries; the conquest strategy by Spain, France, Austria, and Prussia from the seventeenth to the early nineteenth centuries; and the technological strategy by Britain and, later, Western Europe, from the late eighteenth century.

These different dynamic strategies generated very different strategic demands within Western Europe for physical and human capital, for technological, institutional, and strategic ideas, as well as for population which, through strategic substitution, led to different uses of these **strategic instruments**. As far as the commerce strategy is concerned, its pursuit by Western Europe in the seventeenth and eighteenth centuries led to a rapid expansion of acquired territory in the rest of the world (see Figure 13.3). Colonies were required to exploit and protect resources, goods, and trading routes essential to extracting monopoly profits from commerce. And in order to establish and maintain these colonies over the longrun it was necessary to generate an increase in population by widening the gap between fertility and mortality rates in the imperial country. This involved a decision-making process at both the micro and macro levels. Families responded to the growing economic opportunities provided at home and overseas through the commerce strategy by increasing the number of children in order to maximize their probability of survival and prosperity; and the ruling elites, who came from wealthy merchant families, encouraged and facilitated this response (Snooks 1997a: ch. 10).

The commerce strategy was initiated in Western Europe by Portugal in the sixteenth century and was taken over first by the Dutch Republic and, from the mid-seventeenth century, by England. Owing to the dominance of England/Britain throughout much of the seventeenth and eighteenth

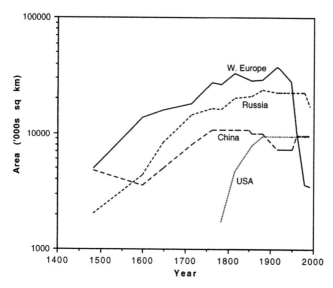

Figure 13.3   Territorial dimensions of the mega-state, 1450–2000: Europe, Russia, China, and USA

Source: Snooks 1997: 426.

centuries it will become our focus here. Figure 13.4 shows that the area of England/Britain's empire increased rapidly during the first half of the seventeenth century, slowed appreciably during that century's second half, resumed its rapid expansion during the first half of the eighteenth century, declined for a generation after the 1760s once the commerce strategy had been exhausted, and only increased again (for a further century) with the discovery and pursuit of the technological strategy.

It is interesting how closely fertility follows that pattern (see Figure 13.5). While the British Empire was expanding in the first halves of the seventeenth and the eighteenth centuries, fertility, particularly in relation to mortality (here measured inversely by changing expectation of length of life at birth), remained at high levels, only falling or stagnating when growth of the Empire stagnated or declined, as in the second half of the seventeenth and the late eighteenth centuries.

Britain's commerce strategy generated population expansion because of new opportunities not only in the Empire but also in the Empire's metropolis. London grew as the Empire grew, to a size that could not be sustained by a pre-industrial technology if the commerce strategy ever exhausted itself (which it did in the mid-eighteenth century). London's population,

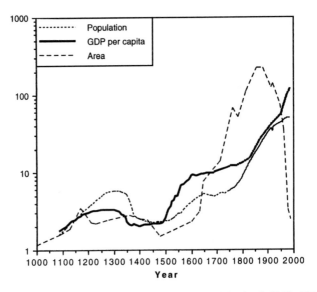

Figure 13.4   Income, population and empire of England, 1000–2000
Source: Adapted from Snooks 1997a: 276.

which had been 50 000 in 1500 (the optimum size warranted by pre-industrial technology), expanded rapidly to 200 000 in 1600, 575 000 in 1700,
and 948 000 in 1800 (Bairoch *et al.* 1988: 33). London's commerce competitors, Lisbon in Portugal and Amsterdam in the Dutch Republic, also
expanded rapidly to 1700 when they were eclipsed by the English.
Between 1500 and 1700 Lisbon increased from 65 000 to 180 000 and
Amsterdam from 15 000 to 200 000; and thereafter they both stagnated.
Through commerce London had become the greatest city in the world.

    Prior to the Industrial Revolution the commerce strategy had no rival in
terms of impact on Western European fertility (see Table 13.2). The conquest strategies of Spain, France, Austria, and Prussia generated economic
growth with a much slower expansion of population than in Britain from
the mid-eighteenth century (Wrigley and Schofield 1981: 214). The underlying reason is that conquest on the limited Western European scale did
not require the sustained increase in fertility (relative to mortality) needed
to build a global commerce empire. Paris, a conquest metropolis that had
always been much larger than London, did double its size to 580 000
between 1500 and 1800, but even so it was surpassed by London in 1700.
By 1800 Paris was only half the size of its old rival. With Spain's pursuit
of conquest from the late fifteenth century, Madrid grew rapidly from
13 000 in 1500 to 140 000 in 1700, but with the exhaustion of that strategy

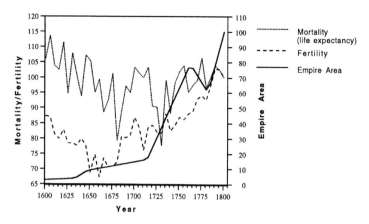

Figure 13.5   Empire area, mortality and fertility of England, 1000–2000
Note: 1801 = 100.
Sources: Wrigley and Schofield 1981: Appendix; Snooks 1997a: 276.

in the late seventeenth century the Spanish capital stagnated (Bairoch *et al.* 1988: 18, 28).

The technological strategy, which was pursued throughout Western Europe during the second half of the nineteenth century, had a similar effect on the mortality, but a differential impact on the fertility, of individual nations. Once again the different fertility responses were due to the different technological substrategies pursued. Each substrategy generated a different form of strategic demand, which had a different population requirement and, hence, a different set of incentives for the families in each society.

The Industrial Revolution was forged in Britain, a society that, through commerce, had created the world's largest empire. It was the exhaustion of the commerce strategy in the mid-eighteenth century that had led the British to seek an alternative way to achieve their materialist objectives (Snooks 1997a: 338–63). While that alternative, the technological strategy, did not require additional territory to generate rapid and sustained economic growth, it was only through territorial control that the new strategy could be defended. In effect it was the extension of the European balance of power concept, which had existed for a millennium, throughout the rest of the world. And it led to a grab for territory by Western Europe (see Figure 13.3). Only after development of nuclear weapons was the empire unnecessary (ibid.: 293–5). As the leading industrial nation throughout the nineteenth century, Britain maintained its world dominance built up before 1760 (see Figure 13.4). This in turn required the maintenance of high fertility rates relative to death rates (see Table 13.3).

Table 13.2   Metropolitan populations in Western Europe and the USA, 1600–1996 (millions)

	1500	1600	1700	1750	1800	1850	1900	1950	1996
London	0.05	0.20	0.57	0.68	0.95	2.23	6.62	10.37	7.6[a]
Britain	5.00	6.25	9.25	10.00	16.00	28.00	42.00	54.00	58.14
London as % of Britain	1.00	3.20	6.16	6.80	5.94	7.96	15.76	19.20	13.07[a]
Amsterdam	0.015	0.05	0.20	0.21	0.21	0.22	0.51	0.86	1.1
The Netherlands	0.9	1.50	2.00	2.00	2.00	3.00	5.25	10.00	15.58
Amsterdam as % of the Netherlands	1.67	3.33	10.00	10.50	10.50	7.33	9.71	8.60	7.06
Paris	0.225	0.30	0.50	0.57	0.55	1.05	3.33	5.53	9.6
France	15.00	10.50	22.00	24.00	29.00	36.00	41.00	42.00	58.33
Paris as % of France	1.50	2.86	2.27	2.38	1.90	2.92	8.12	13.17	16.46
Berlin	0.009	0.01	0.06	0.11	0.17	0.44	2.42	3.35	3.3
Germany	9.00	12.00	13.00	15.00	18.00	27.00	43.00	70.00	81.92
Berlin as % of Germany	0.10	0.08	0.46	0.73	0.94	1.63	5.63	4.79	4.03
Rome	0.055	0.10	0.14	0.16	0.15	0.18	0.49	1.57	2.7
Italy	10.00	12.00	13.00	15.00	19.00	25.00	34.00	47.00	57.23
Rome as % of Italy	0.55	0.83	1.08	1.07	0.79	0.72	1.44	3.34	4.72
New York	—	—	0.02	—	0.59	3.10	7.27	14.83	16.4
USA	—	0.80	1.00	2.00	6.00	24.00	76.00	150.00	269.44
New York as % of USA	—	—	2.00	—	9.83	12.92	9.57	9.89	6.09

Note: [a]Changed boundaries.
Sources: McEvedy and Jones 1978; Bairoch et al. 1988; United Nations 1996; United Nations 1997.

Table 13.3 Average number of children per woman (TFR),
Western Europe, 1750–1950

Country	1750	1775	1800	1825	1850	1875	1900	1925	1950
England	5.28	5.87	5.54	5.05	4.56	3.35	1.96	2.15	2.04
Sweden	4.21	4.34	4.68	4.40	4.28	3.51	1.90	2.05	1.98
Germany	—	—	—	—	5.17	3.98	2.80	2.06	1.69
France	—	—	—	3.42	3.27	2.60	2.14	2.59	2.11
The Netherlands	—	—	—	—	4.98	3.98	2.86	2.76	1.88

Source: Abstracted from Livi-Bacci (1992: 122).

The other major Western European powers, such as France, Germany, and Italy, joined in the scramble for Africa and for other poorer regions of the world, but they had industrialized too late to compete seriously with Britain for overseas territories. Accordingly, their strategic demand for population was considerably less than Britain's at its empire zenith. This can be seen in Table 13.3, which shows the total fertility rate of a range of Western European nations. Britain's fertility rates only remained higher than those of other Western European countries until its empire began declining rapidly from the middle of the nineteenth century. Similarly, the largest cities in continental Europe were unable to rival London until then (see Table 13.2). Only after the exhaustion of Britain's pioneering technological substrategy by the end of the Edwardian period did the growth of London slow down and was it surpassed by the cities of the new world which served the mega-market of North America.

The relationship between strategic demand and fertility suggested by my dynamic model can be tested formally. Of course, as we are dealing with the seventeenth and eighteenth centuries, we need to be sensitive to problems of measurement error, particularly as these may lead to autocorrelation. The dependent variable in my population model is fertility, which has been measured by estimates of the 'gross reproduction rate' (Wrigley and Schofield 1981: 530), and the main explanatory variable is strategic demand, which has been proxied by estimates of empire size in terms of millions of square kilometres (Snooks 1997a: 276). Territory is a good proxy for strategic demand in the pre-Industrial Revolution period, because the dominant dynamic strategies of both commerce and conquest required the continual inflow of external resources to generate economic growth. As we are really trying to explain the changes of fertility in relation to mortality we should rerun the regression using both empire size and mortality (life expectancy) as explanatory variables.

The regression results are presented in Table 13.4. These results confirm the visual examination of Figure 13.5. Using the territorial proxy for strategic demand it is possible to explain up to two-thirds of the variation of fertility throughout the two centuries from 1601 to 1801. All coefficients are highly significant, and the regressions pass the tests for heteroskedasticity and functional form. The only problem is the presence of autocorrelation, probably due to the nature of the data, which affects the efficiency of the estimates but does not deny the nature of the relationship. *Overall it can be concluded that a strong and significant relationship exists between strategic demand generated by the commerce strategy and the resulting fertility in England during the seventeenth and eighteenth centuries.* Interestingly, when we test the strategic-demand/fertility relationship for

Table 13.4   The strategic-demand/fertility relationship, England, 1601–1801

Dependent variable: Fertility (GRR)	Regression 1	Regression 2
Size (sq. km) of territory	7.109	717.09
	(7.782)	(8.600)
Mortality (life expectancy)		0.023
		(2.9742)
Constant	2.052	1.227
	(61.294)	(4.399)
$\bar{R}^2$	0.60	0.67
D–W	0.611	0.839
Heteroskedasticity	0.830–2.321	0.005–2.263
Ramsey Reset	1.796–2.850	0.308–0.543

Notes:
t ratios are in parenthesis.
GRR = gross reproduction rate.

the longer period 1601 to 1871, which covers the entire ascent and initial descent of empire, we are able to explain 82 per cent of the variation in fertility using a polynomial function to the power of four. These results confirm my dynamic-strategy model and refute the 'demographic transition' approach.

In the same way the different strategies employed by Third-World societies have a differential impact on their fertility rates. The fundamental reason for the different overall population response as between the First and Third Worlds (see Figure 13.6) is the very existence of the First World. Mortality in the Third World has been determined by the economic strategies of SCs rather than NSCs. Although expressed differently, this is widely acknowledged (Wrigley 1969; Birdsall 1988; Hayami 1997). Fertility, on the other hand, is determined by the economic strategies of the NSCs, which include nondynamic as well as dynamic strategies.

As we have seen, the Third World consists of NSCs that have failed to adopt successful dynamic strategies, and ESCs that have already embarked upon the GST. Unsuccessful NSCs are generally ruled by rent-seeking elites and are populated by family groups pursuing nondynamic strategies. The main nondynamic strategy is procreation, which is pursued not to gain greater control over unused resources (the objective of the dynamic strategy

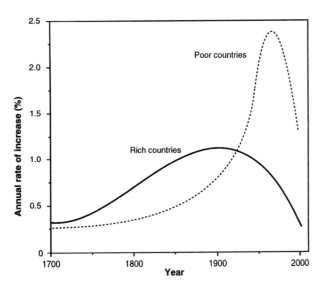

Figure 13.6   Comparison of demographic transitions: rates of increase for poor
and rich populations (1700–2000)
Source: Based on Livi-Bacci 1992: 148.

of family multiplication) but to provide greater security for the family's
patriarch. This is why in Africa, Western Asia, and Southern Asia birth
rates have remained high (29–41 per thousand) despite the fall in death
rates to low levels (7–14 per thousand) (see Table 13.1). This nondynamic
strategy is well known even if the underlying reason for it is obscure – the
wider societal failure of existing dynamic strategies.

By contrast, in ESCs, where dynamic strategies have been successfully
adopted, the ruling elite are profit-seeking rather than rent-seeking, and
families and individuals respond to a strategic demand that calls for a
reduction in previously high fertility levels. The birth rate has fallen to relatively low levels in East Asia (18 per thousand) and even Latin America
(25 per thousand). And the nature of the demographic response in each
ESC will depend upon their particular strategic demand which, as shown
above, is generated by their unfolding dynamic strategy. A more appropriate term, therefore, for the so-called 'demographic transition' is the
'demographic response' to the more fundamental **strategic transition**.

The dynamic-strategy model, therefore, can sort out the existing confusion
about causal relationships between variables such as economic growth,

fertility, mortality, and education. Falling mortality rates in the modern world can be quickly dealt with, as there is little disagreement on this issue. Mortality rates have responded to improving basic infrastructure (sewerage, water supplies), and knowledge communicated from SCs to NSCs. Falling fertility rates, on the other hand, have been more difficult to explain.

The dynamic-strategy model throws much needed light on the obscurities of fertility change. As outlined above, fertility responds to changes in strategic demand rather than to changes in sociopolitical factors such as adult education that are really outcomes of the dynamic process. It is important to realize that fertility control was not invented by modern societies. All viable societies throughout history have effectively controlled their populations – both by increasing and decreasing fertility when deemed necessary – to achieve their common objective of survival and prosperity. A few examples include the hunting societies of Aboriginal Australia, the Bushmen of the Kalahari, the Innuit of North America, and the agricultural societies of the ancient world in Europe, Asia, and the Americas (Snooks 1996: ch. 8). Only the means by which fertility control has been exercised has varied. In human society population has always been an instrument employed to achieve the strategic objectives of its participants.

Economic growth, as measured by real GDP per capita (or real GCI per household) is an outcome of the dynamic process, rather than a cause or a consequence of fertility change. In terms of the dynamic-strategy model it is generated by the interaction between strategic demand and strategic response as the dynamic strategy unfolds. While fertility change is part of this wider dynamic process, it is not directly related to economic growth either as a stimulus or a barrier as is usually argued. The role that fertility change plays as a strategic instrument in the dynamic process depends on the nature of the dynamic strategy being pursued, while the rate of economic growth depends on the degree of success of that pursuit. It is for this reason that a group of individual societies can experience similar rates of economic growth but very different rates of fertility change and population expansion. This is the underlying rationale of substitutability of strategic instruments in the strategy function.

Where, then, does this leave the much-heralded role of adult female education as a means of reducing fertility? In the dynamic-strategy model, education of all types is a response to strategic demand. Human capital, like all other supply inputs, is required to facilitate the effective unfolding of the prevailing dynamic strategy. As these supply inputs are related not directly in a causal way but only indirectly through a third party, namely strategic demand, *adult education is not a determinant of fertility change.*

Both are a response to strategic demand. While fertility control is ageless, adult female education is a modern development.

This raises the important issue of the role of policy. Most demographers argue, in Malthusian spirit, that, in order to achieve more rapid economic growth in the Third World, it is essential to reduce fertility. To do so they usually advocate that governments invest heavily in adult female education. The dynamic-strategy model, however, suggests that such a policy initiative undertaken in NSCs in advance of strategic demand will either fail to reduce fertility, or, if it does, will reduce the survival prospects of the families concerned, and will certainly not generate additional economic growth. Indeed it will have a negative impact on economic growth owing to the misallocation of scarce resources. What NSCs need to do is to adopt viable dynamic strategies that will generate economic growth, a decline in fertility (as the nondynamic strategy of procreation is replaced with a viable dynamic strategy), and also, in due course, an increase in education (including that of adults both male and female). To reverse this order will merely produce a misallocation of scarce resources in NSCs and will delay even further their strategic transition.

13.2   LOW-LEVEL EQUILIBRIUM TRAP OR STRATEGIC DEFICIENCY?

Economists leave the sources of population change to demographers and treat it as an exogenous variable in their growth models. Even development economists who claim that population expansion is a major problem for NSCs deal with it in a fairly mechanical way. The main population model to emerge from development economics is the low-level equilibrium trap model developed by Richard Nelson (1956), which has its roots in the population model developed by Robert Thomas Malthus (1986, orig. publ. 1798). Population is treated in this model as a major obstacle to economic growth, which can only be surmounted by a determined and concentrated effort by the state both to reduce fertility levels and to promote economic growth. It is seen as a major reason for NSCs remaining underdeveloped. The model suggests that as long as GDP per capita remains below a notional threshold level, the rate of population expansion will exceed that of economic growth, and the growing economy will gravitate back to a low-level equilibrium trap. This multiple equilibria model is more complex than – but just as unrealistic as – the single equilibrium neoclassical growth models.

The model can be illustrated by Figure 13.7. Point A represents the population trap at a low level of GDP per capita. It is a stable equilibrium because any deviation from it will generate dynamic forces involving GDP and population that will lead the economy back to point A. At any point between A and B, the population growth rate is greater than the income growth rate, which causes GDP per capita to fall until it reaches A. If the economy, as a result of an exogenous shock, falls below A, these forces are felt in reverse, leading to a movement back to A. But if the economy can, with a intensive effort, get beyond B, the rate of GDP growth will exceed that of population growth and, hence, the economy will experience sustained economic growth.

In terms of this simple model the key question is how an economy can travel from A to B and beyond without being dragged back to A. The overall conception is something like the 'big-bang' theory of the universe: if the momentum imparted to matter in the universe is great enough to pass some threshold beyond which gravity has no further claims, then it will continue to expand forever; if not, then it will be drawn back upon itself. Possibly this natural science analogy informed the policy prescription of the 1960s, that a 'traditional' society could only escape the low-level equilibrium trap by pursuing the 'big-push' approach to industrialization. The 'big push' would be aided by a determined attempt to reduce fertility through a comprehensive family-planning programme.

The low-level equilibrium trap model is highly artificial and simplistic. It involves reducing the NSC economy to a three-variable model that

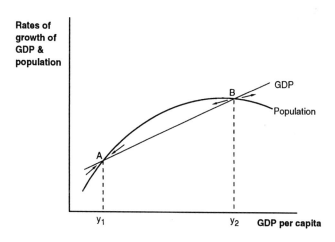

Figure 13.7   The population trap model

mechanistically generates the desired outcome only because the shape of the growth paths of GDP and population have been artificially engineered. Change the shape of these curves and you will get very different outcomes. And as this model has no underlying dynamic theory, there is no valid reason for preferring one set of curves to any other set. In effect the model-builder crafted a mechanism that would give him what he wanted – a low-level equilibrium trap outcome. Of course, this is the standard way of building neoclassical growth models.

Not surprisingly there is no empirical justification for Nelson's model. This would not be a serious objection if the sole objective of the exercise was merely to play a game called: How might we account for the difficulty experienced by NSCs in escaping from the gravity of a 'traditional' cultural background? But it *is* a serious objection if the winner of this game were to use his or her model to propose development policy for a real, poverty-stricken society. Such a policy could lead to a massive waste of scarce resources, to huge debts, and to a postponement of that country's strategic transition for decades, even generations. This appears to have been the case for many NSCs in the 1960s and 1970s.

What we require is a dynamic model that can offer realistic insights into the actual economic predicament of NSCs rather than solutions to intellectual games. The dynamic-strategy model, as we have seen, views the problems of NSCs as outcomes of their inability to successfully adopt an appropriate dynamic strategy. This in turn is due to a failure to take part in an interaction with the global strategic core – to enter into the GST – owing largely to an inappropriate endowment of natural and human resources. What it is not an outcome of is the failure of family planning and adult female education. As suggested already, family planning and adult education will only be effective in promoting economic development when strategic demand for it has been generated. There is no good reason for the confusion expressed by many for the failure of premature policies aimed at reducing fertility in NSCs. Consider the comment by Livi-Bacci (1992: 177) in regard to India: 'In spite of increased resources, the 1980s witnessed "a steep decline in the quality of family planning and public health practice" due to the increasing role played by bureaucrats as opposed to specialists'. As argued here, it was a failure not of supply but of demand.

The concept of the 'big push', promoted by simplistic models of the population-trap variety, is misconceived. Of course, the 'big-push' argument has a long history going back at least to the Bolshevik economist Preobrazhensky, whose ideas were implemented by Stalin from 1929 (Nove 1992: 115–32); and in the West it was championed by Paul Rosenstein-Rodan (1943), Ragnar Nurkse (1953), and Arthur Lewis

(1955). Not only is this idea contrary to the way societies have joined the GST over the past two centuries, it is also an inappropriate policy for NSCs, which possess neither the surpluses nor the specialized human capital required to implement and maintain such a vast development programme. Invariably societies that have attempted to develop in this way – such as the USSR, China, and North Korea – have failed at great cost to their populations in terms of large-scale starvation and massive wastage of scarce resources. While these outcomes are well known, it is important to emphasize that they received encouragement and support from unrealistic and simplistic economic and demographic models.

13.3   CONCLUSIONS

Population is a central if obscure force in the economic development of nations. Demographers study it in isolation from the dynamic processes of human civilization, and economists treat it as a force exogenous to their growth models. Both approaches are misdirected. Population is an integral part of the dynamic process and must be examined in this complex context. Yet it is neither a driving force nor a barrier to the dynamic process. The dynamic-strategy model shows that population change is largely a response to strategic demand that is generated by the unfolding dynamic strategy. This theoretical relationship receives persuasive empirical support from formally testing the relationship in Western Europe between a proxy for strategic demand and fertility change. In the following chapters we will show how other strategic instruments also respond to changes in strategic demand.

14 Capital Accumulation

Capital accumulation has long held pride of place in theories about economic development. This pre-eminence can be traced back to the work of the pioneering economists Adam Smith (1723–1790), David Ricardo (1772–1823), and Karl Marx (1818–1883). The focus of this work is on physical rather than human capital. Even in the modern theory of economic development, which emerged in the 1940s, human capital was largely ignored until the 1970s. And the focus of policy-making bodies, both national and international, followed a similar preoccupation. This chapter examines the development models in which capital plays the central role in explaining the persistence of underdevelopment. It also exposes the limitations of these models, and suggests how they can be resolved.

14.1   THE ROLE OF PHYSICAL CAPITAL

The emphasis on physical capital in modern growth theory as well as in economic development theory has a long history. Adam Smith, in the *Wealth of Nations* (1776), saw capital stock playing a central role in increasing national income by facilitating the division of labour. Increases in capital stock were the outcome of surpluses generated by the abstinence of capitalists – surpluses that could be increased by the removal of artificial privileges of a landowning class dedicated to conspicuous consumption. While Smith (ibid.: chs. 1–3) did discuss human capital involved in the division of labour, the subject was ignored by later economists. Capital accumulation also played a central role in David Ricardo's model of economic growth which, as is well known, was really a model of convergence to the stationary state. Ricardian growth is the temporary outcome of an exogenous shock that operates through the resulting increase in profits. The sequence between static equilibrium positions is as follows: profits rise owing to an exogenous shock → the surplus is invested in capital stock → the demand for labour increases → nominal wages rise → population increases → the margin of cultivation is extended → diminishing returns in agriculture are encountered → production costs rise → profits decline → the rate of capital accumulation falls to zero → the stationary state is reachieved. For Ricardo (1817: ch. 21) stasis is the normal condition of human society – a condition perpetuated by maintaining the equilibrium stock of capital.

Like the classicists, Marx (1867/1961: pt 7) focused on the role of capital. His *magnum opus*, *Capital*, was preoccupied with the production and circulation of capital. He accepted the traditional centrality of the relationship between capital accumulation and profits (although he focused on the *rate* rather than the *size* of profits), but envisaged a greater role for technological change. However, Marx rejected the classical relationship between wages and population expansion, and substituted arguments about both the 'reserve army of labour' and changing labour force participation rates. Despite these modifications to the classical argument, the economic outcome of Marx's model was much the same. Capitalists invest because that is their destiny, and they attempt to maintain profits in the face of continuous investment through innovation. But the growing capital intensity of production (owing to the labour-saving nature of technological change) reduces the profit rate, places increasing pressure on wage rates, increases unemployment and, after the occurrence of increasingly severe fluctuations, leads to the collapse of 'capitalism' and the introduction of 'socialism' and, inevitably, 'communism' – the ultimate stationary state.

During the course of the next century the economics profession turned from the big issues of economic growth and the functional distribution of income to the more manageable issues of microeconomics – the realm of the neoclassical economist. When the concern with development issues resurfaced in the 1940s, orthodox economists once more turned to the central role of capital. The problem they faced was how to explain the persistence of underdevelopment. As suggested in Chapter 2, the fundamental reason for their puzzlement was the lack of a workable theory of global development. If a society is poor, they reasoned, it must be because that society is caught in some sort of low-level equilibrium trap. And, in the absence of a theory of dynamic demand, they argued that it must be the outcome of supply-side forces, namely indivisibilities in the supply of capital or inadequacies in financial markets.

While this narrow, indeed distorted, perception of underdevelopment is shared by orthodox economists both old and new, their suggested solutions to this basic problem have changed with changing fashions. Keynesian economists, who dominated the field between the 1940s and the mid-1970s, thought that escape from this trap could be achieved only by large-scale government investment in massive capital projects, whereas neoclassical economists, who re-emerged in force after that time, believe that only freely operating markets can break down the barriers of development. Neither group, however, possesses a global vision of the development process.

The Keynesian Tradition

The various orthodox explanations of the persistence of underdevelopment can be grouped together under the general rubric of low-level equilibrium models. These models have roots that can be traced back to John Maynard Keynes' *The General Theory* (1936), and even to Thomas Robert Malthus' *An Essay on the Principle of Population* (1798). As is well known, Keynes' theory of effective demand was developed to explain the persistence of the high levels of unemployment that existed throughout the Western world during the 1930s. The Keynesian model explains how equilibrium can be achieved at less than the full-employment level of GDP – in effect a low-level employment trap. It is just a short step from the Keynesian unemployment equilibrium to the underdevelopment equilibrium concept that characterizes development theory.

The low-level equilibrium model emerged during the 1940s and 1950s. It began with the work of Paul Rosenstein-Rodan, which was concerned with the discontinuities or external economies that he thought formed a barrier to economic development. Initially Rosenstein-Rodan (1943) emphasized limitations imposed by the market, but later (1957) he extended his argument to include three forms of indivisibilities concerning the supply of social overhead capital, the complementarity of demand, and the supply of savings. Because of these indivisibilities, he maintained, growth was not a steady process, rather it occurred in a discontinuous way by making relatively large leaps from time to time. Without the momentum required to achieve these economic leaps, the development threshold would not be exceeded and underdevelopment would persist. Rosenstein-Rodan (1957, in Higgins 1968: 328) asserts:

> Proceeding 'bit by bit' will not add up in its effects to the sum total of the single bits. A minimum quantity of investment is a necessary (though not sufficient) condition of success. This is in a nutshell the contention of the theory of the big push.

And the big push required big government just as Keynes had argued in a different context.

In essence, Rosenstein-Rodan argued that the big push was required because of the 'great minimum size' or 'lumpiness' of social overhead capital and because in order for Say's Law to work – for the output of new industries to find a market – it was necessary to invest in a wide range of modern industries that would generate the necessary demand for each other's products. Government effort was required not only to undertake large infrastructure investment with its high social and low private rates of return, but also to orchestrate large-scale investment programmes that enjoyed high private rates of return. Rosenstein-Rodan (ibid.: 330) feared that 'isolated and small efforts may not add up to a sufficient impact on growth', and he believed that 'an atmosphere of development effervescence may also arise only with a minimum speed or size of investment'. In other words, the motivation for, and momentum of, economic development must come from the supply side. Clearly there is no hint here of a general response to dynamic demand; even static demand is supply-generated.

The big-push hypothesis was further developed by Ragnar Nurkse (1953), Hans Singer (1958), and Albert Hirschman (1958). Nurkse, for example, argues that the central problems in underdeveloped countries are twofold: the 'lack of capital', which results from the limited ability of individuals and organizations in poor countries to save; and the lack of inducement to invest, which is a function of the limited size of the commodity market. Nurkse's solution, like that of Rosenstein-Rodan, is to undertake a 'synchronized application of capital to a wide range of different industries' in order to provide both sufficient capital and sufficient intersectoral demand for the output of the newly established industries. In the context of unfavourable terms of trade, this can be achieved only through a programme of import replacement. Nurkse called this the concept of 'balanced growth'.

The response to these ideas was rapid and vigorous, with both Singer and Hirschman separately agreeing that a big investment push was required but arguing that any attempt to achieve it in a balanced way was beyond the capacity of undeveloped countries. Poor countries, they claimed, simply do not have the necessary capital and skills required to develop on the massive scale suggested by Nurkse. Development could only proceed in an unbalanced fashion. Hirschman even attempted to transform this limitation into a virtue by arguing that economic development can best be achieved by pursuing a deliberate policy of unbalancing the economy in order to induce a development response. It is almost as if he was saying: if there is no such thing as dynamic demand – how could there be if the deductivists had not detected it? – then we will have to create it by deliberately unbalancing the economy which will artificially establish demands that require a supply response. It was as if his 'strategy' was born of frustration with the state of reality – when it was really born of an unconscious frustration with the state of deductive theory. Hirschman's 'strategy of economic development' was to focus on a big push in a small number of key industries or sectors that were specially selected to maximize the 'incentives and pressures' on the rest of the economy. These were identified as possessing the greatest forward and backward linkages.

The perennial problem that these early development economists grappled with was where would the funds required for the 'big push' or 'minimum effort' in import replacement come from. It was generally agreed that poor countries are unable to borrow funds from wealthy countries because their surpluses are too small to make repayments of interest let alone principal. The funds, therefore, had to come from internal agricultural surpluses. Of the models developed to show how this could be achieved, the best known are by Arthur Lewis (1954) and J. Fei and G. Ranis (1961). Lewis, who begins with a Ricardian model, argues that savings are made by the small but growing capitalist class, who draw on underemployed rural workers without reducing agricultural productivity owing to their low, even zero, marginal productivity. Fei and Ranis adopted this dual sector model to explain how investment in a closed LDC is financed. They argue, in the Lewis tradition, that, if the marginal product of underemployed agricultural workers is zero, these workers can be attracted to the newly expanding manufacturing sector without reducing the level of agricultural production. Further, by maintaining the same level of consumption per head in the agricultural sector, rural householders can sell excess food to the manufacturing sector and save the resulting money receipts. These savings are then available for lending to the expanding manufacturing sector or for syphoning off by the government through taxation in order to fund the 'big push'. It will be obvious that this labour-surplus economy model is based on some unrealistic assumptions – particularly concerning the decision of rural peasants to save rather than increase their meagre consumption – but so is the balanced growth hypothesis that it was designed to serve.

The various low-level equilibrium hypotheses that focus on the role of capital have been elegantly synthesized by Ben Higgins (1968), with the assistance of Trevor Swan.[1] The first formal version of the low-level equilibrium model by Richard Nelson (1956) was, as we saw in Chapter 13, cast in terms of population and GDP rather than in terms of the demand and supply of investment funds. The Higgins–Swan model is not only more relevant to our discussion of the role of capital formation in economic development but it can be compared directly with the Solow–Swan growth model for developed nations.

The Higgins–Swan low-level equilibrium model is presented in Figure 14.1, showing the 'aggregate net savings' function SS' and the

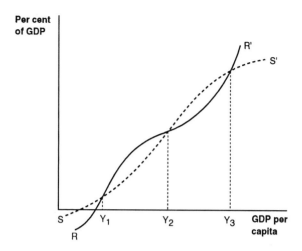

Figure 14.1   The Higgins low-level equilibrium model
Source: Adapted from Higgins 1968: 348.

'capital requirements' function *RR'*, both expressed in terms of percentages of GDP. These curves show the amounts of aggregate saving and capital required at each level of GDP per capita. The capital requirement curve expresses the capital needed to generate various levels of GDP per capita with given rates of growth of both population and productivity. Higgins (1968: 349) claims that it is 'similar in meaning to Harrod's "capital requirements for a natural rate of growth" except that we are expressing requirements in terms of capital per head and allowing for a constant rate of technological progress'.

The low-level equilibrium trap is indicated by Y_1. At this stable equilibrium position the rate of capital accumulation is just sufficient to maintain per capita income slightly above the subsistence level with a 'modest' rate of population growth. Any attempt to increase GDP per capita will be blocked by savings being insufficient to meet the capital requirements stipulated by this model. In order to move from Y_1 to Y_3 it is necessary to initiate a big investment push to generate enough capital to raise income above Y_2 (an unstable income level). Once Y_2 has been surpassed, the economy will automatically gravitate to the stable equilibrium income level Y_3. This can be thought of as convergence to the steady state, and can be safely left in private hands. Of course, the analysis assumes that there is no change in the underlying rate of technological progress, which would lead to a shift in the *RR'* curve.

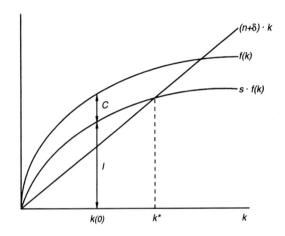

Figure 14.2   The Solow–Swan model
Notes: $k(0)$ is the initial level of the capital/labour ratio (owing to a disruption of some type), k^* is the steady-state level, I and C are the levels of investment and consumption and $f(k)$, $s \cdot f(k)$ and $(n + \delta) \cdot k$ are the production, investment, and depreciation functions.

Clearly the Higgins–Swan low-level equilibrium model has much in common with the Solow–Swan growth model for developed economies. Both focus on the demand and supply for investment funds and both manipulate these functions in an unrealistic way to achieve the desired outcome – either convergence to an equilibrium growth path or convergence to a low-level equilibrium trap. Figure 14.2, which diagrammatically represents the Solow–Swan growth model, shows the saving function $(s \cdot f(k))$ as greater than the depreciation function $((n + \delta) \cdot k)$ until they intersect at k^* (the equilibrium capital/labour ratio), which is the steady-state level. Although expressed in different units, this is the same as the equilibrium at Y_3 in the Higgins–Swan model presented in Figure 14.1 which is automatically achieved once a society has escaped the poverty trap through the 'big push'.

The Neoclassical Tradition

Like its Keynesian rival, the neoclassical tradition in development economics accepts the idea that the persistence of underdevelopment is the outcome of a low-level equilibrium trap. Once again the supply-side poverty trap is an essential concept for economists who do not possess a model of global economic development involving dynamic demand.

Without a poverty trap they are unable to explain why all the nations of the world are not fully developed.

Where the neoclassicals differ from the Keynesians is in their explanation of the low-level equilibrium in Figure 14.1 and the ways in which it might be transcended. The poverty trap, we are told, is an outcome not of market failure as claimed by the Keynesians but of government failure. Hence, the neoclassical prescription is not for a big government push but a reduction of government intervention through a process of 'structural adjustment' whereby budgets and trade accounts are balanced and markets – particularly capital markets – are deregulated. They hold firm to the naive belief that the poverty trap will be eliminated and economic development will be forthcoming if the price mechanism, free from inflation, is allowed to operate without interference in a global context.

The neoclassical approach, which has dominated development thinking among intellectuals and bureaucrats, particularly in the IMF and the World Bank, since the early 1980s can also be related to the Higgins–Swan model in Figure 14.1. By deregulating markets, the neoclassical economist might claim, it is possible to raise the saving function, so that for each level of GDP per capita a higher percentage of GDP will be saved. Also, by exposing underdeveloped countries to global markets, both commodity and financial, they will become recipients of advanced technology, which will cause the capital requirements curve to shift to the right. The combined effect will be to make the demand and supply curves for investment imitate those in the Solow–Swan growth model in Figure 14.2. Accordingly, the underdeveloped country will be able to imitate the developed world by escaping from the poverty trap and converging to the steady state. The only problem is the real-world evidence. During the 1980s and first half of the 1990s, the most impressive growth in the Third World, that of the Asian Tigers, was achieved with considerable government involvement; and countries in Latin America and sub-Saharan Africa, which were forced to take the neoclassical medicine, performed poorly. There must be a better explanation, which can also explain the global dynamic process.

14.2   THE ROLE OF HUMAN CAPITAL

The primary focus of development economists on the role of physical capital in the growth process led to the neglect of human capital until the 1970s. Naturally, scholars were aware of the importance of human skills in the growth process, but it was believed that they would emerge only if higher levels of physical capital accumulation could be achieved. Rarely was human capital included in development models. Only after the failure of big-push policies in the Third World during the 1960s, and after the development of human capital theory in the 1960s and 1970s by Gary Becker (1964), Jacob Mincer (1974), and others, did the focus of development economics shift from physical to human capital.

But, as usual in the world of ideas, the pendulum of intellectual fashion swung to the opposite extreme. Investment in human capital was expected to achieve what the big push in physical capital had been unable to bring about – escape from the poverty trap. Because of the supply-side approach of neoclassical human capital theory, education was expected to generate an increase in agricultural productivity that, in turn, would provide the savings required for economic growth. It was also thought, as we have seen in Chapter 13, that elementary education, particularly of females, would reduce the rate of population increase and, thereby, eliminate the Malthusian crisis. Numerous studies have appeared in the development literature showing the correlation between expenditure on education and increases in GDP. These have been formalized through calculations of rates of return on education that are always high relative to investment in physical assets (Colclough 1982). The problem with these studies of simple correlations is in determining whether education is a cause or a result of higher levels of GDP. In Chapter 13 it was argued that education in ESCs, in the absence of interventionist policies, is a response to strategic demand, and that GDP is the outcome of a dynamic process involving the interaction between strategic demand and strategic response. In other words, they are not *directly* related to each other in a causal way.

We can interpret these neoclassical human capital arguments in terms of the Higgins–Swan model in Figure 14.1. Taking them at face value, it is possible to show that both the increase in farm productivity and the reduction in the rate of increase of population will act to shift the capital requirement curve (RR') to the right. The probable combined effect, our neoclassical economist might claim, will be to eliminate the poverty trap and allow the underdeveloped country to grow rapidly along the lines suggested by the Solow–Swan model in Figure 14.2. But surely there is a difficulty for the neoclassical economist proposing this solution: it is similar to the big-push solution because it requires the government to undertake a massive educational programme at the primary, secondary, and tertiary levels. As shown in the annual *World Development Reports* published by the World Bank, education programmes – particularly at the higher levels – are costly exercises. If education was left to market forces – to the generation of strategic demand for this facilitating instrument – the level of educational investment envisaged by development economists would not be forthcoming. Such big-push educational programmes are bold initiatives, and their economic success will depend on the truth not only of the poverty trap model but also of the idea that economic growth is driven by investment in human capital rather than being merely facilitated by it. I argue that both assumptions are wrong and that, in consequence, such programmes involve a considerable waste of scarce resources. In this they are no different to the big investment push in physical capital. The supply response must follow rather than precede the expansion of strategic demand.

14.3   THE DYNAMIC-STRATEGY SOLUTION

The dynamic-strategy model offers a new way of looking at the role of capital, both physical and human, in the development process. It involves two main elements – the strategic demand–response mechanism, and the substitutability of instruments within the **strategy function**. Both suggest a very different solution to the problem of underdevelopment.

The strategic demand–response mechanism discussed in Chapter 11 makes it clear that the driving force in the strategic transition comes from the demand rather than the supply side. This is an outcome of the **unfolding technological paradigm**. Faced with this reality there is no possibility of forcing the GST forward through supply-side intervention. It is for this reason and not, as it is fashionable to argue today, because of 'government failure' that the big push, either in physical or human capital, has failed to solve the 'problem' of underdevelopment. Indeed, by investing on a large scale ahead of **strategic demand**, many NSCs have squandered scarce financial resources and have created overwhelming debt burdens that have actually slowed the process of **strategic transition**. The implication of treating investment as a response to strategic demand is that gross domestic capital formation (GDCF) can be divided into two parts: direct GDCF which, as a direct response to strategic demand, facilitates the unfolding of the dominant dynamic strategy; and indirect GDCF, which supports the living standards of the population that have been generated by the **dynamic strategy**.

As the working of the strategy function is discussed fully in Chapter 12, I will merely outline its implications for capital accumulation here. It has already been argued that the **strategic instruments**, which respond to strategic demand, are highly substitutable. The logical implication of this is that the 'fixed capital requirement function' does not exist in reality. If aggregate saving proves to be a barrier to a particular way of proceeding, even after the substitution of labour for capital has taken place, other strategic instruments such as **strategic ideas** and **strategic leadership** will be substituted for capital stock. And if the fixed capital requirement function does not exist, then neither does the poverty trap. It is merely a fiction to cover up the absence of any theory in development economics about the GST.

While the role of strategic ideas and strategic leadership will be discussed in detail in later chapters, a brief outline is required here. Strategic ideas are responsible for reshaping the design of the dynamic strategy or substrategy to achieve the same outcome using a different combination of strategic instruments. This is the real source of innovations and organizational arrangements that are capital saving in nature. And strategic leadership is a major way in which new strategic ideas can be implemented. The state is responsible for negotiating/enforcing new economic deals with other nations, for arranging new sources of outside funding to supplement domestic savings, and for generating the legislation required for institutional change.

14.4   CONCLUSIONS

Clearly both physical capital and human capital are important strategic instruments, but they are not as critical for explaining either the growth process or the persistence of underdevelopment as is often claimed. This point can be made about both orthodox and Marxian development theory. Capital is not the main component in the dynamic process. That role is reserved for the interaction between strategic demand and strategic response. In the strategy function other strategic instruments can, up to a point, be substituted quite effectively for capital. The way in which this can be achieved – through the creative use of strategic ideas – is the subject of the next chapter.

15 Technological or Strategic Change?

Most economists today take it for granted that technological change is the key to the dynamics of human society. Innovation is usually treated as a spontaneous outcome of either structural or institutional change. Recently considerable effort has been devoted by different schools to developing 'endogenous' and evolutionary models to suggest that this is an automatic and irreversible process. In this chapter the orthodoxy is challenged on two grounds: first, that technological change is not the key to the dynamic process but merely a major **strategic instrument**; and, secondly, that it is not part of an evolutionary or automatic process but is a response to changing **strategic demand**. The central dynamic mechanism in human society, I will argue, is not technological change but **strategic change**. The belated conversion of neoclassical economists to faith in technology is, therefore, ironical.

Strategic change occurs as materialist man, operating within a competitive environment, adopts new **strategic ideas**. These ideas, which are accumulated in the form of **strategic knowledge** by a variety of organizations, are concerned with new ways of exploiting strategic opportunities in an attempt by individuals to survive and prosper. They are, in other words, a response to changes in strategic demand. New strategic ideas are used to coordinate the changing combination of strategic instruments – such as infrastructure, equipment, human capital, technology, scale of production, institutions, and organizations – in order to maximize the exploitation of strategic opportunities. It is in this way that a society's dynamic strategy and substrategies unfold. Essentially the dynamics of human society is the outcome of a **strategic pursuit** rather than a technological production process.

15.1 THE TRADITIONAL APPROACH TO THE ROLE OF TECHNOLOGICAL CHANGE

Despite the current general belief in the central dynamic role of technological change, the conversion to this view is a recent occurrence. The main reason appears to be that innovation is a real-world disequilibrium process that is not well handled by a discipline whose theoretical foundations are

devoted to the exploration of static issues of equilibrium and resource allocation. The deductive approach is unable to encompass complex historical
processes. The main exceptions are Adam Smith, Karl Marx, and Joseph
Schumpeter – all non-neoclassical economists who had a keen appreciation of history – and most economic historians since Arnold Toynbee snr
(1852–1883). But, until recently, these scholars had little influence on the
thinking of neoclassical economists.

Yet even those economists who do acknowledge the importance of technological change in modern society have failed to see its true role. This is
because all deductive economists focus on production as if it is the prime,
even sole, objective of human society. As suggested earlier, they see society as a factory that is primarily engaged in transforming technical knowledge into production. This is the defining characteristic of both the
neoclassical and the Marxist traditions. Both traditions share the deductive
approach which, by limiting their breadth of vision, leads them to visual-
ize the objective of society as a production process rather than as a
strategic pursuit.

The Focus on Production

One of the turning points in mainstream economics was the decision to
focus on production analysis. As suggested above, this was an outcome of
adopting the deductive method to the total exclusion of the inductive or
historical method (Snooks 1993: ch. 1; 1998b: ch. 5). This deductive
approach began in earnest with David Ricardo (1772–1823), was continued by Karl Marx (1818–1883) and Stanley Jevons (1835–1882), and was
triumphantly consolidated by Alfred Marshall (1842–1924). Of these
deductivists, Marx and Marshall focused largely upon the microanalysis of
capitalist production. Modern neoclassical economics, which has been
built upon this tradition, has continued to treat human society as if it were
a factory.

Marx

The influence of Marx on modern neoclassical economics is not widely
appreciated. This influence can be traced back to Marx's single-minded
focus on the process of production in capitalist societies. To Marx, capitalist society was little more than a giant factory: machine production, which
was the driving force in his model, not only determined capitalist 'value'
but also the production relationships between the two classes of capitalists
and workers. Indeed, the political struggle between capital and labour was

little more than a conflict between the factory owner and his workers writ large. In contrast, the early classical economists, particularly Adam Smith, adopted a more macroeconomic approach together with a wider vision of society.

The three volumes of *Capital* are devoted to showing that value is created only in the process of production. Nothing is added, we are told, by the process of distribution. Because all value is the product of labour – both directly in the form of labour time and indirectly through labour embodied in capital – the appropriation by capitalists of 'surplus value' leads to the exploitation of the workers. This 'contradiction' in capitalism leads to a growing conflict between capital and labour which, aided by unrealistic assumptions about an equal rate of surplus value and a secular decline in profit rates, causes capitalism finally to collapse. Marx's entire analysis of the nature and dynamics of capitalism, in other words, works itself out within the walls of the factory. It is, figuratively, a storm in a teacup. Marx's macroeconomics is merely a projection of his micro-economics.

Economic change in Marx's capitalist system, which is generated by investment in new labour-saving technology, leads to an increase in the ratio of fixed to working capital. In the process, the relationship between capital and labour is transformed owing to changes in the balance between 'necessary' and 'surplus' (or unpaid) labour, between labour employed and labour consigned to the 'reserve army' of the unemployed, between large and small capitalists, and between large and small firms (factories). All this is the outcome of what Marx called 'the progress of machinery' that took place within the factory (Marx 1859/1970: 117; 1867/1961: 357–61). In other words, for Marx, the machine and the factory dominate the destiny of capitalist society.

Jevons, Marshall, and the Modern 'Productionists'

While Ricardo was responsible for changing the method in political economy from induction to deduction, he retained the classical focus on macro-economics. This at least implied a wider sociopolitical system, even if Ricardo neglected to make it explicit. It was Jevons who, in Britain, pioneered the shift from macroeconomics to microeconomics and who dispensed with any discussion of the encompassing sociopolitical system. This was the beginning of the 'marginal revolution' – simultaneously 'discovered' by Karl Menger (1840–1921) in Austria and Léon Walras (1834–1910) in Switzerland – which focused on static issues of resource allocation and the determination of prices in a world of given tastes, income, and technology. While Jevons, like the other 'marginalists', focused on consumer utility – or the static demand side – he did have a theory of the costs of production which, in the labour chapter, was developed in terms of disutility (Black 1970: 19).

But it was Marshall rather than Jevons who laid the foundations for the modern neoclassical approach to economics and to society. Marshall integrated – but, more importantly, subordinated – the new utility theory of Jevons and the other marginalists in order to analyse prices using a partial equilibrium approach. Certainly Marshall gave some attention to marginal utility and consumer demand theory – after all he was responsible for the famous scissors analogy for demand and supply – but he focused mainly on marginal costs and production theory.

Marshall began his analysis of production theory where Jevons left off – with the concept of marginal disutility – and developed the modern foundations of the theory of the firm. This was his abiding interest. Indeed, Marshall's earlier work, *The Economics of Industry* (1879), bore little sign of the new utility theory, and his later work, *Industry and Trade* (1919), returned to a focus on the supply side. None of this, of course, is surprising. Marginal utility theory is unquantifiable, and even its eventual replacement – indifference curve analysis – is merely a convenient, if artificial, way of introducing the demand curve into the theory of the firm. Certainly it is not at all convincing, because consumer demand is left in the realms of psychology rather than being derived from its dynamic origins in strategic demand. In any case, the usual textbook discussion of consumer demand is merely meant to set the stage to enable a focus on what neoclassical economics is all about – the theory of production.

Apart from his influential partial equilibrium analysis, Marshall's most important contribution was to the formulation of a supply-side microeconomics. This contribution included the central production-theory issues of increasing-cost versus decreasing-cost industries, internal versus external economies of scale, the incompatibility between competition and longrun supply curves, quasi-rents, the role of the representative firm, and many more (Blaug 1986: 152). *Hence, what Marx did for the radical tradition in economics, Marshall did for the orthodox tradition – he modelled society as if it were a factory.* Like Marx, he viewed factory production as central to the achievement of mankind's objectives and, again like Marx, he treated technology as a central element in this process. As Marshall (1920: 115) tells us: 'Knowledge is our most powerful engine of production; it enables us to subdue Nature and force her to satisfy our wants.' But, unlike Marx, Marshall did not employ his microeconomics to fashion a dynamic model that would carry human society to its historical destiny.

His effective interest was to model the way capitalism of his day worked, not to analyse the direction it might be taking. Consequently, Marshall pushed the central concerns of classical economics – particularly macroeconomics and dynamics – off centre stage.

Despite the remarkable attempt of J. M. Keynes (1883–1946) to develop a static form of macroeconomics set adrift from Marshallian production theory, his influence on the 'productionists' was limited to the generation following the Second World War. Keynes was able personally to transcend the productionist outlook of the prevailing neoclassical tradition because, like Adam Smith, he possessed a wider vision of human society and of the role and method of economics (as a moral science). But the difficulties experienced by the 'neoclassical synthesis' in coming to grips with the supply-side disturbances emanating from the OPEC oil crisis of the 1970s gave the productionists, who had long been struggling to reinterpret Keynesian macroeconomics in microeconomic terms, the opportunity to reject Keynes and to regain the intellectual high ground.

By the mid-1980s the victory of the productionists was largely complete. Once more the distorting vision of society as a factory prevailed in a profession that is determined to explain macroeconomic developments with microeconomic concepts and to analyse dynamic processes with static production theory. Neoclassical growth theory, as is well known, is based on the restricted forms of various simple production functions. Even the 'endogenous' growth models, which attempt to encompass technological change, begin with the production function (Snooks 1998b: ch. 3). In other words, neoclassical growth theory also treats human society as if it were a factory.

The productionist approach has had a marked influence on both development economics and historical economics. Development economics has taken its lead directly from either the Marxist or the neoclassical traditions, both of which offer this mechanical engineering approach. This is clearly reflected in the development models discussed in Chapter 6 above. While it might be expected in a subject area that employs a deductive method and shares many of the assumptions of theoretical economics, it is disappointing when it also occurs in the field of historical economics which follows a more inductive outlook. Many historical economists employ the neoclassical production-function framework when exploring economic growth. This may not present problems if it is only used as a starting point. But if not transcended during the course of the historical investigation, the neoclassical approach will generate a distorted picture both of human society and its objectives and of the dynamic process.

One historical economist, G. N. von Tunzelmann, in a recent book, *Technology and Industrial Progress*, makes explicit his productionist approach. We are told that:

> The main objective of this book is thus to develop the micro-founda-tions of macro-level growth and development behaviour. The micro-foundations are sought at the level of the *firm* or enterprise, rather than at the level of the *industry*. (1995: 2; his emphasis)

The only way in which the micro-foundations of macro-growth can be developed is to follow Marx, Marshall, and the neoclassicals by treating society as a factory. According to von Tunzelmann, not only are firms treated as 'agents for transforming technologies into products', but 'the dis-cussion of countries has been located at the firm level' because they 'are taken to be the empirical micro-foundations of growth and structural change at the macro level' (ibid.: 21, 389).

For this to be true it is necessary, according to von Tunzelmann, to envisage an 'overall "national system of production", embracing techni-ques, production processes, and administrative and financial organiza-tions' – a system that, we are told, changes through a secular process of industrialization involving an 'interaction between technology and organi-zation'(ibid.: 389–90). Von Tunzelmann (ibid.: 414, 418) insists that 'for industrialization to take hold, the evidence here lies heavily on the side of the significance of production processes'; and that 'to harp again on my main theme, *technological* information is of limited benefit until it is embedded as knowledge in firms and transmuted into *production* knowl-edge permitting the emergence of commercial *products*' (my emphasis). Like Marx and Marshall, he sees *'the machine as a paradigm for technol-ogy and the factory as a paradigm for organization in manufacturing industry'* and, indeed, for the macro-economy (ibid.: 392; my emphasis). While this argument lies firmly within the productionist tradition, von Tunzelmann is unusual in consciously drawing on both its sources in Marx and Marshall.

The Focus on the Machine

Marx and Marshall, the founders of 'productionism', regarded the machine and the knowledge it embodied as a central force in capitalism. Both scholars devoted considerable time to explaining its role in the process of production. Curiously, later generations in this tradition took the role of the machine for granted, largely because they were interested in static allocation and price issues. Even when orthodox economists turned their attention to growth theory they neglected technological change, assuming it was an exogenous force. Nor did development economists pay it more than passing attention, focusing instead on the role of capital. One of the few exceptions was W. E. G. Salter and the sources-of-growth people who followed his lead.

Owing to the severe limitations of static equilibrium theory it is difficult or impossible for orthodox economists to encompass technological change. The one theory that has emerged from this tradition is the concept of induced innovation resulting from an exogenous change in relative factor prices. It was an hypothesis first introduced by John Hicks (1932). His argument was that a relative increase in the price of labour would induce a labour-saving innovation. This simple hypothesis was accepted uncritically for a generation before being challenged by W. E. G. Salter (1960), William Fellner (1961), and Edwin Mansfield (1961), among others. The counter-argument was that a change in relative factor prices will lead to factor substitution rather than innovation, unless there is an increase in total costs which could induce an innovation that is either labour-saving or capital-saving. It was argued that the *nature* of the innovation will depend on technological not economic conditions.

An attempt by Syed Ahmad (1966) to rescue Hicks' hypothesis of induced innovation was made by introducing the concept of the 'historical innovation possibility curve', which is 'an envelope of all alternative isoquants (representing a given output on various production functions) which the businessman expects to develop with the use of the available amount of innovating skill and time'. This curve is 'not the result of any economic choice, it is a purely technological or laboratory question' – the economic choice is made by selecting one of the various isoquants belonging to the innovation possibility curve (ibid.: 347). With this traditional analysis, Ahmad shows that a relative rise in the price of labour will unambiguously lead to an innovation that is necessarily labour-saving only if the innovation possibility curve is technologically unbiased. It is a model recently employed by Yujiro Hayami (1997) to explain economic development. But, as I will argue, this is a static rather than a dynamic model; it relies on many special assumptions, it accepts changing relative factor prices as exogenously determined, and it is an unrealistic supply-side model. The proponents of the induced-innovation hypothesis omit the dynamic element in reality by jumping directly from relative factor prices to technological change – they omit the essential element of strategic demand.

In general, only economic historians have paid much attention to examining the role of technological change in the process of economic growth and development. This appears to be an outcome of their interest in the first Industrial Revolution – which spawned a plethora of new machines embodying new processes – and the way this new factory technology was transmitted from Britain to Europe, North America, and Japan. Historians of various descriptions were the first to analyse the nature of technology transfer and of property rights in knowledge protected by patent laws.[1] When neoclassical theorists became interested both in treating technological change as endogenous and in analysing technology transfer in the late 1980s and 1990s, they relied heavily on this literature because deductive neoclassical production theory has nothing to say about the dynamics of technological change. It is a process that must be observed to be understood.

Yet, although economic historians have been able to describe the real-world processes of technological change and technological transfer, they have not been able to explain it convincingly. In this they have received no help from growth theorists and, until recently (Snooks 1996; 1997a; 1998b), have not possessed an appropriate inductive model. Most technology historians, such as Joel Mokyr (1990), take their lead from neoclassical economics and adopt supply-side explanations that involve the erection and removal of barriers to innovation. Those adopting demand-side explanations – such as Sokoloff and Khan (1990) and Magee (1996) – focus on static market explanations rather than on strategic demand first introduced explicitly in my book *The Dynamic Society* (Snooks 1996).[2] Similarly, those attempting to explain the process of technology transfer between societies at different stages of economic development have experienced difficulties owing to the absence of a suitable model of the global strategic transition. While there are a variety of explanations, none is convincing.

The Focus on Structures

There is, of course, widespread dissatisfaction with the neoclassical tradition's inability to explain economic growth in general and technological change in particular. A recent manifestation of this disquiet is the attempt to develop an evolutionary model of dynamic change. As discussed in detail in *Longrun Dynamics* (Snooks 1998b), there have been two approaches in this field – evolutionary institutionalism and the new evolutionary economics. Evolutionary institutionalism, which includes the work of Thorstein Veblen (1899), Friedrich Hayek (1988), Douglass North (1981; 1990) and their disciples, focuses on the evolution of societal rules (some of which regulate the technological environment); whereas the new evolutionary economics, which includes the work of Richard Nelson and Sidney Winter (1982) and their followers, focuses on the evolution of 'routines' that primarily involve techniques of production. Both are supply-side models.

By substituting the organic analogy of biology for the mechanical analogy of physics, we are told, economics will become a more realistic science. Yet, even if that were true, which it is not, evolution could never be more than a partial theory. In historical biology evolution can explain genetic change but not the fluctuating fortunes of life; and in the social sciences it can encompass only institutional change, not changes in the entire society. What is urgently required in both cases is a more general dynamic model – such as the dynamic-strategy model – that encompasses and transforms these partial supply-side *mechanisms*.

The evolutionary theorists have also introduced some confusion into the economics discipline by advocating the erroneous evolutionary concept of institutional and technological irreversibility. As shown elsewhere (Snooks 1997a), institutional and technological changes can and do experience complete reversals when there is a reversal in the dynamic-strategy sequence, such as conquest commerce conquest. Accordingly, institutional and technological change is not an evolutionary process. It is a function of strategic demand. Further, the economic evolutionists have attempted to replace the existing dynamic form in the neoclassical growth model – the equilibrium growth path – with equally artificial devices such as 'routinized behaviour' (Veblen 1899), punctuated equilibria (Hodgson 1993), and path-dependence (Nelson and Winter 1982; North 1990). While these artificial dynamic structures are necessary supporting devices in a supply-side economics, they have no place in a realistic dynamic theory (Snooks 1998b). Only strategic demand fulfils that role.

15.2 THE DYNAMIC-STRATEGY APPROACH TO TECHNOLOGICAL CHANGE

The dynamic-strategy approach provides an entirely new perspective on technological change and technology transfer. To put this model through its paces I will proceed by posing and answering a number of questions that have arisen in the earlier part of this chapter: Is technological change the key to the dynamic process? Is it an automatic or evolutionary process? Is the production process of which it is a part the central characteristic of human society? How are we to explain the process of technology transfer?

Is Technological Change the Key to the Dynamic Process?

We need to view technological change from a very different perspective. As implied by the **strategy function** in Chapter 12, technological change is not the key to the dynamic process, merely one of a number of instruments needed to facilitate the wider process of strategic change. By saying 'merely', I do not mean to belittle technological change, just to place it in a proper context. Technological change is as important as, but no more so in the modern era than, the other strategic instruments of capital, labour, **strategic institutions/organizations**, **strategic leadership**, and **strategic ideas**. All strategic instruments respond, through the orchestration of prices, to strategic demand as the dominant dynamic strategy/substrategy unfolds. As strategic demand changes so too does the composition of this set of strategic instruments. Technological change may be an important instrument for a society seeking to achieve its objectives of survival and prosperity in one period, but not in another.

An excellent recent example of the fluctuating influence of technological change to the dynamics of society is Hong Kong. When Hong Kong began its phase of rapid and sustained growth in the 1960s, it did so by imitating foreign technology in order to build up a flourishing export base of manufactured goods. But, with the rapid expansion of manufacturing in mainland China from the late 1970s, Hong Kong found it more profitable to transfer resources from manufacturing activities to those of commerce and finance. In this way it adopted a new role as economic mediator between China and the rest of the world. Consequently production-related technological change became a relatively less important strategic instrument in Hong Kong's pursuit of prosperity. In effect, Hong Kong became the modern equivalent of medieval Venice, which acted as the centre of commerce between Europe and the Orient. Indeed, history provides many examples of societies changing their dynamic strategies and, hence, the instruments by which they were pursued. Much of the considerable economic growth experienced in the pre-modern world was generated by the non-technological strategies of conquest and commerce (Snooks 1996; 1997a).

The essential point to note is that, while the importance of individual strategic instruments waxes and wanes, the central role of strategic ideas in coordinating the supply response to changes in strategic demand remains constant. This has been completely overlooked in the past. Hence, we need to shift our attention from technological change and technological ideas to the role of strategic change and strategic ideas.

What are strategic ideas? Quite simply, strategic ideas are views about how best to exploit changing strategic opportunities – how best to employ the available strategic instruments. Strategic ideas are generated by **strategic pioneers** who are struggling with changing economic realities and, when successful, they are adopted by the large numbers of **strategic followers** (Snooks 1997a: ch. 2). New strategic ideas are added to the existing stock of **strategic knowledge** accumulated by organizations at all levels of society. These strategic organizations include political parties, bureaucratic departments, educational and research organizations, employer groups, trade unions, households, and, finally, corporations. Strategic knowledge is employed by these organizations, and the individuals who act within them, in order to respond effectively to changing strategic opportunities.

It will be obvious how the strategic approach differs from the productionist approach. The productionist emphasis on the central role in social dynamics of production and technological change leads to a focus on the role of firms – merely one of many strategic organizations – in accumulating technological knowledge and in transforming it into goods and services. By contrast, strategic organizations at all levels and in all sectors of society accumulate strategic knowledge in order to develop and facilitate a viable strategic pursuit. Societal dynamics is a strategic pursuit, not a process of production.

Is Technological Change either an Induced or an Evolutionary Process?

The conventional wisdom is that technological change is the outcome of supply-side developments. Joel Mokyr (1990: 151), a historical economist, represents this point of view when he argues, in circular fashion, that: 'Human appetites being what they are, necessity is always there; the ability to satisfy it is not ... The "demand" for technology is a derived demand, that is, it depends ultimately on the demand for the goods and services that technology helps produce; there is little or no demand for technology for its own sake'. Even those who consider demand to be important (Sokoloff and Kahn 1990; Magee 1996) focus on the nature of domestic and international markets. The problem they face is that market size and structure are outcomes of the dynamic process of which technological change is a component part – it is an outcome of the interaction between strategic demand and strategic response. As a dynamic outcome the market cannot be an independent determinant of technological change. The problem of causation here is similar to the issue discussed in Chapter 13 of whether fertility reduction (a response to strategic demand) is caused by an increase in adult female education (an outcome, like an increase in real GDP per capita, of the dynamic process). Technological change, like the reduction in fertility, is a direct response to changes in strategic demand, not to consumer demand, which is simply an outcome of the dynamic process.

Deductive economists, as we have seen, also regard technological change as an outcome of supply-side forces. Yet neoclassical economics has little to say on this important topic. The main reason is that, while technological change is a complex disequilibrium process, neoclassical economists persist with a static equilibrium analysis that takes little account of dynamic reality. Their theoretical insights are largely restricted, as shown above, to the concept of induced technological change. Not only is this concept static rather than dynamic, but the changing relative factor prices that induce innovation are exogenously determined. But worse than this, the induced-innovation model is hopelessly misspecified. As the dynamic-strategic model demonstrates, there is no direct relationship between relative factor prices and either factor substitution or technological change. In neoclassical theory it is necessary to postulate this direct relationship – the automatic emergence of innovation – because it lacks both a driving force and a concept of dynamic demand. Yet neoclassical economics is not alone in this: the new evolutionary economics views technological change as a supply-side evolutionary process that is unidirectional.

In the dynamic-strategy model, changing relative prices impact directly not on technological change but on the choice of dynamic strategy and its substrategies. As the chosen dynamic strategy unfolds – or, in static terms, as the strategy function shifts – strategic demand is generated for a variety of strategic instruments including technological change. Hence, it is strategic demand and not relative factor prices that leads directly to a change in technology and to factor substitution. Neoclassical economics omits the dynamic element in its discussion of innovation. And, to confound the evolutionists, technological change can be reversed because it is driven by the process of strategic change rather than biological-like forces. If, following the exhaustion of the dominant dynamic strategy, an earlier strategy is employed as a replacement (as has happened frequently in the past – see Snooks 1997a), institutions and technologies will be thrown into reverse.

Clearly, the attempt by Ahmad (1966) to rescue the Hicksian concept of induced innovation – innovation that occurs mysteriously without human agency – is interesting but ultimately unsuccessful. The model is misspecified. Social dynamics is not just an automatic response to exogenously determined factor prices, but is the predictable outcome of the deliberate and determined efforts of individuals attempting to maximize the probability of survival and prosperity.

Is Social Dynamics a Process of Production?

The Marxist–neoclassical vision of human dynamics as a process of production is not only misleading, it is deforming. The production of commodities is only one aspect of the dynamic process of modern society. This should be particularly clear today when the world's leading nations are service societies because service societies do not fit comfortably into the neoclassical production framework. Of course, production theory can be modified to analyse service activity, but the simple factory–machine relationship in productionist theory breaks down.

A very effective test of modern neoclassical theory of the role of production and technological change is to apply it to pre-modern society. This helps to avoid the myopia that often afflicts us when generalizing about human society from our own limited experience. It is essential to realize that human objectives in pre-modern society – to survive and prosper – were the same as they are today, but that the dynamic strategies by which they were pursued were very different. These different dynamic strategies arise from the different technological paradigms, as shown in Figure 2.1, that have been experienced through time. Yet, because of the similar dynamic conditions pertaining to each of the four dynamic strategies – family multiplication, conquest, commerce, and technological change – a general model must be relevant to them all. If not, the chances are that our model cannot even explain developments in our own era.

The important conclusion of my earlier historical investigations (Snooks 1996: ch. 9) is that in pre-modern societies production technology played a subordinate role in social dynamics to the pursuit of either conquest or commerce. Production in these societies was employed largely for subsistence, whereas conquest and commerce were used to generate economic growth. Hence, the main role for new technological ideas in pre-modern society was to facilitate war and trade rather than production (Snooks 1997a).

What Needs to be Explained: Technological or Strategic Transfer?

Clearly we need to explain how NSCs adopt both viable dynamic strategies *and* effective production techniques. But it is essential to sort out the priority between them. Strategic ideas are, as we have seen, responsible for coordinating the strategic instruments of which technological knowledge is but one. Equally important are the capital needed to make knowledge – both strategic and technical – effective, the institutions and organizations required to facilitate the new strategy (which may or may not be based on technological change), and the government leadership necessary to coordinate, assist, and guide the private strategic pursuit.

Primarily lacking in NSCs are strategic ideas and strategic knowledge. These societies are run by and for rent-seeking antistrategists who are able to grow rich more quickly by exploiting their fellow man than by exploiting available strategic opportunities and, thereby, creating new wealth. Only as NSCs begin to interact with the global strategic core will the grip of the antistrategists be broken and will a demand for strategic ideas and strategic instruments emerge. This outcome turns the exploitation thesis of the dependency theorists on its head. The essential requirement for NSCs at this stage is to acquire and pursue effective strategic ideas in order to enter into the GST.

Strategic ideas determine the development approach that will be followed by an NSC or ESC. Individuals and governments will adopt those strategic ideas – in response to strategic demand – that maximize strategic opportunities in the light of the society's resource endowment and competitive environment. Governments seeking to provide strategic leadership will need to decide what strategic models they should follow: what should be the balance between productionism and commerce, between the production of goods and services, between import substitution and export orientation, between private enterprise and government intervention, between growth and distribution, between domestic savings and foreign borrowing, between capital-intensive and labour-intensive production techniques, between balanced and unbalanced development, between centralized and decentralized institutions and organizations, and so on. In other words, a society's strategic knowledge will provide a framework for, among other things, technology transfer. It will determine the balance between the use of foreign and local technology.

To be more specific, the interaction between strategic demand and strategic ideas will determine the balance in an ESC between the modern manufacturing sector and the more traditional agricultural sector, between the domestic and overseas orientation of manufacturing and agriculture, and between the emphasis on industrialization and trade. In turn, this will determine the need for high-tech foreign production knowledge and low-tech local production knowledge. As Gary Magee (1999) has shown in the case of Australia during the second half of the nineteenth century, considerable invention (and presumably innovation) occurs within an ESC, with local inventors specializing according to their comparative advantage in less sophisticated, resource-oriented activities in the agricultural, pastoral, mining, and household sectors. This local pursuit of inventive and innovative activities requires only limited investment in human capital. On the other hand, foreign technology is associated with more sophisticated manufacturing activities requiring greater investment in human capital. But the balance between these sources of technology will depend on a society's strategic knowledge generated in response to strategic demand. Technology transfer, like technological change, is subordinate to strategic change.

15.3   CONCLUSIONS

The central conclusion of the dynamic-strategy model is that society is not a factory (or a farm or a firm) but a strategic organization. And the dynamics of human society is the outcome not of a production process but of a strategic pursuit. Hence, the centrally important process in human society is not technological but strategic change based on the accumulation of strategic rather than technological knowledge. This has radical implications not only for the way we view the process of economic development but also for development policy.

16 Institutional Response

Institutions have no secure place within the canon of orthodox economics. Mainstream neoclassical economists ignore them, and unorthodox economists explain them with the help of disciplines from beyond the boundaries of the social sciences. It is hardly surprising, therefore, that institutional change has never been explained convincingly by the economics profession. While this may not concern those who live in the virtual world of abstract theory, it is frustrating for those development economists concerned with real-world problems.

To establish and resolve this difficulty, the current approach to institutional change is reviewed, its limitations discussed, and a more realistic theory outlined. It is shown that institutions certainly can be integrated into a general theory of the real economy, but only by employing the inductive method. Accordingly there is no need to go beyond the boundaries of the social sciences and no excuse for importing spurious ideas from the biological sciences.

16.1 ORTHODOX APPROACHES

Institutionalism has a long, if ineffective, tradition in the English-speaking world. Its origins can be traced back to the German and English historical schools of economics in the nineteenth century (Snooks 1993: 26–9). While the historical schools did not survive long into the twentieth century they did give rise to two more robust offspring – the British economic and social history tradition and the North American school of institutional economics. Both, however, were summarily dismissed by the mainstream deductive tradition, particularly during the 'golden era' from 1950 to 1973. Since the 1970s one of these newer traditions, institutionalism, has experienced a renaissance. Yet, the outcome has been unimpressive. This is particularly disappointing for development economics that is forced to deal with the real world.

Surveying the Field

There are three main branches of contemporary institutionalism: the old institutional economics, the modern evolutionary institutional economics, and the new institutional economics. The first of these, the old institutional economics, is usually associated with the names of T. B. Veblen (1857–1929), J. R. Commons (1862–1945), W. C. Mitchell (1874–1948) and, more recently, C. E. Ayres (1891–1972). While there are differences amongst them, they have at least three important aspects in common: like the historicists before them they reject the 'hedonistic' rationality of neoclassical economics and claim (in some instances) that human motivation evolves with human institutions; they focus on collective action arising from institutional constraints, or rules, rather than on the 'atomistic' action of individuals as in mainstream economics; and they reject the equilibrium approach of neoclassical economics in favour of an evolutionary approach. While this work has long been ignored by the economic mainstream, it has influenced recent unsuccessful attempts to build a modern theory of evolutionary economics – a type of neo-Veblenianism – by writers such as G. M. Hodgson (1993). This work, which I have examined in more detail elsewhere (Snooks 1997a: 74–81; 1998b: 51–6), is true to its earlier influences in its entrenched anti-neoclassicism.

The new institutional economics involves an extension of mainstream deductive theory to accommodate some of the views of the old institutionalists. In this field the two most important pioneering figures are F. A. Hayek (1899–1992) and D. C. North (1921–). As is well known, Hayek comes from the neo-Austrian tradition and North is from the neoclassical tradition of deductive economics. They both emphasize different aspects of the old institutionalist school, with Hayek (1988), like Veblen, focusing on a Darwinian evolutionary process, and North, like Commons, opting for an historical process driven by an interaction between institutions and organizations. Recently there has been a *rapprochement*, with signs that North's approach is becoming increasingly evolutionary. The first part of this chapter focuses on the approach taken by North and his followers because of their more explicit interest in the historical development process.[1]

The New Institutional Economics

The new institutional economics in historical development has been pioneered by Douglass North, who adopts a deductive approach to this issue. North begins with the neoclassical model and releases a number of restrictive assumptions that bring institutions into play. These include the assumptions that decision-makers possess perfect information, appropriate models of reality, and perfect information-processing abilities. But, North argues, as the information reaching decision-makers is fragmentary and costly, and as their conceptual models of the world are imperfect, exchange between individuals gives rise to transaction costs which call institutions – or rules of the game – into being. These rules can be either formal, such as those enshrined in the statute books, or informal, such as customs or traditional forms of behaviour.

Emergence of the North Model

North's views on the role of institutions in the dynamic process have changed significantly over the past three decades. Over that time he has moved progressively closer to a social-evolutionary approach. In *The Rise of the Western World* (North and Thomas 1973), it is argued that economic performance is determined by changes in institutions, and that institutional change is largely a function of population change (driven by plagues, wars, and other exogenous events) through its impact upon the labour–land ratio, at least until the Industrial Revolution when technology became the driving force. The main mechanism of change involves relative price changes which create incentives to construct more efficient institutions. North's explanation, in other words, is derived from the deductive neoclassical model which suggests that economically rational decision-makers will adopt the most efficient institutions available in the face of exogenous change. Hence, the persistence of apparently inefficient institutions, such as those in Spain during the pre-modern period and in the Third World, remained as a puzzle that North and Thomas could not solve. As North (1990: 7) later admitted: 'Such an anomaly did not fit into the theoretical framework'. But this was not the only problem (Field 1994). Why, for example, did markets continue to develop after population was halved with the Black Death of 1348 if population growth was the driving force behind the earlier growth of markets? Why was there no reversal in this process over the following century? At the time, he and Thomas attempted to explain away such anomalies in an unsatisfactory *ad hoc* way.

In *Structure and Change in Economic History* North (1981) developed a more sophisticated analysis of institutional change. He moved away from the simple neoclassical efficiency mechanism and closer to the old institutionalists by developing a transaction-costs model that attempted to explain the differential economic performance of societies with both efficient and inefficient institutional frameworks. The perseverance of inefficient institutions is the outcome of leaders devising property rights in their own interests. But he fails to develop an encompassing model to explain why they do so. Further, North's deductive economic model changes abruptly from period to period. For the pre-modern period he adopts an augmented classical model, in which exogenous population growth runs into diminishing returns in the face of the fixed resource of land; and for the modern era he adopts an augmented neoclassical model, which assumes constant returns to scale and embodies a highly elastic supply curve for knowledge (ibid.: 60). Both variations are extended in an *ad hoc* way by theories about institutions and ideology because he believes that the original models cannot explain the totality of the progress of Western society. His aim, he tells us (ibid.: 7), is 'to fill out the gaps in the neoclassical model'. This model, which lacks cohesion, is discussed more completely elsewhere (Snooks 1996: 130–4). To 'illustrate' the general nature of this model North provided an interpretation of institutional change in Western civilization since the Neolithic Revolution. He did not attempt any formal testing of his model. But still a puzzle remained. Why, ultimately, did competitive pressure fail either to eliminate inefficient nations or to force these nations to adopt more efficient institutions? Why was it that all societies did not move to optimal institutional arrangements as predicted by neoclassical theory? Why has economic underdevelopment persisted in the Third World?

By the time *Institutions, Institutional Change and Economic Performance* (North 1990) was published, North believed he had the answer to this final puzzle. It is an answer that involves three elements that are tacked onto the basic neoclassical model: a 'symbiotic' relationship between institutions and organizations; a path-dependence of the institution–organization interaction that leads to a 'lock-in'; and a feedback mechanism involving imperfect information and imperfect conceptual models. Much of the weight of his new approach rests on both the distinction made by Commons some six decades earlier between institutions and organizations, and on the recent path-dependence literature. In other words he has abandoned, as Field (1991: 1000) has noted, the earlier attempt to build a general model of rule variation.

According to North, institutions, in conjunction with the usual economic constraints, provide the economic opportunities in society, while organizations emerge to exploit these opportunities. In this interactive process, maximizing organizations alter the institutions that brought them into existence. This is a type of evolutionary model, inspired by neoclassical economics as well as (indirectly) Darwin, in which the selective device is 'adaptive efficiency'. Owing to different information processes – involving different costs of information and different conceptual models (cultures) – institutional change in different societies takes different evolutionary paths. This is a path-dependent process involving increasing returns and fragmentary information feedback which leads to institutional 'lock-in' that resists competitive pressures. It is North's explanation of why inefficient institutions can persist into the longrun. Hence, in searching for a resolution to the problem of sub-optimal institutional arrangements in the Third World – a problem that has worried him for some three decades – North has moved a long way towards the evolutionary supply-side approach of the old institutionalists. Economic growth, he tells us, is an outcome of the evolutionary interaction between institutions and organizations.

North's Model of Institutional Evolution

North has high ambitions for his model of institutional change which, he claims, plays a central role in the dynamics of human society. North (1990: 107) explains:

> institutions ... are the underlying determinant of the long-run perfor-
> mance of economies. If we are ever to construct a dynamic theory of
> change – something missing in mainstream economics and only very
> imperfectly dealt with in Marxian theory – it must be built on a model
> of institutional change.

And what this model must be able to explain is the inherently incremental process of institutional change. While North grants that wars, revolutions, conquest and natural disasters can lead to discontinuities in institutional change, 'the single most important point about institutional change ... is that institutional change is overwhelmingly incremental ... a gradual restructuring of a framework in which the interconnections between formal and informal constraints and enforcement characteristics evolved over centuries' (ibid.: 89). There is much here in common with the recent evolutionary institutional economists, although they may not welcome the comparison owing to the association with North's neoclassical approach.

North's dynamic model is a supply-side model. While North (ibid.) has recently introduced changes in tastes into the analysis – what passes in neoclassical economics for the demand side – he focuses primarily upon relative prices. His discussion of relative prices includes relative factor prices and what I will call relative institutional prices. Relative factor prices only appear to play a role in North's model prior to the Industrial Revolution when population change – which is an exogenous variable driven by the changing incidence of disease, war, and natural disasters – leads to a change in the land–labour ratio and thereby to a change in institutions.

The second type of relative prices – transaction costs – which is endogenous to North's model is, he claims, more important and universal in its applicability:

> reflecting the ongoing maximizing efforts of entrepreneurs (political,
> economic, and military) that will alter relative prices and in consequence

induce institutional change. The process by which the entrepreneur acquires skills and knowledge is going to change relative prices by changing perceived costs of measurement and enforcement and by altering perceived costs and benefits of new bargains and contracts. (Ibid.: 84)

This operates through a mechanism he calls 'adaptive efficiency'. North (ibid.: 80) explains:

Adaptive efficiency ... is concerned with the kinds of rules that shape the way an economy evolves through time. It is also concerned with the willingness of a society to acquire knowledge and learning, to induce innovation, to undertake risk and creative activity of all sorts, as well as to resolve problems and bottlenecks of the society through time.

It is a concept associated with the interaction between institutions and organizations that operates according to the incentives contained within society's rules.

While relative prices are 'the most important source' of institutional change, changing tastes or preferences for cultural values sometimes play a minor role. But tastes, even then, appear to be influenced by relative prices. North (ibid.: 84) claims: 'We know very little about the sources of changing preferences or tastes. It is clear that changing relative prices play some role in changes in taste.' To illustrate this point he refers to the changing structure of the Western family in the second half of the twentieth century. While this is, he claims, largely due to 'changing relative prices of work, leisure, and contraception', it is also due, in part, to changing ideological attitudes to moral issues and to the role of women in society. This is not a fortunate illustration as I have shown elsewhere (Snooks 1994a: 85–8) that 98 per cent of the shift of women from the home to the market between 1947 and 1990 can be accounted for by changes in the gender demand for labour, which in turn is due to changes in the technological base of society in response to strategic demand. This leaves little room for institutional or ideological variables.

Hence, the only demand-side variable in North's explanation is cultural preferences, and even this is an *ad hoc* variable to be invoked when relative prices are unable to explain most of the observed institutional change. It is interesting that whenever North is unable to explain institutional change with his supply-side model he invokes culture or ideology. As argued below, cultural preference, which is merely the concept of consumer demand derived from static neoclassical theory, does not constitute the dynamic demand for institutions. That arises from society's unfolding dynamic strategy.

On its own, the 'adaptive efficiency' model of institution change is, as North is well aware, unable to account for the persistence of inefficient institutional systems and poor growth performance either in the past or in the contemporary world. North (1990: 93) explains:

> Again going back to the Coase theorem: in a world of zero transaction costs, the efficient solution that produced the highest aggregate income would prevail. But because transaction costs are not zero, we could anticipate differential performance reflecting different degrees of success of institutional frameworks in reducing transaction (and transformation) costs. But why would the relatively inefficient economies persist? What prevents them from adopting the institutions of the more efficient economies?

His latest answer to these questions, which have plagued him over the past 30 years, is the path-dependence of institutional change.

Societies, according to North, get locked into their institutional structures owing to the nature of their evolutionary process. His argument, as mentioned briefly in Chapter 6, is that, in a world of increasing institutional returns and of deficient information feedback, the conceptual models possessed by decision-makers do not converge on the 'true' models. In this explanation, increasing returns reinforce the direction of institutional development once a society begins on a particular path, and incomplete markets, which (together with cultural values) reinforce faulty conceptual models, lead to divergence from the most efficient development path. Hence, inefficient institutional systems persist in some societies and differential growth rates are experienced. North (ibid.: 95–6) explains:

> if the markets are incomplete, the information feedback is fragmentary at best, and transaction costs are significant, then the subjective models of actors modified both by very imperfect feedback and by ideology will shape the path. Then, not only can both divergent paths and persistently poor performance prevail, the historically derived perceptions of the actors shape the choices that they make.

North is optimistic that this path-dependence approach, which was first developed by Arthur (1988) and David (1985; 1993), will finally resolve the problem of persisting inefficient institutional systems and differential economic performance. North (1990: 133) concludes his survey of different approaches to economic development with the statement:

> There is a different, and I think, better story. It concerns the endless struggle of human beings to solve the problems of cooperation so that

they may reap the advantages not only of technology, but also of all the other facets of human endeavor that constitute civilization.

Evaluating the New Institutionalism

The Limitations of Neoclassicism

Most of the problems facing the new institutionalist approach to societal dynamics arise from an inability to throw off the neoclassical framework. While the neoclassical model is an excellent tool for examining shortrun static problems, it is incapable of analysing longrun dynamic issues. It cannot even be used as a foundation on which to build a more realistic dynamic theory as the new institutionalists have attempted. As I argued in *Longrun Dynamics* (Snooks 1998b), we need to make a new beginning by constructing real-world dynamic models using the historical or inductive method. Our dynamic models must emerge from real-world reconstructions, not be imposed upon them.

The neoclassical foundations of North's dynamic model are reflected in his theory of human behaviour and his supply-side approach. Although North claims that some of the assumptions in the Walrasian general equilibrium model are unrealistic, he adopts the neoclassical theory of human behaviour. Hence, he accepts the orthodox view that all individual decision-makers make a conscientious attempt to collect as much cost–benefit information as possible, to process this information using conceptual models of reality, and to correct those models when the outcomes of decisions are known. What he challenges is the neoclassical view that information is perfect, that the conceptual models are comprehensive and correct, and that all information is quickly and correctly processed. By introducing imperfection in the supply and processing of information into the classical model, North introduces transaction costs and on this he constructs his static theory of institutions. He attempts to convert this static theory into a dynamic model by introducing the idea of path-dependence, which he interprets as an interaction between institutions and organizations that produces a development path shaped by increasing returns and deficient feedback. The persuasiveness of North's model depends, therefore, upon the realism of the neoclassical theory of human behaviour. If that theory is false, the foundations for North's models will crumble. In Chapter 10, I argue that the neoclassical theory of human behaviour is incorrect and demonstrate that, by employing the historical rather than the deductive method, it is possible to construct a more realistic theory of human behaviour.

North is also attracted to the idea that institutions are constraints – rather than a means to facilitate the achievement of human objectives – because it fits into the neoclassical framework of production theory. This supply-side approach provides a curious perspective on human society. Individuals accept the limitations imposed by constraints on their individuality in order to make society work. But, apart from some sort of interventionist god, whose objective is it to make society work? Decision-makers are interested not in making society work, but in achieving their materialist objectives by using rules to facilitate their dynamic strategies. That society works is an unengineered by-product of the individual's pursuit of survival and prosperity. This is the argument outlined briefly in *The Dynamic Society* (Snooks 1996) and developed fully in *The Ephemeral Civilization* (Snooks 1997a). The nature of institutions and institutional change can be more convincingly explained as a supply response to strategic and tactical demand. In *The Dynamic Society* I argue that institutions emerge largely in response to strategic demand generated by the fundamental dynamic process. Why has North overlooked this dynamic demand? Primarily, I believe, because he is 'constrained' by the supply-side approach of neoclassical economics. North argues, as we have seen, that institutions are required because imperfect information and decision-making lead to transaction costs. Only formal and informal rules can reduce the risk and the uncooperative behaviour that occurs in a world where transaction costs are positive. And these rules change over time largely under the influence of supply-side forces. Apart from a short discussion of cultural tastes or preferences, even static demand does not play much of a role – and then only in an *ad hoc* way – in North's thinking. North is a captive of the neoclassical paradigm.

In order to account for matters that cannot be explained by his supply-side model, North is forced to develop separate and *ad hoc* theories of the role of the state and of ideology. Once again this is a legacy of the neoclassical paradigm. According to North the role of the state is to enforce constraints, and the role of ideology (moral and ethical codes) is to provide social stability. North calls upon both, in an *ad hoc* way, to explain the persistence of inefficient institutions. In my model both the state and ideology are the instruments of those attempting to implement their dynamic strategies and tactics. They are, therefore, integral and endogenous elements in my dynamic model rather than exogenous appendages as in North's explanation.

Finally, is it true, as North claims, that this static neoclassical approach can be transformed into a dynamic model by utilizing the concept of path-dependence? North (1990: 112) asserts: 'Path dependence is the key to an analytical understanding of long-run economic change.' In my opinion, path-dependence is a further supply-side concept that constrains the independent action of individuals and their society: they get 'locked into' a particular development path. There is a strong hint of historical inevitability about this argument. If individuals are free to choose, what does path-dependent 'lock-in' really mean? It can only mean that there are no other more profitable development paths open to them. In this context, 'lock-in' has little meaning. My model provides a very different explanation. The absence of profitable alternatives in any society is demand-determined owing to the exhaustion of the dominant dynamic strategy rather than supply-determined through a deficiency of information.

Foundations for a Dynamic Model

North claims that the past can only be made intelligible as a story of institutional evolution. The institutional framework provides the changing incentives and opportunities required for decision-makers to achieve their objective. I disagree. The only way the past can be made intelligible is by focusing upon the primary dynamic mechanism that underlies both institutional change and economic performance. Incentives and opportunities in society are provided by the unfolding dynamic strategy which, in turn, depends upon changing relative factor prices and the changing competitive environment. These opportunities are realized by competing decision-makers through investment in the infrastructure and technology of dynamic strategies. These strategies drive the changes in institutions, organizations, and economic performance. Hence, the main interaction is not between institutions and organizations, as North claims, but between the unfolding dynamic strategy on the one hand and *both* institutions and organizations on the other. I have called this interaction the 'secondary dynamic mechanism' (Snooks 1996; 1997a). In this mechanism, while there is some feedback from institutions to the primary dynamic process, the overwhelming direction of causation is from strategies to institutions. In the dynamic-strategy model the development path of society depends not upon increasing institutional returns and deficient feedback but upon the unfolding and, ultimately, exhaustion of dynamic strategies. North sees the dynamic process as an endless struggle of human beings to achieve their objectives by solving the problems of cooperation, whereas I see it as an eternal struggle to survive and prosper by investing in, and gaining political control of, the dominant dynamic strategy.

The Determinants of Economic Performance

Throughout his work North, as we have seen, associates poor economic performance with inefficient institutional structures. Differential growth rates between nations, he claims, can be explained by the different types of societal rules that these nations adopt. Favourite contrasting examples are Spain and England in the early-modern period, and today's developed and Third-World nations. This coincidence, of course, is not proof of a causal relationship between the two. It is quite possible that both the efficiency of institutional frameworks and the differential rates of economic growth are jointly determined by an omitted variable in North's analysis. The dynamic-strategy model suggests that, as will be discussed later in the chapter, the differences in both institutional efficiency and growth rates in the examples North uses were a function of the different dynamic strategies chosen and of the success of those strategies. It has nothing to do with the concept of path-dependence. One cannot, therefore, agree with North, or his followers (such as Yeager 1995), that 'incorporating institutions into history allows us to tell a much better story than we otherwise could' (North 1990: 131). A better story can only be told if we turn away from the various deductive schools of economics and of biology and look to reality itself. This is the subject of the rest of the chapter.

16.2   THE STRATEGIC APPROACH

The basic argument in this chapter is that institutions and organizations emerge and change in the longrun primarily in response to changing **strategic demand** generated by an unfolding dynamic strategy. Only their superficial, ephemeral forms are shaped by what I have called relative institutional prices. Hence, in a competitive environment, strategic demand for both institutional and organizational support will be met in the most efficient way possible at the time, in response to the relative costs of various possible alternatives that reflect factor endowments and prior historical developments. This has been demonstrated exhaustively in my recent book *The Ephemeral Civilization* (Snooks 1997a).[2]

Societal rules, both formal and informal, will be established and constantly altered to carry out the dynamic strategies by which decision-makers attempt to maximize their chances of survival and prosperity. These rules are required, as argued in Chapter 10, in order to economize on that scarcest of resources, the intellect. Similarly, societal organizations of all types – economic, political, social – also respond largely to these dynamic strategies, rather than to institutions as new institutionalists like Douglass North (1990) argue. The incentives to which organizations respond, therefore, are to be found in the strategic opportunities rather than the opportunities provided by institutions. Societal rules do not provide opportunities or incentives of their own volition, they merely communicate the opportunities generated by the fundamental dynamic forces. There will, of course, be a degree of interaction between these demand and supply forces, but causality flows overwhelmingly from the former to the latter. Also, rules do not evolve in a Darwinian manner as Friedrich Hayek (1988) argues.

It is in the process of **strategic imitation**, by which the vast majority of decision-makers emulate the action of the successful **strategic pioneers**, that societal rules are employed. Institutions are needed not only to economize on intelligence (not on information), but also to achieve strategic objectives through order and control. Hence the rule-makers, who are the strategic followers and the apostles of order, constitute the vast majority of decision-makers. Rules, therefore, are essential to the dynamics of human society even though they are purely derivative of it.

While these variables will be modelled more fully later in the chapter, enough has been said to provide a framework for categorizing institutions and organizations in order to see how institutional change occurs. Institutions and organizations are dealt with together here because both respond to strategic demand in similar ways, and because the new institutionalist focus on institutional rules is too narrow. They are jointly determined by strategic demand, and any *independent* interaction between them is relatively minor.

Strategic Institutions

Strategic institutions are those formal and informal rules of conduct that are required to support the emergence and development of the **dynamic strategies** of family multiplication, conquest, commerce, and technological change. These institutions, which operate at both the macro/micro and national/regional levels, cover the full societal spectrum of economic, social, and political activities. They include the economic and political systems; the rules by which business is conducted; the way goods, services, and factors of production are bought and sold; the way business is financed; the rules of monetary supply; the way property rights are allocated; the way politics is conducted; and the way people interact at a social level. The type of dynamic strategy pursued by a particular society has a characteristic and predictable impact upon all these institutions.

In simple societies the demands made upon intellectual faculties are *relatively* light and, hence, the role of formal rules is relatively unimportant; informal rules and custom are sufficient. As the society becomes increasingly complex, **strategic costs** (interpreted by institutionalists as transaction costs) will rise with the increasing demands made upon intellectual

resources. This will lead to the growing importance of formal institutions
or rules. This is not, as Mark Casson (1991: 3) has argued, a result of
declining 'mutual trust'; nor does it endanger the viability of that society.
What endangers society is the exhaustion and non-replacement of the
dominant dynamic strategy. This leads directly not to a reduction in trust,
but to a decline in **strategic confidence**. It is the decline in confidence in
the prevailing strategy by decision-makers that leads to a loss of trust and
societal order.

The variable nature of society's strategic institutions have been discussed in detail in *The Ephemeral Civilization* (Snooks 1997a). The four
main dynamic strategies generate demands for different types of societal
rules, in order to facilitate very different approaches to the eternal pursuit
of survival and prosperity. A few examples will suffice to illustrate my
point. As far as the economic and political system is concerned, a conquest
strategy will lead to central economic and political control by a military
strongman (king or dictator) because of the monopoly of economic ownership; the commerce strategy will see the emergence, owing to a more
widespread ownership of economic resources, of a regulated market system with a wider political franchise which, depending on the era, will
range from elected merchant princes in democratic city-states to parliamentary systems with an upper middle-class franchise in nation-states; and
the technological strategy results in a market system with a parliamentary
democracy based upon universal franchise owing to the universal system
of economic democracy. In Third-World (or transitional) societies entering
into the GST this will involve a shift from controlled (or command) systems to increasingly democratic economic and political systems. While
this set of relationships between the dominant dynamic strategy and the
economic and political system is not entirely precise at the detailed level,
it is quite clear in bold outline. The same is true of the different systems of
exchange, property rights, law, and social intercourse.

These relationships are not accidental. Different strategies can best be
implemented with different economic and political systems. A society that
switches from a commerce or a technological strategy to a conquest strategy, for example, will see the emergence of a new ruling elite; it will experience significantly less freedom of political or economic expression;
control over its rules of exchange will pass from private (free markets, private monopolies, guilds) to public (forced labour, plunder, state distribution) bodies; its property rights will change from a widespread (or even
universal) to a restrictive and authoritarian basis; and its democratic rules
of social exchange will be replaced by autocratic decree. Changes of this
nature can be seen throughout the historical record, as in the case of

Carthage (after 300 BC) and of Greece (after 338 BC) as they turned increasingly from commerce to conquest; and in the case of Germany and of Japan after the mid-1930s as they turned from the technological to the conquest strategies. These reversals, which were due to changing dynamic strategies, cannot be explained by evolutionary institutionalism. The same is true of more minor institutional changes taking place in modern society in response to the development and replacement of technological substrategies.

Strategic Organizations

As in the case of institutions, the various dynamic strategies call forth a set of characteristic and predictable organizations. In *The Ephemeral Civilization* (Snooks 1997a) I divide strategic organizations into two main categories – major strategic organizations, and support organizations. The major strategic organizations are those demanded by decision-makers to implement and expand society's dominant dynamic strategy. For societies pursuing the family-multiplication strategy, this involves the kinship teams required for hunting and gathering; for those pursuing conquest, it covers military and imperial organizations; for those pursing commerce, it includes trading and financial organizations together with state naval and foreign service organizations; and for those societies pursuing the technological strategy, it encompasses industrial and commercial organizations together with a comprehensive state bureaucracy. These strategic organizations are important not only because they facilitate the exploitation of strategic opportunities, but also because they are custodians of strategic and technological knowledge. As discussed in Chapters 12 and 15, **strategic knowledge** is central to the coordination and flexibility of the supply-side response to strategic demand, while technological knowledge is one of a number of strategic instruments that also include capital and labour.

Any society changing its dominant strategy would also need to change its major strategic organizations. A society, for example, switching from commerce to conquest – such as Athens during the Peloponnesian wars – would gradually replace its commercial organizational structure with a military structure; while a society switching from commerce to technological change – such as Western Europe between the eighteenth and nineteenth centuries – would replace its commercial structure with an industrial system. And we could expect to see a massive change in our present organizational structure if, under pressure from an eco-dictator, the technological strategy collapsed and, by default, was replaced by the conquest strategy (Snooks 1996: ch. 13). In this event the industrial–commerce complex would be subordinated to a military–imperial system. The effect would be similar to that achieved partially in both Europe and Asia in the 1930s and 1940s which saw the emergence of dictators pursuing irrational objectives such as racial purity. Finally, a Third-World nation, switching from antistrategic to strategic policies as it enters into the global strategic transition, will replace its organizations of exploitation with market-oriented organizations of industry and commerce.

Support organizations also depend upon the type of dynamic strategy pursued by any society. The nature of education and training, the type of manufacturing concerns, the character of research and development, and even the forecasting methods employed (compare the non-scientific forms employed in the conquest societies of both Nazi Germany and ancient Rome) depend on the dominant strategy. Once again this can best be seen in a society switching its dynamic strategy. With a shift from commerce to conquest – which can be seen in Carthage in the third century BC or Greece in the fourth century BC, or Venice in the early sixteenth century – the support organizations shift from a preoccupation with the development of skills and the manufacture of products required in trade to a focus on activities needed for war. This was also experienced in Western democracies during the Second World War.

Quite clearly, the strategic and support organizations of society depend upon the opportunities and incentives generated not by institutional constraints, as argued by Douglass North and other new institutionalists, but by its dynamic strategies. And changes in these organizations are driven not by forces on the supply side favoured by these institutionalists, but by the forces of strategic demand generated by an unfolding dynamic strategy. The role of supply forces – relative institutional prices – is limited to considerations of organizational design.

Changes in Institutions and Organizations

The key to understanding institutions is the realization that they can only achieve the objectives of those who employ them if they are relatively stable. It is not possible to conduct business successfully if the rules of the game, such as property rights and market regulations, are constantly changing. Continuous revolution, as the Chinese discovered in the 1960s and 1970s, is bad for business. Institutions, therefore, are of no use unless a degree of stability can be attained. But we know that they do change over time. The argument developed in *The Dynamic Society* (Snooks 1996) and *The Ephemeral Civilization* (Snooks 1997a) is that this change in the longer term is driven by strategic demand and shaped by relative institutional prices. As we have seen, dynamic demand changes when, and only when, there is a change in the fortunes of a strategy. Hence, those periods of relative stability in society's institutions reflect the stability of strategic demand rather than the stasis that, we are told by the evolutionary institutionalists, is supposed to characterize the Darwinian process of institutional change. Relative institutional prices, which are the costs of alternative institutions that can be adopted to facilitate the dynamic strategies, change owing to changes in economies of scale and technology that arise from the dynamic processes of the real economy.

Strategic Demand

Strategic demand for institutional and organizational structures is, as indicated above, generated by the dynamic process of the real economy. It is an outcome of the major dynamic strategies of family multiplication, conquest, commerce, and technological change. This is the 'fundamental law of institutional change' (Snooks 1998a: 233–4). It is the law on which all other institutional laws – such as those of democratization, social complexity, social cohesion, social unrest, and political collapse – are based. Shifts in strategic demand occur due to the changing fortunes – or unfolding – of the dominant dynamic strategy, and to the transition from one strategy to another. In turn these developments depend upon changes in relative factor endowments and in the wider competitive environment. As shown in Chapter 11, strategic demand is very different from the orthodox concept of aggregate demand, which is merely an outcome of the dynamic system at any point in time. Aggregate demand, which can be thought of as 'static demand', is both narrower than, and derivative of, strategic demand.

We need to consider both the nature of strategic demand and the forces that cause it to shift over time. Changes in institutions and organizations are achieved by human agents wanting to invest in the dominant dynamic strategy and needing to establish stable rules and organizations to do so. It is important to realize that this is not an evolutionary or unidirectional process, as institutional change will be reversed if there is a breakdown of the dynamic strategy or a reversal of the strategic sequence. The demand for relevant organizations is quite straightforward. Individuals form associations with each other – such as trading, financial, shipping, insurance, industrial, and military organizations – to enable investment in, and the operation of, the dominant dynamic strategy. The demand for institutions, however, is more complex because the procedure involved is less direct.

To change the formal strategic rules it is necessary to influence those who hold political power. This can be achieved either by tempting or pressuring the political leaders. Temptation can be exercised by giving the political leaders a share of the strategic profits either through bribery or through legal business arrangements. Political pressure is exercised by lobby groups who threaten to divert the political support of their strategic backers to the political opposition. In Third-World countries this is usually achieved by eventually sweeping away the old ruling antistrategists. The struggle for strategic control of the sources of wealth is tackled in Chapter 17.

Institutional Supply

While the primary dynamic mechanism generates a changing demand for institutions and organizations to facilitate the objectives of materialist man, their design is shaped by supply-side forces. Basically these forces involve costs associated with the range of feasible rules and organizations that could be employed in any particular society to meet the change in strategic demand. The forms chosen will depend upon which of the available alternatives meet the prevailing strategic demand most efficiently and hence maximize material advantage. This 'law of institutional economy' (Snooks 1998a: ch. 10) takes into account past decision-making and the general cultural context. In other words, the most efficient institution or organization 'available' to a particular society at a point in time is not necessarily the most efficient form available in a timeless sense. While a society's history of decision-making does not lock it into a particular development path, as many under the influence of recent ideas about 'path-dependence' claim, it does affect the costs of alternatives.

Within the limits provided by the strategic-demand framework, changes in institutions and organizations will also occur as relative institutional prices change. These prices change whenever there is a change in technology broadly conceived to include ideas relevant to the structure of human society. But even these changes depend upon the primary dynamic mechanism. Enough has been said about the supply side, as this has been discussed at length in the works of the new institutional economics. Yet a new perspective and orientation that gives pride of place to strategic demand is required in institutional analysis. Until now we have lacked a persuasive account of the demand side.

Only strategic demand can, for example, solve the puzzle in Douglass North's work of why apparently inefficient institutions persist in the longer term, particularly in the Third World. The model developed here suggests that inefficient institutions persist in societies where formerly successful dynamic strategies have been exhausted, or where dynamic strategies have never been successful. In these circumstances of *strategic* failure, the most profitable *tactic* for the ruling class is rent-seeking. And this rent-seeking generates a demand for tactical instruments – rules and organizations – that are, in comparison with societies employing success-ful dynamic strategies, relatively inefficient. Rent-seeking is a tactic rather than a strategy because it aims not to increase prosperity through the growth of real GDP per capita but merely to redistribute wealth more inequitably.

While the institutions associated with rent-seeking might seem ineffi-cient to the successful dynamic strategist, they are effective instruments in the hands of either failed strategists (as in many Third-World societies today), or dedicated antistrategists (as in the former USSR or in Communist China), in their attempt to gain a greater share of existing wealth. This model can, therefore, effectively account for the differences in institutions, organizations, and economic performance between England and Spain in the pre-modern period, or between developed and Third-World countries in the late twentieth century, that have puzzled North (1990: 113–17). Spain's earlier successful conquest strategy had been exhausted by the early seventeenth century and, in the competitive circumstances of the time, could not be replaced with the commerce strategy so effectively used by England throughout the sixteenth and seventeenth centuries. This pro-duced in Spain a level of performance and an efficiency of structure that compared unfavourably with England's, particularly as the exhausted commerce strategy in the eighteenth century gave rise to the technological strategy we know as the Industrial Revolution. The Spanish ruling elite, however, was able to use new and existing institutions quite effectively in redistributing wealth in their own favour and in maintaining the existence of a less-efficient economic system. North's explanation, that Spain's poor performance was the result of its culturally determined inefficient institutions, is not at all persuasive. It is not valid to use the coincidence of poor performance and 'inefficient' institutions as evidence for the institu-tional hypothesis for societal dynamics. Both are jointly determined by the dynamics of the real economy. The same is true for the continuing contrast between First- and Third-World nations. Only when Third-World countries enter into the GST will the balance between antistrategists and strategists change in favour of the latter, who will generate a growing strategic demand for strategic rather than antistrategic institutions and organiza-tions. Institutions are not a barrier to economic development but rather a reflection of it.

16.3 CONCLUSIONS

Institutions are important, but only in their facilitation of the strategic pursuit. They are not the centre of an evolutionary process as the institutionalists claim. Rather they are strategic instruments that respond to changes in strategic demand, which in turn is the outcome of the global strategic transition. An important part of their role is the accumulation of strategic ideas that are vital to strategic change. Nor are they the determinant of economic performance, as both are outcomes of the strategic pursuit. By treating human society as a strategic organization rather than a factory or a subject of Darwinian evolution, it has been possible to locate institutions securely in the process of social dynamics in developing nations.

17 Government and Strategic Leadership

Interpretations of the appropriate role for government in both **strategic countries (SCs)** and **nonstrategic countries (NSCs)** differ markedly. While some scholars view the state as a corrective for the excesses and failures of the market, others see it as the very source of these problems. More recently the World Bank (1997b) has adopted a compromise stance between these extreme positions. Yet none of these viewpoints captures the real role of the state in the Third World. The reason, as we have come to expect, is that economists have no general model of development that encompasses both the **global strategic transition (GST)** and the national process by which the reins of power pass between economic groups in society. Their views about the state are either ideologically or philosophically based.

The objectives of this chapter are to outline the various orthodox views of the role of government, to show how these fail to penetrate to the real issue, and to outline a more effective alternative approach. There are four main economic interpretations of the role of government: the neo-Keynesian, the 'socialist', the neoclassicist, and the institutionalist. The neo-Keynesians, as is well known, favour government intervention to enable escape from the low-level equilibrium trap; the socialists, including Marxists, dependency theorists, and humanists, insist that governments should either take control of the development process by formulating and implementing economic plans or, at the very least, ensuring equity before economic growth; the neoclassicists argue that government interference with market forces is the root cause of persistent underdevelopment; and the institutionalists, including those currently at the World Bank, claim that government has a positive role to play by facilitating rather than directing the development process. While these interpretations have waxed and waned over the past half century, currently the neoclassical view is in the ascendancy. But there are signs that it is being challenged by the institutionalist compromise.

As will become clear, none of these factions is able to satisfactorily relate the role of government to the wider development process. Accordingly, their suggestions for reform, which have been acted on by international organizations such as the IMF, the World Bank, and some luckless NSC governments, are damaging to the development process. In order to provide advice that is not damaging and may even be helpful, it is essential to consider the role of government within the framework of a global dynamic model that is also capable of analysing individual NSCs. Our analysis provides a new perspective on the objectives and role of government in the Third World as well as on policy.

17.1 THE ORTHODOX APPROACH TO GOVERNMENT

The four main interpretations of the role of government are briefly surveyed. While some of these issues have been discussed in earlier chapters we need to draw the threads together here. It can be seen that none of these orthodox viewpoints is based on a general model of economic development.

The Neo-Keynesians

The dominant theme in this orthodox faction is market failure. Persistent underdevelopment is interpreted as an outcome of markets failing to provide the incentives, information, and resources required to break free from the low-level equilibrium trap discussed in Chapters 13 and 14. They conclude that the only way to do so is by a 'big push' mounted by the central government. While this argument emerged from the influence of Keynes' *The General Theory* (1936) – in which it was argued that equilibrium could be achieved at less than the full-employment level of income owing to the failure of labour and money markets to clear – the concept of market failure can be traced back to Friedrich List (1789–1846).

List provided theoretical justification for countries, such as Germany, France, and the USA in the mid-nineteenth century, that were struggling to industrialize in the face of competition from Great Britain. In essence this was an attack on the British deductive school of economics – mainly Adam Smith – which advocated *laissez-faire* and free trade. While this trade policy was clearly in the interests of Britain, which had pioneered the First Industrial Revolution, it was not in the short-term interests of nations that were struggling to industrialize. Although List did not precisely formulate the famous 'infant industry' argument, it was the concept towards which he was struggling (Blaug 1986: 129–30). He argued that, left to itself, the market in an underdeveloped country would fail to give rise to firms and industries that could be internationally competitive with a limited period of initial protection. Accordingly, List argued, there was good reason for governments in underdeveloped countries, like Germany in the mid-nineteenth century, to actively pursue industrialization policies that included import duties and embargoes. Only once countries like Germany were able to compete with Britain, List argued, would international free trade be a desirable goal. Further, he claimed that the concept of welfare maximization arising from free trade is only valid under shortrun static conditions characterized by fixed production costs, and that it did not apply to the dynamic conditions of economic development (Hayami 1997: 208).

The big-push economists – including Rosenstein-Rodan (1943; 1957), Nurkse (1953), Singer (1958), and Hirschman (1958) – carried the concept of government intervention in the development process considerably further than did List. Together with socialists of various descriptions, they provided the intellectual rationale for the government-led economic development that predominated in intellectual and bureaucratic circles, international organizations, such as the IMF and the World Bank, and in the Third World for three decades following the Second World War. Despite the enthusiasm and optimism of this post-war generation, underdevelopment was still widespread in the mid-1970s. Indeed, the development prospects of some regions, such as Latin America, had even deteriorated. This failure, which has been blamed upon the neo-Keynesian policies, is regarded as 'government failure', as opposed to the market failure they had attempted to overcome.

The 'Socialists'

This is a rather diverse group. It includes Marxists who advocated the centrally determined model developed by the USSR, those who favoured a system of central planning consistent with a market economy and, more recently, those who maintain that economic development programmes should 'put people first' by placing equity before growth.

Neo-Marxist writers, in accordance with the master's analysis, anticipate that all countries will inexorably proceed through the 'historical' stages of capitalism, socialism, and communism. In other words, each and every underdeveloped society will pass through a development process that leads to the end of history – which is human freedom. The fact that this has not happened during the past half century has compelled Marxists of various descriptions to explain this failure. Unimaginative Marxists have actually blamed capitalists in the Third World for failing to fulfil their historical destiny. Accordingly they have advocated the Soviet model of dictatorship by the proletariat through revolution to force the pace of industrialization. It is a model that involves a system of central planning and control in order to achieve high rates of capital accumulation, modern capital-intensive technologies in the high priority capital goods sector, heavy investment in technical skills, the collectivization of agriculture, and import substitution. While many became increasingly disillusioned with this approach as applied in some Latin American and Southeast Asian countries, it lost all credibility when the USSR and Eastern Europe collapsed in the early 1990s.

Less orthodox Marxists, like Gunder Frank (1967), often called 'dependency theorists', offer a more sophisticated explanation of the persistence of underdevelopment. They view the development of capitalism as a dualistic process, by which the growth of Europe and North America has created a 'process of underdevelopment' in Africa, Asia, and Latin America. Underdevelopment, according to this interpretation, is an outcome of a process of dependency in which Third-World countries become appendages to the developed countries. And the economic development of these countries is distorted by this dependency. As decisions about development issues are made by external individuals and organizations, NSC surpluses are appropriated by the First World. The solution, we are told, is to eliminate the 'dependency relations' by developing self-reliant, non-dictatorial socialist systems in the Third World and by embracing a New International Order of national equality. Needless to say, this call for change is both idealistic and excessively optimistic.

Finally there are those who favour government intervention to tame rather than to transform capitalism. In the past this involved the advocacy of indicative planning to rationalize and help direct market forces. And, more recently, it has led to the argument that, in a new global order of cooperation and concern, governments should pursue equity before economic growth. Some influential orthodox development economists have promoted this humanist side of the development debate. Paul Streeten (1995), for example, has put forward a passionate and idealistic programme for human development in the Third World, and takes a stand against the economic rationalism of the neoclassicists. Essentially, he advocates a role for collective action through special organizations at both the national and global levels. At the national level Streeten believes that, through the 'empowerment' of the people, central governments would be able to pursue 'human development' and the 'elimination of poverty' rather than economic growth. Streeten (ibid.: 135) claims that 'economic growth is a side-effect, not the aim, of a rational economic policy'. The human development objectives of national governments, he assures us, will be supported by a new 'global order' based on fairness, equality, and human solidarity, which in turn will employ policy instruments such as a 'global monetary authority' and a 'global civil service' that must be responsible to the 'world community'. This, it need hardly be added, is a vision driven not by a realistic model of global dynamics but by humanist ideology. It is this type of unrealistic philosophical approach that has led some countries to establish 'centres for democratic institutions' aimed at 'promoting democracy, human rights, and effective governance' in developing countries.[1] Such policy, as we shall see later in this chapter, is based on a total misunderstanding of the relationship between economic development and political change and, therefore, it will only serve to exacerbate the underlying cause of underdevelopment and to waste resources that could be better used in other ways.

The Neoclassicists

The neoclassical viewpoint found expression throughout the second half of the twentieth century, but it became dominant only after the 1970s when the prevailing neo-Keynesian approach began to founder. This apparent failure was evident in both the First and Third Worlds. The reason for the persistence of underdevelopment, according to the neoclassical tradition, is not market failure as claimed by the neo-Keynesians but 'government failure'. Governments are not only less efficient than the private sector in the provision of goods and services, we are told, but their intervention is responsible for encouraging rent-seeking governments to grow out of control by seeking to maximize revenue in a manner unconstrained by 'moral rules'. This makes it possible for lobby groups to invest time and resources in persuading politicians in power to redistribute income in their favour through tariffs, subsidies, tax concessions, and export bounties. The end result, they claim, is to divert resources from their most efficient use. Hence, in order to eliminate the poverty trap in which Third-World countries are caught, it is necessary to eliminate market distortions introduced and maintained by governments, and to promote globalization.

Market distortions can only be eliminated by reducing the role of government to the bare minimum. This requires – according to James Buchanan (Buchanan *et al.* 1980) and other public choice theorists – restricting government activity to the provision of public goods, including the protection of individuals and property rights, and the enforcement of private contracts. As governments are predatory by nature they can only be restrained by developing constitutional rules that reflect the electorate's preferences. In effect, the public choice theorists refuse to recognize that governments can play a positive, proactive role in both the First and the Third World.

The promotion of 'globalization' involves opening up Third-World countries to global market forces. This requires the removal of all obstacles to trade and factor flows, such as tariffs and subsidies, together with controls over the exchange rate and the free movement of capital and labour. In this respect, neoclassical economists look to Adam Smith and David Ricardo who analysed the issues of government failure and free trade, rather than to Friedrich List and J. M. Keynes, as do the advocates of government intervention.

The Institutionalists

Like the public choice theorists, Douglass North (1981; 1990), one of the leading contemporary institutionalists, focuses on the central role of the state, but unlike them he invests government with the potential to play a positive as well as a negative role in economic development. North's theory of the state is based on the central idea that it is an organization trading revenue for 'protection and justice' – which includes establishing and supervising property rights and contracts – with a population of individuals pursuing wealth maximization (North 1981: 23). This exchange is an outcome of the economies of scale associated with the provision of these services. The state's objective is to maximize revenue, which it pursues by 'acting like a discriminating monopolist, separating each group of constituents and devising property rights for each'. But, in contrast to the public choice theorists, he quite rightly rejects the notion that there are no constraints on the state's desire for predatory power. North (ibid.: 35–6) explains that 'the state is constrained by the opportunity cost of its constituents since there always exist potential rivals to provide the same set of services', because revenue-seeking generates market inefficiency. The rivals, ever present in the wings waiting for their opportunity to occupy centre stage, include potential leaders within society and aggressive states without. As an economic historian, North has a much better understanding of reality than the public choice theorists.

A tension exists in North's model between the revenue-maximizing objectives of the state and the wealth-maximizing motives of its citizens. On the one hand, the state needs to establish a set of property rights specifying the ownership structure of both the factor and commodity markets to maximize the rents that it can extract; and, on the other, it must reduce transactions costs both to satisfy its clients and to increase output so as to enjoy growing revenues. But as the property rights structure that will enable the ruler to maximize rents conflicts with the most efficient structure that will maximize economic growth, the political and economic outcomes will be unstable. It is this instability that, according to North, explains the persistence of underdevelopment. Those Third-World nations able to resolve this conflict will be more successful in the struggle for economic development.

Clearly North's interpretation of the role of the state in Third-World countries has been influential, not least with those who compiled the 1997 World Development Report entitled *The State in a Changing World*, which also emphasizes the positive role of the state in economic development.[2] In effect, the World Bank takes a compromise stance between the neo-Keynesians and the neoclassicists. The World Bank (1997b: 1) claims:

> An effective state is vital for the provision of the goods and services – and the rules and institutions – that allow markets to flourish and people to lead healthier, happier lives. Without it, sustainable development, both economic and social, is impossible. Many said much the same thing fifty years ago, but then they tended to mean that development had to be state-provided. The message of experience since then is rather different: that the state is central to economic and social development, not as a direct provider of growth but as a partner, catalyst, and facilitator.

Growth, therefore, is to be generated by the market, while the state is to help out where it can without creating serious distortions.

The World Bank has no global model of economic development, nor does it appear to possess a realist theory of the role of the state. It views the state within a political philosophy framework – a deductive framework – asking what is an ideal state and how can Third-World governments achieve this ideal. They are not troubled by the realistic conflict raised by North, nor by the dynamic process of strategic struggle discussed in the second part of this chapter. They ignore existing political and economic realities and propose measures by which Third-World governments could, if they were disinterested and altruistic, improve the development performance of their nations. The authors' philosophical approach is reflected in the title of Part I of the World Bank's report – '*rethinking* the state', rather than *reconstructing the real role* of the state.

The basic message of the World Bank's report (1997b: 3–4) is that, in order 'to make every state a more credible, effective partner in its country's development', governments need to 'match the state's role to its capability' and to 'raise state capability by reinvigorating public institutions'. In the first place, therefore, Third-World governments should not overreach themselves. They should do the important things such as 'to deliver basic services, provide infrastructure, regulate the economy' and leave the rest to the market. By 'getting the fundamentals right', the World Bank means establishing a foundation of law; maintaining 'a nondistortionary policy environment', including macroeconomic stability; investing in 'basic social services and infrastructure'; protecting the vulnerable; and protecting the environment. They stress that the state must be aware of its own limits, that it need not be the sole provider of public utilities, and that it should cooperate with private interests.

The World Bank's definition of 'institutional capability', however, is totally unrealistic. The report claims (ibid.: 110) that 'a state that ignores the needs of large sections of the population in setting and implementing policy is not a capable state'. On this definition no pre-modern state could be regarded as 'capable', because all pre-modern societies were ruled by very small proportions of their populations. By this definition Rome (or Greece, Egypt, Assyria, Akkad, Carthage, China, or Tenochtitlan) could not be regarded as capable states despite the fact that they ruled most of the known world for much longer than any modern equivalent. Confusion exists in this report between a 'capable' state, which Rome certainly was, and a 'democratic' state, which Rome certainly was not. It is a confusion central to the flaw in contemporary development policy. To compound this confusion the report (ibid.: 111) also claims that 'throughout history nearly all societies have grappled with how to make the state reflect the needs and interests of the population'. This is a complete distortion of history and, if acted upon, will lead to a distortion of the development process. The report has confused the 'population' with the 'strategist'. In all pre-modern societies the strategists constituted only a tiny proportion of the population. This is critically important as societies – as we shall see – are ruled by and for the dynamic strategists, not for the population at large. Only in advanced technological societies are the strategists and the population virtually identical. This fundamental misinterpretation of reality reflects a misunderstanding of the objectives and role of government as well as the nature of the development process.

The second main thrust of the World Bank's recommendations is that a continuing attempt should be made to improve the 'capability' of Third-World states. This can be done 'by providing incentives for public officials to perform better while keeping arbitrary action in check'. These incentives include: effective rules and restraints, greater competitive pressure, and increased citizen voice and partnership. These more effective rules concern the separation of powers between the judicial, legislative, and executive branches of government, together with controls over discretionary authority to eliminate corruption. Greater competitive pressure must be imposed on the state by introducing and enhancing a system of merit in the public service, and by breaking the monopoly of state providers of public goods and services. The state should also be brought 'closer to the people by increasing consultation in policy-making and by decentralising its spending powers to the local level'. While these objectives are laudible, there is no way they will be effective unless they are introduced in response to strategic demand.

A strong sense of unreality pervades the World Bank report. This arises inevitably from the total absence of realistic models of global economic development and of the role of the state. As mentioned earlier, the method the authors of the report have employed is to outline how Third-World states can be transformed to match an unexplored philosophical ideal. This ideal appears to be based on Western ideas about what constitutes good democratic government rather than an evaluation of the realistic role played by governments in the global strategic transition. They make the same error as those countries which want to export democratic values rather than strategic ideas to NSCs.

This lack of reality also arises from the implicit focus of the report. It is difficult to see to whom the advice is being directed. The report's authors seem to believe, totally unrealistically, that in Third-World countries there exist influential, disinterested, and altruistic people who have the desire and power to reform their states. All they lack, apparently, is the wisdom or information so to do. And they must believe that the extent of this ignorance is infinite because they acknowledge that 'so few developing countries have managed to create effective state institutions' (ibid.: 144). The reality is that Third-World nations are controlled by ruling elites that may be influential, but are, quite naturally, the very reverse of disinterested and altruistic. Their concern is not to transform their states to conform with some sort of Western philosophical ideal but to employ them as instruments in the pursuit of their own self-interested objectives. This is how ruling elites have always acted (Snooks 1997a). To pretend otherwise is worse than unhelpful. The only way in which the World Bank's vision can be implemented is not through persuasion but through Western hegemony. Instead they rather lamely suggest that reforms might be adopted, despite all the acknowledged evidence to the contrary, in the event of economic crisis, external threat, the emergence of 'reform-oriented political leaders and elites', or through 'globalization'. This is merely the wishful thinking required to justify a deeply flawed analysis. What they have overlooked is the dynamic mechanism of strategic struggle to which we shall now turn.

17.2   THE STRATEGIC APPROACH TO GOVERNMENT

The strategic approach to government is touched upon in Chapter 12 where it is argued that government leadership is an important part of the **strategy function**. As we have seen, in the dynamic-strategy model the nature and changing role of government is a response to **strategic demand**. It is the role of the state to facilitate the dynamic pursuit of society's strategists. The state, therefore, is run by strategists for the benefit of strategists and not necessarily by and for the entire population as political philosophers often claim. Dynamic-strategy theory contains two key mechanisms that can be employed to explain the changing role of government. The first of these is the concept of **global strategic transition (GST)**, by which NSCs are drawn into the development process, and the second is the concept of the **strategic struggle**, by which the nature of government is transformed. They are interactive mechanisms.

The Global Strategic Transition

We can be brief because the GST mechanism has already been outlined in detail in Chapter 2. The process of economic development for an NSC begins when it interacts with countries that form the **global strategic core**. Essentially this occurs when SCs find they have something to gain from sustained economic exchange with an NSC. For the NSC there is little real discretion in this process. While an NSC can attempt to promote its attractions, in terms of natural resources, cheap labour supplies, or strategic location, it must wait until it gets drawn into the global development process before it can have an influence on development outcomes. Nevertheless, once under way economic development is generated from a mutual interaction between the strategic core and the **global strategic fringe**.

Evidence for the causal sequence outlined here can be found in the entire history of mankind (Snooks 1996; 1997a) and, more recently, in the many costly development failures over the past fifty years. Following the end of the Second World War there was considerable optimism about the ability of the First World to force the pace of development in the Third World. This was a natural outcome of the success achieved both in Europe and Japan in the wake of massive aid by the USA and the newly formed international organizations such as the IMF and the World Bank. If the war-ravaged developed world could be so quickly reconstructed, it was reasoned, it should be possible to release the Third World from its poverty trap.

By the mid-1970s it was clear that this early optimism was an illusion. Much of the Third World remained in poverty despite a massive injection of aid, capital investment, and technical training and advice by the First World. But there was a new element in this apparently unchanging situation – the crippling burden of debt under which the Third World now laboured. The drive against underdevelopment had not only failed but had actually made the economic circumstances of many poor countries even worse. The underlying problem, which was unrecognized then and remains unrecognized now, is that economic development as a whole cannot proceed any faster than the pace at which the global technological paradigm unfolds. Clearly individual countries that are particularly favoured can develop more rapidly than the average. Europe and Japan, for example, were able to recover rapidly after the Second World War because they were integral parts of the global strategic core, whereas most of the Third World was unable to develop because they had not even begun to interact systematically with this core. Attempts to force the pace were counterproductive because they only helped to distort and delay the transition process.

It is probably necessary to repeat an important point made earlier in Chapter 2, that there is nothing inevitable or preordained about the GST. This process is the outcome of individuals throughout the world exploring and investing in strategic opportunities in order to survive and prosper in a competitive world. This process can and does falter, and it can even be thrown into reverse, as has occurred in the past (Snooks 1997a: ch. 10). It did falter during the 1940s when the world advanced the war front rather than the strategic front. And it faltered again during the 1970s and 1980s following the OPEC oil crises and the failed attempt to force the pace of economic development in the Third World. And it will falter again in the future if there is any concerted international attempt to constrain growth-inducing technological change in the misguided belief that this action will save the planet. Neither is the entry of individual NSCs into the global strategic transition inevitable or preordained. While enlightened policy will not advance the timing of an NSC's development, misguided policy certainly will delay, even postpone indefinitely, this process.

One of the most important problems encountered by those international organizations and developed nations that attempted to force the pace of economic development was the fact that NSC ruling elites and their governments saw little advantage, and great personal danger, in promoting the development of their countries. NSCs are usually run by antistrategic ruling elites who attempt to exploit and control potential strategists in their society. This begins to change only when the interaction between the global strategic core and an NSC gets underway. In other words, the wider global strategic process is essential to changing the attitudes, institutions, and politics in the NSC. Yet even this is a slow process as it takes time for the new strategists to accumulate economic wealth that can be translated into political power through the strategic struggle; and, of course, the antistrategists can be counted on to resist these changes with all their influence and power. This is why those, like current officers in the World Bank, who argue that existing governments in the Third World can be reformed by visionary leaders or by external shocks are well wide of the mark. The key to political reality is the strategic struggle that we will now explore.

The Strategic Struggle

The second major mechanism transforming the role of government, therefore, is the strategic struggle. It is through this competitive process that control of the **dynamic strategy** passes from one group to another. To understand how this mechanism operates we need to consider this issue – first presented in my *The Ephemeral Civilization* (Snooks 1997a) – in some detail.

The process of political transformation in any society is dominated by the struggle between various socioeconomic groups for control of the dynamic strategy. To control the dynamic strategy is to control a society's sources of income and wealth. The strategic struggle is, therefore, fundamentally an economic struggle – a struggle for survival and prosperity – despite its use of political instruments. This struggle is one of the 'primary laws of history' (Snooks 1998a: ch. 8). The groups involved in this struggle can be classified as follows:

- the strategists (or profit-seekers):
  - old strategists – supporters of the traditional strategy;
  - new strategists – supporters of the emerging strategy;
- the nonstrategists (coerced workers and dependents);
- the antistrategists (or rent-seekers):
  - conservative antistrategists;
  - revolutionary antistrategists.

All societies at any given time include representatives of these strategic groups, which are involved in a continuous struggle against each other for influence and control over the sources of income and wealth, and against governments that fail to provide either effective strategic leadership or good strategic value for taxes. The relative importance in society of these strategic groups changes considerably over time, not as a simple progression but as a complex yet predictable function of the unfolding dynamic strategy. And in turn, this unfolding is an outcome of the interaction between an NSC and the global strategic core.

These strategic categories require definition. The **strategists** are the driving force in society who invest time and resources in pursuing and profiting from the existing dynamic strategy and its substrategies. They are profit-seekers because the returns they seek are from investments that generate growth rather than a redistribution of a given GDP per capita in their favour. Strategic investment includes both physical and human capital. This is not a homogeneous group, as it consists of old strategists, who support the traditional strategy, and of new strategists, who explore the emerging strategy. As the old strategy shows signs of exhaustion, these two groups struggle for power, with the outcome determining the society's future. The mechanism by which the new strategy spreads throughout society is called the process of **strategic imitation**, and it involves (as shown in Chapter 10) the imitation of the success of the **strategic pioneers** by vast numbers of followers eager to share in the spoils. But, of course, the problem in NSCs, in contrast to SCs, is that the strategists are a tiny proportion of the total population, and they are kept in their place and exploited by the rent-seeking ruling elite who are the antistrategists.

The **nonstrategists** are unable to invest in the prevailing dynamic strategy largely because they are controlled and exploited by the strategists. There is no competititve demand for their services. While this is not a very large group in modern SCs – being restricted to minors and social deviants – it can form the majority in NSCs. Similarly, in the West in pre-modern times it also included the great majority of the population. Yet, rather than declining over time in a linear fashion, the role of the non-strategist has described a great circle from early hunter–gatherer societies, when the family controlled economic activities and the participation rate was high, to ancient and medieval societies, when small ruling elites forcibly employed large numbers of dependent labourers and slaves; to today when the great majority actively participate in the prevailing strategy. Today's NSCs have yet to complete this circle, and nonstrategists remain to be exploited by their ruling elites. While they continue to exist, so will their predators. It is a vicious, symbiotic relationship.

The **antistrategists** are interested not in economic growth but in distributing existing income even more completely in their favour. In an NSC, rent-seeking is a rational pursuit prior to a society being drawn into the global strategic transition, because there are few attractive profit-making opportunities to excite the attention of the ruling elite. As mentioned earlier, the antistrategists thrive off the nonstrategists (or potential strategists), and will continue to exist as long as their prey. In ESCs and SCs the antistrategists exist in two forms, the conservative antistrategists who pursue their objectives peacefully within the law, and the revolutionary antistrategists who attempt to hijack the dynamic strategy. The revolutionary anti-strategists comprise that small but extremely ruthless minority dedicated to overthrowing the dynamic strategy for their own rent-seeking purposes. While this group is always present in ESCs and, even, SCs, it comes to prominence during times of crisis, for example the Bolsheviks in Russia in 1917, the Nazis in Germany in the 1930s, and the militarists in Japan in the 1930s. Essentially they hijack the strategic struggle between the old and new strategists. In doing so they recreate in industrial societies conditions that exist in NSCs. It is a reversion to earlier forms of repression.

The problem for NSCs is that the strategic struggle is in abeyance. Small antistrategic ruling elites dominate populations in which the great majority of people are nonstrategists. The potential strategists – those with the human capital and inclination to invest in profit-seeking activities – exist in such small numbers and in such grinding poverty that they are not in a position to overthrow the antistrategists. They just do not have sufficient economic power. In these circumstances there is no way that the ruling elites are going to voluntarily hand over power to the people as suggested by the World Bank (1997). Even external crises will not change this situation as they claim: the ruling *dynasty* may be swept aside, but it will be replaced not by new strategists, as there is no new strategy, but by another *dynasty* of antistrategists. There is no point in lecturing NSC elites on democracy when the potential strategists do not possess the economic power to move to centre-stage. The strategic struggle must precede any political transformation.

As suggested earlier, the antistrategists will not be removed until our NSC has been converted into an ESC by being drawn into the global strategic transition. In the process, nonstrategists are converted into strategists, who grow in numbers and economic power, partly at the expense of the existing antistrategists. Eventually the strategists will be able to sweep the antistrategists aside, just as they will soon do in China, where the strategists have been rapidly multiplying and growing more wealthy since the late 1970s.

It is just not possible to democratize NSCs that have not entered into the global strategic transition. Advice to the contrary by well-meaning intellectuals and humanitarians can only lead to a distortion of the strategic process. This form of **strategic distortion** is far more serious than the market distortion resulting from government intervention that has been identified by neoclassical economists. Even if the institutional framework of democracy is retained by an NSC pressured by international interests, it will merely be a hollow form that disguises the exploitation of the antistrategists. All that will be achieved is a slowdown in the real force of democratization – the strategic struggle. It is, therefore, essential that developed countries refrain from the desire to recreate the world in their own image. While the desire is natural, it demonstrates a complete lack of understanding of the history of even their own societies.

In this context it is important to emphasize that the political transformation is not an evolutionary process. An example from the First World will clarify the issue. Despite the apparent evolutionary progression in English political institutions over the past millennium, **strategic reversals** are possible. While England, the world's first industrial nation, has experienced a conquest commerce technological strategic sequence, there was nothing inevitable about this. It was the outcome of a particularly fortuitous and happy coincidence: the exhaustion of the commerce strategy in the mid-eighteenth century coincided with the exhaustion of the neolithic technological paradigm (Snooks 1997a: 292–302). Had the exhaustion of England's commerce strategy occurred prior to the end of the neolithic technological paradigm, the strategic sequence would have been conquest commerce conquest, as it was for ancient Greece and as was feared in Britain by Adam Smith's contemporaries. Such a strategic reversal would have led to a reversal of sociopolitical forms possessing the same function as similar sociopolitical forms in earlier times. In these circumstances, old commerce strategists would have been overwhelmed by a new military (rather than industrial) elite that would have required different political, social, and economic institutions. In particular, democratic institutions would have been dismantled and replaced by more repressive institutions controlled by the new men of conquest, as happened in ancient Greece under the Macedonians.

The strategic reversal, therefore, leads to a reversal of strategic demand and, hence, of institutions. As far as ESCs are concerned, the important point is that if the global strategic transition falters, as it did in the 1970s, the radical antistrategists may sweep back into power and reverse the process of political democratization. The progress of democratization is not inevitable as it depends on the fluctuating fortunes of the unfolding dynamic strategy. Elsewhere I have called this 'the law of democratization', which applies to all political, economic, and social institutions and organizations.

While the changing political process is similar at both the strategic and substrategic level – both are outcomes of the strategic struggle – there is a major difference. Generally speaking, at the strategic level the struggle is between supporters of entirely different strategies – in the case of NSCs between the old antistrategists and the new antistrategists – whereas at the substrategic level it takes place between factions within a single strategy. In other words, at the substrategic level all participants accept and support the existing economic/social/political system, and the strategic struggle involves the pursuit of more advantageous positions within that system. Accordingly, neither the new or old **strategic factions** wish to pursue their struggle to the point where the existing system breaks down. Instead they seek resolution of their differences through existing political structures – although they will need to modify them in the process – to achieve a marginal redistribution of income from one faction to another. Those factional struggles only become central in ESCs when it is generally accepted that these societies have entered securely into the global strategic transition.

Clearly the dynamic-strategy model is diametrically opposed to Karl Marx's concept of class and class struggle. In my model the defining characteristic of a strategist is that he or she invests in either physical or human capital which is required in the *pursuit* of a society's dynamic strategy. By contrast, Marx's concept of class and class struggle is based on ownership of the means of *production*; hence, the population of a modern technological society (misleadingly called 'capitalist' by Marx) is divided into 'capitalists' and 'workers' involved not in a *strategic pursuit* but in a *process of production*. Marx failed to realize two essential matters. First, that the dynamics of human society is an outcome of a strategic pursuit rather than a process of production; and secondly that all 'classes' in the technological society are part of the same strategist group because they invest time and resources in the prevailing substrategy and they benefit from the returns to this strategic investment. Rewards depend not on the type of ownership of the means of production as Marx argued, but on the amount and quality of strategic investment. Workers as well as capitalists have a stake in the technological society and neither group has any intention of destroying it.

In the dynamic-strategy model, therefore, there is no fundamental conflict between 'capital' and 'labour', because they all accept, pursue, and benefit from the technological strategy. The objective of the struggle between strategic factions in contemporary society in both SCs and ESCs is to marginally influence the distribution of a growing national product, not to derail the technological strategy. Both 'capital' and 'labour' are on the same side in the more critical struggle against rent-seeking antistrategists. This is why there has been no real proletarian revolution – only antistrategic takeovers in the name (only) of the proletariat – in any technological society. It is for this reason that Marx was wrong about the future of 'capitalism'. Quite incorrectly he saw all 'capitalists' as rent-seekers – as exploiters of labour – rather than as profit-seekers; and he viewed 'class struggle' incorrectly as the central mechanism in the rise and fall of capitalism rather than as a secondary process in the transfer of political power.

17.3   STRATEGIC LEADERSHIP

The primary role of government is to provide **strategic leadership**. This involves facilitating the achievement of the materialistic objectives of society's dynamic strategists. While important, the governmental functions of protecting property rights, supervising contracts, providing public goods, and delivering welfare services are secondary. As I have shown in *The Ephemeral Civilization* (Snooks 1997a), the very reason for the emergence of central governments was to coordinate and promote the interests of those investing in society's dominant dynamic strategy. In essence, the state is and has always been an instrument of the strategists – it is run by and for the strategists at the expense of the nonstrategists (or dependent workers and slaves). Only during the mature phase of the modern technological strategy, when virtually the entire population of SCs had been drawn into the dynamic strategy and, hence, had become strategists, did the state represent all the people. Only then did it become a provider of universal protection and welfare.

NSCs, however, are not modern technological societies. As they have yet to be drawn into the GST they are in a similar position to Western societies before – long before – the Industrial Revolution. It should be realized, however, that while their initial circumstances are similar they are able to transform themselves more rapidly than in the past through the mechanism of **strategic imitation**. Essentially they are dominated by either antistrategists or narrowly based strategic elites, and the majority of their populations can still be classified as nonstrategists. Strategic leadership in NSCs, therefore, is for the benefit of the minority, as it has been through most of human history.

But once a society has been drawn into the GST, its burgeoning strategic group begins to exert an influence on its pre-modern government. Governments in these ESCs are expected to provide strategic leadership by clearing away obstacles to development and by helping to chart a new economic course. If they fail to respond to this strategic demand, political pressure builds through the opposition of the strategists that will eventually sweep the antistrategists away. By doing so, the new strategists capture the state and turn it to facilitating their economic interests. This is what we can expect to see in China and Southeast Asia (including Indonesia) in the near future.

Once the state has been captured by the strategists it is expected to provide strategic leadership. Needless to say this is not an easy transition. If the prevailing political faction, through ignorance or incompetence, is unable to satisfy the majority of the strategists it will be replaced with one that can. As the transition proceeds and a growing proportion of the population enter into the strategic ranks, the political complexion of the state will change. What never changes, however, is the expectation that it must serve the interests of the strategists by providing strategic leadership. Needless to say this expectation is not clearly articulated, rather it is 'expressed' through the primeval process of the strategic struggle. Until now, this reality has not been spelt out in intellectual terms. The prevailing political philosophy is in the deductive Platonic tradition that views the essence of the state in idealistic rather than realistic terms.

What is strategic leadership? As suggested already, it involves state action that facilitates the private exploitation of strategic opportunities. This can only be effectively achieved by government if it is in tune with the desires and needs of the strategists and if it provides the type of leadership that assists their interests. Government survival depends on this. If the state cannot provide acceptable and effective strategic leadership it can do nothing. And its central concern must be to assist in the development of strategic ideas and strategic knowledge. This is the essential platform from which economic development must proceed. Strategic ideas, which can be used to reshape the strategy function, can only be usefully formulated, however, in cooperation with existing and emerging strategists.

What in practice do we mean by strategic ideas? Many of the issues involved have been touched upon already in preceding chapters. Basically they are concerned with whether private and public bodies should focus on:

- a broad or a narrow economic front;
- manufacturing or agriculture;
- capital-intensive or labour-intensive technologies;
- import substitution or export promotion;
- domestic savings or foreign borrowing;
- foreign or domestic technology;
- rapid or slow population growth.

These general considerations will be dealt with in the context of those specific activities that provide the greatest return on the investment of time and capital, given the NSC/ESC resource endowment and its competitive environment. The dynamic substrategies chosen and strategic leadership provided will depend on the particular circumstances in which Third-World countries find themselves. Each society is unique. Hence, only the general principles can be dealt with in this book.

Strategic leadership, as shown by a systematic study of history (Snooks 1997a), can take a variety of forms. Essentially it embraces central decisions about how a society can be organized to achieve the best outcomes for its supporting strategists. This can take the form of central planning, mixed private–public enterprise, or minimal government involvement. Invariably the first and last of these three approaches have failed.

The Failure of both Central Planning and Neoliberalism

The last decade has witnessed massive planning failures in the USSR and Eastern Europe together with their Third-World satellites. The usual neoclassical argument is that state control is a relatively easy matter in simple economies, but as those economies mature and become more sophisticated governments need to relax their controls and allow the market to assume its rightful place. Unless this occurs, we are told, the lack of sufficient information and the high transactions costs will cause a centrally determined economy to grind to a halt (Hayami 1997: 219–20). The real reason for the collapse of the Second World, however, is quite different: basically, the command model is incompatible with the competitive pressure to survive and prosper. The truth is that the Stalin model is very good at achieving the objectives of the radical antistrategists, which is to prevent the reemergence of the strategists from whom they hijacked society and to maximize the extraction of rents from the nonstrategists. What the antistrategic society is not good at, in contrast to the strategic society, is in delivering high and sustained rates of economic growth. In an antistrategic world this would not matter, but in the real world of highly competitive strategic societies the antistrategic society is just not able to keep up in the longer term. The command system fails for strategic rather than institutional reasons.

Strategic societies in which governments persistently fail to understand the role of strategic leadership will also suffer in the global struggle to survive and prosper. This is a danger that, at the end of the twentieth century, faces many SCs and NSCs alike. Seduced by prevailing neoclassical views and with an affinity for unimaginative, hair-shirt policies of containment and deflation, many governments around the world have accepted the neoliberal view that the state should take a minimalist stance consistent with static efficiency. The fundamental problem is that it is inconsistent with dynamic progress. Neoliberal views are based not only on a failure to recognize the dynamic role of strategic leadership but also on flawed theories about the relationship between economic growth, unemployment, and inflation (Snooks 1998b). By rejecting the role of strategic leadership – which involves promoting the interests of strategists – and striving for static efficiency – which blocks the interests of strategists – economic growth slows and unemployment rises. Yet, perversely, this is seen as the signs of success by governments and their neoclassical advisers who are confused about the real role of inflation.

Unfortunately these static policies have been forced on the Second and Third World by the leading lending nations and by international organizations like the IMF and the World Bank. It has become the condition for access to ready sources of funds. In this way the First World has contributed to the slowing down of the GST. It is a very dangerous approach. In the first place it will lead to a degree of political instability in the First World as governments are continually being swept away but, in the absence (at least until now) of any recognized alternative, the old destructive policies are being maintained. And secondly it will lead to a faltering of the GST and, hence, to the reemergence of the antistrategists in ESCs. To avoid this potentially disastrous outcome, neoclassical policies in SCs, ESCs, FASCs, and NSCs must be abandoned in favour of strategic policies that emphasize the concept of strategic leadership.

The Role of Trade Protection

The second main issue of strategic leadership is that of protection or free trade. As we have seen, neoclassicists regard government failure (distorting the market) as a greater problem than market failure (market malfunctions). The problem of underdevelopment can be resolved, they tell us, by opening up the Third World to free trade rather than by following the downward path of protection. In today's jargon that means connecting the Third World to the process of globalization. The usual argument is that global income per capita will increase owing to the increasing international specialization according to comparative advantage and to the reduction in rent-seeking as government-induced market distortions are eliminated.

In a static world these conclusions have some force, but in a dynamic world they need to be modified. Tariffs are a policy instrument that has been effectively employed in the past to enable latecomers to industrialize in the face of keen competition from the global strategic core. Successful examples of this tactic can be found in the cases of Germany, which used tariffs to protect its 'infant' industries from British exports in the mid-nineteenth century; of the USA, which employed the same tactic in the second half of the nineteenth century to protect its industrialization process from West European competition; and of Australia in the interwar years, especially against competition from the USA (Snooks 1997a). The same valid tactics are also available to the Third World today provided they are only regarded as a first step in the development of a genuine technological substrategy, as was done in East Asia. On the other hand, if protectionism is indefinitely maintained, as in Latin America, the development process will stall. The fundamental point is that tariffs, like all other policy measures, can be used for good or ill. There is nothing inevitable about government failure, except when the role of strategic leadership is rejected.

The historical evidence (Snooks 1996; 1997a) suggests that real government failure – when societies falter and even collapse – is an outcome not of intelligent government intervention but of an inability or refusal to provide strategic leadership. *A government that meets all the neoclassical criteria for static efficiency but does not provide strategic leadership is a failure and it will be swept away.* And a society that continues to ignore the obvious lessons and refuses to abandon neoclassical policies will be severed from the GST and, hence, will suffer life-threatening political instability. Dynamic failure in the real world is more important than static failure in the neoclassicists' virtual world.

17.4 CONCLUSIONS

Strategic leadership is fundamental to the success of societies engaging with the GST. This is true at all times and in all places. The primary role of government is to facilitate the exploitation of strategic opportunities, which is best done in close collaboration with their society's dynamic strategists. And the central part of that function is the selection and application of strategic ideas. Strategic leadership involves using whatever tactics are required to enable an NSC to enter into the strategic transition. This will involve transcending the pseudo-puritanical strictures of the apostles of static efficiency and embracing the dynamic proficiency of the strategic approach. The very real threat to our age arises from a situation in which strategists are able to remove offending political dynasties but are not able to replace their policies with those that will lower the barriers to the GST. This is because, until now, there has been no alternative set of theoretically grounded policy principles to neoliberalism. The latter is the subject of the final chapter.

Part VI
Conclusion

18 Strategic Predictions and Policies

In this final chapter consideration is given to the predictions and policies that arise from the dynamic-strategy model of economic development. Not only is this an important role for economic and political modelling, it is also a critical test of the usefulness of such work. If a model cannot be used to make sensible predictions and propose useful policy then it is unlikely to be able to provide even a satisfactory explanation of the present and the past. This inadequacy may not be otherwise discernible owing to the sophisticated modelling techniques, particularly of advanced mathematics, employed by contemporary economists. In Chapters 7 and 8 it is shown that traditional economics, both orthodox and radical, is unable to provide either a satisfactory vision of the future or useful principles for formulating policy regarding economic development.

18.1   STRATEGIC PREDICTIONS OF THE FUTURE

It is clear from the discussion in Chapter 8 that the traditional approach to economic growth and development has been unable to provide convincing predictions about the future for countries at any stage of development. The reason is that it has failed to successfully model the global dynamic process. Neoclassical theorists have limited their focus to the modern economy's system of production, which is merely the means whereby the exogenous dynamic impetus is translated into a greater per capita surplus. As these models do not address the core dynamic mechanism they are unable to tell us anything about the future of **nonstrategic countries (NSCs)**, **emerging strategic countries (ESCs)**, **former antistrategic countries (FASCs)**, or even **strategic countries (SCs)**. Historicists, such as Marx and Rostow, have been equally unsuccessful in predicting future economic change because they have either adopted metaphysical explanations, or have merely extrapolated past patterns of events into the future.

   The only way to successfully explore the past, present, and future is by constructing a general dynamic model that can embrace the entire development experience at both the national and global levels. The dynamic-strategy model developed in this book has strong empirical roots and it encompasses the entire dynamic mechanism rather than just the means by which an exogenous dynamic impetus is converted into a larger surplus, together with sociopolitical as well as economic forces, and the dynamic process at the global as well as the national level. Two aspects of the strategic vision of the future are examined here: the future development of the **global strategic transition (GST)** and the coming of the next **technological paradigm shift**. Both issues arise from the logical operation of the dynamic-strategy model and *not* from the extrapolation of past patterns into the future.

The Future of the GST

The dynamic-strategy model provides a theoretical account of the GST that can be tested against real-world experience. In Chapter 2 it is argued that the modern GST is the outcome of the **unfolding industrial technological paradigm** that began with the Industrial Revolution in the late eighteenth century and that will be exhausted in the not-too-distant future. It is a highly competitive process driven by individuals and their political representatives, who adopt effective technological substrategies in order to survive and prosper. The resulting strategic struggle at the global level generates an intense interaction within and between the **global strategic core** consisting of wealthy SCs and its **strategic fringe** consisting of ESCs and NSCs. It is from this strategic core–fringe interaction that the GST progresses, drawing into its vortex an increasing number of NSCs.

When an NSC enters into the global strategic transition, it adopts a viable **technological substrategy** that is part of the wider process of strategic core–fringe interaction. Economic development is, therefore, the outcome of a strategic pursuit, not of a production process. As this substrategy unfolds it generates a changing national **strategic demand** for a range of factor, technological, institutional, and strategic inputs and it generates a growing **strategic confidence** that guarantees trust and cooperation. A central part of this strategic demand–response mechanism, which provides the necessary incentives, is the generation of **strategic inflation**. As the dynamic strategy unfolds, a growing proportion of the population in our society is drawn into its orbit because they invest time and resources in its operation and share in its success. In an attempt to secure control over the sources of their income and wealth, the new strategists come into conflict with the old antistrategists. From this **strategic struggle**, the new strategists gain political power to protect their wealth. Unless reversed by a military takeover, the growing 'strategization' of society leads increasingly to the democratization of sociopolitical institutions. Steadily the NSC is transformed into an ESC and, finally, an SC. Of course, there will be many difficulties on the way, including some major reversals as being experienced in Indonesia today. The GST must not be thought of as an inevitable or irreversible process.

The evidence presented in Chapter 3 shows how far the modern GST has progressed since the late eighteenth century. The fact that this progress is not arbitrary or accidental but rather systematic and continuing has significance in terms of the persistent attempt by the development community to 'come to the aid' of the Third World with their interventionist agenda (even the neoliberals). It does not seem to faze them that their agenda has *never* been successful. The reason for the development community's continuing interest is that they are pursuing their own materialist objectives. At the national and international level, the superpowers and development organizations employ aid for wider strategic purposes such as the exercise of control over essential resources (such as oil) and key locations (such as military intervention in Japan, Korea, Vietnam, Afghanistan). It is a significant fact that the concept of economic development emerged as a subject of interest for the superpowers as their direct territorial control through colonialization declined. And at the individual level, there is much to be gained by intellectuals, bureaucrats, and politicians from the continued fiction that economic development can only be achieved through their involvement. The reverse is true.

The dynamic-strategy model is able to show that the GST is a self-generating process that does not require any intervention by the development community. Indeed, this type of intervention leads only to a waste of development resources, to a delay in economic development, and even to a temporary reversal of this process. Surely if the development community was really concerned with ensuring that the Third World join the First World as quickly as possible, a much greater effort would have been devoted to understanding the global dynamic process. Ironically, now that a general dynamic model is available, it can be seen that the GST is a self-reinforcing process that has been successfully completed on three former occasions in human history even without the existence of a development community or a development industry.

I anticipate that the modern GST will be largely complete by the end of the twenty-first century. By this I mean that most countries will have achieved SC status, but, as in all forms of human endeavour, there will be failures. This is not to suggest that there will be an equality of outcomes. There will always be some societies that are more enterprising or lucky than most, just as there will be others that are considerably less enterprising or lucky. It is the same for societies at the global level as it is for individuals at the national level. And there will be fortunately placed societies at the leading edge of the next **technological paradigm shift**.

The Future Technological Paradigm Shift

The dynamic-strategy model shows that once the industrial technological paradigm has been fully exploited, the pressures will mount for the forging of a new paradigm. The outcome will take the form of a technological paradigm shift – popularly known as an economic revolution – that will open up vast new possibilities from the innovative use of the world's natural resources. The only alternative for a world unable to stand still is reversion to the conquest strategy, which could lead to nuclear holocaust and to the destruction of civilization and even of life. These conclusions arise from the logical operation of the dynamic-strategy model and not from the extrapolation of patterns from the past, although they are supported by the historical record.

I have no intention of devoting much time to this aspect of my theory here. It has been developed at some length in both *The Dynamic Society* (Snooks 1996: ch. 13) and *The Ephemeral Civilization* (Snooks 1997a: ch. 13) in both theoretical and empirical terms. There are two reasons for raising the issue again in this book. First, it is the logical outcome of the GST, which is responsible for spreading the underlying technological paradigm throughout the globe. As each NSC becomes absorbed into the global strategic core, the day draws closer when the industrial technological paradigm will be exhausted. While-ever there are underutilized natural resources somewhere in the world it is more economical for the strategic core to extend its existing influence than to invest in a new technological paradigm. But there will be strategic hot spots that may lead to the beginning of a new economic revolution before the GST has been entirely worked out. In this case the spread of the new paradigm will be delayed until the old paradigm has reached the ends of the Earth. This will place the lagging countries in an even more difficult economic situation. In the past these strategic hot spots involved limited geographical areas – **funnels of transformation** – that were subject to a high degree of interaction and cross-fertilization and, hence, exhausted the existing paradigm more quickly. In the past these funnels of transformation included the rift valley of East Africa, the fertile crescent in the Middle East, the Meso-American isthmus, and the North Sea. The future is another matter.

The second reason for introducing the technological-paradigm-shift concept is that it is essential to a full understanding of the issue of environmental degradation. Only with the use of the dynamic-strategy model is it possible to distinguish between the unnecessary degradation of natural resources that must be addressed with restorative action, and the depletion of natural resources owing to pressures generated by an exhausting technological paradigm. The dynamic-strategy model suggests that the future will be similar to the situation in Western Europe, and particularly Britain, during the second half of the eighteenth century when organic resources were severely depleted owing to the exhaustion of the neolithic technological paradigm. This pressure was not released until the technological paradigm shift, popularly known as the Industrial Revolution, occurred. In the future, continued progress of the GST will release pressure on organic resources in the Third World by eliminating the need for population expansion and by shifting strategic demand from organic to inorganic resources; but at the same time it will increase pressure on inorganic resources and will further contribute to problems such as global warming and the diminishing ozone layer. Only with the future technological paradigm shift will these environmental problems be solved by the introduction of entirely new energy sources (solar power) and construction materials (Snooks 1997a: 492–8). The worst thing that policy-makers could do would be to ban or restrain growth-inducing technological change in the mistaken belief that this will save the environment. In fact only the completion of the GST will both save the environment and transform the living standards of the Third World.

18.2 STRATEGIC POLICY

Traditional development policy is, as shown in Chapter 7, in a complete muddle. There is no integrated approach to development policy, which has fragmented into a large number of inconsistent issues. Once again the reason for this is the failure of orthodox economists to construct a general economic and political model of the development process. Indeed, traditional development policy is employed as a substitute for such a model in order to leap over the enormous gaps in development knowledge. Instead of attempting to understand the dynamic process and subsequently to remove barriers to its effective operation, traditional policy-makers rush in with little more than their faith that they can kick-start Third-World economies. The legacy of this approach is the disruption of the **national strategic transition (NST)** of individual NSCs and the displacement of the GST.

In this book the approach taken is diametrically opposite to that of the traditionalists. An attempt is made to model the entire development process and to identify barriers to its effective progress that require removal. In tackling the policy implications of this approach consideration is given to both the GST and the technological paradigm shift.

Policy for the GST

Development policy should be considered within the context of the dynamic-strategy model. This involves the recognition that economic development is a global process that is the outcome of the unfolding industrial techno-logical paradigm driven by an interaction between (and within) the global strategic core and its fringe. Owing to this strategic interaction a growing number of NSCs gain entry into the global strategic transition and are transformed from NSCs to ESCs and, finally, to SCs. Economic develop-ment, in other words, is a self-generating and continuing, if not a continu-ous, process. It is not something that has to be created or forced by intellectuals, bureaucrats, and international organizations. Indeed, it cannot be created in this way because the process is not properly understood by the development community, and because even if it were it would still not be possible to provide any short cuts to SC status. This is the old problem of spontaneous order with which Adam Smith and Friedrich Hayek were preoccupied, except that it concerns a dynamic rather than a static order (Snooks 1998b: pt III). The unavoidable and unalterable truth is that eco-nomic development is the unconscious outcome of the desires of humankind rather than the conscious outcome of our intellect. This is always difficult for academics and intellectuals to accept. The best we can do in these cir-cumstances, therefore, is to understand what the dynamic process involves and to ensure that policy is used to remove obstacles in its path rather than to intervene blindly and unnecessarily thereby diverting it from its path.

Policy Principles

The dynamic-strategy model provides both a new basis for analysis and, accordingly, a new set of policy principles relevant to economic develop-ment. In *Longrun Dynamics* (Snooks 1998b: 232–40), I reviewed the gen-eral principles underlying orthodox economic policy for developed countries. These principles are based on the static concepts of efficiency and market flexibility. Neoclassical economists would prefer to deal with the first of these – efficiency – in terms of a social welfare function that can be maxi-mized subject to the usual economic constraints. As a unique social welfare function does not exist – see Arrow's Impossibility Theorem – neoclassical economists are thrown back on the concept of Pareto optimality, by which any change can only be regarded objectively as an improvement if it makes someone better off without anyone else becoming worse off. Although it was developed for shortrun analysis, Pareto optimality is also applied to the longrun, mainly in support of notions of free trade and globalization. The second orthodox policy principle of market flexibility is essential in neoclassical economics because it helps to prop up a supply-side theory. If supply is to create its own demand, the shape of the aggregate supply curve must be vertical, and this requires flexible markets. In turn this has led to the adoption of the concept of the natural rate of unemployment, or the 'nonaccelerating inflation rate of unemployment' (NAIRU), that has caused the disruption of economic growth in the First and Third Worlds alike.

These artificial orthodox concepts, made necessary by a supply-side theory with no role for dynamic demand, have encouraged a policy stance that emphasizes stability at the expense of dynamics. This has led to the use of what I call the policy rules of the four zeros – zero government deficits, zero government debt, zero inflation, and zero market imperfection. It is as if neoliberals, frustrated that their models do not look like the real world, are attempting to make the real world look like their models. And the attempt to do so in the Western world since the 1970s through anti-inflation and, hence, antigrowth policies has led to the deflation of **strategic confidence** and the undermining of longrun viability.

This discussion is relevant to the Third World because neoliberals have exercised considerable influence over international development organizations such as the IMF and the World Bank during the past two decades. This accounts for the structural adjustment programmes that these international organizations have imposed on the Third World whenever the latter required financial aid. These static, supply-side programmes are an attempt to reshape the Third World in the image of neoclassical theory. Such policy is fatal to the longrun economic development of these countries, because it imposes stability at the expense of dynamics. It also leads to the disruption and delay of the GST.

What is urgently needed is a new key policy principle, together with policy rules, based on an appropriate general dynamic model. In *Longrun Dynamics* (Snooks 1998b: ch. 17) I proposed the **strategic optimization principle**, which involves maximizing the sustainable exploitation of strategic opportunities and which is measured by real GDP per capita, not HDI. This is consistent with the GST coefficient calculated in Table 4.3 for countries throughout the world. Based on the dynamic-strategy model, this policy principle is relevant to a dynamic rather than a static world. Hence, the **strategic test** replaces the Pareto efficiency test.

In a dynamic world, efficiency of production and distribution is secondary to strategic development. The dynamic-strategy approach also demolishes the NAIRU rule of thumb by undermining the causal relationship between unemployment and inflation. Strategic inflation is, as shown in Chapter 11, a central part of the strategic demand–response mechanism, while unemployment is a static outcome of the dynamic process at a particular point in time. They are not directly related in a causal sense and, hence, the Phillips curve has no meaningful existence. We should, therefore, think of a viable First-World economy as one in successful pursuit of its dynamic strategy, experiencing relatively rapid growth of real GDP per capita (say 2–3 per cent per annum), with low levels of unemployment (3–4 per cent), and moderate levels of strategic inflation (4–6 per cent).

While this new policy principle arose from the application of the dynamic-strategy model to the First World, it is just as relevant to the Third World. Just as relevant and even more crucial. All countries in the world are part of the same GST process. Accordingly, the appropriate test of performance for ESCs is just the same as that for SCs – the strategic test of whether the exploitation of strategic opportunities is being maximized in a sustainable way. In the case of ESCs they should expect to experience rates of economic growth and strategic inflation substantially higher than those in SCs (see Chapter 11). ESCs have entered into the GST, but unless they maximize strategic exploitation they could well slip back into the NSC category. Certainly they will have little prospect of catching up to and joining the SCs. And the same is true for FASCs that are struggling to substitute strategic for antistrategic development programmes. Neither group can afford the luxury of wasting resources either through speculation or through the pursuit of mistaken orthodox policies involving overinvestment in education, equity, or environmental programmes. Even the strategic test for NSCs is but a variation on that for all other analytical categories. In this case it is not so much the maximization of strategic opportunities, as maximizing the growing signs of individual and group strategic (profit-seeking) activity as preparatory to entering into the GST.

How are Third-World countries to score well in terms of the strategic test? In *Longrun Dynamics* (Snooks 1998b: 242) I suggested that SCs needed to ensure that static issues such as economic stability and external and internal balance should not be allowed to overwhelm the continuous exploitation of strategic opportunities. I argued that governments should provide strategic leadership rather than just good economic housekeeping. Strategic leadership involves facilitating the objectives of society's strategists by

actively promoting their cause. This includes investing in strategic infrastructure (research, educational, transport and communication facilities)
where the social return is expected to exceed the private return; encouraging domestic innovation and facilitating technological transfer; spearhead-
ing the penetration of new markets by negotiating external trade and
technological deals on behalf of the strategists; protecting the dynamic
strategy at home and abroad; and operating proactively to secure control
over external strategic resources or strategic locations. A government supplying strategic leadership, therefore, will respond to the demands of
strategists (profit-seekers) rather than antistrategists (rent-seekers). And in
difficult times strategic leadership will involve going beyond the Keynesian
policy prescription of augmenting aggregate demand by detecting the
strategic cause of downturn and assisting in the replacement of exhausted
with new technological substrategies. It is essential to realize that **strategic
distortion** created by disrupting the dynamic process is far worse than
market distortion that may be created by this level of government intervention. Clearly strategic leadership requires a dynamic role for government denied in the Western world by neoclassical models.

Strategic leadership is just as central and even more crucial for the future
of Third-World countries. It is essential that the governments of ESCs
respond to the requirements of their strategists rather than to the demands
of international organizations such as the IMF and the World Bank that are
influenced by economic ideologues, or to the advice of 'experts' in the
wider development community. By providing strategic leadership, ESC
governments will be following their own self-interest because their rent-
seeking can be maximized only if economic growth is maximized. Their
rule, however, will be limited. As a growing proportion of the population
is drawn into the dynamic strategy, the strategists will assume greater
political control, either gradually or following some sort of revolution, and
will provide their own strategic leadership. It is possible that the old ruling
elite may avoid being swept away if they also become strategists themselves by giving up rent-seeking for profit-seeking and by adopting more
democratic political institutions. Whatever the pathway to strategic control, it is essential that ESC governments reject the debilitating neoliberal
policies currently in vogue in the First World and in its interventionist
international organizations. To fail in this will be to substitute static man-
agement for strategic leadership and to experience stasis rather than
dynamics. The same is true for FASCs.

But what about NSCs? In the absence of successful strategists in
NSCs, the ruling elites focus on rent-seeking. They are not committed
antistrategists of the Bolshevik kind, just opportunists that pursue the

most remunerative pursuits. Only when a sizeable and growing proportion of the population turn to strategic pursuits will the ruling elite find it expedient to take account of the needs of the strategists. They do this because the taxing of strategists becomes the most rapidly growing source of their revenues. Until this time NSC governments do not provide any form of strategic leadership, nor will it be possible to induce them to do so. But from this time on, perceptive NSC leaders will become increasingly interested in removing obstacles to strategists pursuing their profit-seeking objectives. Even so, the ruling elite will view its relationship with the strategists as exploitive and they will regularly intervene to provide preferential treatment to favourites willing to provide extra gratuities and/or support. But gradually the ruling elite will become directly involved in strategic activities, granting themselves and their families substantial monopolies. Only when the strategists gain greater economic power will they challenge these corrupt practices and, eventually, insist that the ruling elite supply proper strategic leadership that is relatively free from corruption, cronyism, nepotism, and preferential treatment – leadership that is aimed at facilitating the objectives of the strategists. But, by this time, our NSC will have become an ESC. Strategic leadership has small beginnings in an NSC, but it expands as the society's technological substrategy unfolds.

It is essential to realize that the changing political situation of NSCs is a response to an unfolding dynamic strategy. Hence, it is not appropriate for outsiders to suggest, as they regularly do, that the political system that has emerged in the most advanced SCs should be adopted by ESCs, FASCs, and even NSCs. There are some who naively argue that the adoption of democratic institutions will increase a country's rate of economic growth. This is based not on a general economic and political model of development but rather on simple correlations between the two variables. What is not understood is that both these economic and political results are outcomes of the modern dynamic process and are not causally related. In the early modern and pre-modern worlds – the greater part of human experience – it was possible to achieve high rates of economic growth with very undemocratic institutions. It all depends on the nature and success of the strategic pursuit. It is essential that political institutions be shaped by strategic demand rather than ideology, because the adoption of inappropriate institutions under external pressure either will be totally ineffective as the ruling elite employs its unequal power to reassert control or will be disruptive of the strategic transition.

Policy Issues

No attempt will be made to provide detailed policy prescriptions. While I have outlined clear policy principles for the Third World, these must be employed flexibly in different circumstances. There are no standard policy programmes that should be followed by all countries in all circumstances. It is essential to resist the temptation to mindlessly follow the flavour of the month – for example, the so-called 'Asian model' (*The Economist*, 20 December 1997: 15) – without investigating closely the relevance of such an approach. The central policy objective always is to respond to the society's strategists and to facilitate their objectives. In effect this means responding to changing strategic demand as the country's technological substrategy unfolds in the context of the developing GST. The essence of the strategic response is flexibility. Policies must not be perpetuated beyond their strategic effectiveness, as happened with ISI policies in Latin America. This can best be avoided by governments listening closely to their own strategists rather than to so-called 'experts' either local or foreign.

What can be done profitably here is to employ the dynamic-strategy model to integrate the fragmented traditional policy prescriptions and to provide a consistent policy focus for all these areas. In particular I will consider briefly the interventionist–neoliberal debate, together with traditional policy prescriptions concerning population, human capital, technological change, domestic and foreign sources of funds, equity versus growth, and environmental degradation.

Neither side in the interventionist–neoliberal debate has much to recommend it. In the end, both are disruptive of the GST because they both misunderstand the real nature of the development process. The interventionists wanted to intervene in the operation of Third-World countries in a massive way through the 'big push' in order to kick-start these economies. This was a blind leap of faith because they had no workable model of the development process. They viewed economic growth as the outcome of a production process rather than as a strategic pursuit. They thought that by building infrastructure and factories on a massive scale, the Third World would overcome its poverty trap and 'take off' into rapid and sustained economic growth. Central planning, which was developed to achieve this objective, degenerated into an engineering exercise concerned with production inputs and outputs rather than a creative exercise concerned with the strategic pursuit. The strategic pursuit generates and sustains economic growth, which is something an engineered production system cannot do.

The neoliberal approach is, ironically, just as interventionist as the despised interventionist approach, and just as disruptive. The neoliberal focus on structural adjustment programmes by the IMF and the World Bank are responsible for destroying strategic confidence and for undercutting the longrun viability of the Third World. This is an outcome of the neoliberal attack on both strategic inflation and strategic leadership, which disrupts the strategic demand–response mechanism. The neoclassical vision on which this policy is based is seriously at variance with reality. It is a vision of a perfectly competitive production system that attains optimal efficiency, measured in Paretian terms, when it is in equilibrium. In reality, economic development is a disequilibrium process – an opportunistic strategic pursuit rather than an efficient production process.

Strategic leadership, in contrast to both the interventionist and neoliberal approaches, is based on a realistic analysis of the dynamic process. It does not impose an unrealistic production approach on an NSC, nor does it force an ESC to disrupt its own strategic demand–response mechanism. It accepts the reality of the strategic pursuit and it reinforces strategic confidence and facilitates the operation of the dynamic mechanism by assisting strategists to achieve their objectives. Strategic leadership requires intervention, but only to focus the efforts of the strategists and, thereby, facilitate the unfolding of the dynamic strategy. The success of such policy can be seen reflected in rapid and sustained rates of economic growth.

The dynamic-strategy model also enables us to draw a variety of detailed policy issues together by viewing them as **strategic instruments** that respond to changes in strategic demand. These strategic instruments include population, human capital, investment, technology, and institutions. The same is true of the supply-side sources of these strategic instruments, such as fertility, immigration, education and technical training, savings and foreign capital, together with knowledge and invention. In the light of the dynamic-strategy model we need to add strategic ideas/knowledge, strategic institutions, and strategic leadership.

While the traditional approach is to seek intervention on the supply side, the dynamic-strategy approach is to argue that if we take care of strategic demand the supply response will take care of itself. At best, the supply-side approach – emphasizing the reduction of fertility through female education, growth through overinvestment in schooling, investment through promoting the saving rate, economic development through equity and democracy – will merely waste scarce resources and disrupt the development process. At worst it will derail it entirely.

The dynamic-strategy model shows that with the unfolding technological substrategy a Third-World country will experience changes in strategic demand that call forth a supply response articulated through strategic inflation. The essential requirement of policy-makers is that they recognize the true nature of this process and attempt merely to remove any stubborn institutional obstacles that might complicate or delay the response of these various strategic instruments. This includes the reduction, if not elminiation, of **nonstrategic inflation** through a more sensible monetary policy. The greatest error they can possibly make is to employ stabilization policies to eliminate strategic, rather than nonstrategic, inflation. By interfering with the strategic demand–response mechanism in this way, the development process will be disrupted – and it will be derailed permanently if this disastrous neoliberal policy thrust is maintained indefinitely, as 'experts' in the IMF are attempting to do.

Policy and the Technological Paradigm Shift

Dynamic-strategy theory can make a unique contribution to the environmental debate because it is able to model the critically important process of technological paradigm shifts. As argued earlier, the exhaustion of the current industrial technological paradigm will place considerable pressure on natural resources leading to inevitable environmental degradation. The essential point is that there is no way of avoiding these consequences. But there is cause for optimism, because paradigmatic exhaustion, by generating radical changes in relative factor prices, will lead the way to the next – the fourth – technological paradigm shift. It is impossible to leap over this stage not only because there is insufficient information about both the timing and the nature of this revolution but also because, even in the event of this information being available, there is no possibility that changes of this complexity can be engineered by human beings. The failure of the Soviet Union testifies to this.

The only rational response in the face of this difficult and uncertain future is to do as we have always done – to select the most efficient solution to the problems that emerge in order to maximize individual material advantage. The worst possible response would be to do as the ecological engineers of the *Limits to Growth* (Meadows *et al.* 1972) and *Beyond the Limits* (Meadows *et al.* 1992) variety have insisted we must – abandon all growth-inducing technological change and attempt to create the stationary state. As I have argued in *The Dynamic Society* (Snooks 1996) and *The Ephemeral Civilization* (Snooks 1997a), this could only be achieved if an eco-dictator of the Stalinist variety – the archetypal antistrategist – assumed control of a global state; and once achieved it would lead to the emergence of regional warlords pursuing the ancient dynamic strategy of conquest. This would be disastrous both for human society and the ecology.

It is possible and desirable, however, to ease the burden of paradigmatic exhaustion. Human society should, and appears to want to, devote some of its GDP to repairing the damage inflicted upon the environment by its pursuit of economic growth. This desire is reflected not only in the growing public agitation over environmental issues but also in the growing attention that neoclassical economics, as discussed in Chapter 7, is devoting to this subject. While traditional economics cannot tell us much about longrun dynamics, it can sort out the benefits and costs of restoring the environment, which can be treated as a shortrun static issue.

In this respect, however, neoclassical economists have overlooked two important problems. By employing partial and general equilibrium models and ignoring issues of longrun dynamics, they have failed to recognize the possibility that environmental damage is not just a matter of efficient markets for environmental services, but also the outcome of early paradigmatic exhaustion. What this means is that it is not possible to eliminate environmental damage by making markets more efficient. And as paradigmatic exhaustion emerges, this problem will become increasingly significant.

This has led to a second problem whereby environmental economists wish to take account of intergenerational transfers, because they sense that otherwise even efficient markets will not prevent the deterioration of natural resources. The intergenerational equity argument is, in the light of my dynamic-strategy model, highly dangerous because it supports the demands of the ecological engineers to override the objectives of current decision-makers in the name of unborn generations. This is very similar to earlier arguments of the Bolsheviks in Russia who claimed to be making decisions on behalf of the vast unconsulted majority of the Russian people – in Marx's words – through the 'dictatorship of the proletariat' (actually the dictatorship of the Bolsheviks and, ultimately, of Stalin). It is the usual ploy of antistrategists. It must be realized that we are not only ignorant of what future generations might choose but also run the risk of derailing the Dynamic Society by delaying the next paradigm shift and, in the process, setting loose the forces of war and conquest. Quite clearly this would make future generations worse off. A dynamic perspective suggests that the best outcome for current and future generations is to remove any obstacles to the unfolding industrial technological paradigm and to ensure that the preferences of present decision-makers for material and environmental outcomes can be taken into account through more effective markets. This will both save the environment and transform the living standards of the great proportion of the world's population trapped in the Third World.

18.3 CONCLUSIONS

In this book it has been argued that to understand the development process it is necessary to develop a dynamic model that can simultaneously explain the economic and political dimensions involved. A critical test for such a model is whether it can make sensible predictions about the future. Not being able to do so would call into question its credentials for explaining the past and present and for formulating useful policy principles. It is the claim of this book that dynamic-strategy theory can pass this critical test, that it can resolve the current development dilemma, and that its policy principles will be of use to countries that have yet to enter into the GST. Needless to say, the theory presented here will need to be rigorously tested at the detailed societal level in the Third World before these claims will be widely accepted. What it does provide now is a new vision of the global development process and a new hope for the Third World.

Notes

1 Economic Development Redefined

1. There are exceptions to this generalization, such as Arndt (1987), Clark (1940), and Maddison (1995b).

2 The Global Strategic-Transition Model

1. In the New World an entirely independent neolithic revolution began in the Mesoamerican isthmus about 7000 years ago.
2. This argument was first presented in Snooks (1996: ch. 12).

3 The Unfolding Technological Paradigm

1. 'The law of diminishing strategic returns' encompasses the classical law of diminishing returns based upon the misleading assumption of a fixed supply of land (or natural resources). The classical version is a special case of this more general law as it is based upon conditions specific to a rare and restricted period in human history. While it has only occurred twice in the last 11 000 years, on the cusp between two technological paradigms, we may be approaching a third occurrence. The classical economists focused upon a world of technological transition between an exhausted neolithic and a yet to be realized industrial technological paradigm. At this rare historical moment all former dynamic strategies – conquest, commerce, and neolithic technology – had been exhausted, and it appeared that the stock of natural resources was finite in an absolute sense. In fact the supply of natural resources depends upon the dynamic strategies of materialist man. *Hence diminishing returns at the societal level are experienced not on natural resources but on dynamic strategies.* Owing to their myopic historical focus the classical economists thought that the diminishing returns they actually detected were due to land being a fixed factor of production rather than to the exhaustion of the neolithic paradigm.

    This dynamic law also resolves the difficulty inherent in the neoclassical version of diminishing returns which transfers the law from a situation where land is in fixed supply in the longrun to a situation where all factors of production are in fixed supply in the shortrun. While diminishing returns on fixed factors can only be established in the shortrun (because only in the shortrun can factors be fixed), it is only in the longrun, when substitution of factors can occur, that the concept has any operational significance. This dilemma is resolved when we see diminishing returns at the macro level as an outcome of exhausting dynamic strategies rather than either exhausting natural resources or fixed factors in the shortrun. The continued introduction of new technology prevents the exhaustion of the modern dynamic strategy and hence prevents the emergence of diminishing returns at the societal level. (But, of course, diminishing returns occur on individual investment projects as those projects are exhausted.)

2. See the Preface and Chapter 8 for discussions of Adam Smith's detection and resolution of the unease felt in England in the mid-eighteenth century arising from the exhaustion of the commerce strategy and the emergence of militarism.

3. This section is based on the important quantitative work of Angus Maddison (1995a) in constructing comparable statistical series since 1820 of the levels and rates of change of real GDP per capita for all the main countries of the world using purchasing power parity converters (PPPs).

4   The State of the Third World

1. For a discussion of the Chinese system in a dynamic-strategy framework – past, present, and future – see Snooks (1997a: ch. 12).

2. Since writing the text of this chapter, Indonesia, under pressure from the IMF to introduce policies of strategic adjusmtent and democratization, has experienced escalating social unrest and political uncertainty. While part of this can be viewed as an outcome of the strategic struggle between the old antistrategists and the new strategists, a growing and unnecessary part must be regarded as the predictable response to neoliberal policies forced on Indonesia by the IMF and the superpowers. These interventionists, therefore, should be prepared to shoulder some of the responsibility for the social cost that will undoubtedly follow (20 May 1998).

5   The State of the Second World

1. What does this law imply about China, another antistrategic society? Unlike the USSR it has been able to introduce economic reforms without political collapse, but only because it earlier failed to effectively introduce a centrally determined command system. Without a self-sustaining system of rent-seeking, the post-1978 reforms in China were not completely frustrated as they were in the USSR after 1965. But, according to this law, the emergence of strategists since those reforms will eventually sweep the remaining antistrategists (the Chinese Communist Party) from power. This is the ultimate outcome of the strategic struggle between old antistrategists and new strategists. Throughout history, ruling elites that refused to lead the emerging new dynamic strategy have been removed (for example, Charles I in 1649 and James II in 1688 in England; and Louis XVI in 1791 in France).

2. While the antistrategist takeover is a fascinating issue, it can be dealt with only briefly here. For greater detail see Snooks (1997a: 440–65).

6   Traditional Development Theory

1. Good surveys of traditional development theory can be found, for example, in Higgins (1968), Ghatak (1995), Cypher and Dietz (1997), and Pomfret

(1997). The emergence of economic development as an idea is elegantly discussed by Arndt (1987).

2. Ben Higgins (1968: 63) has been followed in this formulation. The classical model received a late extension by Bensusan-Butt (1960) who showed how the stationary state could be achieved by introducing structural change. But like the rest he adopts a supply-side productionist approach.

3. The notation here follows that by Barro and Sala-i-Martin (1995). The derivation and proofs of these equations are given in that source.

4. See the pioneering article by Dowrick and Nguyen (1989).

5. The Prebisch–Singer hypothesis has its origins in Prebisch (1950) and Singer (1950). Also see Singer and Sharma (1989) for further development of this argument.

7 Traditional Development Policy

1. More detail can be found in Snooks (1998b: 81–8).

2. For an excellent discussion of these issues together with Adam Smith's philosophical system, see Fitzgibbons (1995).

9 The Global Dynamic-Strategy Model

1. Efficiency is measured here in cost–benefit terms as between alternative dynamic strategies. This is worked out not by rational calculation but by trial and error. In this context, efficiency is a relative rather than an absolute concept. A strategy is chosen because, at that point in time, it is more efficient than the alternatives, not because in some timeless sense it is absolutely the most efficient strategy.

10 The Driving Force

1. 'The law of human motivation', which underlies my general dynamic model, was derived from an historical examination not only of human society over the past two million years, but of the emergence of life over the past few billion years. As scarcity is demand-determined this condition will always be with us (Snooks 1996).

2. The use of the term 'economic distance' in the concentric spheres model (Snooks 1994a) predated my knowledge of the kinship selection model which uses the term 'genetic distance'. It is an interesting parallel.

3. Further discussion of the concentric spheres model can be found in Snooks (1997a: ch. 2).

4. The way ideology is employed to raise strategic confidence is discussed more fully, and illustrated extensively, in Snooks (1997a).

5. Our modern epoch is not unique in this respect. All ages abound with information about successful individuals and the sources of their success, rather than about theoretical models and the data required to apply them to reality.

Imitative information in conquest societies focuses on successful military and state leaders, in commerce societies on successful commercial leaders and practices, and in technological societies on successful money-making practices. See Snooks (1997a: 43–5) for a discussion of imitative information in pre-modern societies.

6. Intellectual economizing is explained in greater detail in Snooks (1997a: 46–9).

11 The Global Strategic Demand–Response Mechanism

1. The regression results for the Third-World growth–inflation curve, which imposes a 10 per cent inflation ceiling, for 1983 to 1993 are:

$$y = 3.874 + 0.343\,x$$
$$(3.264)\ (1.283)$$

- $\bar{R}^2 = 0.08$
- It passes all the heteroskedasticity and Ramsey reset specification tests.
- The t ratios are in parentheses.

2. It is possible to allow for nonstrategic inflation by including as explanatory variables both changes in the money supply (M_3) and nominal wages. This improves the goodness-of-fit coefficients (up to 0.45) and the t ratios.

12 The Strategy Function

1. A fascinating example of strategic substitution in the pre-modern world is the type of strategic design adopted for conquest. Between 1325 and 1519, Aztec society pursued the dynamic strategy of conquest. In contrast to Rome they chose the hegemonic (intimidation) rather than the territorial (occupation) form of conquest, precisely because the resulting strategic demand for physical capital was considerably less. A territorial empire required heavy investment in permanent territorial armies, fortified garrisons, permanent bases, and colonial public buildings and bureaucracies; whereas a hegemonic empire was held together with the threat of military retaliation in the event of revolt. While a hegemonic empire could be sustained by a part-time army of warrior–farmers following traditional small-scale agriculture, a territorial empire required a professional standing army and a form of large-scale capitalist agriculture (Snooks 1997a: ch. 7).

13 Population

1. Elsewhere I have called this 'the law of strategic crisis', which states that the exhaustion of a dominant dynamic strategy in a competitive world leads not to the stationary state but to a strategic crisis that threatens the

very existence of the society. The reason that stasis turns into crisis is that specialization in commerce (or conquest) invariably encourages a society to exceed its optimum size (as determined by the prevailing technological paradigm) which is unsustainable once the dominant strategy has been exhausted. The reason this law replaces the Malthusian crisis is that the longrun decline in real GDP per capita is due not to the continued pressure of population on resources but to the downsizing required to regain the optimum economy size. This in turn operates according to 'the law regulating the optimum size of societies' (Snooks 1998a: 217–18). It is necessary to draw a distinction between crises that result from exhausting dynamic strategies and exhausting substrategies. The latter are less serious and unlikely to lead to collapse.

2.   The contrast in titles between my *Portrait* (Snooks 1994a) and Becker's *Treatise* (Becker 1991) was intentional. A treatise is an abstract exercise (deduction), whereas a portrait is a picture of reality (induction). For a methodological discussion of these issues see Snooks (1994a: ch. 1).

3.   The econometric results are shown in Table N.1.

Table N.1   Determinants of household size, Australia, 1946–90

	Constant	KLR	FMW	$HHS_{(-1)}$	$HHS_{(-2)}$	$\bar{R}^2$	D–W
β_1	4.823	−0.0002	−0.808			0.988	0.393
β_2	1.031	−0.00003	−0.186	1.266	−0.479	0.998	1.901
t_1	65.017	−16.188	−5.964				
t_2	3.771	−3.401	−2.721	9.271	−3.880		
E_1		−0.164	−0.177				
E_2		−0.037	−0.041	1.275	−0.485		

Notes

a. The results corrected for autocorrelation (β_2, t_2, E_2) are shown immediately below the uncorrected results (β_1, t_1, E_1).

b. β gives the parameter estimates of the intercept or constant and the following explanatory variables: the market capital/labour ratio (KLR), and the female/male wage rate in nominal terms (FMW).

c. t gives the conventional t-ratios.

d. E gives the partial elasticities of household size (HHS) evaluated at the sample means of the explanatory variables.

e. D–W is the Durbin–Watson statistic to test for autocorrelation.

Source: Snooks 1994a: 68.

14   Capital Accumulation

1.   Higgins (1968: 348–9), commenting on the origin of his low-level equilibrium diagram says 'in the working out of these diagrams, the author has had

invaluable assistance from Professor Trevor Swan'; and also refers to 'an unpublished paper [by Swan] presented to an M.I.T. seminar'. Hence the co-discoverer of the famous Solow–Swan neoclassical growth model also had a hand in formulating a general version of the low-level equilibrium model in development economics.

15 Technological or Strategic Change?

1. See, for example, Gomme (1946), Habakkuk (1962), Landes (1969), Rosenberg (1970), Higgs (1971), David (1975), Headrick (1981), Headrick (1988), Hindle (1981), Jeremy (1981), Stapleton (1987), MacLeod (1988), Sokoloff (1988), and Mokyr (1990).
2. Actually, the concept of strategic demand is implicit in the analysis of the Total Economy in my earlier book, *Portrait of the Family* (Snooks 1994a). See Chapter 13 above.

16 Institutional Response

1. F. A. Hayek's work has been considered in more detail in Snooks (1997a: 81–4) and Snooks (1998b: 56–9).
2. While a similar discussion has appeared in Snooks (1998b), it needs to be repeated here owing to the novelty of the theory and the different reader-ship.

17 Government and Strategic Leadership

1. This is nationalist propaganda disguised as aid. It will have no beneficial effect and may even lead the ruling elite in developing countries to distrust the advice from their own strategists. It is essential that governments continue to listen to their strategists and not foreign, or local, 'experts'.
2. The World Bank team that prepared *The State in a Changing World* (World Bank 1997b) was led by Ajay Chhibber and comprised Simon Commander, Alison Evans, Harald Fuhr, Cheikh Kane, Chad Leechor, Brian Levy, Sanjay Pradhan, and Beatrice Weder. They acknowledged the 'valuable contributions' of Jean-Paul Azam, Ed Campos, Hamid Davoodi, Kathleen Newland, Kenichi Ohno, Dani Rodrik, Susan Rose-Ackerman, Astri Suhrke, and Douglas Webb; together with the 'assistance' of Ritu Basu, Gregory Kisunko, Une Lee, Claudia Sepulveda, and Adam Michael Smith. Stephanie Flanders was the principal editor. The work was carried out under the general direction of the late Michael Bruno, Lyn Squire, and Joseph Stiglitz. The authors also acknowledged 'useful advice' from a panel of external experts comprising Masahiko Aoki, Ela Bhatt, Kwesi Botchwey, Peter Evans, Atul Kohli, Klaus König, Seymour Martin Lipset, Douglass North, Emma Rothschild, Graham Scott, and Vito Tanzi.

Glossary of New Terms and Concepts

As longrun dynamics is a new area of study it has been necessary to develop and employ a range of new terms and concepts in this book. To assist the reader, these terms and concepts have been brought together and briefly defined in this Glossary. When a new term or concept is first mentioned in a chapter it has been printed in bold type. Italics in the Glossary have been used to indicate that additional concepts are also defined here. Unfamiliar terms not included here can be found in the glossaries of *The Dynamic Society* (Snooks 1996), *The Ephemeral Civilization* (Snooks 1997a), and *Longrun Dynamics* (Snooks 1998a). In this study 'longrun' is a single word because it refers to an important and integrated concept.

Antistrategic countries (ASCs) are societies that have been hijacked by radical organizations interested only in rent-seeking and in suppressing the potential *strategists*. It is important to draw a distinction between *ASCs* or command economies and antistrategic policies that are adopted by Third-World countries that may be rent-seeking but do not attempt to suppress emerging strategists. China, Vietnam, and Cuba are remaining examples of old *ASCs* that are either in transition or in danger of collapse. See also *SCs*, *ESCs*, and *FASCs*.

Antistrategic crisis is an outcome of the failure of antistrategic policies in both Second-World and Third-World countries. In the Second World we have seen the terminal crises of *ASCs* in the Soviet block owing to their inability to compete economically with *SCs* of the First World. In the Third World, *ESCs* in Latin America have experienced reversible crises that arose in the second half of the twentieth century owing to the pursuit of heavily protectionist policies. See also *strategic crisis*.

Antistrategists comprise those ruling elites who assume control of societies during times of strategic crisis and engineer repressive economic and political systems. These command systems are designed to eliminate existing *strategists*, to prevent the re-emergence of potential strategists, and to facilitate rent-seeking. Examples of societies dominated by antistrategists include Rome from the time of Claudius, Soviet Russia, Nazi Germany, and Maoist China. Control by antistrategists is the outcome of a military-backed takeover by a small band of professional revolutionaries who are able to exploit the chaos that emerges when the new strategists are unable to overwhelm the old strategists during the course of a difficult *strategic transfer*.

Concentric spheres model of human behaviour In this model the self is at the centre of a set of concentric spheres that define the varying strength of co-operative relationships between him or her and all other individuals and groups in society. The strength of the economic relationship between the self and any other individual or group – measured by the *economic distance* between them – will depend on how essential they are to the maximization of his or her utility. Those aspects of his or her objective function – such as the generation of love, companionship, and children – will be located on spheres with the shortest distance from the centre, with other relatives, friends, neighbours, workmates, members of various religious and social clubs, city, state, nation, group of nations, and so on occupying spheres that progressively radiate from the centre (see Figure 10.1). As the economic distance increases, the degree of cooperation diminishes. The force keeping the spheres apart is the incessant desire of the self to survive and prosper, and the force preventing the spheres flying into space (the model's economic gravity) is *strategic confidence* – the basis of trust and cooperation – generated by a successful dynamic strategy.

Dynamic order is the process by which economic agents, all attempting to maximize the probability of their individual survival and prosperity, cooperate to achieve rapid and sustained economic growth. This is the outcome of an unfolding dynamic strategy that generates changes both in *strategic demand* for a wide range of inputs including institutions and organizations, and in *strategic confidence* concerning the future. While the strategic unfolding continues and society prospers, strategic confidence remains high, generating trust and cooperation between individuals at all levels of society and stability in its institutions. But when this unfolding falters, confidence will decline, causing a deterioration in former trust, cooperation, and institutional stability and, hence, in dynamic order.

Dynamic strategies are those wide-ranging programmes employed by decision-makers attempting to maximize the probability of survival and prosperity. In the Dynamic Society these strategies include family multiplication, conquest, commerce, and technological change. The adoption of any one of these strategies will depend upon factor endowments and, hence, relative factor prices, and will require investment in specialized infrastructure. This investment generates a stream of positive net returns. Economic growth, therefore, is strategy-led. A dominant dynamic strategy will be pursued until it has been economically exhausted, which will occur when the marginal cost of investment in this strategy equals its marginal revenue. This leads not to collapse but to stagnation. Over time any dominant strategy will consist of a sequence of substrategies by which the economic possibilities of the former are explored. For the modern era these substrategies have been called *technological styles/technological substrategies*.

Economic distance is the measure of the strength of material relationships between the self and all other individuals and groups in society. Economic distance is inversely related to the importance of other individuals and groups in maximizing the material objectives of the self. Hence family and friends occupy the spheres closest to the self, and strangers are to be found on the most distant spheres (see Figure 10.1). It is an important component of the *concentric spheres model of human behaviour*.

Economic resilience is the command nations have over material goods and services, and is measured by GDP per capita. It is a measure of society's ability to compete and survive, and should be contrasted with the concept of quality of life, which has little to do with survival in the longrun. Economic resilience is the power of nations, and of human society itself, over longrun survival.

Emerging strategic countries (ESCs) are societies that have entered into the *global strategic transition (GST)* and are experiencing rapid and sustained economic growth. This is an outcome of a continuing interaction with *SC*s that constitute the *global strategic core*. There are two types of *ESC*: Type I includes those *ESC*s that have adopted their own *technological substrategy*; and Type II includes those *ESC*s responding solely to the dynamic strategy of the strategic core. The latter are always in danger of reverting to the ranks of the *NSC*s – there is nothing inevitable about the strategic transition – while the former aspire to the ranks of the *SC*s.

Former antistrategic countries (FASCs) are societies that were formed when countries of the former Soviet block collapsed. Currently they are in a state of transition, but their destination is uncertain. Occupying a living-standard range similar to the *ESC* category, some (the Czech Republic, Hungary, Poland) appear to be in transition to the ranks of the *SC*s and others (Azerbaijan, Kyrgyz Republic, and Uzbekistan) to the ranks of *NSC*s. The rest will probably maintain their existing ranking, equivalent to *ESC*s, for some time.

Funnel of transformation This is a physical environmental factor that helped to determine where the Neolithic Revolution would occur when the palaeolithic technological paradigm was approaching economic exhaustion. In the Old World this was the Fertile Crescent and in the New World it was the Meso-american isthmus. It is highly likely that the rift valley of east Africa played a similar role in the Palaeolithic Revolution (the shift from scavenging to hunting). These were corridors of heightened competition, appropriate resources, and exchange of ideas through which peoples from several continents had to pass. They were the sites of technological revolution and the sources of its transfer to the rest of the known world.

Global strategic core This consists of a steadily growing number of *SC*s that constitute the dynamo of global economic change. It is not only responsible for driving the *unfolding technological paradigm* but is gradually drawing *NSC*s into its orbit. The latter group of countries are called the *global strategic fringe*. This growing global interaction between the core and the fringe generates the *global strategic transition (GST)*, which is responsible for what is popularly known as economic development.

Global strategic demand See *strategic demand*.

Global strategic fringe This consists of those *NSC*s and *ESC*s that are drawn into a spiralling orbit around the strategic core. It is an interaction driven by *global strategic demand* generated within the core, some of which is met by the fringe. This interaction takes place through international trade and factor movements. International trade, therefore, is driven not by comparative production costs – the traditional explanation of neoclassical *productionists* – but by global strategic demand. This constitutes a new theory of international trade.

Global strategic imitation See *strategic imitation*.

Global strategic transition (GST) is the focus of this book. It is a complex dynamic process by which an increasing number of *NSC*s are drawn into the vortex of dynamic interaction between the world's most economically advanced nations. This dynamic process is an outcome of the global unfolding of the technological paradigm as *materialist man* in the leading *SCs* explores the existing strategic potential. The resulting transition from *NSC* to *ESC* to *SC* is what is popularly known as economic development. See also *national strategic transition (NST)*.

Growth–inflation curve This is the empirical reflection of the strategic demand–response mechanism that was discovered in *Longrun Dynamics* (Snooks 1998b). It is important to realize that this curve describes the relationship between the rate of growth of real GDP per capita and *strategic inflation* (not total or *nominal inflation*). The econometric problem involves filtering out *nonstrategic inflation* from available data. While this can be done roughly for *SCs* and some *ESCs* (Type I) it is impossible for *NSCs*. Also it is essential to realize that this curve is not the strategic demand–response model, it is merely a rough test of its existence.

Imitative information, in contrast to the information required by the neoclassical model, is readily available and easily evaluated. It is gained from direct observation of those around us, from professional advice, from the media, and from books, magazines, and electronic sources. What we need to know is: who is successful and why, not how, to calculate accurate rate of return calculations.

Intellectual economizing This is the core of my theory about the imitation mechanism in human (and animal) decision-making. It is based on the historical observation that the world's scarcest resource is the intellect, and that decision-makers economize on this resource by making rules and by imitating the successful actions of others. This is the basis for the process of *strategic imitation* by which the *strategic pioneers* are followed by large numbers of *strategic followers*.

Materialist man is a central concept in longrun dynamics. Materialist man is related, yet very different, to the neoclassical concept of *homo economicus*. Rational economic man is not a dynamic force in society, but rather an abstract collection of preferences and rational choices concerning consumption and production. Economic theorists have divorced these behavioural outcomes from more fundamental human motivational impulses. Materialist man on the other hand is a real-world decision-maker who attempts to survive and, with survival, to maximize material advantage over his lifetime. This does not require perfect knowledge or sophisticated abilities to rapidly calculate the costs and benefits of a variety of possible decision-making alternatives, just an ability to recognize and imitate success. Materialist man includes the *strategic pioneers* who explore strategic opportunities, and the *strategic followers* who imitate their success and provide the energy for the *unfolding dynamic strategy*.

National strategic transition (NST) This is the dynamic process through which an individual society passes as its *dynamic strategy* (or substrategy) unfolds. It is driven by *materialist man* in pursuit of his desire to survive and prosper. It is also part of the wider dynamic process of the *GST*.

Nominal inflation This is total inflation which is composed of *strategic inflation* and *nonstrategic inflation*, a distinction that arises from the dynamic-strategy model.

Nonstrategic countries (NSCs) are those Third-World societies that have yet to enter into the *GST*. The ruling elites of *NSCs* adopt, for economically rational reasons, rent-seeking policies rather than viable *technological substrategies.* Accordingly *NSCs* do not experience rapid and sustained economic growth. See also *SCs, ESCs, ASCs,* and *FASCs.*

Nonstrategic crisis is the economic crisis that emerges in an *NSC* owing to the failure to enter into the *GST* by pursuing a viable *dynamic strategy.* The ruling elites, generally the military class or with support from that class, pursue rent-seeking objectives, and the people (*nonstrategists*) pursue family multiplication. While both groups are acting rationally in a pre-*GST* environment, the outcome, as in sub-Saharan Africa, is extremely poor growth punctuated by wars, disease, and famine. See also *strategic crisis* and *antistrategic crisis.*

Nonstrategic inflation is that part of *nominal inflation* not generated directly by the dynamic process. Instead, nonstrategic inflation is the outcome of exogenous shocks (such as wars, epidemics, and resource bonanzas/crises) and institutional problems (such as inappropriate action by central banks, trade unions, and arbitration commissions).

Nonstrategists are those groups in society that are unable to freely invest in, or profit from, the prevailing dynamic strategy. They are controlled and manipulated by the *strategists* or *antistrategists* who exercise a monopoly over society's resources and wealth. The nonstrategists are the dependent agricultural workers in medieval society, slaves in both the pre-modern and modern world, and the 'people' in modern command systems such as Stalin's USSR or Mao's China. It would be a mistake to think that the role of the nonstrategist has evolved over time. Quite the reverse. The last twelve thousand years have seen the nonstrategist follow a great circle. In the palaeolithic era, most adults were freely involved in the dominant strategy of family multiplication; in the neolithic era, very small ruling elites controlled either the conquest or commerce strategies; and only during the modern era have these elites given way to the democratic control of the technological strategy.

Productionists is the term used here to classify economists in both the orthodox and Marxist traditions who regard production and technology – the factory and the machine – as the core of the dynamic process. Essentially the productionists see economic growth as the outcome of an engineering relationship between factor inputs, technology, and the output of goods and services. Neoclassical economics, which constructs its macroeconomic theory from the building blocks of production theory, is really a branch of production engineering. The *stratologists* have different visions of both human society and its dynamic processes.

Strategic change occurs when new *strategic ideas* are applied successfully by a nation in the *strategic pursuit* of its objectives. In formal but static terms it amounts to a shift of the *strategy function,* which embodies the relationship between *strategic instruments* and the *strategic outcome.* In dynamic terms it is an outcome of the response of strategic ideas to changes in *strategic demand* as the *dynamic strategy* unfolds. See also *strategic substitution.*

Strategic confidence, which is the outcome of a successful *dynamic strategy,* is the force that keeps human society together. A successful dynamic strategy leads to a workable network of competitive/cooperative relationships, together with all the necessary rules and organizations. In economic transactions, individuals relate directly to the successful strategy and only indirectly to each other. It is not a matter of mutual 'trust' as such – of having confidence in the nature of other individuals – but rather having confidence in the wider dynamic strategy in which they are all involved and on which they all depend. What we know as 'trust' is derived from strategic confidence. Once the dynamic strategy has been exhausted and cannot be replaced, strategic confidence declines and, in extreme cases, disappears. And as strategic confidence declines, so too does 'trust' and cooperation. Strategic confidence is communicated directly to individuals in a society by the rise and fall in material standards of living and indirectly and less effectively through religious and secular ideology.

Strategic costs rise as the *dynamic strategy* unfolds and society becomes increasingly complex. The reason is that increasing demands are made upon intellectual resources. Strategic costs have been viewed by institutionalists as transaction costs. These costs must be offset by rising benefits from the *unfolding dynamic strategy*.

Strategic countries (SCs) are those societies that have been fully inducted into the *GST* through their successful pursuit of the prevailing technological strategy. They do so by adopting one of a range of *technological substrategies*. Accordingly, SCs enjoy rapid and sustained economic growth over the longrun. These societies constitute the steadily growing *global strategic core*. Also see *ESCs*, *FASCs*, *ASCs*, and *NSCs*.

Strategic crisis This occurs when a society's dominant dynamic strategy (or substrategy) is economically exhausted. This point is reached when the marginal costs of the dominant strategy (or substrategy) equals its marginal revenue. The approaching strategic crisis leads to a deceleration of the upswing and to eventual downturn. Any future recovery must await the emergence of a new strategy (or substrategy). The exhaustion of a strategy has more serious implications for any society than the exhaustion of a substrategy. Contrast with the *antistrategic crisis*.

Strategic demand is the central concept in the dynamic-strategy model. It is an outcome of the *unfolding dynamic strategy*, and exerts a longrun influence over both the employment of resources and the institutional and organizational structure of society. Shifts in strategic demand occur as the dominant dynamic strategy unfolds and as one dynamic strategy replaces another. These shifts elicit changes in society's use of resources and its strategic institutions and organizations.

Strategic distortion is the disruption or perversion of the process by which the dynamic strategy unfolds in an *ESC* owing to any external attempt to accelerate the process of democratization. Such intervention causes a disruption of the *strategic struggle* which is the real force of democratization. This outcome is far more serious than any market distortion resulting from inappropriate government intervention noted by neoclassical economists.

Strategic factions Although the changing political process is similar at both the strategic and substrategic levels – as it is the outcome of the *strategic struggle* – there is a major difference. At the strategic level the struggle is between supporters of entirely different strategies (such as conquest and commerce or commerce and technological change), whereas at the substrategic level it takes place between 'factions' within a single strategy. Hence, at the substrategic level, all participants accept and support the existing economic/social/political system, and the strategic struggle involves the pursuit of more advantageous positions within that system. Rather than pursue their struggle to the point where the existing system breaks down, the old and new strategic factions pursue their differences through existing democratic structures to achieve a marginal redistribution of income.

Strategic followers travel in the wake of the *strategic pioneers*. They seek information not about the costs and benefits of various investment alternatives, but about who and what is successful and why. When the pioneers earn extraordinary profits, they are emulated by large numbers of followers. This is the process of *strategic imitation*.

Strategic ideas   This new concept is concerned with the alternative ways in which the *strategic instruments* can be brought together to effectively pursue the strategic objective of survival and prosperity. They enable *strategic substitution* between these instruments in this pursuit. The accumulated flow of strategic ideas is the state of *strategic knowledge*, which defines the *strategy function*. Strategic ideas may obtain a limited momentum of their own in the shortrun, but over the longer haul they are driven by *strategic demand* generated as individual strategists and their leaders attempt to exploit strategic opportunities in the face of competition and scarce resources. Strategic ideas are concerned with how best to exploit these opportunities.

Strategic imitation is the process by which *strategic followers* emulate the activities of the successful *strategic pioneers*. The followers attempt to imitate not the intellectual mechanism of digital computers but the *dynamic strategies* of successful pioneers. And as the followers successfully imitate the successful pioneers, a new dynamic strategy emerges to challenge the old. This concept is based on the demonstrable fact that the human species is driven not by ideas but by desires. We develop rules not to economize on information and 'trust' but on the world's scarcest resource, intelligence. See also *intellectual economizing*.

Strategic inflation   In the dynamic-strategy model, the role of prices is central to the interaction between *strategic demand* and *strategic response*. The unfolding dynamic strategy generates an increase in strategic demand that places pressure on existing resources, technologies, and institutions, thereby leading to an increase in prices and extraordinary profits. This provides the incentives for the strategic response. It is the systematic increase in prices, which arises from the dynamic process, that constitutes strategic inflation. The more erratic impact of exogenous forces (war, epidemics, and natural resource bonanzas/crises) and of institutional difficulties is called *nonstrategic inflation*. Total inflation is called *nominal inflation*.

Strategic institutions are those formal and informal rules of conduct required to support the emergence and development of the various *dynamic strategies*. They include the economic and political system; the rules by which business is conducted; the way goods, services, and factors of production are bought and sold; the way business is financed; the way property rights are allocated; the way politics is conducted; and the way people interact at a social level. The type of dynamic strategy pursued has a characteristic and predictable impact upon all those institutions.

The need for these rules increases as the dynamic strategy unfolds and *strategic costs* rise owing to increasing demands made upon scarce intellectual resources. See also *unfolding dynamic strategy.*

Strategic instruments include the usual factors of production such as land, labour, and capital (both physical and human), together with the more novel *strategic ideas, strategic leadership, strategic institutions,* and *strategic organizations.* These instruments, which can be substituted one for the other in order to achieve the same *strategic outcome* or increased in quantity and/or quality to generate an improvement in outcome, respond to changes in *strategic demand.* In the dynamic-strategy model, as in the real world, strategic demand is the driving force. Say's Law exists only in the minds of the *productionists.*

Strategic knowledge, which is the outcome of the accumulation of *strategic ideas,* defines the *strategy function.* A change in strategic knowledge, therefore, causes a shift in the strategy function. This knowledge is accumulated by *strategic organizations.*

Strategic leadership is a fundamentally important concept in this study. It is essential in facilitating the pursuit of the society's dominant *dynamic strategy.* This role exceeds the minimum laid down by neoliberal advocates of all kinds, including neoclassical economists and constitutional economists such as James Buchanan. The test of strategic leadership is not that of static efficiency (Pareto optimality) but of effective and sustained development of the dominant dynamic strategy (strategic progress). Strategic leadership is also important in generating and maintaining *strategic confidence,* which binds society together through a network of cooperative relationships. It is strategic leadership rather than 'moral leadership' (Casson 1991: 3) that is essential for the wellbeing of society. Like 'trust', the moral integrity of society is an outcome of a successful dynamic strategy.

Strategic optimization principle This policy principle, which was first proposed in *Longrun Dynamics* (Snooks 1998b: ch 17), involves maximizing the sustainable exploitation of strategic opportunities. It is measured by real GDP per capita, not HDI. Based on the dynamic-strategy model, this policy principle is relevant to a dynamic rather than a static world. It requires the replacement of the Pareto efficiency test with the *strategic test.*

Strategic organizations are developed to facilitate the unfolding *dynamic strategy.* They emerge, in other words, in response to changes in *strategic demand.* For societies pursuing the family-multiplication strategy these organizations involve kinship teams required for hunting and gathering; for conquest societies they include military and imperial organizations; for commerce societies they include trading and financial organizations, together with state naval and foreign service organizations; and for technological societies they involve industrial and commercial organizations together with state bureaucracies. See also *unfolding dynamic strategy.*

Strategic outcome is the result of the *strategic pursuit* which embodies the attempt by *materialist man* to maximize the probability of survival and prosperity. In dynamic terms strategic outcome, which can be proxied by real GDP (or GCI), is generated by the strategic demand–response mechanism, and in static terms it is the outcome of the *strategy function*. It is, therefore, a measure not of 'wellbeing' but of 'economic resilience' – the ability to survive and prosper.

Strategic pathways are the trajectories traced out by the dynamic processes of societies pursuing one of the four *dynamic strategies* (or one of the more numerous substrategies). They are the outcome of the *strategic demand–strategic response* mechanism. For technological societies these pathways are best measured by real GDP and real GDP per capita, while for commerce and conquest societies they are best measured by territorial size as these strategies involve imperial expansion. See also *unfolding dynamic strategy*.

Strategic pioneers are those innovators who successfully invest in aspects of a new and emerging dynamic strategy. They operate not on detailed information about benefits and costs, but on intuition about outcomes and faith in their own abilities. They embody the various available investment alternatives. They are but a small proportion of other equally optimistic risk-takers – the ones who got it right at the right time. The rest are weeded out by competitive forces. Their reward is to reap the extraordinary profits of which they dreamed. They confound the supporters of rational expectations.

Strategic pursuit   The central focus of the dynamic model developed in this book is the strategic pursuit. Human society is viewed as a *strategic organization* dedicated to the strategic pursuit, in which the pioneering strategists explore the economic potential of the most effective dynamic strategy and its substrategies. These strategies have included family multiplication, conquest, and commerce in the past, as well as technological change in the present. It is important to focus on the strategic pursuit rather than the means by which this driving force is translated into a material surplus. By focusing on the system of production instead, the *productionists* fail to come to grips with the dynamic process in their own, or any other, era.

Strategic response is the supply response of the *strategic instruments* to changes in *strategic demand*. This concept undermines Say's Law – adopted explicitly by the classical economists and implicitly by the neoclassical economists – which states that supply creates its own demand. To the contrary, strategic demand creates its own supply through the process of *strategic inflation*.

Strategic reversals   These occur when a traditional *dynamic strategy* exhausts itself and the only viable replacement strategy is one used in the past. An example is the conquest   commerce   conquest strategic sequence in ancient Greece or medieval Venice, or the family-multiplication   conquest   family-multiplication sequence in China after AD 500. This leads to the reversal of the earlier victory of one group of strategists over another, such as merchants over warriors followed by warriors over merchants – as in Greece and Venice. It leads to a corresponding reversal in institutional development, which confounds the idea of social evolution.

Strategic struggle   The strategic struggle is a contest between various groups in society for control of the sources of society's resources and wealth. Although it employs political instruments it is fundamentally an economic struggle – a struggle for survival and prosperity in the face of scarce resources. This struggle involves a contest between either the new and old *strategists*, or between the strategists and the *antistrategists*. If the transfer of control between the old and new strategists does not occur smoothly, the strategic struggle will lead to civil wars or revolutions. And if the new strategists are not sufficiently powerful economically to overwhelm the old strategists quickly, the antistrategists may exploit the situation by hijacking the revolution through manipulation of the *nonstrategists*, and by creating a command system.

Strategic substitution is what happens when we move along a given *strategy function*. It involves the substitution of one strategic instrument for another without reducing the *strategic outcome*. It is the reason that shortages of one instrument, say savings, will not prevent the achievement of a desired strategic outcome.

Strategic test The dynamic-strategy model introduces a new central policy principle, namely maximizing the sustainable exploitation of strategic opportunities, which is measured in terms of GDP per capita. But it should be emphasized that this is not equivalent to the optimum growth path idea, because such a path can be identified neither in prospect nor retrospect. In the dynamic-strategy model the 'strategic test' replaces the 'Pareto efficiency test' (as efficiency of production and distribution is secondary to strategic development), and the 'Wicksell test' advocated by constitutional economists (because it provides the ultimate and measurable basis for 'unanimity and consensus'). It is a test relevant to the longrun as well as the shortrun.

Strategic transfer This is the process by which strategic control passes from the old *strategists* to the new strategists. This transfer may take place relatively smoothly if the new strategists are absorbed into existing institutions of power; it may take place violently through civil war and revolution if the old strategists are able to make a determined stand; and it may break down altogether and be hijacked by the *antistrategists* if the new strategists are not able to take control quickly. In the last two cases the strategic transfer turns into a *strategic crisis*. Strategic transfer is a critical phase in the history of any society, for it can lead to the continued development of more democratic institutions or to a return to more autocratic institutions.

Strategists comprise the dynamic group in society that invests time and resources in pursuing and profiting from one of the four *dynamic strategies*. The strategists are a diverse group. We must distinguish between the *strategic pioneers* (the more ambitious and risk-averse) and the *strategic followers*; and between the old strategists (supporters of the traditional strategy) and the new strategists (supporters of the emerging strategy). While there is synergy between the pioneers and the followers, the old and new strategists are generally involved in a struggle for control of society's dominant dynamic strategy. This *strategic struggle* is at the core of institutional change and has been responsible for civil wars and revolutions. See also *nonstrategists* and *antistrategists*.

Strategy function This function describes the relationship between the *strategic outcome* of survival and prosperity, and the *strategic instruments* by which it is achieved. While it is a static concept – analysing this relationship at a point in time – it is determined by the *unfolding dynamic strategy*. This relationship is more complex than that envisaged by the *productionists*, and it is based on a new vision of human society as an organization dedicated to the creative pursuit of strategic objectives rather than a giant factory dominated by the machine.

Stratologists   The new vision of human society as an organization dedicated to the pursuit of strategic objectives is the focus of interest in the study of stratology. The stratologist is contrasted with the *productionist* with his more restricted vision of human society – a vision that fails the test of reality.

Surplus-generating medium   This is the device through which the *strategic pursuit* of *materialist man* is transformed into the material surplus that satisfies his desire to survive and prosper. While the strategic pursuit has existed throughout the entire history of human society, the surplus-generating medium varies with the dynamic strategy being pursued. Since the Industrial Revolution this has been the industrial production system, but in pre-modern society it was either the conquest or commerce systems, and in pre-civilization society it was the hunter–gatherer system. Clearly none of these surplus-generating systems should be viewed as the dynamic core of human society. The reason orthodox economics is unable to satisfactorily analyse the dynamics of human society is because the *productionists* have focused exclusively on the system of production.

Technological paradigm shifts   The progress of human society takes place within a dynamic structure defined by the great technological paradigm shifts in which growing resource scarcity is transcended by mankind breaking through into an entirely new technological era, thereby opening up extended possibilities for further economic growth. This involves the introduction of an entirely new set of techniques, skills, institutions, and outcomes. There have been three great technological paradigm shifts in human history: the palaeolithic paradigm shift when hunting displaced scavenging; the neolithic paradigm shift when agriculture displaced hunting; and the industrial paradigm shift when urban centres displaced rural areas as the major source of growth. See also *unfolding technological paradigm*.

Technological strategy   This strategy is the dominant dynamic impulse of modern society and, in the past, has been employed by economic decision-makers to transcend exhausted technological paradigms. It was at the very centre of the palaeolithic (hunting), neolithic (agricultural), and modern (industrial) revolutions or *technological paradigm shifts*. And it will be the dominant dynamic strategy of the future. Unlike the conquest and commerce strategies it leads to an increase in material living standards not only for its host civilization, but for human society as a whole. See also *technological styles/technological substrategy*.

Technological styles/technological substrategy   Within the modern technological paradigm, the dynamic *strategists* of competing nation-states attempt to secure a comparative advantage in their pursuit of extraordinary profits by developing new technological substrategies or technological styles. These technological styles/ substrategies – which historically have included: steam-powered iron machinery using coke (1780s–1830s); steel, synthetic chemicals, and complex machinery (1840s–1890s); electricity and the internal combustion engine (1900s–1950s); automated processes, microelectronics, lasers, new construction materials, and biotechnology (since 1950s) – emerge within the existing industrial paradigm as it unfolds at the global level. In turn they comprise a large number of 'strategic projects' that are coordinated through *strategic imitation*. See also *technological strategy*.

Unfolding dynamic strategy   It is important to realize that when I refer to the 'unfolding' of a dynamic strategy I do *not* mean that the strategy is tracing out some preordained pattern of change like the emergence of a plant from a seed or the opening of a flower. A dynamic strategy 'unfolds' because economic decision-makers, operating in a competitive environment and responding to changing relative prices, attempt to achieve their objectives of maximizing the probability of survival and prosperity by exploring all the possibilities provided by a particular dynamic strategy at a given time or place. There is nothing inevitable or unilinear about this process. See also *dynamic strategies*.

Unfolding technological paradigm   This is the global process by which the potential of a *technological paradigm shift* is fully exploited. It is this process that generates the *global strategic transition*, by which an increasing number of societies are drawn into the *global stategic core* – a process popularly known as economic development. This unfolding process is neither inevitable nor smooth, a reality reflected in the fluctuating fortunes of the world economy throughout the history of civilization. As there have been four technological paradigms in human history – the pre-palaeolithic (scavenging), palaeolithic (hunting), neolithic (agricultural), and modern (industrial), see Figure 2.1 – there is nothing unique about economic development in the modern era. This fact has important implications for development policy.

Bibliography

Agence France-Presse, 23 February 1998.

Aghion, P. and P. Howitt (1992), 'A model of growth through creative destruction', *Econometrica*, **60** (2):323–51.

Ahmad, S. (1966), 'On the theory of induced invention', *Economic Journal*, **76** (302):344–57.

Ake, C. (1996), *Democracy and Development in Africa* (Washington, DC: Brookings Institution).

Alejandro, C. F. D. (1970), *Essays on the Economic History of the Argentine Republic* (New Haven and London: Yale University Press).

Amalrik, A. (1970), *Will the Soviet Union Survive 1984?* (New York: Harper & Row).

Amsden, A. (1994), 'Why isn't the whole world experimenting with the East Asian Model to develop? Review of the East Asian miracle', *World Development* (22): 627–33.

Arndt, H. W. (1987), *Economic Development: The History of an Idea* (University of Chicago Press).

Arndt, H. W. (1992), 'The economics of globalism', *Banca Nazionale del Lavoro Quarterly Review*, **180** (March):103–12.

Arndt, H. W. (1993), *Fifty Years of Development Studies* (Canberra: National Centre for Development Studies, Research School of Pacific Studies, Australian National University).

Arrow, K. J. (1962), 'The economic implications of learning by doing', *Review of Economic Studies*, **29**:155–73.

Arthur, W. B. (1988), 'Competing technologies: An overview', in G. Dosi, R. Nelson, G. Silverberg and L. Soete (eds), *Technical Change and Economic Theory* (London and New York: Pinter), pp. 590–607.

Åslund, A. (1995), *How Russia Became a Market Economy* (Washington, DC: Brookings Institution).

Bairoch, P., J. Batou and P. Chèvre (1988), *The Population of European Cities, 800–1850: Data Bank and Short Summary of Results* (Geneva: Droz).

Bagnoli, P., W. J. McKibbin and P. J. Wilcoxen (1996), 'Global economic prospects: medium term projections and structural change' (unpublished paper, revised version of paper presented to United Nations University Conference on the Sustainable Future of the Global System, Tokyo, 16–18 October 1995).

Baran, P. A. (1957), *The Political Economy of Growth* (New York: Monthly Review Press).

Barro, R. J. and X. Sala-i-Martin (1995), *Economic Growth* (New York: McGraw-Hill).

Bauer, P. T. (1948), *The Rubber Industry* (Cambridge, Mass.: Harvard University Press).

Bauer, P. T. (1954), *West African Trade: A Study of Competition, Oligopoly, and Monopoly in a Changing Economy* (Cambridge University Press).

Bauer, P. T. (1971), *Dissent on Development* (London: Weidenfeld & Nicolson).

Bauer, P. T. (1984), 'Remembrance of studies past: Retracing first steps', in G. M. Meier and D. Seers (eds), *Pioneers in Development* (New York: Oxford University Press for the World Bank), pp. 27–43.

Becker, G. S. (1964), *Human Capital: A Theoretical and Empirical Analysis with Special Reference to Education* (New York: Columbia University Press for the National Bureau of Economic Research).

Becker, G. S. (1976), 'Altruism, egoism, and genetic fitness: Economics and socio-biology', *Journal of Economic Literature*, **14** (3):817–26.

Becker, G. S. (1981), *A Treatise on the Family* (Cambridge, Mass.: Harvard University Press).

Becker, G. S. (1987), 'Family', in J. Eatwell, M. Milgate and P. Newman (eds), *The New Palgrave: A Dictionary of Economics* (London: Macmillan), vol. 2, pp. 281–6.

Becker, G. S. (1991), *A Treatise on the Family* (enlarged edn; Cambridge, Mass.: Harvard University Press).

Bensusan-Butt, D. M. (1960), *On Economic Growth: An Essay in Pure Theory* (Oxford: Clarendon).

Bergstrom, T. C. (1995), 'On the evolution of altruistic ethical rules for siblings', *American Economic Review*, **85** (1):58–81.

Berman, B. J. and C. Leys (eds) (1994), *African Capitalists in African Development* (Boulder: L. Rienner).

Birdsall, N. (1988), 'Economic Approaches to Population Growth', in H. Chenery and T. N. Srinivasan (eds), *Handbook of Development Economics*, 2 vols (Amsterdam: North Holland), pp. 477–542.

Black, R. D. C. (1970), 'Introduction', in W. S. Jevons, *The Theory of Political Economy* (Harmondsworth: Penguin), pp. 7–40.

Blaug, M. (1986), *Great Economists Before Keynes: An Introduction to the Lives and Works of One Hundred Economists of the Past* (Atlantic Highlands, NJ: Humanities Press International).

Booth, A. (1991), 'The economic development of Southeast Asia: 1870–1985', in G. D. Snooks, A. J. S. Reid and J. J. Pincus (eds), *Exploring Southeast Asia's Economic Past* (Melbourne: Oxford University Press), pp. 20–52.

Booth, A. (1998), *The Indonesian Economy in the Nineteenth and Twentieth Centuries: A History of Missed Opportunities* (New York: St Martin's; London: Macmillan).

Boserup, E. (1965), *The Conditions of Agricultural Growth: The Economics of Agrarian Change Under Population Pressure* (Chicago: Aldine).

Brown, I. G. (1997), *Economic Change in South-East Asia, c.1830–1980* (New York: Oxford University Press).

Buchanan, J. M. (1987), 'Constitutional economics', in J. Eatwell, M. Milgate and P. Newman (eds), *The New Palgrave: A Dictionary of Economics* (London: Macmillan), vol. 1, pp. 585–8.

Buchanan, J. M., R. D. Tollison and G. Tullock (eds) (1980), *Toward a Theory of the Rent-seeking Society* (College Station, Texas: Texas A & M University).

Bulmer-Thomas, V. (1994), *The Economic History of Latin America Since Independence* (Cambridge University Press).

Byrnes, R. F. (ed.) (1983), *After Brezhnev: Sources of Soviet Conduct in the 1980s* (Bloomington: Indiana University Press).

Cardoso, F. H. and E. Faletto (1979), *Dependency and Development in Latin America* (Berkeley: University of California Press).

Casson, M. (1991), *The Economics of Business Culture: Game Theory, Transaction Costs and Economics* (Oxford: Clarendon; New York: Oxford University Press).

Chen, E. K. Y. (1997), 'The total factor productivity debate', *Asian-Pacific Economic Literature*, **11** (1):18–38.

Chesnais, J. C. (1986), *La Transition démographique: Etapes, formes, implications économiques: Etude de séries temporelles (1720–1984) relatives à 67 pays* (Paris: Presses Universitaires de France).

Clapham, J. H. (1926, 1932, 1938), *The Economic History of Modern Britain*, 3 vols (Cambridge University Press).

Clark, C. G. (1940), *The Conditions of Economic Progress* (London: Macmillan).

Clark, C. G. and M. R. Haswell (1964), *The Economics of Subsistence Agriculture* (London: Macmillan).

Cline, W. R. (1992), *Global Warming: The Economic Stakes* (Washington, DC: Institute for International Economics).

Coghlan, T. A. (1918), *Labour and Industry in Australia, from the First Settlement in 1788 to the Establishment of the Commonwealth in 1901*, 4 vols (London and New York: Oxford University Press).

Colclough, C. (1982), 'The impact of primary schooling on economic development: a review of the evidence', *World Development*, **10**:167–85.

Collins, S. and B. Bosworth (1996), 'Economic growth in East Asia: accumulation versus assimilation', *Brookings Papers on Economic Activities*, **2**:135–91.

Cypher, J. M. and J. L. Dietz (1997), *The Process of Economic Development* (London and New York: Routledge).

David, P. A. (1975), *Technical Choice, Innovation and Economic Growth: Essays on American and British Experience in the Nineteenth Century* (Cambridge University Press).

David, P. A. (1985), 'Clio and the economics of QWERTY', *American Economic Review*, **75** (2), pp. 332–7.

David, P. A. (1993), 'Historical economics in the longrun: some implications of path-dependence', in G. D. Snooks (ed.), *Historical Analysis in Economics* (London and New York: Routledge), pp. 29–40.

Dawkins, R. (1989), *The Selfish Gene* (new edn; Oxford University Press).

De Gregorio, J. (1993), 'Inflation, taxation, and long-run growth', *Journal of Monetary Economics*, **31**:271–98.

Denison, E. F. (1962), *The Sources of Economic Growth in the United States and the Alternative Before Us* (New York: Committee for Economic Development).

Denison, E. F., assisted by J. Poullier (1967), *Why Growth Rates Differ: Postwar Experience in Nine Western Countries* (Washington, DC: Brookings Institution).

Denison, E. F. and W. K. Chung (1976), *How Japan's Economy Grew So Fast: The Sources of Post War Expansion* (Washington, DC: Brookings Institution).

Dobb, M. (1960), *Soviet Economic Development Since 1917* (5th edn; London: Routledge & Kegan Paul).

Dornbusch, R. and J. M. Poterba (eds) (1991), *Global Warming: Economic Policy Responses* (Cambridge, Mass.: MIT Press).

Dowrick, S. and D. T. Nguyen (1989), 'OECD comparative economic growth 1950–85: Catch-up and convergence', *American Economic Review*, **79** (5):1010–30.

Dunlop, J. B. (1993), *The Rise of Russia and the Fall of the Soviet Empire* (Princeton University Press).

Dutt, A. K. (1992), 'Two issues in the state of development economics', in A. K. Dutt and K. P. Jameson (eds), *New Directions in Development Economics* (Aldershot, Hants, and Brookfield, Vt: E. Elgar), pp. 1–34.

European Bank for Reconstruction and Development (1994), *Transition Report, October 1994: Economic Transition in Eastern Europe and the Former Soviet Union* (London: European Bank for Reconstruction and Development).

Fei, J. C. H. and G. Ranis (1961), 'A theory of economic development', *American Exonomic Review*, **51**:533–65.

Fei, J. C. H. and G. Ranis (1964), *Development of the Labor Surplus Economy: Theory and Policy* (Homewood, Ill.: R. D. Irwin).

Fellner, W. (1961), 'Two propositions in the theory of induced innovations', *Economic Journal*, **71** (282):305–8.

Field, A. J. (1991), (Review of D. C. North, *Institutions, Institutional Change, and Economic Performance*), *Journal of Economic History*, **51** (4):999–1001.

Field, A. J. (1994), 'North, Douglass C.', in G. N. Hodgson, W. J. Samuels and M. R. Tool (eds), *The Elgar Companion to Institutional and Evolutionary Economics: L–Z* (Aldershot: Edward Elgar), pp. 134–8.

Fischer, S., R. Sahay and C. A. Végh (1996), 'Stabilization and growth in transition economies: the early experience', *Economic Perspectives*, **10** (2):45–66.

Fitzgibbons, A. (1995), *Adam Smith's System of Liberty, Wealth, and Virtue: The Moral and Political Foundations of The Wealth of Nations* (Oxford: Clarendon).

Frank, A. G. (1967), *Capitalism and Underdevelopment in Latin America: Historical Studies of Chile and Brazil* (New York: Monthly Review Press).

Frech, H. E. (1978), 'Altruism, malice, and public goods', *Journal of Social and Biological Structures*, **1** (2):181–5.

Friedman, M. and A. J. Schwartz (1982), *Monetary Trends in the United States and the United Kingdom, Their Relation to Income, Prices, and Interest Rates, 1867–1975* (University of Chicago Press).

Gerschenkron, A. (1962), *Economic Backwardness in Historical Perspective* (Harvard University Press).

Ghatak, S. (1995), *An Introduction to Development Economics* (3rd edn; London and New York: Routledge).

Gomme, A. A. (1946), *Patents of Invention: Origin and Growth of the Patent System in Britain* (London: Longmans, Green for the British Council).

Griffiths, I. L. (1995), *The African Inheritance* (London and New York: Routledge).

Grossman, G. M. and E. Helpman (1991), *Innovation and Growth in the Global Economy* (Cambridge, Mass.: MIT Press).

Habakkuk, H. J. (1962), *American and British Technology in the Nineteenth Century: The Search for Laboursaving Inventions* (Cambridge University Press).

Hadjor, K. B. (1993), *Dictionary of Third World Terms* (London and New York: Penguin).

Hamilton, W. D. (1964), 'The genetical evolution of social behaviour (I and II)', *Journal of Theoretical Biology*, **7**:1–16, 17–52.

Hayami, Y. (1997), *Development Economics: From the Poverty to the Wealth of Nations* (Oxford: Clarendon).

Hayek, F. A. von (ed.) (1935), *Collectivist Economic Planning: Critical Studies on the Possibilities of Socialism by N. G. Pierson, Ludwig von Mises, Georg Halm, and Enrico Barone* (ed., with an introduction and a concluding essay, by F. A. von Hayek; London: Routledge).

Hayek, F. A. von (1988), *The Fatal Conceit: The Errors of Socialism* (ed. W. W. Bartley; London: Routledge; New York: Routledge, Chapman & Hall).

Headrick, D. R. (1981), *The Tools of Empire: Technology and European Imperialism in the Nineteenth Century* (New York: Oxford University Press).

Headrick, D. R. (1988), *The Tentacles of Progress: Technology Transfer in the Age of Imperialism, 1850–1940* (New York: Oxford University Press).

Hicks, J. R. (1932), *The Theory of Wages* (London: Macmillan).

Higgins, B. H. (1959), *Economic Development: Principles, Problems and Policies* (London: Constable).

Higgins, B. H. (1968), *Economic Development: Principles, Problems, and Policies* (revised edn; New York: W. W. Norton).

Higgs, R. (1971), 'American inventiveness, 1870–1920', *Journal of Political Economy*, **79** (3):661–7.

Hindle, B. (1981), *Emulation and Invention* (New York University Press).

Hirschman, A. O. (1958), *The Strategy of Economic Development* (New Haven: Yale University Press).

Hodgson, G. M. (1993), *Economics and Evolution: Bringing Life Back into Economics* (Oxford: Polity).

Howarth, R. B. and R. B. Norgaard (1992), 'Environmental Valuation under Sustainable Development', *American Economic Review*, **82** (2):473–7.

International Bank for Reconstruction and Development (1997), *World Development Report 1997: The State in a Changing World* (New York: Oxford University Press for the World Bank).

International Monetary Fund (various years), *International Financial Statistics Yearbook* (Washington: International Monetary Fund).

Jeremy, D. J. (1981), *Transatlantic Industrial Revolution: The Diffusion of Textile Technologies Between Britain and America, 1790–1830s* (Oxford: Blackwell).

Kaldor, N. (1956), *Indian Tax Reform: Report of a Survey* (New Delhi: Department of Economic Affairs).

Kelman, S. (1981), *What Price Incentives? Economists and the Environment* (Boston: Auburn House).

Kendrick, J. W. (1964), 'Comments', in J. Vaizey (ed.), *The Residual Factor and Economic Growth* (Paris: OECD), pp. 216–17.

Kennedy, P. M. (1989), *The Rise and Fall of the Great Powers: Economic Change and Military Conflict from 1500 to 2000* (London: Fontana).

Keynes, J. M. (1936), *The General Theory of Employment, Interest, and Money* (London: Macmillan).

Killick, T. (1995), *IMF Programmes in Developing Countries* (London: Routledge).

Killick, T., M. Malik and M. Manuel (1992), 'What can we know about the effects of IMF programmes?' *World Economy*, **20** (September):575–97.

Lal, D. (1983), *The Poverty of 'Development Economics'* (London: Institute of Economic Affairs).

Landes, D. S. (1969), *The Unbound Prometheus: Technological Changes and Industrial Development in Western Europe from 1750 to the Present* (London: Cambridge University Press).

Lenat, D. B. (1996), 'Artificial intelligence', *Key Technologies of the 21st Century – Scientific America: A Special Issue* (New York: W. H. Freeman & Co.), pp. 15–18.

Leontief, W. W. (1951), *Input–Output Economics* (San Francisco: W. H. Freeman).

Lewis, W. A. (1954), 'Economic development with unlimited supplies of labour', *Manchester School*, **20**:139–91.

Lewis, W. A. (1955), *The Theory of Economic Growth* (London: Allen & Unwin).

Livi-Bacci, M. (1992), *A Concise History of World Population* (Cambridge, Mass., and Oxford: Blackwell).

Lucas, R. E., Jr (1988), 'On the mechanics of economic development', *Journal of Monetary Economics*, **22** (1):3–42.

McEvedy, C. and R. Jones (1978), *Atlas of World Population History* (London: Allen Lane).

MacLeod, C. (1988), *Inventing the Industrial Revolution: The English Patent System, 1660–1800* (Cambridge University Press).

Maddison, A. (1992), *The Political Economy of Poverty, Equity, and Growth: Brazil and Mexico* (Oxford University Press for the World Bank).

Maddison, A. (1995a), *Monitoring the World Economy, 1820–1992* (Paris: Development Centre of the Organization for Economic Co-operation and Development).

Maddison, A. (1995b), *Explaining the Economic Performance of Nations: Essays in Time and Space* (Aldershot, Hants, and Brookfield, Vt: E. Elgar).

Magee, G. B. (1996), 'Patenting and the supply of inventive ideas in colonial Australia: evidence from Victorian patent data', *Australian Economic History Review*, **36** (2):30–58.

Magee, G. B. (1997), *Productivity and Performance in the Paper Industry: Labour, Capital, and Technology in Britain and America, 1860–1914* (Cambridge University Press).

Magee, G. B. (1999), *Knowledge Generation, Technological Change and Economic Growth in Colonial Australia* (forthcoming).

Malthus, T. R. (1986; first publ. 1798), *The Works of Thomas Robert Malthus*, vol. 1: *An Essay on the Principle of Population as it Affects the Future Improvement of Society* (ed. E. A. Wrigley and D. Souden; London: W. Pickering).

Manne, A. S. and R. G. Richels (1992), *Buying Greenhouse Insurance: The Economic Costs of Carbon Dioxide Emission Limits* (Cambridge, Mass.: MIT Press).

Mansfield, E. (1961), 'Two Propositions in the theory of induced innovation', *Economic Journal* (June):305–8.

Marshall, A. (1919), *Industry and Trade: A Study of Industrial Technique and Business Organization; and of Their Influences on the Conditions of Various Classes and Nations* (2nd edn; London: Macmillan).

Marshall, A. (1920; orig. publ. 1890), *Principles of Economics: An Introductory Volume* (8th edn, reset and repr. 1949; London: Macmillan).

Marshall, A. and M. Paley (1879), *The Economics of Industry* (London: Macmillan).

Marx, K. (1947; Orig. publ. 1891), *Critique of the Gotha Program* (Moscow: Foreign Languages Publishing House).

Marx, K. (1961; Orig. publ. 1867), *Capital*, vol. 1: *A Critical Analysis of Capitalist Production* (Moscow: Foreign Languages Publishing House).

Marx, K. (1970; Orig. publ. 1859), *Contribution to the Critique of Political Economy* (ed. Maurice Dobb; Moscow: Progress Publishers).

Massel, B. (1960), 'Capital formation's technological change in United States manufacturing', *Review of Economics and Statistics*, **42** (2):182–8.

Meadows., D. H. *et al.* (1972), *The Limits to Growth: A Report for the Club of Rome's Project on the Predicaments of Mankind* (New York: Universe).

Meadows, D. H. *et al.* (1992), *Beyond the Limits: Confronting Global Collapse, Envisioning a Sustainable Future* (Post Mills, Vt: Chelsea Green).

Mehmet, O. (1995), *Westernizing the Third World: The Eurocentricity of Economic Development Theories* (London and New York: Routledge).

Meier, G. M. and D. Seers (eds) (1984), *Pioneers in Development* (New York: Oxford University Press for the World Bank).

Mill, J. S. (1875; Orig. publ. 1843), *A System of Logic, Ratiocinative and Inductive: Being a Connected View of the Principles of Evidence and the Methods of Scientific Investigation*, 2 vols (9th edn; London: Longmans, Green, Reader & Dyer).

Mill, J. S. (1909; orig. publ. 1848), *Principles of Political Economy with Some of Their Applications to Social Philosophy* (ed. and intro. W. J. Ashley; London: Longmans, Green).

Mincer, J. (1958), 'Investment in human capital and personal income distribution', *Journal of Political Economy*, **66**:281–302.

Mincer, J. (1974), *Schooling, Experience and Earnings* (New York: National Bureau of Economic Research, distributed by Columbia University Press).

Mises, L. E. von (1958), *Theory and History* (London: J. Cape).

Mokyr, J. (1990), *The Lever of Riches: Technological Creativity and Economic Progress* (New York: Oxford University Press).

Morris, D. R. (1994), *The Washing of the Spears: A History of the Rise of the Zulu Nation under Shaka, and its Fall in the Zulu War of 1879* (London: Pimlico).

Morrison, J. R. (1995), 'Record of IMF-supported adjustment programs assessed', *IMF Survey*, **24** (15):233–6.

Mosley, P., J. Harrigan and J. F. J. Toye (1991), *Aid and Power: The World Bank and Policy-based Lending*, 2 vols (London: Routledge).

Murrell, P. (1996), 'How far has the transition progressed?' *Economic Perspectives*, **10** (2):25–44.

Myint, Hla (1954), 'An interpretation of economic backwardness', *Oxford Economic Papers*, **6** (2):132–63.

Myrdal, G. (1957), *Economic Theory and Under-developed Regions* (London: Duckworth).

Myrdal, G. (1968), *Asian Drama: An Inquiry into the Poverty of Nations* (London: Penguin).

Myrdal, G. (1984), 'International inequality and foreign aid in retrospect', in G. M. Meier and D. Seers (eds), *Pioneers in Development* (New York: Oxford University Press for the World Bank), pp. 151–65.

Nelson, R. R. (1956), 'A theory of the low-level equilibrium trap in undeveloped economies', *American Economics Review*, **46** (5):894–908.

Nelson, R. R. and S. G. Winter (1982), *An Evolutionary Theory of Economic Change* (Cambridge, Mass.: Belknap Press of Harvard University Press).

Nordhaus, W. D. (1991a), 'To slow or not to slow: the economics of the greenhouse effect', *Economic Journal*, **101** (407):920–37.

Nordhaus, W. D. (1991b), 'The cost of slowing climate change: A survey', *Energy Journal*, **12** (1):37–65.

Nordhaus, W. D. (1991c), 'A sketch of the economics of the greenhouse effect', *American Economic Review*, **81** (2):146–50.

North, D. C. (1981), *Structure and Change in Economic History* (New York: Norton).

North, D. C. (1990), *Institutions, Institutional Change, and Economic Performance* (Cambridge and New York: Cambridge University Press).

North, D. C. and R. P. Thomas (1973), *The Rise of the Western World* (Cambridge University Press).

Nove, A. (1972), 'Economic reforms in the USSR and Hungary: A study in contrasts', in A. Nove and D. M. Nuti (eds), *Socialist Economics: Selected Readings* (Harmondsworth: Penguin), pp. 335–62.

Nove, A. (1992), *An Economic History of the USSR, 1917–1991* (3rd edn; Harmondsworth: Penguin).

Nurkse, R. (1953), *Problems of Capital Formation in Underdeveloped Countries* (Oxford: Blackwell).

Pares, B. (1966), *A History of Russia* (New York: Knopf).

Pastor, M. (1987), *The International Monetary Fund and Latin America: Economic Stabilization and Class Conflict* (Boulder, Colo.: Westview).

Petty, W. (1691), *The Political Anatomy of Ireland: With the establishment for that kingdom when the late Duke of Ormond was the lord lieutenant. Taken from the records To which is added Verbum sapienti; or an account of the wealth and expences of England, and the method of raising taxes in the most equal manner. Shewing also, that the nation can bear the charge of four millions per annum, when the occasions of the government require it* (London: printed for D. Brown and W. Rogers, at the Bible without Temple-bar, and at the Sun over-against St Dunstans Church, Fleetstreet).

Plato (1892), 'Republic', in *The Dialogies of Plato, Translated into English with Analyses and Introductions by B. Jowett*, vol. III (Oxford: Clarendon), pp. 1–338.

Pomfret, R. W. T. (1995), *The Economies of Central Asia* (Princeton University Press).

Pomfret, R. W. T. (1997), *Development Economics* (London and New York: Prentice Hall).

Prebisch, R. (1950), *The Economic Development of Latin America and Its Principal Problems* (New York: United Nations Department of Economic Affairs).

Ragsdale, H. (1996), *The Russian Tragedy: The Burden of History* (Armonk, NY: M. E. Sharpe).

Rebelo, S. (1991), 'Long-run policy analysis and long-run growth', *Journal of Political Economy*, **99** (3):500–21.

Reid, A. J. S. (1988), *Southeast Asia in the Age of Commerce, 1450–1680*, vol. 1: *The Lands Below the Winds* (New Haven: Yale University Press).

Reid, A. J. S. (1993), *Southeast Asia in the Age of Commerce, 1450–1680*, vol. 2: *Expansion and Crisis* (New Haven: Yale University Press).

Ricardo, D. (1817), *On the Principles of Political Economy and Taxation* (London: J. Murray).

Romer, P. M. (1986), 'Increasing returns and long-run growth', *Journal of Political Economy*, **94**:1002–37.

Romer, P. M. (1987), 'Growth based on increasing returns due to specialization', *American Economic Review*, **77** (2):56–62.

Romer, P. M. (1990), 'Endogenous technological change', *Journal of Political Economy*, **98** (5), part II:S71–S102.

Rosenberg, N. (1970), 'Economic development and the transfer of technology: Some historical perspectives', *Technology and Culture*, **11** (4):550–75.

Rosenstein-Rodan, P. N. (1943), 'Problems of Industrialization of Eastern and South-Eastern Europe', *Economic Journal*, **53**:202–11.

Rosenstein-Rodan, P. N. (1957), *Notes on the Theory of the 'Big Push'* (MIT, CIS).

Rostow, W. W. (1975), *How It All Began: Origins of the Modern Economy* (London: Macmillan).

Rostow, W. W. (1990; orig. publ. 1960), *The Stages of Economic Growth: A Non-Communist Manifesto* (3rd edn; Cambridge University Press).

Salter, W. E. G. (1960), *Productivity and Technical Change* (Cambridge University Press).

Samuelson, P. A. (1983), 'Complete genetic models for altruism, kin selection and like-gene selection', *Journal of Social and Biological Structures*, **6** (1): 3–15.

Schelling, T. C. (1992), 'Some economics of global warming', *American Economic Review*, **82** (1):1–14.

Schultz, T. W. (1960), 'Capital formation by education', *Journal of Political Economy*, **68**:511–83.

Schultz, T. W. (1961), 'Investment in human capital products', *American Economic Review*, **51** (1):1–17.

Schultz, T.W. (1964), *Transforming Traditional Agriculture* (New Haven: Yale University Press).

Schumpeter, J. A. (1934; orig. publ. 1912), *The Theory of Economic Development: An Inquiry into Profits, Capital, Credit, Interest and the Business Cycle* (Cambridge, Mass.: Harvard University Press).

Schumpeter, J. A. (1939), *Business Cycles: A Theoretical, Historical and Statistical Analysis of the Capitalist Process* (New York: McGraw-Hill).

Schumpeter, J. A. (1943), *Capitalism, Socialism, and Democracy* (London: George Allen & Unwin).

Scitovsky, T. (1954), 'Two concepts of external economies', *Journal of Political Economy*, **17**: 143–51.

Sheshinski, E. (1967), 'Optimal accumulation with learning by doing', in K. Shell, (ed.), *Essays on the Theory of Optimal Economic Growth* (Cambridge, Mass.: MIT Press), pp. 31–52.

Singer, H. (1950), 'The distribution of gains between investing and borrowing countries', *American Economic Review*, **40** (2):473–85.

Singer, H. (1958), 'The concept of balanced growth and economic development: theory and facts', paper given at University of Texas Conference on Economic Development (April).

Singer, H. W. and S. Roy (1993), *Economic Progress and Prospects in the Third World: Lessons of Development Experience, 1945–1992 and Beyond* (Aldershot, Hants, and Brookfield, Vt: Edward Elgar).

Singer, H. W. and S. Sharma (eds) (1989), *Economic Development and World Debt* (London: Macmillan).

Smith, A. (1961; orig. publ. 1776), *An Inquiry into the Nature and Causes of the Wealth of Nations*, 2 vols (5th edn repr., ed. E. Cannan; London: Methuen).

Smith, A. (1976; orig. publ. 1759), *The Theory of Moral Sentiments* (ed. D. D. Raphael and A. L. Macfie; Oxford: Clarendon).

Smith, A. (1978), *Lectures on Jurisprudence* (ed. R. L. Meek, D. D. Raphael and P. G. Stein; Oxford: Clarendon).

Snooks, G. D. (1993), *Economics Without Time. A Science Blind to the Forces of Historical Change* (London: Macmillan; Ann Arbor: University of Michigan Press).

Snooks, G. D. (1994a), *Portrait of the Family Within the Total Economy. A Study in Longrun Dynamics, Australia 1788–1990* (Cambridge University Press).

Snooks, G. D. (1994b), 'New perspectives on the Industrial Revolution', in G. D. Snooks (ed.), *Was the Industrial Revolution Necessary?* (London and New York: Routledge), pp. 1–26.

Snooks, G. D. (1996), *The Dynamic Society. Exploring the Sources of Global Change* (London and New York: Routledge).

Snooks, G. D. (1997a), *The Ephemeral Civilization. Exploding the Myth of Social Evolution* (London and New York: Routledge).

Snooks, G. D. (1997b), 'Strategic demand and the growth–inflation curve: New theoretical and empirical concepts', *Working Papers in Economic History*, 195 (RSSS, Australian National University, July).

Snooks, G. D. (1998a), *The Laws of History* (London and New York: Routledge).

Snooks, G. D. (1998b), *Longrun Dynamics. A General Economic and Political Theory* (London: Macmillan; New York: St Martins Press).

Sokoloff, K. L. (1988), 'Inventive activity in early industrial America: Evidence from patent records, 1790–1846', *Journal of Economic History*, **48** (4): 813–50.

Sokoloff, K. L. and B. Z. Khan (1990), 'The democratization of invention during early industrialization: Evidence from the United States, 1790–1846', *Journal of Economic History*, **50** (2):363–78.

Solow, R. M. (1956), 'A contribution to the theory of economic growth', *Quarterly Journal of Economics*, **70**:65–94.

Solow, R. M. (1957), 'Technical change and the aggregate production function', *Review of Economics and Statistics*, **29** (3):312–20.

Stapleton, D. H. (1987), *The Transfer of Early Industrial Technologies to America* (Philadelphia: American Philosophical Society).

Streeten, P. P. (1980), *Development Perspectives* (London: Macmillan).

Streeten, P. P. (1995), *Thinking About Development* (Cambridge and New York: Cambridge University Press).

Streeten, P. P., S. J. Burki *et al.* (1981), *First Things First: Meeting Basic Human Needs in the Developing Countries* (New York: Oxford University Press for the World Bank).

Swan, T. W. (1956), 'Economic growth and capital accumulation', *Economic Record*, **32**:334–61.

Syme, D. (1871), 'On the method of political economy', *Westminster Review*, pp. 206–18.

Syme, D. (1876), *Outlines of an Industrial Science* (London: Henry S. King & Co).

Toynbee, A. (1969; orig. publ. 1884), *Toynbee's Industrial Revolution: A Reprint of Lectures on the Industrial Revolution* (New York and Newton Abbot: David & Charles).

Tunzelmann, G. N. von (1994), 'Technology in the early nineteenth century', in R. Floud and D. McCloskey (eds), *The Economic History of Britain Since 1700*, vol. 1: *1700–1860* (2nd edn; Cambridge University Press), pp. 271–99.

Tunzelmann, G. N. von (1995), *Technology and Industrial Progress: The Foundations of Economic Growth* (Aldershot, Hants, and Brookefield, Vt: E. Elgar).

United Nations (1989), *World Populations Prospects 1988* (New York: United Nations).

United Nations (1996), *World Population 1997* (New York: United Nations).

United Nations (1997), *Urban Agglomerations* (New York: United Nations).

United Nations Development Programme (various years), *Human Development Report* (New York: Oxford University Press).

Veblen, T. B. (1899), *The Theory of the Leisure Class: An Economic Study of Institutions* (New York: Macmillan).

Viner, J. (1953), *International Trade and Economic Development: Lectures Delivered at the National University of Brazil* (Oxford: Clarendon).

Warr, P. G. (ed.) (1993), *The Thai Economy in Transition* (Cambridge University Press).

Witt, U. (ed.) (1993), *Evolutionary Economics* (Aldershot, Hants, and Brookfield, Vt: E. Elgar).

World Bank (various years), *Annual Report* (New York: World Bank).

World Bank (various years), *World Debt Tables, vol. 1* (New York: World Bank).

World Bank (1993), *World Development Report* (New York: Oxford University Press).

World Bank (1995), *World Development Report* (New York: Oxford University Press).

World Bank (1997a), *Global Development Finance, vol. 1* (New York: World Bank).

World Bank (1997b), *World Development Report: The State in a Changing World* (New York: World Bank).

Wrigley, E. A. (1969), *Population and History* (London: Weidenfeld & Nicolson).

Wrigley, E. A. and R. S. Schofield (1981), *The Population History of England, 1541–1871: A Reconstruction* (London: Edward Arnold).

Yeager, T. J. (1995), 'Encomienda or slavery? The Spanish Crown's choice of labour organisation in sixteenth-century Spanish America', *Journal of Economic History*, **55** (4):842–59.

Index

adaptive efficiency, and institutional change, 285–6
Africa, economic growth of and interaction with global strategic core, 62; economic growth of, 31, 32, 204, 205, 207; growth rate of ESCs in, 58, 59; and GST, 39, 40; *see also* sub-Saharan Africa
aggregate demand, and strategic demand, 295
aggregate production function, 224–8; and technological knowledge, 224, 225
altruism, 177, 178, 187
aid, *see* foreign aid
antistrategic collapse, law of, *see under* laws of history
antistrategic containment, and clash with strategic pursuit in USSR, 80–2
antistrategic core, and stage three of GST, 40; *see also* Union of Soviet Socialist Republics (USSR)
antistrategic countries (ASCs), 68, 79, 317; defined, 11–12, 344; *see also* former antistrategic countries (FASCs)
antistrategic crisis, defined, 344; of Latin America, 65–71
antistrategic fringe, 85
antistrategic global process, 80; history of, 85–100; *see also* Union of Soviet Socialist Republics (USSR)
antistrategic institutions, 70, 121–2, 297; *see also* command economy
antistrategic paradox, and USSR, 98
antistrategic struggle, in USSR, 90
antistrategists, and command system in USSR, 89–92, 317; defined, 344; and ecological engineers, 336; and exploitation of nonstrategists, 89, 94, 311, 317; and exploitation of strategists, 80, 81, 311; in Germany, 312; and industrialization

in USSR, 89; in Japan, 312; in Latin America, 67; and neoliberalism, 318; in NSCs, 278, 311; role of, 311–12; and rules/institutions, 200, 201; ruling elites of NSCs as, 278, 296, 309–10, 311, 312, 315; in Russia, 90, 97, 98, 100, 312; in SCs and ESCs, 311–12; and strategic struggle, 97, 98, 310; and suppression of strategists, 12, 80, 81, 88, 89, 94; takeover of Russia by, 86–9; in Third World, 121; and USSR, 88–9, 91–2, 94, 297, 336, 344; *see also* antistrategic countries (ASCs); command economy; conservative antistrategists; rent-seeking; revolutionary antistrategists; strategic struggle; strategic transfer
antistrategy, import replacement as, 67
Argentina, 58, 66, 67–8, 68
ASCs, *see* antistrategic countries
Asia, economic growth of, 31, 32, 204, 205–7; financial crisis, 41; *see also* 'Asian meltdown'; and stage three of GST, 40; *see also* East Asia; Southeast Asia
'Asian meltdown', 36, 41, 59, 73, 74, 141; dynamic-strategy explanation of, 75–6, 77, 77–8; IMF and, 133; neoclassical economics and, 75, 76, 161; neoliberal explanation of, 75, 76, 77
'Asian miracle', 36, 41, 59, 76; and 'imitation model', 140; neoclassical economics and, 261
Australia, as commerce colony, 66; growth of, 68; HDI and GST rankings, 57; household change in and dynamic-strategy model, 239; and import replacement, 117; and stage one of GST, 37–8; and trade protection, 319

Index

transformation, funnels of, *see* funnels
of transformation
transition, conventional interpretation
of, 82–5; conventional policies
regarding, 83–4, 102–3; and
FASCs, 79–82, 83, 84, 100–1,
102–3; and strategic demand, 84,
98; and struggle of new strategists
and antistrategists, 98–100; *see
also* demographic transition;
global strategic transition (GST);
strategic transition
trust, and strategic confidence, 189,
349; *see also* cooperation

underdevelopment, and big-push model,
6, 7, 137–8, 251, 252–3, 256–8,
301; and capital accumulation,
254–64; and capitalism, 119,
138–9; classical/neoclassical
development economics and,
5–6; and colonialism, 120–2;
'cumulative circular causation'
hypothesis and, 120–2;
dependency theorists and, 6–7,
118–19, 139, 302; and free trade
and Third World, 318–19; global-
polarization theorists and, 6–7,
116–19; humanists and, 302–3;
and 'imitation model', 140–1;
institutionalists and, 6–7, 119–25,
139–40, 304; Keynesian
economics and, 7, 115, 255,
256–60; and low-level equilibrium
models, 256–7; and market
failure, 300; neo-Marxists and,
301–2; neoclassical economics
and, 255, 303–4; path-dependence
and, 122–5; policy, 136–41;
poverty-trap theorists and, 6,
115–16; structuralists and, 6,
116–18, 138–9; World Bank and,
305–7
unemployment, dynamic-strategy
model and, 330; and inflation, 330
unfolding dynamic strategy, 179;
defined, 355; and democratization,
77; and institutional change, 71;
and institutions and organizations,

289; and strategic confidence,
180–1; and strategic demand,
180–1, 181; and strategic
pioneers, 192; and supply-side
variables, 183
unfolding technological paradigm,
13–14, 17–21, 31–42; defined,
355; and economic development,
309; and global strategic demand,
202; and GST, 180
Union of Soviet Socialist Republics
(USSR), as antistrategic core, 40,
85; and antistrategic paradox, 98;
antistrategic struggle in, 90; and
antistrategic takeover, 86–9; and
antistrategists, 88–9, 91–2, 94,
344; and big push, 252, 253; and
clash of strategic pursuit and
antistrategic containment, 80–2;
collapse of and stage four of GST,
41; and command system, 89–92,
92–5, 95–8, 317; dissolution of,
96; economic growth in, 91, 93,
94; and first Five-Year Plan,
90–1; and Gorbachev 'reforms',
95–7; history of, 85–100; and
industrialization, 89; institutions
of command economy of, 91–2;
and Khrushchev 'reforms', 93–4;
and Kosygin 'reforms', 94; and
Marxism, 82; middle classes and
command economy of, 89; and
New Economic Policy (NEP), 90;
and nonstrategists, 88, 348; and
War Communism, 90; *see also*
Russia; Russian Revolution
United Arab Emirates, 58
United Nations Development
Programme, and human
development index (HDI),
44–5
United States of America (USA), and
3rd technological substrategy
(1870s–1920s), 24, 221–2, 223;
and 4th technological substrategy
(1950s–1980s), 24–5, 205, 222;
and 5th technological substrategy
(since 1980s), 25, 222; as
commerce colony, 66; and GST,